TABLE OF CONTENTS

A Guide To STARTING A BUSINESS IN MINNESOTA

Twentieth Edition, January 2002

Charles A. Schaffer
Madeline Harris
Ann M. Wilczynski

ISBN 1-888404-25-6

PREFACE

This twentieth edition of ***A Guide to Starting a Business in Minnesota***, like its predecessors, is intended to provide a concise, summary discussion of the major issues faced by those starting a business in Minnesota. This edition of the Guide contains three major sections: the narrative text; a Resource Directory, which provides addresses and telephone numbers of organizations referenced in the text; and the Directory of Licenses and Permits, which lists all business licenses and permits required by the State of Minnesota, the state agency which issues or administers the license or permit, and a telephone number for obtaining more information. Topics presented in the narrative text are presented in the order in which the new business owner typically must address them. Note that a business that will have operations or a physical presence (with the possible inclusion of an Internet presence) in another state should check with the government authorities in that state to obtain information on licensing, tax and other issues. We hope this organization is useful.

While no one publication can answer every question for every kind of proposed business, this Guide does respond to the questions and concerns most frequently raised. While it tries to be both timely and comprehensive, this Guide is not intended as a final statement on any one subject. In particular, users should be aware that the formal legal requirements for business start-up and operations may change from time to time. Specific updates and additional information may be obtained from the many sources listed.

Before engaging in any business venture, it is advisable to seek both legal counsel and advice from an accountant. Both professionals can advise you as to the best course you might take in establishing your business. The information provided in this Guide is not intended to replace that kind of advice and assistance.

We wish to express our thanks and appreciation to all who have contributed their time, effort, and expertise in the compilation of this Guide. A particular note of thanks must go to: Bert Black of the Office of the Secretary of State; Kevin Amundson, Charlie Anderson, Dave Anderson, Kathleen Cheney, Doug DeGrole, Keith Getschel, Ann Gravelle, Rick Groger, Rolf Larson, Don Martin and Marilyn Sheffield of the Department of Revenue; Daniel Sexton and Ann Hagestad of the Department of Commerce; Steve Lapinsky and Melanie Miles of the Department of Human Rights; Mary Brunkow, John Thomas and Deb Serum of the Department of Economic Security; James Honerman of the Department of Labor and Industry; Laura Wojtowicz of the Department of Administration; Michael Nelson of the Pollution Control Agency; George Saumweber of the U.S. Small Business Administration; David Gaffaney of the U.S.D.A. (Rural Development); Janis Rannow of Minnesota Technology, Inc.; Ann P. Makres of the Internal Revenue Service; Bonnie Florello of Minnesota Project Innovation; Deb McKinley of MnTAP; Thersa Gaffey of the Office of Environmental Assistance; District Director Denise C. Scharlemann and Amee Christensen of the U.S. Department of Labor; Charles Nidby of the U.S. Immigration and Naturalization Service; Daphne Fuller of the Minnesota Society of Certified Public Accountants; James Young of the Minnesota State Bar Association; Carol Halvorson and Mike Bublitz of the Minnesota Society of Enrolled Agents; and Ann Silgen of the Minnesota State College & University System.

Particular thanks go to Mary Kruger for the sections on "Business Taxes" and "Choosing The Form of Business Organization." We would also like to thank Millie Caballero, Michael Myhre and Mark Simmer for their numerous contributions to the compilation of this Guide.

Charles A. Schaffer
Madeline Harris
Ann M. Wilczynski

Editor's Note: Throughout the year and as warranted, we will post on our website (www.dted.state.mn.us) updates to this Guide.

CHOOSING THE FORM OF BUSINESS ORGANIZATION

TAX AND NON-TAX CONSIDERATIONS

INTRODUCTION

One of the fundamental initial decisions a new business owner faces is choosing the form of organization for the business. Generally speaking, a person should consider himself or herself to be "in business" once they have begun the operation of an activity for which they expect to be paid. This is true whether or not that person terminates other employment (such as a job that brings a paycheck), or intends to operate that business on a seasonal or short-term basis. For most businesses, the choices are:

Sole Proprietorship. In a sole proprietorship, the business is owned and controlled by one individual. This person alone receives the profits and bears the losses from the business, and this person alone is responsible for the debts and obligations of the business. Income and expenses of the business are reported on the proprietor's individual income tax return, and profits are taxed at the proprietor's individual income tax rate. **If a husband and wife wish to own a business together, they must either form a partnership, corporation or limited liability company (in order to have each of them be an owner of the business) or a sole proprietorship (in which case only one of them will be an owner of the business).**

Partnership. A **general partnership** is a business owned by two or more persons who associate to carry on the business as a partnership. Partnerships have specific attributes, which are defined by statute. All partners in a general partnership share equally in the right, and responsibility, to manage the business, and each partner is responsible for all the debts and obligations of the business. Distribution of profits and losses, allocation of management responsibilities, and other issues affecting the partnership usually are defined in a written partnership agreement. Income and expenses of the partnership are reported on federal and state "information" tax returns, which are filed by the partnership. The partners are taxed on their respective share of the partnership's profits at their individual income tax rates.

Starting in calendar year 2002 Minnesotans may form partnerships only under the Revised Uniform Partnership Act, Minnesota Statutes Chapter 323A.

Partnerships formed under Chapter 323 (the old Act) may have changed to the new Act by amending their partnership agreement at any time before January 1, 2002. Those partnerships that did not do so were brought under Chapter 323A on January 1, 2002.

These two Acts are somewhat different, and **due to the many changes instituted by the new Act, it is recommended that you consult with your attorney about the new partnership law.**

Limited Liability Partnerships. A general partnership may register as a **limited liability partnership (LLP)** by filing a limited liability partnership registration. In limited liability partnerships, the personal assets of the partners are shielded against liabilities incurred by the partnership in tort or contract situations. This is different from a general partnership, in which partners are personally liable to an unlimited extent for the debts and obligations of the partnership. It should be noted that limited liability partnerships are a relatively new type of entity and certain aspects, such as tax aspects, of such entities are not yet fully developed or understood.

Limited liability partnership status affords protection to the individual partner from liability for partnership obligations in tort and contract. An LLP files with the Secretary of State an annual report. There is a one-year grace period for retroactive reinstatement after revocation of LLP status for failure to file the annual report.

There is an additional provision (Minnesota Statutes section 322A.88) allowing a limited partnership to elect limited liability partnership status under Chapter 323A. This allows for limited liability protection for both general and limited partners and this type of partnership is called a limited liability limited partnership. Limited liability limited partnerships are discussed below.

A **limited partnership** is a type of partnership in which the limited partners share in the partnership's liability only up to the amount of their investment in the limited partnership. By statute, the limited partnership must have at least one general partner and one limited partner. The general partner has the right and responsibility to control the limited partnership, and is responsible for the debts and obligations of the limited partnership. The limited partner, in exchange for limited liability, is usually not involved in the day-to-day management and control of the business. Limited partnerships must be established in compliance with statutory requirements, including requirements of tax and securities laws. Because of their complex nature, limited partnerships should not be undertaken without competent professional advice.

Note that a limited partnership is governed by Chapter 323A for certain matters not addressed by Chapter 322A.

As mentioned above, limited partnerships, just like general partnerships, may elect limited liability partnership status under Chapter 323A of the Minnesota Statutes. A limited partnership that does so is known as a limited liability limited partnership. In other words, a limited liability limited partnership (L.L.L.P.) is a limited partnership because it has a certificate of limited partnership on file with the Secretary of State's Office (pursuant to Chapter 322A, the Minnesota Statute dealing with limited partnerships) and it has also filed, pursuant to Minnesota Statutes section 322A.88, a Statement of Qualification as a limited liability partnership. In all instances, however, the partnership remains a limited partnership governed by Chapter 322A (except to the extent that Chapter 323A addresses certain matters that Chapter 322A does not), and must meet all the requirements that limited partnerships must meet.

Care should be taken in naming a limited liability limited partnership; the name must contain either, the words "limited partnership, limited liability partnership" (or the abbreviation "L.P., L.L.P." or the words "limited liability limited partnership" (or the abbreviation "L.L.L.P.").

It is important to note that if a limited liability limited partnership chooses the L.L.L.P. designation, that partnership should also use that designation in its name as listed on its certificate of limited partnership. There are two reasons for this. First, without doing so, the Secretary of

State's office might not accept the partnership's Statement of Qualification, because it is not clear that the entities are one and the same. Second, there could be questions about what standard of personal liability to apply to the partnership and the partners, and what entity is responsible for the partnership's actions, because the partnership's filings with the Secretary of State's office are inconsistent.

Corporation. A corporation is a separate legal entity. It is owned by one or more shareholders. The corporation must be established in compliance with the statutory requirements of the state of incorporation. The shareholders elect a board of directors which has responsibility for management and control of the corporation. Because the corporation is a separate legal entity, the corporation is responsible for the debts and obligations of the business. In most cases, shareholders are insulated from claims against the corporation.

It is worth noting here that because a corporation is an entity separate from its owners, if the owner (and/or members of the owner's family) performs services for the corporation, these persons are considered to be employees of the corporation. Thus, the corporation will be required to comply with most of the laws and regulations and reporting requirements applicable to employers.

The corporation, as a separate legal entity, is also a separate taxable entity. The corporation may be taxed under Subchapter C of the Internal Revenue Code (a "C corporation") or Subchapter S of the Code (an "S corporation"). Minnesota tax laws provide for comparable treatment. A C corporation reports its income and expenses on a corporation income tax return and is taxed on its profits at corporation income tax rates. The corporation income tax is sometimes called a corporate franchise tax. Profits are taxed before dividends are paid. Dividends are taxed to shareholders, who report them as income, resulting in "double taxation" of profits which are paid as dividends. If the corporation meets the statutory requirements for S corporation status, the shareholders may elect to be taxed as an S corporation. Under the Internal Revenue Code, an S corporation may have only one class of stock, no more than 75 shareholders, and no shareholders that are nonresident aliens or non-individuals (e.g., corporations, partnerships, limited liability companies) except for certain estates, trusts and certain tax exempt entities. The S corporation is taxed in much the same manner as a partnership, i.e., the S corporation files an information return to report its income and expenses, but it generally is not separately taxed. Income and expenses of the S corporation "flow through" to the shareholders in proportion to their shareholdings, and profits are allocated and taxed to the shareholders at their individual tax rate. S corporations are described in more detail in later sections of this Guide.

A **closely held corporation** is any corporation whose shares are held by a relatively small number of shareholders. The Minnesota Business Corporation Act defines a closely held corporation as one which does not have more than 35 shareholders. Most closely held corporations are relatively small business enterprises, in which all shareholders tend to be active in the management of the business. The closely held corporation can provide many of the advantages of incorporation, such as limited liability for shareholders and S corporation status for tax purposes (if an S corporation election is made under the Internal Revenue Code) while retaining many of the simplified, less formal operating procedures of sole proprietorships and partnerships. Some states provide a separate, less formal, less restrictive set of laws for closely-held corporations. Minnesota does not. In Minnesota, the business corporation law is geared to small corporations, so a separate law is not necessary, and all corporations operate under one law.

Limited Liability Company. A Minnesota business also may organize as a limited liability company. A limited liability company is a form of business organization that is designed to combine the tax treatment of a partnership with the limited liability characteristics of a corporation. A limited liability company may have one or more members. As described further in the section on tax considerations in choosing the form of organization, organizers of Minnesota limited liability companies have some flexibility with respect to the federal income tax treatment of such entities due to the Treasury Regulations on entity classification. These Regulations appear in 26 C.F.R. § 301.7701-1 et. seq. (effective since January 1, 1997).

Limited liability companies with more than one member, like partnerships and limited partnerships, may choose to be taxed as partnerships or corporations. (In either event, the limited liability company must obtain both federal and state tax identification numbers, even if it has no employees). **A limited liability company with only one member may be taxed as a corporation or as a sole proprietorship. A limited liability company with one member that chooses to be taxed as a sole proprietorship generally does not obtain a federal or state tax identification number.** Business income and losses of the limited liability company that chooses to be taxed as a partnership or as a sole proprietorship may be passed through to the owners of the business. A limited liability company that chooses to be taxed as a partnership or as a sole proprietorship is not taxed at the entity level, eliminating the double taxation of profits that occurs with a C corporation. Income is then taxed at the owners' individual tax rate. Like a corporation, liability for business debts and obligations generally rests with the entity rather than with individual owners. A limited liability company is not subject to many of the restrictions that apply to S corporations. Unlike a limited partnership, all members of a limited liability company may participate in the active management of the company without risking loss of limited personal liability. It is managed by a board of governors and an active manager.

Other Forms of Organization. Other forms of organization available to Minnesota businesses include professional organizations (discussed further in this Guide), cooperative associations, business trusts, and certain variations of these forms of organization. These types of organizations are established and regulated by statute and involve complex legal, financial and accounting issues. Organizing under any of these forms should not be attempted without competent professional advice. Because of their highly specialized nature, these forms of organization are not addressed in detail in this Guide.

Changing the Form of Organization. Note that although the discussion in the above paragraphs is also applicable when changing the form of business organization, (e.g., when converting a sole proprietorship to a corporation), a business owner is strongly urged to seek professional assistance when doing so, because unintended consequences may result. As an example, contracts entered into by the business may or may not be assignable to the new entity; also, there may be a tax cost to changing the form of organization, such as when an S corporation becomes a C corporation.

NON-TAX FACTORS IN CHOOSING THE FORM OF ORGANIZATION

In choosing the most appropriate form of organization, the business owner will want to consider a variety of factors, including: complexity and expense of organizing the business; liability of the business owner; distribution of profits and losses; management control and decision making; financing startup and operation of the business; transferability of ownership interest; continuity of the business entity following withdrawal or death of an owner; complexity and expense of terminating or reorganizing the business; extent of governmental regulation, and tax considerations.

These factors should be examined carefully in light of the objectives of the business owner. Competent legal, accounting and tax professionals can provide valuable advice and assistance in selecting the most appropriate form of organization.

As with many business decisions, choosing a form of organization involves weighing the advantages and disadvantages of each alternative before selecting the form most appropriate to the business owner's situation. No one form of organization will be appropriate to all situations, and as the business expands a change in the form of organization may be necessary. The discussion which follows examines the differences in each of the above factors for proprietorships, partnerships, corporations, and limited liability companies.

Complexity and Expense of Organizing the Business

All businesses, regardless of their form, will encounter certain organizational costs. These costs can include developing a business plan, obtaining necessary licenses and permits, conducting market research studies, acquiring equipment, obtaining the advice of counsel, and other costs.

Sole Proprietorship. The sole proprietorship is the simplest form of organization, and the least expensive to establish. There are no statutory requirements unique to this form of organization. From a regulatory standpoint, the business owner only needs to obtain the necessary business licenses and tax identification numbers, register the business name, and begin operations. Many individuals begin their business as a sole proprietorship. As the business expands or more owners are needed for financial or other reasons, a partnership or corporation may be formed.

Partnership. A **general partnership** is more complex to organize than a sole proprietorship, but involves fewer formalities and legal restrictions than a limited partnership, corporation, or limited liability company. Basic elements of partnership law are established by statute, but most issues can be determined by agreement of the partners. A written partnership agreement is highly recommended, but is not legally required. Factors to consider in a partnership agreement are listed in a later section of this Guide. The partnership agreement is not required to be filed with any governmental entity. Note that under the Revised Uniform Partnership Act of 1997, (RUPA) Minnesota Statutes Chapter 323A, partnerships have the option of filing with the Secretary of State certain statements regarding the authority and liability of partners as well as the status of the partnership.

A **limited partnership** must meet specific statutory requirements at the time of organization, and the offering of ownership interests in the limited partnership is subject to tax and securities laws. Accordingly, the limited partnership will be more complex and expensive to organize than a general partnership.

Limited Liability Partnership and Limited Liability Limited Partnership. An existing general partnership may elect limited liability partnership status by filing a limited liability partnership registration with the Secretary of State. Such registration is effective for an indefinite period of time. Limited liability limited partnerships are also permitted. Anyone interested in forming an

LLP or an LLLP is advised to seek the advice of counsel. Note also under RUPA (i.e., Chapter 323A), limited liability limited partnership registrations have an indefinite term, although the Secretary of State's Office will revoke LLP or LLLP status if the required annual registration is not filed. Limited liability partnerships generally follow partnership law with specific exceptions as provided by law.

Corporation. The corporation is a formal and complex form of organization, and accordingly can be expensive to organize. Procedures and criteria for forming the corporation and for its governance are established by statute. **FAILURE TO FOLLOW THE STATUTORY FORMALITIES CAN RESULT IN LOSS OF CORPORATE STATUS AND IMPOSITION OF PERSONAL LIABILITY ON THE INCORPORATORS OR SHAREHOLDERS.** The S corporation faces further complexity in that the election of S corporation status for federal tax purposes must be filed with the Internal Revenue Service in a timely fashion. In addition, care must be taken in the transfer of shares not to inadvertently lose S corporation status.

Because of the complexities involved in incorporating, corporations often will make greater use of professional advisors, which will increase costs. Other costs associated with incorporating include filing fees, which are greater for corporations, and the costs associated with tax compliance and preparing various government reports. If the corporation does business in other states, it generally will be required to register to do business in those states, thus further increasing the cost and complexity of incorporation. And, if the corporation will raise capital by selling securities, the compliance costs involved will be substantial.

Minnesota has attempted to simplify the incorporation process by including in the Minnesota Business Corporation Act all of the rules pertaining to the internal governance of the corporation. A corporation that agrees to be governed as specified in the statute need only file standard form articles of incorporation with the Secretary of State. The corporation that wishes to vary the statutory requirements generally must do so in its articles of incorporation. Prior consultation with legal counsel can assist the incorporators in determining which approach is most appropriate for the corporation. Further information on incorporating appears in the section of this Guide titled Forming a Minnesota Business Corporation.

Limited Liability Company. The limited liability company combines aspects of the partnership and the corporation. It can be expected to be similar to a corporation in complexity and cost to organize. As with a corporation, the procedures and criteria for forming a limited liability company are specified by statute. **FAILURE TO FOLLOW THE STATUTORY REQUIREMENTS CAN RESULT IN LOSS OF LIMITED LIABILITY COMPANY STATUS AND IMPOSITION OF PERSONAL LIABILITY ON THE ORGANIZERS AND MEMBERS OF THE COMPANY.** There is very little case law to guide organizational and operational decisions although the limited liability company law is modeled on the business corporaton law. For this reason, owners of a limited liability company may need to consult often with their professional advisors, increasing their costs.

Under the Treasury Regulations dealing with the federal income tax classification of business entities, the organizers of a Minnesota limited liability company have some flexibility in choosing the tax status of their entity. Professional advice in this area is strongly encouraged.

As is the case for Minnesota corporations, organizers of a limited liability company may agree to have the company governed by the provisions of Minnesota statutes. In that case, standard form articles of organization may be used to organize the company.

Further information on forming a limited liability company appears in the section of this Guide on Forming a Minnesota Limited Liability Company.

Liability of the Business Owners

Sole Proprietorship. The sole proprietor is personally liable for the debts of the business, even if those debts exceed the owner's investment in the business. All of the owner's assets – both those used in the business and personal property (subject to certain exemptions) – can be attached by creditors and sold to pay business debts. The sole proprietor may be able to minimize certain risks such as property loss, personal injury or product liability by obtaining adequate insurance.

Partnership. In a **general partnership**, each partner is personally liable for the full amount of the partnership's debts, even if the debts exceed his or her investment and even if the partner did not personally consent to the debt. This is because, unless care is taken in the partnership agreement to limit a partner's authority and potential creditors are notified of the limitation, any partner may bind the partnership. The partner with greater personal assets thus risks losing more than a partner with fewer personal assets. As with a sole proprietorship, many business risks can be lessened by obtaining adequate insurance.

However, in a Minnesota **limited liability partnership,** partners are not personally liable for the wrongful acts or omissions in the ordinary course of business of other partners, for the misuse of money or property of a non-partner by another partner, or for the debts or obligations of the partnership, subject to certain exceptions. It is uncertain how this kind of partnership will be treated in other states, although most states have adopted some form of limited liability partnership legislation.

In a **limited partnership**, so long as the statutory formalities are met and the limited partner is not relied upon by others as a general partner, the limited partner generally is not liable for the obligations of the limited partnership. Thus the limited partner risks loss only up to the amount of his or her investment. The general partner retains full liability as in any other partnership. In **limited liability limited partnerships** general partners will enjoy the same protections from liability enjoyed by limited partners.

Corporation. The corporation is a separate legal entity, and in most cases is the entity that is liable for the debts of the business. The shareholders generally are exempt from personal liability for those debts and thus risk loss only up to the amount of their investment in the corporation. This is the case for both the C corporation and the S corporation. It should be noted, however, that in a small, closely held or newly created corporation without an established credit history, some or all of the shareholders may be expected to personally guarantee repayment of certain corporate debts as a condition of obtaining a loan or credit. Also, under certain circumstances such as fraud or personal wrongdoing, shareholders may be held personally liable for wrongful acts. Finally, it is possible for courts to "disregard" the corporate entity and make shareholders liable under certain circumstances.

Limited Liability Company. Liability of the owners of a limited liability company generally is the same as for shareholders of a corporation; that is, absent fraud, personal wrongdoing or disregard of the entities, they generally are not held personally liable for the debts and obligations of the business. They therefore risk loss only up to the amount of their investment. As is the case for corporations, owners of small, closely held, or newly organized limited liability companies may be required to give personal guarantees of repayment to secure financing or credit.

Distribution of Profits and Losses

Sole Proprietorship. The sole proprietor receives all the profits from the business, and bears all the losses, which may exceed the proprietor's investment in the business.

Partnership. In the general partnership, the limited liability partnership, the limited liability limited partnership and the limited partnership, profits and losses are passed through to the partners as specified in the partnership agreement. If left unspecified, profits and losses are shared equally among the partners.

Corporation. In a **C corporation**, profits and losses belong to the corporation. Profits may be distributed to shareholders in the form of dividends, or they may be reinvested or retained (within limits) by the corporation. Except upon sale of stock or liquidation of the corporation, losses by the corporation are not claimed by individual shareholders. In an **S corporation**, profits and losses flow through to shareholders in proportion to their shareholdings.

Limited Liability Company. Profits and losses of a limited liability company generally are allocated among the members in proportion to the value of their contributions. The articles of organization or the board of governors, under circumstances specified in the statute, may provide for a different allocation.

Management Control and Decision Making

Sole Proprietorship. The sole proprietor has full and complete authority to manage and control the business. There are no partners or shareholders to consult before making decisions. This form of organization gives the proprietor maximum freedom to run the business and respond quickly to day-to-day business needs. The disadvantage of this form is that the sole proprietor, as just one person, will have limited time, energy and expertise to devote to the business. His or her experiences may not provide the breadth of skills and knowledge necessary to deal with all phases of the business. Further, because the sole proprietor is the only person authorized to act on behalf of the business, he or she may be unable to leave the business for extended periods of time without jeopardizing its operations. As the business expands, the proprietor may be able to hire managers to perform some of these functions and provide additional expertise, but in the early years of the business, the sole proprietor often will perform many of these tasks alone.

Partnership. The general rule of management is that in both a **general partnership** and a **limited liability partnership**, all partners share equally in the right, and responsibility, to manage and control the business. The partnership agreement may centralize some management decisions in a smaller group of partners, but all partners continue to share ultimate responsibility for these decisions. By statute, certain management decisions require unanimous consent of the partners. Other decisions may be made by consent of a majority of the partners. The right to share equally in decisions can make the decision making process cumbersome, and the risk of major disagreements can impair effective operation of the business. An advantage of the partnership that is not present in a sole proprietorship is that the partnership, with its several owners, can bring a broader range of skills, abilities and resources to the business. The owners' combined experiences also can promote more informed decision making. In addition, the workload can be shared to lessen the physical and other demands on the individual owners.

However, under the Revised Uniform Partnership Act, Minnesota Statutes Chapter 323A (RUPA), a system of formal filings has been established that allows the partnerships to limit the authority of certain partners to third parties as well as to limit the liability of partners for obligations incurred after a partner has left the firm. In order to use this system, the partnership must first file with the Secretary of State an assumed name certificate or limited liability partnership statement of qualification. After that filing has been made, the partnership may again file any of the following statements with the Secretary of State:

- **Statement of Partnership Authority**. This allows the partnership to either restrict or specifically expand the authority of particular partners to conduct various transactions, particularly real estate transactions.

- **Statement of Denial.** This allows a partner to deny partnership status or the conferral of authority upon the partners by a Statement of Partnership Authority.

- **Statement of Dissociation.** This allows a partner who is withdrawing from the partnership to avoid liability for obligations for the partnership incurred after the partner has withdrawn, and also allows the partnership to eliminate the authority of that partner to bind the partnership.

- **Statement of Dissolution.** This allows the partnership to notify the world that it is dissolving and that partners will no longer have authority to act on behalf of the partnership.

The following are also permitted:

- **Statement of Merger.** This allows partnerships and limited partnerships to merge with each other.

- **Statement of Qualification.** This statement establishes a Minnesota limited liability partnership under Chapter 323A.

- **Statement of Foreign Qualification.** This statement registers a non-Minnesota limited liability partnership.

Any of these seven statements may also be amended or cancelled.

In order for any Statement to have an effect on real property transactions, a certified copy of the Statement, obtained from the Secretary of State, must be recorded in the office where land records for the county in which the real property is located, and, if applicable, has been memorialized on the certificate of title for that real property.

In a **limited partnership**, the limited partners generally do not participate actively in the management and control of the limited partnership. The general partners perform this function.

The limited partnership thus provides a vehicle for raising capital without diluting control of the firm.

Corporation. The rules for corporate decision making are established by statute, but many rules may be modified by the articles of incorporation or bylaws. Shareholders elect the board of directors, which in turn manages the operation of the business. The corporation also must have one or more natural persons exercising the functions of chief executive officer and chief financial officer. Except in very small corporations in which the shareholders are also the directors, shareholders as a group generally will not directly participate in management decisions. This concentration of decision making in a relatively few individuals promotes flexibility in decision making, but also can result in overruling of minority interests or in some cases manipulation or exploitation of minority shareholders. To resolve this problem, corporations may adopt provisions in the articles of incorporation or bylaws to give minority shareholders a stronger voice in management decisions. Decision making authority also may be delegated by the shareholders and/or directors to hired managers, who may or may not be shareholders. This delegation further removes decision making authority from the shareholders. Like a partnership, the corporation can draw on the skills and expertise of more than one individual in running the business. This can broaden the base of information for decision making and reduce workload demands on individual managers.

The articles of incorporation, by-laws or state business corporation act establish procedures and criteria for decision making, such as meeting and quorum requirements, voting margins, and the like, which may make decision making in the corporation more cumbersome than in a sole proprietorship or partnership.

Limited Liability Company. Like a corporation, a limited liability company has centralized management. By statute, a limited liability company is managed by or under the direction of a board of governors, comprised of one or more individuals. In addition, the limited liability company must have one or more individuals exercising the functions of chief manager and treasurer. Additional managers and agents may be appointed by the board. The limited liability company act also authorizes members of the limited liability company to make management decisions under certain circumstances. As with a corporation, many of the rules governing the management of the limited liability company are specified in the articles of organization, by-laws, or the limited liability company statute.

Financing Startup and Operation of the Business

A startup business, regardless of form, generally will find it difficult to obtain outside financing. The statistical failure rate for new businesses is high, and many lenders view financing the startup business venture as extremely risky. Banks and other creditors generally will require a significant capital investment by the business owner, and a personal guarantee that the owner will repay the loan. Corporations may issue securities to pool capital from a large number of investors; however, the costs of complying with complex federal and state securities laws may be prohibitive, and there is no guarantee that a market will exist for the securities of a new firm. Likewise, limited liability companies may increase capital by admitting more members, but will need to offer prospective members some likelihood of return on their investment. Thus as a practical matter, startup financing for the new venture – whether it is a sole proprietorship, a partnership, a corporation or a limited liability company – often is limited to what the owner and others closely associated with the venture are able to raise.

The discussion which follows addresses the relative ease with which firms with established credit histories may be able to attract financing.

Sole Proprietorship. The sole proprietor's ability to raise capital generally is limited to the amount he or she can personally secure. Accordingly, the sole proprietorship ordinarily will have less capital available to finance operations or expansion than will other forms of organization that may be able to attract outside investors.

Partnership. In most cases, a partnership will be able to raise capital more easily than a sole proprietorship, but not as easily as a corporation. The borrowing power of each partner may be pooled to raise capital, or additional partners may be admitted to increase this pooled borrowing power. Or, if the partnership does not wish to distort the ownership position of the original partners, a limited partnership may be established to raise capital. Unlike a corporation, however, partnership assets generally will not be accepted as collateral by a lender. Instead, assets of the individual partners are used to secure loans, which are made to the partners in their individual capacity.

Corporation. The corporation generally is the easiest form of organization for raising capital from outside investors. Capital may be raised by selling stocks or bonds to investors. As noted in the section of this Guide on securities registration, the sale of securities is regulated by federal and state laws. Due to the complexity of these laws, the sale of securities is expensive, and the cost may be prohibitive for startup firms. Long term financing by lending institutions is easier for a corporation to structure because corporate assets may be used to secure the financing. Personal assets of the principals of the corporation and its shareholders also may be used to guarantee loans to the corporation.

The number of shares of stock a corporation may issue must be authorized by the articles of incorporation. If a corporation has issued all of its authorized shares, it is necessary to amend the articles of incorporation to authorize additional shares. The amended articles of incorporation must be filed with the Secretary of State, and a filing fee paid. The corporation can avoid paying this additional filing fee by authorizing a large number of shares at the time of incorporation.

An S corporation may have only one class of stock outstanding. This may limit the financing alternatives available to the S corporation.

Limited Liability Company. The limited liability company is financed by contributions from members. It also may invest its own funds, borrow money and trade in the securities of other organizations and the government. The limited liability company offers more flexibility in structuring outside financing than does the S corporation. The S corporation is limited by the single class of stock rule and it generally must allocate profits and losses proportionately. The limited liability company may create multiple membership classes and series, and may provide in its articles of organization that profits and losses may be allocated other than in proportion to the value of a member's contribution. (Tax counsel should be consulted on the tax consequences of a disproportionate allocation.)

Limited liability company members do, however, have preemptive rights to increase their own contributions to the company before the company accepts contributions from outsiders. Also, the articles of organization may need to be amended to allow the limited liability company to create additional membership classes or series of membership interests. Another potential issue in attracting outside financing is that lenders and venture capitalists may not be familiar with the limited liability company as a form of organization. They thus may be unwilling to finance a deal without substantial equity participation and personal guarantees by limited liability company members or principals.

Transferability of Ownership Interest

Sole Proprietorship. A sole proprietor transfers ownership of the business by transferring the assets of the business to the new owner. The prior proprietorship is terminated and a new proprietorship is established under the new owner.

Partnership. The transfer of a partner's economic interest in a partnership is determined by the partnership agreement, or by statute if there is no partnership agreement. Unless permitted by the partnership agreement, no person may become a partner without the consent of all the other partners. If a partner attempts to transfer his or her interest in the partnership without such an agreement, the transferee does not become a partner but instead becomes entitled to receive the profits which the transferring partner otherwise would receive. A properly drawn partnership agreement will address the conditions under which an ownership interest may be transferred, and the consequences to the transferee and to the partnership.

Corporation. Ownership in a corporation is transferred by sale of stock. A change in ownership does not affect the existence of the corporate entity. Technically, shares of stock in a corporation are freely transferable. As a practical matter, however, the market may be limited for shares of stock in a small corporation that is not publicly traded. In addition, shareholders in a new venture often will want to prevent unrestricted transfer of shares and thus may provide in the articles of incorporation or bylaws for transfer restrictions or buy-sell and redemption agreements, further limiting transferability. In an S corporation, shares of stock also are freely transferable. However, the S corporation election may be inadvertently terminated if the entity to which the shares are transferred does not qualify as an S corporation shareholder.

Limited Liability Company. Membership rights in a limited liability company consist of financial rights and governance rights. Financial rights are the rights to share in the profits, losses and distributions of the limited liability company. Governance rights are the rights to vote and to manage the business. Unless the articles of organization or operating agreement provide otherwise, a member may assign or transfer financial rights. Such a transfer gives the transferee all the rights to profits and distributions that the transferor had. The transfer does not create membership rights in the transferee, nor can the transfer allow the transferee to directly or indirectly exercise governance rights. Governance rights can only be transferred if all members give their written consent. The articles of organization may provide for less-than-unanimous consent.

Continuity of the Business Following Withdrawal or Death of an Owner

Sole Proprietorship. The business entity terminates at the death of the proprietor or if the proprietor becomes unable to manage it.

Partnership. General partnerships and **limited liability partnerships** under the Revised Uniform Partnership Act (Chapter 323A) do **NOT** automatically cease to exist when a partner dies or otherwise withdraws from a partnership. The partnership continues, unless certain other events occur. A **limited partnership** does not terminate when a limited partner dies or becomes disabled. The limited partner's interest may be assigned, and if the limited partner dies, his or her legal representative may exercise all the partner's rights for purposes of settling the estate.

Corporation. A corporation is a separate legal entity, and therefore the death, disability or withdrawal of an owner has no legal effect on the business entity's existence. As a practical matter, however, many small businesses depend heavily on the efforts of one or two individuals, and the death or disability of one of those key individuals can seriously impair the economic viability of the business. For this reason, a small business corporation, like a partnership, often will obtain life insurance on key shareholder-employees. The articles of incorporation may provide for share purchase agreements or other restrictions on the transferability of stock in order to retain control of the firm by the remaining key individuals.

Limited Liability Company. For limited liability companies formed before August 1, 1999, the termination of membership of a member by any means is an event of dissolution which generally terminates the existence of the limited liability company. If the articles of organization permit remaining members to give dissolution avoidance consent, or to enter into a business continuation agreement, the limited liability company, or its business, may be continued following an event of dissolution. If at least two members remain following the event of dissolution, and all remaining members unanimously consent within 90 days of the termination of membership, the limited liability company's existence and business can be continued. (The articles of organization may provide for less-than-unanimous consent to continue the limited liability company.) Even if the limited liability company's existence is terminated, if the articles of organization permit it, the remaining members may continue the business by merging the limited liability company into another Minnesota limited liability company or into a Minnesota or foreign corporation.

For limited liability companies formed on or after August 1, 1999, the termination of membership of a particular member is an event of dissolution only to the extent specified in the articles of organization or in a member control agreement, or if the membership of the last member terminates and no new members are admitted within 180 days of that termination. Otherwise, the termination of a member's interest does not affect the existence of the limited liability company.

Complexity and Expense of Terminating the Business

Sole Proprietorship. There are no federal or state regulations governing termination of the sole proprietorship itself. The sole proprietor simply winds up the affairs of the business and discontinues operations. If the business had employees, the owner must notify federal and state taxing authorities that the proprietor is no longer operating the business and paying employees. See also the section of this Guide entitled "Business Taxes – Income Tax Withholding – Withholding Tax Penalties and Interest". The final report of income and expenses attributable to the business is included in the proprietor's individual income tax return, which is filed at the usual time. No final return or early filing is required. Tax consequences may flow from the sale or other disposition of assets used in the business.

Partnership. The partnership, because it is a more formal structure than a sole proprietorship, is more complex to terminate. RUPA identifies several ways in which dissolution may occur, but the partners may provide for continuation of the partnership even if an act of dissolution occurs. The consequences of causing the dissolution of a partnership also are specified in RUPA. The statute addresses the allocation and distribution of partnership property upon dissolution, liability of persons continuing the business, and other rights and liabilities of the partners. However, the statute does not address procedural matters such as filing final tax returns, notifying taxing authorities of the termination for employment tax purposes, notification of creditors and similar matters involved in winding up the affairs of the partnership. Assistance with these matters may be obtained from legal counsel. Tax consequences may apply to the disposition of partnership assets, and those tax consequences will flow through to the partners. The **general partnership** may file a Statement of Dissolution with the Secretary of State but generally otherwise need not file notice of dissolution or termination of the partnership with any governmental entity. The **limited partnership** must formally cancel the certificate of limited partnership and file the cancellation with the Secretary of State. A **limited liability partnership** will revert to a general partnership upon voluntarily terminating limited liability partnership status, which is done by filing a withdrawal or termination statement with the Secretary of State. Limited liability partnerships do not expire unless the partnership fails to file the annual registration, in which case the limited liability partnership status is terminated and the partnership reverts to general or limited partnership status.

Note that the Revised Uniform Partnership Act, Minnesota Statutes Chapter 323A, also allows for mergers of partnerships which terminates all but the surviving partnerhsip.

Corporation. The corporation is the most complex business form to terminate. Formal dissolution procedures are specified by statute, and include, for example, filing notice of intent to dissolve the corporation and articles of dissolution with the Secretary of State, notification of creditors, disposition of assets, and distribution of the proceeds to shareholders. Tax consequences will affect both the corporation and its shareholders. Because of the complexity of the statutory procedures and tax implications, professional legal and accounting advice is highly recommended.

Limited Liability Company. As is the case with partnerships, limited partnerships, and corporations, the procedures for dissolving a limited liability company are spelled out in the governing legislation. Different procedures apply, depending on when the limited liability company is dissolved (e.g., before or after membership contributions are accepted), and who dissolves it (e.g., the organizers, the members, or the court). The law specifies the notices to be given (e.g., to members and creditors), filings with the Secretary of State and procedures for winding up the business of the limited liability company.

Subsequent Reorganization of the Business. If the business is being terminated because the owner wishes to do business under a different type of entity (such as converting a sole proprietorship to an S corporation), special issues might need to be addressed. For instance, when an S corporation is converted to a C corporation, adverse tax consequences often result. Also, certain assets of the business may not be transferable; for example, any contract that the business has entered into might or might not be transferable if the business is terminated and reorganized. Many other issues could arise when a business is terminated and begun again under a different form of organization. Although generally speaking an owner is permitted to change the form of his or her business at any time, a business owner is advised to seek professional assistance when considering changing the form of his or her business.

Extent of Government Regulation

Certain types of government regulation will apply to the business regardless of the form of organization. Licenses or permits, where required, will be required of all business entities conducting the regulated activity. Note that businesses operating in multiple jurisdictions (whether cities, states or counties) should inquire about licensing requirements imposed by each of those jurisdictions. This is equally true of businesses using the Internet.[1] Federal, state and local consumer protection laws regulate business relationships with the public, without regard to the form of organization. Every business that hires employees will be required to comply with certain federal and state labor and tax laws governing the employment relationship. The following paragraphs identify the major differences in the extent of regulation of the form of organization itself.

Sole Proprietorship. The sole proprietorship, as a form of business organization, is not generally regulated by the state. Other than tax filings and specialized reports applicable to certain kinds of businesses (e.g., hazardous waste generators), no special governmental filings or reports are required, making the sole proprietorship the least restrictive, most private form of organization.

Partnership. A **general partnership,** like a sole proprietorship, operates with relatively few governmental controls. RUPA provides statutory rules for basic questions of partnership management and relationships between the partners and third persons, but most issues are determined by the partnership agreement. No special partnership reports to or filings with government existing are required, but an assumed name certificate may be required, depending upon the partnership name. **Limited liability partnerships** and **limited liability limited partnerships** must file with the Secretary of State on a yearly basis in order to retain their special status. **Limited partnerships** are more closely regulated than general partnerships, and public filings remove some of the privacy associated with sole proprietorships and general partnerships.

Corporation. Rules governing the corporation are established by laws of the state of incorporation and the corporation's articles of incorporation. These rules are more formal and complex than those governing partnerships and limited partnerships. In addition to complying with laws and regulations applicable to similarly situated businesses, any corporation that issues registered securities will be required to make periodic filings with state and federal regulators and must comply with other reporting requirements. Tax laws applicable to corporations generally are more complex than those applicable to proprietorships and partnerships and specific statutory procedures apply to dissolving the corporate entity. Most governmental filings are public documents, making the corporation the least private form of organization. The S corporation must meet specific requirements to qualify for S corporation tax treatment, and S corporation status may be terminated when these requirements are not met.

Limited Liability Company. Rules governing the limited liability company are established by statute and by the limited liability company's articles of organization and operating agreement (if any). These rules are similar in complexity to those governing partnerships and corporations.

---

[1] For more information about using the Internet, see *A Legal Guide to the Internet* available without charge from the Minnesota Small Business Assistance Office, 500 Metro Square, 121 E. Seventh Place, St. Paul, MN 55101, telephone (651) 296-3871 or (800) 657-3858 (ask for Small Business) or available from the website www.dted.state.mn.us

TAX CONSIDERATIONS IN CHOOSING THE FORM OF ORGANIZATION

n the Internal Revenue Code and Minnesota tax laws are periodically revised. Every effort has been made to incorporate these changes into this section. However, because of the complexity and potential impact of the changes, consultation with a professional advisor on any tax matter is highly recommended.

This section discusses the major tax considerations for the sole proprietorship, partnership, and corporation. For limited liability companies, the Internal Revenue Service has adopted rules (which appear in 26 C.F.R. 301.7701-1 et. seq.)) that allow the organizer(s) to select the federal tax treatment for the LLC: either as a sole proprietorship or a corporation, in the case of LLCs with only one member; or as a partnership or a corporation, in the case of LLCs with at least two members. (The Minnesota Department of Revenue, in Revenue Notice 98-08, has stated that except for entities organized outside the United States and which have only one owner, which is a C corporation, the Department of Revenue will for Minnesota tax purposes respect the choice made under the Federal Regulations). Thus because LLCs are treated as either sole proprietorships, corporations, or partnerships, they are not specifically described in the following text. However a business is treated for federal tax purposes, it also will be so treated for state tax purposes. Detailed advice on specific situations should be obtained from a competent tax advisor.

Considerations addressed in this section include:

- Who is the Taxpayer?
- What Tax Forms Are Used?
- Tax Rates
- Tax Impact
- Selection of the Tax Year
- Compensation for Services
- Employment Taxes and Workers' Compensation Insurance
- Employee Retirement Benefit Plans
- Fringe Benefits
- Capital Gains and Losses
- Net Operating Loss
- Estimated Tax Payments
- Disposition of Ownership Interest

Who Is the Taxpayer?

Sole Proprietorship. In a sole proprietorship, the taxpayer is the individual business owner. The proprietor is taxed on the entire net income from the business, regardless of whether the income is withdrawn for personal use or retained in the business. This is the case for both federal and Minnesota tax purposes.

Partnership. The partnership itself is not a taxable entity. The partnership serves as a conduit through which income, deductions and credits are passed through to the individual partners. Each partner is taxed on his or her share as defined in the partnership agreement. All income of the partnership is taxed to the partners, whether or not it is actually distributed. The partnership itself files an information return which reports partnership income and distributions to the partners. This is the case for both federal and Minnesota tax purposes.

Corporation. A corporation is a separate legal and taxable entity. For tax purposes, the corporation may be a "C corporation" (taxed under Subchapter C of the Internal Revenue Code and corresponding sections of Minnesota Statutes) or it may elect to be treated as an "S corporation" (taxed under Subchapter S of the Internal Revenue Code and corresponding sections of Minnesota Statutes). Both C corporations and S corporations file federal and Minnesota tax returns. In a C corporation, the corporation itself pays tax on corporate profits. After taxes are paid, remaining corporate profits may be distributed to shareholders in the form of dividends. The shareholders are then taxed on the dividends they receive from the corporation. In general, an S corporation is taxed in a manner similar to a partnership; that is, the income, deductions and credits of the corporation are passed through to shareholders, and are taxed to shareholders at their individual tax rates.

Note: It is possible that each of the above-listed entities, other than a sole proprietership, may be subject to a Minnesota minimum fee. See the discussion of "Tax Rates," which follows after the discussion of "What Tax Forms are Used?"

What Tax Forms Are Used?

Note: Income tax forms identified here apply to the 2002 tax year. Amendments to the Minnesota tax laws and federal Internal Revenue Code may change these requirements.

Sole Proprietorship. Federal: The sole proprietor reports income and expenses from the business on Schedule C or Schedule C-EZ (Form 1040) and any related forms and schedules. The net income or loss from the business is then transferred to the proprietor's individual Form 1040. The sole proprietor uses Schedule SE to report net self employment income for purposes of computing the Social Security and Medicare self employment tax. **Minnesota:** There is no separate form for reporting proprietorship income. To compute Minnesota income tax, the proprietor uses Form M-1, the individual income tax form. A copy of the federal Form 1040, including a copy of Schedule C or Schedule C-EZ, plus Schedule SE, if appropriate, must be attached to Minnesota Form M-1. Minnesota does not impose a self employment tax.

Partnership. Federal: The partnership files Form 1065, which is an information return. No tax is paid by the partnership with this return. Other forms and schedules may be required, including Schedules K and K-1. Individual partners use Schedule E (Form 1040) which is prepared with information from their Schedule K-1 of Form 1065, to report their distributive share of partnership income, deductions, credits and losses on their individual Form 1040. Schedule SE (Form 1040) is used to compute Social Security and Medicare self employment tax. **Minnesota:** The partnership files Form M-3. Taxes paid by the partnership with such return are: Minnesota Minimum Fee; Minnesota Composite Income Tax; and Withholding for Nonresident Partners, which is described in the Tax Rates section of this Guide. Form M-1 is used to compute the partners' individual income tax. Schedules M-KPI and M-KPC are supplemental K-1 type schedules used to report modifications to federal tax computations of partnership income, and the other information a partner needs to complete the Minnesota individual income tax return. Schedule M-KC is used for computing the Minnesota Composite Income Tax. Schedule MW-3NR is used for the Withholding for Nonresident Partners. Minnesota does not impose a self employment tax.

C Corporation. Federal: The C corporation reports its income, deductions and credits, and computes its tax, on Form 1120 or Form 1120-A. Supporting forms and schedules may be required. If the corporation issues dividends, it must annually send its shareholders Form 1099-DIV, stating the amount of dividends paid. A copy also is filed with the Internal Revenue Service and the Minnesota Department of Revenue. The shareholder reports dividends received from the corporation on his or her individual Form 1040. **Minnesota:** The corporation files Minnesota Form M-4. Dividends paid to shareholders also must be reported to the Department of Revenue. Form M-1 is used to compute the shareholder's individual Minnesota income tax.

S Corporation. Federal: The S corporation files Form 1120S and supporting forms and schedules, including Schedules K and K-1 (Form 1120S). The S corporation generally is not separately taxed. Individual shareholders report their share of the S corporation's income, deductions and credits on their individual Form 1040, using information contained on the Schedule K-1. **Minnesota:** For Minnesota income tax purposes, the S corporation files Form M-3S-4. Taxes paid by the S corporation with that return are: Minnesota S Corporation Taxes, which apply only if the S corporation is paying federal income tax; Minnesota Minimum Fee; Minnesota Composite Income Tax; and Withholding for Nonresident Shareholders, which is discussed in the Tax Rates section of this Guide. Form M-1 is used to compute the shareholder's individual income tax. Schedule M-KS is a supplemental K-1 type schedule used for reporting modifications to federal income tax computations of S corporation income, and the other information a shareholder needs to complete the Minnesota individual income tax return. Schedule M-KC is used for computing the Minnesota Composite Income Tax. Schedule MW-3NR is used for the Withholding for Nonresident shareholders.

Tax Rates

The rate of tax paid on income from the business activity depends on whether the business is organized as a sole proprietorship, a partnership, an S corporation, a C corporation, or a limited liability company. Income from a sole proprietorship, partnership, S corporation, or limited liability company is taxed to the owner at individual tax rates. A C corporation's income is taxed to the corporation at corporate tax rates. Dividend income paid by the C corporation is taxed to shareholders at individual tax rates.

Federal Individual Income Tax Rates. For the period July 1, 2001 through December 31, 2002, in each year there are six federal tax rates for individual income tax: 10 percent, 15 percent, 27 percent, 30 percent, 35 percent and 38.6 percent. Tax brackets are indexed for inflation.

Minnesota Individual Income Tax Rates. Minnesota individual income tax rates are 5.35 percent, 7.05 percent, and 7.85 percent. Partnerships and S corporations that have nonresident individual partners or shareholders are allowed to pay a composite income tax, on behalf of such nonresident partners or shareholders, on the partnership's or S corporation's return. In that event, the nonresident partners or shareholders do not have to file separate Minnesota income tax returns. The tax rate for the Minnesota Composite Income Tax is 7.85 percent of the individual's "Minnesota source" income. In addition, a partnership or S corporation that does not pay a composite income tax on behalf of nonresident individual partners or shareholders must withhold tax at a rate of 7.85 percent from such an individual's "Minnesota source" income.

Federal Corporate Income Tax Rates. There are seven federal tax rates for corporate income tax for C corporations. They are 15 percent, 25 percent, 34 percent, 39 percent and (due to phase-outs of the lower rates for taxable incomes above certain thresholds), 34 percent, 35 percent and 38 percent. Special rules apply to personal holding companies, corporations with excess accumulated earnings, and to certain other situations.

Minnesota Corporate (Franchise) Income Tax Rates. The Minnesota corporate income tax rate is 9.8 percent. Corporations are subject to an alternative minimum tax based on Minnesota alternative minimum taxable income at the rate of 5.8 percent. The amount due is the excess of the alternative minimum tax liability over the firm's regular franchise tax liability.

Minnesota Minimum Fee Rates. A graduated minimum fee is imposed by Minnesota on corporations, S corporations, partnerships, and limited liability companies. The fee is based on Minnesota payroll, property and sales and is in addition to any regular or alternative minimum tax liability the business may have. Note that for partnerships, the minimum fee is the joint and several liability of the partners. The minimum fee schedule is as follows:

Minnesota Payroll, Property and Sales	Fee
Less than $500,000	$ 0
$500,000 to $999,999	$ 100
$1 million to $4,999,999	$ 300
$5 million to $9,999,999	$1,000
$10 million to $19,999,999	$2,000
$20 million or more	$5,000

Tax Impact

Many factors determine the full tax burden on a business. Some of these factors – such as treatment of capital gains, deductibility of certain items, and the availability of certain credits – will vary depending on the form of organization. Other factors, such as employment taxes attributable to non-owner employees or property taxes, will apply regardless of the form of organization. For detailed analysis of these factors in the context of the specific business, a competent tax advisor should be consulted. The following paragraphs describe the major differences in tax impact attributable to the form of organization.

Sole Proprietorship. Net income or loss from the business is combined with the proprietor's income and losses from other sources to determine the proprietor's income for tax purposes. The proprietor is taxed on the net income of the business, regardless of whether the income is withdrawn for personal purposes or retained in the business. Because income or loss from the business is combined for tax purposes with income and losses from other sources, the tax impact on income from the business may be different than if the business were taxed as a separate entity. However, because only the proprietor and not the business entity is taxed, there is no double taxation on profits of the business paid to the owner. Another advantage of the sole proprietorship compared with the C corporation is that not only the amount but the character of various income items, deductions, and credits may be claimed by the business owner. In a C corporation, items are claimed by the corporation on its tax return and are not passed through to shareholders.

Partnership. Partnership income is taxable to the partners regardless of whether it is actually distributed or retained in the business. The partners report their distributive share of partnership income, deductions and credits on their individual income tax returns, where these items are combined with income and losses from other sources. This income is taxed at the individual income tax rate applicable to the partner's tax bracket. The partners may allocate their distributive share of partnership income, deductions and credits for tax purposes in the partnership agreement. So long as there is "substantial economic effect" to the allocation (as defined by tax laws and Internal Revenue Service regulations), the partnership may offer greater opportunity for tax planning than the proprietorship or corporate form of organization. By "substantial economic effect" the Internal Revenue Service essentially means that the allocation made in the partnership agreement may actually affect the dollar amount of the partner's share of the partnership income or loss independently of any tax consequences. As with the proprietorship, both the amount and character of various income and deduction items are passed through to shareholders. However, certain deductions may not be permitted, certain items must be separately stated, and a partner's ability to claim his or her share of partnership losses generally is limited to the partner's adjusted basis in the partnership.

C Corporation. C corporations are separate taxable entities. The C corporation's taxable income, and tax, are determined prior to distribution of profits to shareholders. Profits which are distributed to shareholders in the form of dividends are then taxable to the shareholders at their individual income tax rate. Thus these dividends are subject to double taxation: once on the corporation's income tax return and once on the individual shareholder's income tax return. In addition, the dividends are taxed to the shareholder as ordinary income: capital gains, charitable contributions and other income and deduction items do not retain their character when passed to shareholders in the form of dividends. Similarly, individual shareholders do not share a corporation's losses for tax purposes.

C corporations offer some opportunity for tax planning in that dividends may be accumulated by the corporation rather than paid to shareholders, thus postponing double taxation. However, Internal Revenue Service regulations limit the amount of accumulated earnings that may be retained by the corporation. An accumulated earnings tax may be imposed on excessive accumulated earnings. Because all income of the sole proprietorship, partnership, and S corporation is taxable to the owners whether or not it is distributed, these entities are not subject to the accumulated earnings tax. The C corporation also may pay a salary to owner-employees. Salaries are deductible by the corporation and thus are not included in the corporation's taxable income. However, the Internal Revenue Service may treat as dividends excessive salaries that appear designed to avoid double taxation.

S Corporation. Like a partnership, the S corporation is a conduit through which the firm's income and deductions flow to the shareholders. Income items (including capital gains) and deductions generally retain their character when passed through to shareholders, although special reporting rules apply and the opportunity to fully claim a share of the S corporation's losses may be limited. Unlike a partnership, allocations to S corporation shareholders must be in proportion to their shareholdings. Thus this form of organization may offer less attractive tax planning opportunities.

A shareholder's pro rata share of S corporation income and deductions is combined with income and losses from other sources and reported on the shareholder's individual income tax return. The total taxable income is taxed at individual income tax rates applicable to the shareholder's tax bracket.

Selection of the Tax Year

The business figures its taxable income and files a tax return on the basis of an accounting period called a tax year. A tax year usually is 12 consecutive months, although in some cases a 52-53 week year or a short tax year may be permitted. A **calendar** tax year is 12 consecutive months ending December 31. A **fiscal** tax year is either 12 consecutive months ending on the last day of any month other than December, or a 52-53 week year. To use a fiscal tax year, the business must keep its books on that basis. Once a tax year is established, the business generally may not change it without Internal Revenue Service approval. The application to change the tax year must show a substantial business purpose for the change, and that no significant tax advantage will result.

Sole Proprietorship. Like most individual taxpayers, sole proprietors generally use the calendar year as their federal and Minnesota tax year. The sole proprietor must report income from all sources on the basis of the same tax year.

Partnership. In general, the partnership must use the same tax year as the partners who own a majority interest in partnership profits and capital. If those partners have different tax years, the partnership must use the same tax year as its principal partners. Principal partners are defined by the Internal Revenue Service as those having an interest of five percent or more in partnership profits or capital. If the principal partners have different tax years, the partnership generally must use the calendar tax year. However, a partnership may adopt a fiscal tax year if it can establish to the satisfaction of the Internal Revenue Service that it has a business purpose for using a fiscal tax year. If a business purpose for using a fiscal tax year cannot be shown, a partnership that would otherwise be required to use a calendar tax year may in some cases elect a fiscal tax year by filing with the IRS Form 8716, Election to Have a Tax Year Other than a Required Tax Year. This election is called a "Section 444 election." A partnership that makes the Section 444 election must in some cases make a payment to the government that reflects the value of the tax deferral obtained by the partners as a result of the partnership's use of a fiscal tax year. A partnership uses the same tax year for both federal and Minnesota income tax purposes.

C Corporation. A C corporation establishes its tax year when it files its first income tax return. The first tax year must end not more than 12 months after the date of incorporation. A C corporation that is not a personal service corporation may choose a calendar tax year or a fiscal tax year, so long as the tax year selected does not distort income. This allows the corporation to establish a tax year in conformity with its natural business cycle. C corporations that are personal service corporations must use a calendar tax year unless the corporation establishes to the satisfaction of the IRS that it has a business purpose for using a fiscal tax year, or makes a Section 444 election.

S Corporation. S corporations must use a calendar tax year unless there is a business purpose for using a fiscal tax year, and the Internal Revenue Service approves. If the S corporation cannot establish a business purpose for using a fiscal tax year, it may be eligible to make the Section 444 election described above. The corporation uses the same tax year for both federal and Minnesota tax purposes.

Compensation for Services

A business may use a variety of methods to compensate persons who provide services to it. Some of these methods include salaries or wages, personal draw, cash for services, and property for services. This section discusses the tax consequences of compensation for services provided by the owner of the business. Compensation to non-owner third parties, including the spouse or children of a sole proprietor, generally will be a deductible expense so long as compensation is reasonable and the services are necessary to the business.

Sole Proprietorship. A sole proprietor is not considered an employee of the business and does not receive wages or salary for tax purposes. A sole proprietor is subject to tax on the net income of the business as it is earned, regardless of whether it is withdrawn. Compensation for services or other amounts withdrawn from the business thus are considered withdrawals of income and are not again taxed at the time of withdrawal.

Partnerships. Like sole proprietors, partners of a general partnership are not considered employees of the business and do not receive wages or salary for tax purposes. The partners are subject to tax on their share of partnership income as it is earned, regardless of whether it is withdrawn. Amounts withdrawn by a partner for compensation or other purposes are considered withdrawals of income and are not again taxed at the time of withdrawal. However, withdrawals in excess of a partner's basis are taxed.

C Corporations. Payments to owners: Payments to shareholder-employees in the form of salary or wages are deductible by the corporation in determining taxable income. As with other wages and salaries, these payments are taxed to the recipient as wage or salary income. Payments must be reasonable and the services must be necessary to the business. Compensation to shareholder-employees which is found by the Internal Revenue Service to be unreasonable may be reclassified as a dividend. This is to prevent using salary payments as a device to avoid double taxation of corporate profits.

S Corporations. Payments to owners: The payment of wages or salary to S corporation employees, including owner-employees, is deductible by the corporation in determining taxable income. These payments are then taxed to the recipient as wage or salary income. Payments must be reasonable and the services must be necessary to the business. The question of unreasonably large salaries to shareholder-employees of S corporations is not as important as it is in C corporations, because the S corporation generally pays no taxes at corporate rates. However, the Internal Revenue Service may challenge salaries which are used as a device to shift income to shareholders in lower income tax brackets.

Note: Special rules apply to tax treatment of property, such as stock, received for services. Business owners contemplating such transfers should consult with their tax advisor prior to the transfer.

Employment Taxes and Workers' Compensation Insurance

Employment taxes include income tax withholding, Social Security and Medicare taxes and federal and state unemployment compensation taxes. Although workers' compensation insurance technically is not a tax, coverage is required for most employees. Employment taxes and workers' compensation insurance are deductible business expenses in determining net income.

Note: The following information on employment taxes and workers' compensation insurance applies only to businesses that have employees. Sole proprietors and partners that provide services to the business are not considered employees for purposes of paying unemployment taxes or obtaining workers' compensation insurance coverage for themselves. They may, however, be liable for Social Security and Medicare self employment tax. (See the discussion of the self employment tax below.) Shareholders in a C corporation or an S corporation who perform services for the corporation generally will be considered employees of the corporation and therefore will be subject to employment taxes. In most situations, workers' compensation coverage for these shareholders also will be required.

Self Employment Tax. Although sole proprietorships and partnerships that do not have employees are not required to pay employment taxes, the sole proprietor or partners may be liable for Social Security and Medicare self employment tax. For 2002 the Social Security and Medicare self employment tax rate is 15.3 percent.

Social Security and Medicare Tax. Social security and Medicare taxes are paid by both the employer and the employee. The Social Security tax rate for 2002 for both the employer and the employee is 6.2 percent of the first $84,900 in wages. The Medicare tax rate for 2002 for both the employer and the employee is 1.45 percent on all wages. Social Security and Medicare taxes are not required for a sole proprietor's children under age 18 who work in the sole proprietorship.

Federal Unemployment Taxes. Employers generally are liable for both federal and Minnesota unemployment taxes. The federal unemployment tax rate is 6.2 percent of the first $7,000 in wages paid each employee. A credit of up to 5.4 percent may be allowed for state unemployment taxes paid. Wages paid to a spouse or child under age 21 who works in a sole proprietorship owned by the spouse or parent are not subject to federal unemployment taxes; other exceptions also may apply.

Minnesota Unemployment Tax. State unemployment tax rates are discussed in the business tax section of this Guide. Different rates apply to new businesses, the construction industry, and businesses which have an established experience rating. The wage base to which the tax applies also depends on the experience rating of the business. Wages paid by a sole proprietor for services performed by a parent, spouse or child under the age of 18 are not subject to Minnesota unemployment taxes. Other exceptions also may apply.

Workers' Compensation Insurance. Workers' compensation insurance rates depend on the nature of the work performed by the employee and the employer's experience rating. A sole proprietor or partner may elect to obtain workers' compensation coverage for an employee who is a spouse, parent or child of the owner, but coverage for these family employees is not required. In addition, certain closely held corporations may elect coverage for executive officers who own at least 25 percent of the stock of the corporation.

Retirement Benefit Plans

Retirement benefit plans include qualified employee benefit plans, nonexempt trusts and annuity plans, self-employed retirement plans, individual retirement arrangements, and simplified employee pension plans. The tax treatment of contributions to these plans is highly technical; also there are frequent changes in tax laws that affect the treatment of those contributions. A business owner contemplating such a plan or making deductions for contributions to the plan should obtain the advice of competent counsel.

Note: Whenever the term "IRA" is used in the following paragraphs, generally speaking the discussion applies to both conventional IRAs and Roth IRAs.

Sole Proprietorship. A sole proprietor may establish and contribute to a Keogh retirement plan. Depending on the proprietor's adjusted gross income and net earnings from self-employment, he or she may open and contribute to an individual retirement account (IRA) in addition to or in place of the Keogh plan. Qualified contributions to the sole proprietor's own Keogh plan or IRA are deductible (with some exceptions) in determining the proprietor's adjusted gross income on Form 1040. Those contributions are not considered expenses of the business, however, and therefore are not deductible in computing net income from the business on Schedule C. Minnesota generally follows IRS rules in the tax treatment of Keogh and IRA contributions. A sole proprietor who has employees may establish a qualified retirement plan for the employees. Contributions to the plan, if they meet IRS requirements, are deductible from business income reported on Schedule C.

Partnership. Like sole proprietors, working partners in a partnership may contribute to a Keogh plan established by the partnership. They also may open and contribute to an IRA if they meet income limitations for such contributions. Qualified contributions by each partner may be deducted (with some exceptions) in computing their individual adjusted gross income on Form 1040. Contributions by or on behalf of partners to their own retirement plans are not deductible from partnership income. Minnesota generally follows IRS rules. Retirement plans which are established for employees must comply with Internal Revenue Service requirements. Contributions to qualified plans on behalf of employees are deductible business expenses.

Corporation. Generally, contributions by the corporation to qualified pension plans and qualified profit sharing plans will be deductible by the corporation. The plan must be approved by the Internal Revenue Service.

Note: Master and prototype retirement plans may be available to the business. In many cases, it will be easier to use these samples rather than setting up a new plan. Master and prototype plans may be sponsored by trade or professional organizations, banks, insurance companies, or regulated investment companies. These entities usually will have applied for, and received, an IRS opinion letter on the plan. Using one of these master or prototype plans does not mean that the plan is automatically qualified. The plan still must meet all IRS requirements. However, the master or prototype may offer a firm some guidance in developing its own plan.

Fringe Benefits

Fringe benefits include items such as accident and health insurance, medical savings accounts, group term life insurance, salary continuation plans, reimbursements for educational expenses, dental insurance, death benefits, day care programs, supplemental unemployment benefits, "cafeteria plan" programs, and others. As with employee retirement benefit plans, the tax treatment of fringe benefits is a highly technical area. Accordingly, it is recommended that the advice of competent counsel be obtained prior to structuring such plans.

The following paragraphs discuss the tax treatment of providing fringe benefits to owners of the business. The cost of providing fringe benefits to employees generally will be a deductible business expense if reasonable in amount and in compliance with federal and state tax codes and other statutory requirements. In some cases the benefits may be taxable to the employee and subject to income tax withholding.

Sole Proprietorship. Sole proprietors generally may not deduct as a business expense the cost of obtaining fringe benefit items for themselves, although items such as day care for the proprietor's children may be eligible for a tax credit if they otherwise meet IRS requirements. Beginning with the 1999 tax year, for federal tax purposes sole proprietors may deduct up to sixty percent of the cost of medical insurance premiums paid for themselves, assuming IRS requirements are met. The deductible percentage increases each year, reaching 100% in 2003. Note that this issue is frequently the subject of legislation in Congress, so anyone interested should monitor developments. Note that for Minnesota income tax purposes, in some cases amounts paid by a sole proprietor for health insurance are subtracted from federal taxable income for purposes of computing Minnesota taxable income. That calculation is made on Schedule M-1H to a sole proprietor's Minnesota income tax return.

Partnership. Working partners of a partnership are considered self employed individuals, and are subject to the same rules on deductibility of fringe benefits as sole proprietors.

C Corporation. The C corporation may deduct the cost of providing fringe benefits to all employees, including shareholder employees. To be deductible, the fringe benefit plan must meet requirements of the federal and state tax laws, including nondiscrimination in favor of executive or highly compensated employees. Employee health plans also must comply with applicable state statutory requirements to be deductible for Minnesota income tax purposes.

S Corporation. An S corporation may deduct the cost of providing fringe benefits that it pays to all employees, including shareholder employees. However, the cost of fringe benefits paid for employee shareholders who own more than two percent of the company's stock must be included in the income of the shareholder. Typically, this is reported on the shareholder employees' Form W-2 in addition to their normal salary.

Capital Gains and Losses

A business that sells or otherwise disposes of capital assets will have a capital gain or capital loss from the transaction. Capital assets are defined by Internal Revenue Service regulations and generally include everything a business owns except property held for sale to customers, most accounts or notes receivable, real and depreciable personal property used in the business, copyrights and similar intellectual property, and certain government publications.

Sole Proprietorship. For individuals, the maximum tax rate on long-term capital gains is 20 percent (10 percent for individuals in the 15 percent bracket). In order to qualify as a long-term capital asset and thus subject to these more favorable rates, the asset must be held at least twelve months. Note that for sales after December 31, 2000, of assets held more than five years, the tax rate drops to 18 percent (8 percent for individuals in the 15 percent bracket).

Generally speaking, capital gains and losses are offset against each other, and a net capital loss can be used to offset up to $3,000 of ordinary income ($1,500 for married individuals filing separately). Capital losses that are not fully used in a tax year may be carried over to future years until offset entirely.

Partnership. Gains and losses from the sale or exchange of capital assets are reported on the partnership return and retain their character when passed through to the partners. The partners treat capital gains and losses that pass through to them in the same manner as other individuals. (See discussion of Sole Proprietorships, above.)

C Corporation. A corporation's capital gains are taxed at the corporation's regular tax rate. Thus the maximum federal tax rate on a corporation's capital gain is 35 percent. A corporation may deduct capital losses only up to the amount of its capital gains. If a corporation has a net capital loss, the loss cannot be deducted in the current tax year but instead must be carried to other tax years and deducted from capital gains that occur in those years. This is the case for both federal and Minnesota tax purposes.

S Corporation. S corporations may pass capital gains through directly to shareholders, although the S corporation must make the determination of when the long-term capital gain is taken into account on its own books.

Net Operating Loss

If the taxpayer's deductions for the year exceed gross income, the taxpayer may have a net operating loss (NOL). The NOL is used to reduce taxable income in other years. There are limits on the kinds of deductions, and the amounts, that can be used in computing an NOL. These limits are different for individuals and for corporations and for federal and Minnesota returns. For C corporations, if the NOL is attributable to business carried on both in and outside Minnesota, a computation allocating a portion of the NOL may be required on the Minnesota return.

Sole Proprietorship. The NOL is determined on the proprietor's gross income from all sources as reported on the Form 1040, not just on the income or loss from the business reported on Schedule C. In general, an NOL is computed in the same way taxable income is computed: deductions are subtracted from gross income, and if deductions exceed gross income there is a net operating loss. However, there are rules that limit what deductions may be taken in computing an NOL. In general, these rules do not permit a deduction for net capital losses, nonbusiness losses, nonbusiness deductions, personal exemptions and NOL carryovers or carrybacks from previous years. Some deductions also must be modified in taking the NOL. Internal Revenue Service regulations and those of the Minnesota Department of Revenue determine the years to which the NOL is carried, and the order in which NOLs are deducted.

Partnership. A partnership is not allowed to take an NOL deduction. All losses to the partnership for tax purposes are passed through to the partners each year. The partners may use their separate shares of the partnership's loss to compute their individual NOL. The rules for sole proprietors discussed above apply.

C Corporation. For federal tax purposes, a C corporation determines and deducts an NOL in much the same way an individual does. The same carryback and carryover periods apply and the same rules apply when two or more NOLs are carried to the same year. A corporation's NOL differs from an individual's NOL in three ways. First, a corporation is allowed to take different deductions in figuring an NOL. Second, a corporation must make different modifications to its taxable income in the carryback or carry forward year when figuring how much of the NOL may be deducted. Third, Minnesota does not permit carryback of an NOL. (An NOL may be carried forward 15 years.) Because the corporation is a separate taxable entity, the NOL is deducted by the corporation and is not passed through to shareholders. Minnesota's tax laws must be followed in taking the NOL deduction for Minnesota income tax purposes.

S Corporation. The S corporation, like a partnership, is not allowed to take an NOL deduction. If the S corporation incurs a loss for the year, it is passed through to shareholders in proportion to their shareholdings. The shareholders of the S corporation may use their share of the corporation's loss to compute their individual NOL.

Estimated Tax Payments

Sole Proprietorship. The sole proprietor generally will be required to make federal and Minnesota estimated tax payments if his or her income tax and (for federal purposes) self employment tax will exceed taxes paid through withholding and credits by $1,000 or more. The tax is determined on income from all sources, including income from the business. A penalty may be imposed on underpaid estimates.

Partnership. The partnership itself is not required to make estimated tax payments. However, for Minnesota tax purposes, a partnership is required to pay quarterly estimated tax if its Minnesota minimum fee is $500 or more or if it has a nonresident partner whose share of the composite income tax is $500 or more. As with the sole proprietorship, individual partners generally will be required to make estimated tax payments if their income tax and self employment tax will exceed taxes paid through withholding and credits by $1,000 or more. The tax is based on taxable income from all sources, not just the income from the partnership. If the tax is underpaid, a penalty may be imposed on the partner. As with the sole proprietorship, both federal and Minnesota estimates generally will be required.

C Corporation. Federal: A C corporation whose estimated tax is expected to be $500 or more is required to make estimated tax payments. Federal estimated tax payments are deposited with an authorized financial institution or Federal Reserve Bank. **Minnesota:** A corporation with an estimated tax of $500 or more must make Minnesota quarterly estimated tax payments. In addition, a C corporation with more than $20,000 in tax liability must make **all** its tax payments via electronic funds transfer. These payments are filed with the Minnesota Department of Revenue. For both federal and Minnesota purposes, a penalty may be imposed for failure to pay the correct estimated tax on or before its due date.

S Corporation. The S corporation is not subject to estimated tax on income which passes through to shareholders. For Minnesota tax purposes, an S corporation is required to pay quarterly estimated tax if its S corporation taxes and minimum fee is $500 or more or if it has a nonresident shareholder whose share of the composite income tax is $500 or more. A penalty may be applied if the estimated taxes are underpaid.

Disposition of Ownership Interest

Sole Proprietorship. The sole proprietor who sells the business is treated as selling the individual assets of the business. The income tax treatment of the sale will depend on whether or not the property is a capital asset, and the length of time the property has been held. The assets may also be subject to state sales tax. A sole proprietor also may change the form of the business without selling its assets, such as by joining with one or more persons to form a partnership or a corporation, and then transferring the assets of the sole proprietorship to the new organization. The tax consequences of such a transfer should be discussed in advance with a competent tax advisor.

Partnership. The sale or exchange of a partner's interest in a partnership ordinarily results in capital gain or loss on the difference between the amount realized and the adjusted basis of the partner's interest in the partnership. Special rules apply to exchanges of an interest in one partnership for an interest in another, liquidation of a partner's interest, and the treatment of unrealized receivables and inventory items. Tangible assets sold as part of the transaction also may be subject to state sales tax. Because of the complexity of the tax laws affecting the disposition of a partnership interest, the tax consequences of such a disposition should be thoroughly explored in advance with a competent tax advisor.

Note also that under the Revised Uniform Partnership Act, Minnesota Statutes Chapter 323A, (RUPA) mergers of partnerships are allowed. Again, because of the complexity of tax laws, a competent tax advisor should be consulted when considering a merger of partnerships.

Corporation. Disposition of an ownership interest (shares of stock) in a corporation must be distinguished from liquidation of the corporation. Individual shareholders who sell their stock generally will recognize capital gain or capital loss on the sale of their shares. The gain or loss will be long term or short term, depending on the length of time the shares were held. An interest in a corporation also may be disposed of by complete or partial liquidation of the corporation. In liquidation, the corporation may either dispose of its property for cash, and distribute the cash to its shareholders, or it may distribute its property to the shareholders in exchange for the corporation's capital stock held by those shareholders. In either case, the distribution generally will result in capital gain or capital loss to the shareholders. Tangible assets sold as part of the transaction also may be subject to state sales tax. In some cases, the timing of the transaction may affect the tax consequences. The tax consequences of corporate liquidations and stock redemptions for both C corporations and S corporations and their shareholders can be complex. For this reason, it is advisable to consult with a competent tax advisor prior to attempting to liquidate the corporation or dispose of corporate assets.

CERTIFICATE OF ASSUMED NAME

When Filing is Required

An individual or partnership that conducts or transacts business in Minnesota under a name that is different from the full, true name of each business owner must register the name of the business by filing a certificate of assumed name with the Secretary of State. A corporation, limited partnership, limited liability partnership or limited liability company that conducts business under a name that is different from the its exact, legal name likewise must file a certificate of assumed name for the business name.

An assumed name filing is also required when a general or limited partnership that is not also a limited liability partnership (or its partners) wishes to file statements of partnership authority, statement of denial, statements of merger, statements of dissociation, statements of dissolution or amendments or cancellations of those statements. (Note that such a partnership is not "assuming" a business name by making these filings; instead, the reason for making the certificate of assumed name filing is that the Secretary of State's Office requires it to be filed before any such statements may be filed.)

For example, if John Smith, a sole proprietor, does business under "Smith's Realty," he must file a certificate of assumed name. Filing is not required, however, if John Smith, a sole proprietor, does business as "John Smith Realty." Likewise, if Able Building Company, a corporation, does business as "ABC Construction," it must register the assumed name "ABC Construction." If, however, Able Building Company does business under the name Able Building Company, it is not required to file a certificate of assumed name.

Restrictions on Assumed Names

An assumed name may include a designation required to be in the name of a business entity only if the business owner using the assumed name is that type of entity. For example, ABC Incorporated, a corporation, may file the assumed name XYZ Limited, because Limited is a corporate designation and the business owner is a corporation. If, however, John Smith is an individual in the realty business, the assumed name cannot be registered as "Smith Realty, Inc." Also, assumed names may not include in their names a geographic reference to a place or community if the business is not located in that community. Finally, financial institutions wishing to use an assumed name must first receive approval from the commissioner of the Department of Commerce.

Reason for Filing

The reason for filing a certificate of assumed name is to provide information to the consumer on the identity of the business owner. **Registration of the assumed name does not protect the name against use by other persons.** The Secretary of State's office will, however, inform the first person to file the name of every later filing of that name or similar names. It is up to the individual to decide whether to take legal action to prevent use of the name. An attorney can provide advice on the likelihood of success and potential costs of such a lawsuit. **Note also that registering a domain name or trademark is a process completely separate from making any filing with the Secretary of State's Office.**

Determining Whether an Assumed Name is Available

An assumed name will not be accepted for filing if it is the same as, or is not distinguishable from, the name of a corporation, limited liability company, limited partnership, limited liability partnership or trademark on file with the Secretary of State. (See the section titled "Determining Whether the Name is Distinguishable" later in this chapter.)

Business owners may call the general information line of the Secretary of State's office (651) 296-2803, or access Secretary of States website, www.sos.state.mn.us, prior to registration to determine whether a name is available. The Secretary of State's office will perform a preliminary check but does not guarantee that the name will be available at the time of filing. There is no procedure for reserving an assumed name. A sole proprietorship or partnership that intends to incorporate at a later date may, however, reserve the corporate name by filing a reservation of corporate name with the Secretary of State. This procedure is described in the section of this Guide on forming a corporation.

Filing Procedure

A simple, one-page certificate of assumed name form can be downloaded from the Secretary of State's web site at www.sos.state.mn.us/business/forms.html, and is also available by fax from the Fax Forms Library at (651) 296-2803, and by mail from that office. The business owner completes and signs the form and files it with the Secretary of State, along with a filing fee. The Secretary of State's office then processes the form. After the Secretary of State notifies the business owner that the filing is accepted, the business owner must have the certificate published for two consecutive issues in a newspaper qualified to print legal notices (sometimes called a "legal newspaper") in the county where the registered office or principal place of business is located. A qualified newspaper is one which meets the statutory standards established by Minnesota Statutes Chapter 331A. The cost of publishing this notice is set by the newspaper and paid for by the person or entity making the assumed name filing. The Secretary of State's Office maintains a list of "legal newspapers."

Failure to publish the notice renders the assumed name filing invalid. A business that fails to file its assumed name as required by law will be assessed $250 in costs at the time of any subsequent lawsuit by or against the business.

Duration of Filing Period; Filing Amendments

A certificate of assumed name is valid for ten years from the date of filing, unless there are changes in the information provided on the certificate. The Secretary of State's office mails the business a renewal form six months prior to expiration of the certificate. For this reason, it is important to notify the Secretary of State's Office each time a business changes its address.

If the information provided on the certificate of assumed name changes, the business must file within sixty days an amendment with the Secretary of State's office.

See the Secretary of State fee schedule later in this Guide for filing fees.

NAMING A CORPORATION, LIMITED LIABILITY PARTNERSHIP OR LIMITED LIABILITY COMPANY

Statutory Requirements

Name requirements for corporations, limited liability partnerships and limited liability companies are established by statute.

The name of a corporation must:

- Be in the English language or any other language expressed in English characters;
- Contain the words "corporation", "incorporated", or "limited", or an abbreviation of one or more of these words, or the word "company" or the abbreviation "Co." if that word or abbreviation is not preceded by "and" or "&" or in the case of a professional corporation, the words "professional association," or "chartered," or the abbreviation "P.A.";
- Not contain a word or phrase indicating that the corporation conducts a business that is not a legal business purpose; and
- Be distinguishable from the name of each domestic or foreign corporation, limited liability company, limited partnership, limited liability partnership or any reserved name, assumed name, trademark or service mark on file with the Secretary of State.

The name of a limited liability partnership must:

- Be in the English language or any other language expressed in English characters;
- Contain the words "limited liability partnership" or the abbreviation "L.L.P." or in the case of a professional limited liability partnership the choices already stated or the words "professional limited liability partnership" or the abbreviation "P.L.L.P.";
- Not contain a word or phrase indicating that the limited liability partnership conducts a business that does not constitute a legal business purpose;
- Be distinguishable from the name of each domestic or foreign corporation, limited liability company, limited partnership, limited liability partnership or any reserved name, assumed name, trademark or service mark on file with the Secretary of State; and
- If the limited liability partnership is also a limited partnership, contain either the words 'limited partnership, limited liability partnership' (or the abbreviation 'L.P., 'L.L.P.') or the words 'limited liability limited partnership' (or the abbreviation 'L.L.L.P.').

The name of a limited liability company must:

- Be in the English language or any other language expressed in English characters;

- Contain the words "limited liability company" or the abbreviation "LLC", or in the case of a professional limited liability company the words "professional limited liability company" or the abbreviation "PLC";
- Not contain the words "corporation" or "incorporated" or the abbreviations of either or both words;
- Not contain a word or phrase that indicates or implies that the limited liability company is organized for a purpose other than a legal business purpose; and
- Be distinguishable from the name of each domestic or foreign limited liability company, corporation, limited partnership, limited liability partnership or any reserved name, assumed name, trademark or service mark on file with the Secretary of State.

Determining the Availability of a Corporate Name or Limited Liability Company Name

The Secretary of State's office will not accept for filing articles of incorporation for a corporation, articles of registration for a limited liability partnership or articles of organization for a limited liability company if the name of the corporation, limited liability partnership or limited liability company is the same as, or not distinguishable from, the name of a Minnesota or foreign corporation, limited liability company, limited partnership, limited liability partnership or reserved name or trademark. (See the section titled "Determining Whether the Name is Distinguishable" later in this chapter.)

The Secretary of State's office will perform a preliminary check to determine the availability of a corporation, limited liability partnership or limited liability company name before the articles of incorporation, registration or organization are filed. Business owners may call the Secretary of State's office, or access that Office's website, www.sos.state.mn.us, prior to filing to determine whether the name is available. The telephone number to call is (651) 296-2803. The Secretary of State's office does not guarantee that the name will be available at the time of filing, however. Incorporators or organizers who wish to place a hold on a name before proceeding with formation of a corporation or limited liability company may file a name reservation with the Secretary of State's office. (See the section of this chapter below on Reserving a Corporate Name or Limited Liability Company Name.)

Warning

As is the case with filing a certificate of assumed name, the registration of a corporate name or limited liability partnership or limited liability company name does not necessarily mean that the name can be used without penalty. There may be existing users of that name who have perfected a prior federal trademark or common law right to the name without filing with the Minnesota Secretary of State. Note also that registering an Internet domain name is a process completely separate from making a filing with the Minnesota Secretary of State. These users may be able to use the courts to prevent the incorporators, organizers, or business entity from actually using the name even though it may be available for registration with the Secretary of State.

Reserving a Corporate Name or Limited Liability Company Name

A corporate name or limited liability company name may be reserved by an individual or entity in one of the eligible categories listed below. The reservation is made on a form available from the Secretary of State, and is effective for 12 months. The reservation may be renewed for an unlimited number of 12 month periods. The fee for reserving the name appears in the Secretary of State fee schedule later in this Guide.

Eligible categories are:

- A person doing business in this state under the desired name (the term "person" includes a corporation or unincorporated association);
- A person intending to incorporate under Minnesota Statutes Chapter 302A or form a limited liability company under Minnesota Statutes Chapter 322B;
- A domestic corporation or domestic limited liability company intending to change its name;
- A foreign corporation or foreign limited liability company intending to apply for a certificate of authority to transact business in Minnesota;
- A foreign corporation or foreign limited liability company authorized to transact business in Minnesota and intending to change its name;
- A person intending to incorporate a foreign corporation or foreign limited liability company and intending to have that entity apply for a certificate of authority to transact business in Minnesota; or
- A foreign corporation or foreign limited liability company doing business under that name or a name deceptively similar to that name in one or more states other than Minnesota and not described above.

DETERMINING WHETHER A NAME IS DISTINGUISHABLE

General Rule

In general, any name which contains a different word from existing names on file with the Secretary of State is distinguishable and the name is acceptable for filing as an assumed name or as the name of a corporation or limited liability partnership or limited liability company. Exceptions to this general rule are stated in the following section.

Exceptions

Names which are identical except for the following are not distinguishable and will not be accepted for filing:

- Corporate endings regardless of where they appear in the name. These include Incorporated, Corporation, Company, Limited, Limited Liability Company, Limited Liability Limited Partnership, Professional Limited Liability Company, Limited Liability Partnership, Professional Limited Liability Partnership, Professional Association, Limited Partnership and their abbreviations, and Chartered.
- The inclusion or omission of articles of speech, conjunctions, contractions, prepositions or punctuation. An article of speech is any one of the words "a," "an," or "the." A conjunction is a word or symbol that joins clauses, phrases or words together. Examples include and, or, as, because, but, +, –, &. A contraction is the shortened form of a word such as ass'n. for association and dep't. for department. A preposition is a word which expresses the relationship between a noun and another word. Examples are at, by, in, up, of, to.
- The abbreviation versus the spelling out of a word or different tenses of the same word. An abbreviation is the shortened form of a word or a recognized shortening of a word to an unrelated combination of letters, e.g., Mister to Mr., pound to lb., Brothers to Bros.
- The spacing of words, the combination of commonly used two-word terms or the splitting of words usually found in compound form.
- An obvious misspelling or alternative spelling or homonym.
- The use of the word or numerals (including Roman) for the same number, e.g., "two," "2," or "II."

Examples:

Corporate Endings – Not Distinguishable
Sunshine Service Corporation
Sunshine Service Ltd.
Sunshine Service Co.

Mooty and Mooty P.A.
Mooty and Mooty Inc.
Mooty and Mooty Limited
Mooty and Mooty Limited Liability Partnership

Conjunctions – Not Distinguishable

Mooty and Mooty P.A.

Mooty, Mooty P.A.

Professional Cleaners Co.
Professional Cleaners Company

Respectful Cemetery Co.
Respectful Cemetary Inc.

Tenses – Not Distinguishable

Advance Security Co.
Advanced Security Corp.

Abbreviations – Not Distinguishable

G/C Enterprises Co.
G.C. Enterprises Corporation
G.C.'s Enterprises Inc.

Stop and Shop Ltd.
Stop 'N Shop Corp.

Mister Softy Inc.
Mr. Softie Corp.

Saint Paul Shoe Co.
St. Paul Shoes Inc.

Hilltop Stables Inc.
Hill Top Stables Inc.

Outbound Travel Co.
Out Bound Travel Inc.

Spacing of Words – Not Distinguishable

Mid Co. Inc.
Mid Co Inc.

Plural vs. Singular – Not Distinguishable

Hill Market Inc.
Hills Market Co.
Hills Market Ltd.

Contractions – Not Distinguishable

The Graphics Department Inc.
Graphics Dep't. Ltd.

National Association of Novelists
Nat'l Ass'n. of Novelists Inc.

Prepositions – Not Distinguishable

A Galaxy of Homes Inc.
Galaxy Homes Inc.

Widget Mfg. of Saint Paul Inc.
Widget Mfg. – St. Paul Co.
Widget Mfg. / St Paul Inc.

Obvious Misspellings – Not Distinguishable

Concept Log Homes Inc.
Concep Log Homes Inc.

Words vs. Numerals – Not Distinguishable

Movie Madness Two Inc.
Movie Madness II Co.
Movie Madness 2 Corp.

Alternative Spellings – Not Distinguishable

Color My Hair, Inc.
Colour My Hair, Co.

Quick Stop Co.
Quik Stop Inc.
Kwik Stop Ltd.

Homonyms – Not Distinguishable

Blue Moon Dust Co.
Blew Moon Dust Co.

Hare Care Inc.
Hair Care Co.

Right Press Inc.
Write Press Corporation

Options for Dealing With Names Which Are Not Distinguishable

A business that wishes to use a name that is not distinguishable from a name that is already on file with the Secretary of State has several options. These include changing the name, obtaining and filing consent to use the name, filing a court order, and filing a statement of dormant business. A fee is charged for each filing.

Changing the Applied-For Name. The name may be changed by adding or deleting words to distinguish the name.

Filing Consent to Use the Name. Written consent may be obtained from the holder of the conflicting name and filed with the Secretary of State. A form for this purpose is available from the Secretary of State's office. Applicants for a trademark may not obtain consents, but they may submit affidavits from themselves and from holders of conflicting names describing the nature of the businesses and the geographic and market area served as evidence that the marks will not be confusingly similar. There is no fee for filing these affidavits, although a fee is charged for filing a consent.

Filing a Court Order. An applicant for a name who obtains a court order establishing a prior right to use of that name may file the name. The court order must be attached to the filing.

Filing a Statement of Dormant Business. To use this method, the applicant must file a signed affidavit stating that: the existing corporation or business has been in existence for three years or more and is on file with the Secretary of State; the existing corporation has not filed anything with the Secretary of State in the past three years; the applicant mailed a written notice by certified mail return receipt requested, to the registered office of the existing corporation or business, and the notice has been returned as undeliverable; the applicant has made a diligent inquiry and has been unable to find a telephone listing for the existing corporation or business in the county of its registered office; and the applicant has no knowledge that the existing corporation or business is still operating.

POST-FILING NAME ISSUES

Filing with the Secretary of State does not confer upon the applicant any right to "use" a name in public commerce. Citizens with names in use can challenge subsequent "uses" by others by either a lawsuit in district court, or by using the "name appeal", an informal process through the Secretary of State, as described in Minnesota Statutes Section 5.22.

FORMING A SOLE PROPRIETORSHIP

As noted in the section on choosing the form of organization, a sole proprietorship is the simplest form of business organization. There are no statutory requirements unique to this form of organization. From a regulatory standpoint, the business owner only needs to register the business name as an assumed name (if it does not contain the business owner's first and last names), obtain business licenses and tax identification numbers if necessary, and begin operations.

A list of business licenses required by the state of Minnesota appears in the Directory of Licenses and Permits section of this Guide. Procedures for registering the business name as an assumed name are discussed in the previous section of this Guide.

The sole proprietor must obtain federal and state tax identification numbers if the business has employees even if those employees are members of the sole proprietor's family. A sole proprietor who will hire employees also will need an unemployment compensation tax number and must secure workers' compensation insurance for employees. A sole proprietor who will be selling a product or service that is subject to sales tax will need to register for sales and use tax purposes. These taxes and procedures for obtaining tax numbers are discussed in the section of this Guide on business taxes.

Sole proprietors who will be hiring employees also should review the section of this Guide on issues for employers.

FORMING A PARTNERSHIP

There are two types of partnerships: general partnerships and limited partnerships. Both general and limited partnerships can elect certain legal rules that give partners in these partnerships greater protection against personal liability. A general partnership that makes this election is called a "limited liability partnership"; a limited partnership that makes this election is called a "limited liability limited partnership."

A general partnership that is formed in a state other than Minnesota, or in a foreign country, is called a foreign general partnership. A limited partnership that is formed in a state other than Minnesota, or in a foreign country, is called a foreign limited partnership and is subject to additional regulatory requirements. A limited liability partnership (or limited liability limited partnership) formed in a state other than Minnesota, or in a foreign country, is called a foreign limited liability partnership (or foreign limited liability limited partnerhship) and is subject to additional regulatory requirements.

GENERAL PARTNERSHIPS

A general partnership is a business that is owned by two or more persons who associate to carry on the business of the partnership. General partnerships have specific attributes, which are defined by Minnesota Statutes Chapter 323A. The general rule is that in a general partnership all partners share equally in the right, and responsibility, to manage the business, and each partner is responsible for all the debts and obligations of the business. General partnerships that have elected limited liability partnership status operate much like general partnerships, but generally partners in limited liability partnerships are not personally liable for the wrongful acts of other partners or for the debts or obligations of the partnership.

Regulatory Requirements

From a regulatory standpoint, a partnership must obtain business licenses if necessary, obtain federal and state tax identification numbers and an unemployment compensation number and will need to register the business name as an assumed name, unless the first and last name of each partner is included in the name of the partnership. Note that, as explained below, it is also strongly recommended that the partnership (no matter what type) draw up a written agreement addressing key issues like the allocation of management responsibilities, the distribution of profits and losses, and rights upon termination. The partnership agreement is not filed with the state, however. Issues commonly addressed in a partnership agreement are discussed in the next section.

A list of business licenses required by the state of Minnesota appears in the section of this Guide titled Directory of Licenses and Permits. Procedures for registering the business name as an assumed name are discussed in the previous section of this Guide.

Note that any partner of a general partnership that has elected limited liability partnership status, or professional limited liability partnership status, is jointly and severally liable for contributions or reimbursement, including interest, penalties and costs with respect to reemployment benefits if the partnership, as an employer, does not pay any amounts with respect to reemployment benefits due the Department of Economic Security.

Although the partnership itself is not a taxable entity, it must file an annual federal and state "information" return with the Internal Revenue Service and the Minnesota Department of Revenue. For this reason, both federal and state tax identification numbers must be obtained by the partnership. A partnership that will be selling a product or service that is subject to sales tax also will need to register for purposes of Minnesota sales and use tax. A partnership that will hire employees, even if those employees are members of a partner's family, must secure workers' compensation insurance covering employees. These taxes and procedures for obtaining tax numbers are discussed in the section of this Guide on business taxes.

Partnerships that will be hiring employees also should review the section of this Guide on issues for employers.

Registration of Domestic and Foreign Limited Liability Partnerships

In order to become a limited liability partnership, a Minnesota general partnership must file a registration to that effect. A form that includes the specifically required language is available from the Secretary of State's web site at www.sos.state.mn.us/business/forms.html, or by fax from the Fax Forms library at (651) 296-2803, or by mail from the office. The partnership is subject to limited liability partnership rules of law on and after the date the registration is filed. That registration is valid indefinitely as long as the annual registration for the partnership is filed on a calendar year basis.

Non-Minnesota limited liability partnerships must similarly register with the Secretary of State and must attach to the registration a certificate of good standing or status from the state or province where the foreign limited liability partnership is formed.

The Partnership Agreement

The partnership agreement addresses a number of issues relating to the management and operation of the partnership. In drawing up the partnership agreement, the prospective partners should consult with legal counsel to assure that the needs and desires of the partners and relevant legal issues are addressed. Some of the issues typically addressed in a partnership agreement include:

- Name of the partnership.
- Duration of the partnership.
- Location of its place of business.
- Capital contribution of each partner.
- Whether partners may make additional contributions.
- The level at which capital accounts of the partners must be maintained.
- Participation of each partner in profits and losses.
- The amounts of any regular drawings against profits.
- Responsibilities and authority of each partner.
- Amount of time to be contributed by each partner.
- Prohibition of partners' outside business activities which would compete with the partnership business.
- Name of the managing partner and method for resolving management disputes.
- Procedure for admitting new partners.
- Method of determining the value of goodwill in the business, in case of death, incompetence, or withdrawal of a partner or dissolution of the partnership for any other reason.
- Method of liquidating the interest of a deceased or retiring partner.

- Circumstances under which a partner must withdraw from active participation, and arrangements for adjusting the partner's salary and equity.
- Whether or not surviving partners have the right to continue using the name of a deceased partner in the partnership name.
- Basis for expulsion of a partner, method of notification of expulsion, and the disposition of any losses that arise from the delinquency of such a partner.
- Period of time in which retiring or withdrawing partners may not engage in a competing business.
- Procedures for handling the protracted disability of a partner.
- How partnership accounts are to be kept.
- The fiscal year of the partnership.
- Whether or not interest is to be paid on the debit and credit balances in the partners' accounts.
- Where the partnership cash is to be deposited and who may sign checks.
- Under what conditions limited partners may be accepted into the firm, and, if so, who shall be designated as the general partner.
- Prohibition of the partners' pledging, selling, hypothecating, or in any manner transferring their interest in the partnership except to other partners.
- Identification of material contracts or agreements affecting the liability or operation of the partnership.

LIMITED PARTNERSHIPS

A limited partnership is a type of partnership in which the limited partners share in the partnership's liability only up to the amount of their investment in the limited partnership. By statute, the limited partnership must have at least one general partner and one limited partner. The general partner has the right and responsibility to control the limited partnership, and is responsible for the debts and obligations of the limited partnership. The limited partner, in exchange for limited liability, generally does not participate in the day-to-day management and control of the business.

Regulatory Requirements

As is the case with general partnerships, a limited partnership will need to obtain business licenses if necessary, obtain federal and state tax identification numbers and may need to register the business name as an assumed name. A limited partnership that will hire employees, even if those employees are members of a partner's family, must obtain an unemployment compensation tax number and worker's compensation insurance for those employees. The limited partnership must file a certificate of limited partnership with the Secretary of State's office before commencing business. The filing requirements are discussed in the next section.

A limited partnership that will be selling shares in the limited partnership to the public likely will be required to register with the federal Securities and Exchange Commission and the Minnesota Department of Commerce. Persons contemplating such an offer or sale should consult with legal counsel well in advance of the offering to assure that it complies with federal and state securities laws.

Certificate of Limited Partnership

A limited partnership must file a certificate of limited partnership with the Secretary of State. Minnesota Statutes § 322A.11 sets forth the minimum content requirements of the certificate. A form containing these requirements is available from the Secretary of State's web site at www.sos.state.mn.us/business/forms.html or by fax from the Fax Forms library at (651) 296-2803 or by mail from the office. A limited partnership is formed at the time the certificate of limited partnership is filed with the Secretary of State or at a later time specified in the certificate.

In addition to the certificate of limited partnership, the limited partnership may also adopt a limited partnership agreement. As is the case with a general partnership agreement, the limited partnership agreement governs the details of the partnership and the management arrangement between the general partners and the limited partnership. Issues and concerns to be addressed in the limited partnership agreement as well as consideration of securities law requirements and tax consequences should be discussed with legal counsel.

In order to become a limited liability limited partnership, the first step is to establish the limited partnership, second, it is necessary to follow the procedures required for creating a limited liability partnership described in the preceding sections of this Guide. It is recommended that the name of the limited partnership and the name on the limited liability limited partnership registration match so that there is no question whether the limited partnership entity has elected limited liability partnership status.

FOREIGN LIMITED PARTNERSHIPS

A limited partnership that does business in Minnesota and is formed in another state or country must register with the Secretary of State as a foreign limited partnership. Filing requirements are established by Minnesota Statutes § 322A.70. A registration form containing the required information is available from the Secretary of State's office by mail, fax, or from the website. The foreign limited partnership must attach to its registration a certificate of good standing (sometimes called a certificate of status) from the state or province where the foreign limited partnership is formed.

A foreign limited partnership also must obtain a Minnesota tax identification number. If the foreign limited partnership has employees, even if those employees are members of a partner's family, it must obtain an unemployment compensation tax number and workers' compensation insurance covering its employees.

FORMING A MINNESOTA BUSINESS CORPORATION

A corporation is a separate legal entity that is owned by one or more shareholders. The shareholders elect a board of directors which is responsible for the management and control of the corporation. As a separate legal entity, the corporation is responsible for the debts and obligations of the business. In most cases the shareholders are insulated from personal liability for claims against the corporation.

A corporation is formed according to the laws of the state in which it is organized. In Minnesota the business corporation statute is Minnesota Statutes Chapter 302A. The following material describes the process for incorporating a business in Minnesota and some of the post-incorporation issues faced by new corporations. Other issues are described in the sections of this Guide on choosing the form of business organization, business taxes, and issues for employers.

ARTICLES OF INCORPORATION

A corporation is formed by one or more incorporators filing articles of incorporation with the Secretary of State and paying the filing fee. Incorporators must be at least 18 years of age. Minimum requirements are satisfied by an articles of incorporation form that is available from the Secretary of State's web site at www.sos.state.mn.us/business/forms.html or by fax from the Fax Forms library at (651) 296-2803 or by mail from the office. Incorporators may, in the articles of incorporation, add to or modify many of the basic statutory provisions set forth in the Minnesota Business Corporation Act. If the incorporators choose to modify the statutory provisions, they must draft their own articles of incorporation; they cannot use the form provided by the Secretary of State. An attorney can assist in determining whether modifications are needed and in drafting articles of incorporation.

Corporate Name

Requirements for the corporate name are discussed in the section on naming the business entity, earlier in this Guide.

Registered Office

A corporation must maintain a registered office located in the state of Minnesota. The address of a registered office must set forth the complete office address (**not a post-office box**). This address may be a street address, a rural route **and** rural route box or fire number, or directions from a landmark. If directions are given, a mailing address in the same town or in an adjacent area must also be given. All addresses **must** have a zip code.

Registered Agent

The corporation is not required to name a registered agent in the articles of incorporation, but if the corporation decides to name an agent, the articles must list the name of the agent and the agent must be located at the registered office.

Corporate Seal

The corporation is no longer required to have a corporate seal.

Number of Authorized Shares of Stock

A corporation may authorize any number of shares of stock. The articles of incorporation require only the total number of shares authorized. Neither a par value nor a stated value is required, although the articles may include par value if shares are to have a par value. Corporations that plan to do business in another state should consider including a provision specifically stating that shares have a par value of one cent per share for franchise fee purposes. This is a restatement of Minnesota Statutes § 302A.401, subd. 2(c) and may enable the corporation to avoid paying excess franchise fees in other states.

Note: While the number of authorized shares is fixed in the articles, the decision to issue shares is up to the directors, who may reserve shares for later issuance. The board must approve each issuance and ensure that the corporation receives fair value for its shares.

Names, Addresses and Signatures of Incorporators

The articles must list the names and complete mailing addresses, including zip codes, of each of the incorporators. There must be at least one incorporator. Each incorporator must be a natural person of at least 18 years of age and must sign the articles.

Other Provisions

There is no publication (i.e., no "legal advertisement") requirement for corporations incorporated under Minnesota Statutes Chapter 302A. There is also no statutory minimum capital requirement for these corporations.

There are a number of provisions of Minnesota Statutes Chapter 302A that may be altered or adopted in the articles of incorporation, but that need not appear in the articles in order to properly form a corporation. A brief description of each of these provisions appears in Minnesota Statutes § 302A.111, subdivisions 2, 3 and 4. Some of these provisions include:

- The power to adopt, amend, or repeal the bylaws is vested in the board of directors (Minnesota Statutes § 302A.181);
- Directors serve for an indefinite term that expires at the next regular meeting of shareholders (Minnesota Statutes § 302A.207);

- A corporation must allow cumulative voting for directors (Minnesota Statutes § 302A.215);
- Absent directors may be permitted to give written consent or opposition to a proposal (Minnesota Statutes § 302A.233);
- A larger than majority vote may be required for board action (Minnesota Statutes § 302A.237);
- The affirmative vote of a majority of directors present is required for an action of the board (Minnesota Statutes § 302A.237);
- A written action by the board taken without a meeting must be signed by all directors (Minnesota Statutes § 302A.239);
- All shares have equal rights and preferences in all matters not otherwise provided by the board (Minnesota Statutes § 302A.401);
- A shareholder has certain preemptive rights, unless otherwise provided by the board (Minnesota Statutes § 302A.413);
- The transfer or registration of transfer of securities may be restricted (Minnesota Statutes § 302A.429);
- Regular meetings of shareholders need not be held, unless demanded by a shareholder under certain conditions (Minnesota Statutes § 302A.431);
- Unless otherwise provided by law not less than ten days notice is required for a meeting of shareholders (Minnesota Statutes § 302A.435, subd. 2);
- The affirmative vote of the holders of a majority of the voting power of the shares represented and voting at a duly held meeting is required for an action of the shareholders, except where this chapter requires the affirmative vote of a majority of the voting power of all voting shares (Minnesota Statutes § 302A.437, subd. 1);
- A larger than majority vote may be required for shareholder action (Minnesota Statutes § 302A.437);
- The number of shares required for a quorum at a shareholders meeting is a majority of the voting power of the shares entitled to vote (Minnesota Statutes § 302A.443); and
- Indemnification of certain persons is required (Minnesota Statutes § 302A.521).

Amending the Articles of Incorporation

A corporation may amend its articles of incorporation to include or modify any provision that is required or permitted to appear in the articles or to omit any provision not required to be included in the articles. Amendments are required when any changes are made in the articles of incorporation. Common reasons for amending the articles include: changing the corporate name or registered address; increasing the number of authorized shares; and changing other provisions affecting the rights of shares and shareholders.

A corporation amends its articles of incorporation by submitting the amendment to the shareholders at a regular or special meeting called with proper notice and having the amendment approved by the required number of votes. Proper notice means the corporation mailed information on the meeting time and other agenda items and a brief description of the amendment to each shareholder entitled to vote at least ten days before the meeting, unless other laws or the articles or bylaws permit a shorter time for notice.

The amendment may be approved by the holders of a majority of the voting power unless the articles require a larger majority or the amendment will either increase or reduce a majority already required in the articles or required by Minnesota Statutes Chapter 302A. In that case the amendment must receive the approval of the higher of the two, if the corporation is not publicly held. A publicly held company requires the approval of a simple majority.

The articles of amendment must include the name of the corporation (which must be identical to the name on file with the Secretary of State), the text of the amendment, and a statement that the amendment was adopted pursuant to Minnesota Statutes Chapter 302A. There is a filing fee. Amendment forms are available at the Secretary of State's web site at www.sos.state.mn.us/business/forms.html or by fax from the Fax Forms library at (651) 296-2803 or by mail from the Secretary of State's Office.

A corporation may also restate its articles of incorporation in their entirety. In addition to stating the name of the corporation and reciting that the restatement was approved pursuant to Minnesota Statutes Chapter 302A, all articles are presented in the language as amended. In other words, all changes are combined in one document. A restatement that includes substantive amendments must be approved by the shareholders in the same way any other amendment is approved. If the purpose of the restatement is only to combine all previous changes into one document, only the board of directors need approve it.

Articles of amendment must also be signed by a person who has been authorized by the corporation to sign corporate documents.

Change of Registered Office or Registered Agent

Every time a corporation moves or changes its registered office or agent it must file a Statement of Change of Registered Office or Agent with the Secretary of State. The Statement of Change of Registered Office or Agent must state the name of the corporation; the new address of the registered office, if the registered office is being moved; the name of the new registered agent, if a new agent is being appointed; and that the change of office or agent was approved by the board of directors. Change of Registered Office or Agent forms are available at the Secretary of State's web site at www.sos.state.mn.us/business/forms.html or by fax from the Fax Forms library at (651) 296-2803 or by mail from the Secretary of State's office.

The statement must be signed by an authorized representative of the corporation. There is a filing fee.

The registered office or registered agent may also be changed by amending the articles of incorporation that sets forth the registered office or registered agent. To do this, the corporation must follow the procedure for amending articles of incorporation.

POST-INCORPORATION ISSUES

General Considerations

When a corporation is formed, it becomes a legal entity that is separate from the owners or shareholders. The corporation can only act, however, through the individuals who are the incorporators, officers, directors, or shareholders. As part of the process of organizing the corporation, those individuals address a number of organizational matters, such as planning the capitalization, choosing the state of incorporation, selecting and reserving the corporate name, and drafting articles of incorporation and bylaws. Once the corporation is formed, those individuals will need to start up and operate the corporation. Specific guidance may be obtained from the firm's legal and tax advisors. In general, start-up and maintenance tasks include:

- Obtaining federal and state tax identification numbers and an unemployment compensation identification number for the corporation.
- Issuing shares of stock in conformity with the articles of incorporation; note also that federal and state securities laws apply to the issuance of corporate shares. Corporate shares may be represented by share certificates or may be "uncertificated." Uncertificated shares do not have certificates but are still reflected on the records of the corporation. As stated elsewhere in this Guide, these laws are complex, and the advice of knowledgeable professionals should be obtained before attempting to issue corporate securities.
- Setting up and maintaining corporate books and records, including books of account, shareholder records, and corporate minute books.
- Calling and conducting the initial meeting of the board of directors or shareholders in conformity with the articles of incorporation and applicable laws.
- Assuring that all actions taken and decisions made by the corporation through its directors, officers and shareholders conform with the articles of incorporation, by-laws, and applicable law. All actions and decisions should be recorded in the corporation's minute book.

Annual Registration

Minnesota corporations are required to file an annual registration form once each calendar year. The form must be returned directly to the Secretary of State. There is no charge for filing the registration, which asks for the name of the corporation; its registered office address; the address of the principal executive office, if it is different from the registered office address; and the name and business address of the chief executive officer. Failure to file the registration form in any calendar year results in loss of good standing. A corporation may return to good standing by completing a current registration and paying a $25 fee. After failure to file for three consecutive years a postcard notice is sent to the corporation, giving twelve months' notice of dissolution. **A corporation dissolved for failure to file annual reports may not be reinstated after dissolution.**

Business Activities Report

Every corporation that does business in Minnesota must annually file with the Department of Revenue a business activities report. Corporations are exempt from this requirement if they:

- File a Minnesota corporate income tax return on time;
- Possess a certificate of authority to do business in Minnesota;
- Are a tax-exempt corporation;
- Are engaged solely in secondary market activity in Minnesota; or
- Are financial institutions that annually conduct business with less than 20 persons, and have total assets and deposits of less than $5 million.

A corporation that is required to file a business activities report and fails to do so is prohibited from prosecuting any cause of action upon which it may bring suit under Minnesota law. In addition, those corporations generally are barred from using Minnesota courts for contracts executed and causes of action arising during the violation period. The Commissioner of Revenue may disclose to litigants whether a business activities report has been filed by a party to a lawsuit.

Copies of Form M-4R, the Business Activities Report, may be obtained from the Minnesota Department of Revenue, Forms Distribution Office at the address and telephone number listed in the Resource Directory section of this Guide.

SUBSIDIARIES

When a corporation extends into a new product line or a new geographic area, it frequently establishes a "subsidiary" corporation. A subsidiary corporation is a separate legal entity which happens to be controlled by another corporation (its "parent") that owns enough shares of the subsidiary's stock to dictate policy. Some subsidiaries are wholly-owned, some are not. As a separate entity, separate records and management are required, although consolidated financial and tax reporting may be possible under certain circumstances. Subsidiaries may also serve to insulate the parent corporation from liability for the action of the subsidiary under certain circumstances.

FOREIGN CORPORATIONS DOING BUSINESS IN MINNESOTA

A corporation that is organized under the laws of a state other than Minnesota that transacts business in Minnesota must apply for a certificate of authority before doing business in Minnesota. The requirements for obtaining the certificate of authority are specified by Minnesota Statutes Chapter 303, and are set forth on a required form available from the Secretary of State's web site at www.sos.state.mn.us/business/forms.html or by fax from the Fax Forms library at (651) 296-2803 or by mail from the Secretary of State's office. A recently-issued (within the past 90 days) certificate of existence from the state of incorporation must accompany the application.

The term "transacting business" is not clearly defined in statute, but the standard used in making the determination is the "minimum contacts" standard used in determining jurisdiction. Under this standard the facts are analyzed to determine whether the business or its local agents have conducted a continuous course of business in Minnesota or with Minnesotans sufficient to justify being governed by Minnesota law. This analysis will not be performed by the Secretary of State's Office or any other state executive agency; each business is responsible for performing its own analysis on the topic.

Neither the Secretary of State's office nor any other state agency will make a determination as to whether a particular organization should register as a foreign corporation. As a general rule, doubts should be resolved in favor of registering the organization. Minnesota Statutes § 303.03 establishes certain activities as exceptions to the registration requirement. Corporations organized outside Minnesota should consult with their legal counsel to determine whether any of the exceptions apply.

A foreign corporation also must file with the Secretary of State an annual registration and pay a $115 fee. Annual registration forms are sent by the Secretary of State to the registered agent and office address of the corporation in Minnesota. The forms are also available at the Secretary of State's web site at www.sos.state.mn.us/business/forms.html or by fax from the Fax Forms library at (651) 296-2803 or by mail from the Secretary of State's office. However, foreign nonprofit corporations are exempt from this requirement. Failure to file the annual registration in a calendar year will result in revocaton.

In addition to obtaining the certificate of authority, a foreign corporation must obtain a Minnesota tax identification number from the Department of Revenue. If the corporation will have employees in Minnesota, it also must obtain a Minnesota employer withholding tax number and an unemployment compensation tax number and arrange for workers' compensation insurance. The procedure for obtaining these numbers is described in the section of this Guide on business taxes and the Checklist for Hiring an Employee.

Foreign corporations also must obtain any state and local business licenses necessary to conduct business operations. Information on business license requirements may be obtained from the Minnesota Small Business Assistance Office at the address and telephone number provided in the Resource Directory section of this Guide.

Finally, the Minnesota Department of Revenue has the power to order the Secretary of State of Minnesota to revoke a foreign corporation's certificate of authority to do business in Minnesota if that corporation "fails to comply with any tax laws" administered by the Department of Revenue.

FORMING A MINNESOTA LIMITED LIABILITY COMPANY

A limited liability company is a form of business organization that generally combines the limited liability of a corporation with the tax status of a partnership. The formation and operation of a Minnesota limited liability company is governed by Minnesota Statutes Chapter 322B.

As with a partnership, business income and losses of the limited liability company are passed through to the owners of the business (except for single-member limited liability companies that elect to be taxed as corporations). As with a corporation, liability for business debts and obligations generally rests with the entity rather than with individual owners. Except for single-member limited liability companies that elect to be taxed as corporations, the limited liability company's income is taxed at the owners' individual tax rate, rather than at the entity level, eliminating the double taxation of profits that occurs with a C corporation. A limited liability company is not subject to many of the restrictions that apply to S corporations, such as a maximum of 75 shareholders, a single class of stock, and limited types of non-individual shareholders. Unlike a limited partnership, all members of a limited liability company may participate in the active management of the company without risking loss of limited personal liability.

Like a corporation, which may have only one shareholder, a limited liability company may have only one member or may have two or more members. A limited liability company's life ends more easily and may happen at the occurrence of an outside event. For example, the life of a limited liability company formed before August 1, 1999, ends at the death, retirement, resignation, bankruptcy, or expulsion of any member. Once dissolution has occurred, the members of the limited liability company need to wind up the affairs of the limited liability company and terminate the organization's existence. Termination can be avoided if there are two or more members remaining and they agree to continue the business of the limited liability company. An attorney can assist in assuring the limited liability company's existence will continue following an event of termination.

Major changes in the limited liability company law, especially concerning limited liability companies formed after August 1, 1999, were passed as part of Chapter 85, 1999 Session Laws of Minnesota. For example, a limited liability company formed after August 1, 1999, is not subject to dissolution (except if specifically provided in its articles of organization or bylaws) upon the termination of any specific member of the limited liability company.

Under the entity classification rules set out in certain Treasury Regulations, it is generally possible for the organizers of a limited liability company to choose how that entity will be treated for tax purposes. Those Regulations appear at 26 C.F.R. section 301.7701-1 *et seq.* The Minnesota legislature has determined that a Minnesota limited liability company should file the same type of return for Minnesota purposes as it does for federal purposes and it will be classified for Minnesota purposes in the same way it is classified for federal purposes. Anyone interested in a limited liability company is strongly advised to seek the advice of tax counsel.

A limited liability company that transacts business in a jurisdiction that does not recognize limited liability companies risks the possibility that the other jurisdiction will treat the company as a partnership and thus not accord its owners the immunity from personal liability that Minnesota grants to owners of limited liability companies.

ARTICLES OF ORGANIZATION

A limited liability company is formed by filing articles of organization with the Secretary of State and paying the filing fee. Minimum requirements for the articles of organization are provided on an articles of organization form that is available from the Secretary of State's web site at www.sos.state.mn.us/business/forms.html or by fax from the Fax Forms library at (651) 296-2803 or by mail from the Secretary of State's office. The articles of organization may add to or modify many of the basic statutory provisions set forth in the Minnesota Limited Liability Company Act. An attorney can assist in drafting articles of organization to assure that the needs and desires of the members, as well as legal requirements, are met. Organizers of a limited liability company must be at least 18 years of age.

Limited Liability Company Name

Requirements for the limited liability company name are discussed in the section on naming the business entity, earlier in this Guide.

Registered Office

A limited liability company must have a registered office located in the state of Minnesota. The registered office may be the place where the business is located or it may be in a different location. The registered office address must be the address of a physical location where a person who represents the limited liability company can be found. A registered office address cannot be a post office box. Acceptable registered office addresses include a complete street address, a rural route and rural route box or fire number or directions from a landmark to the office location. If directions are given, a mailing address in the same or an adjacent town must be given. All addresses must have a zip code.

Registered Agent

The limited liability company is not required to name a registered agent in the articles of organization, but if the limited liability company decides to name an agent, the articles must list the name of the agent and the agent must be located at the registered office.

Names, Addresses and Signatures of Organizers

The articles of organization must list the names and complete mailing addresses, including zip codes, of each of the organizers. There must be at least one organizer. Each organizer must be a natural person who is at least 18 years old. Each organizer must sign the articles.

Other Provisions

There are a number of provisions that may be altered in the articles of organization but need not appear in the articles in order to properly form a limited liability company. A brief description of each of these provisions appears in Minnesota Statutes § 322B.104 subdivisions 2, 3, and 4. Some of these provisions include:

- The power to adopt, amend or repeal the operating agreement is vested in the board of governors (Minnesota Statutes § 322B.201);
- Governors serve for an indefinite term that expires at the next regular meeting of the members (Minnesota Statutes § 322B.606);
- A limited liability company must allow cumulative voting for governors (Minnesota Statute § 322B.610);
- Absent governors may be permitted to give written consent or opposition to a proposal (Minnesota Statutes § 322B.615);
- A larger than majority vote may be required for board of governor action (Minnesota Statutes § 322B.617);
- The affirmative vote of a majority of governors present is required for an action of the board of governors (Minnesota Statutes § 322B.617);
- A written action by the board of governors taken without a meeting must be signed by all governors (Minnesota Statutes § 322B.618);
- All membership interests have equal rights and preferences in all matters not otherwise provided for by the board of governors (Minnesota Statutes § 322B.401, subdivision 5, clause 2);
- A member has certain preemptive rights, unless otherwise provided by the board of governors (Minnesota Statutes § 322B.310);
- The voting power of each membership interest is in proportion to the value reflected in the required records of the contributions of the members (Minnesota Statutes § 322B.318);
- Members share in distributions in proportion to the value reflected in the required records of contributions of the members (Minnesota Statutes § 322B.501);
- Members share in profits and losses in proportion to the value reflected in the required records of the contributions of the members (Minnesota Statutes § 322B.309).

Amending Articles of Organization

A limited liability company may amend its articles of organization to include or modify any provision that is required or permitted to appear in the articles or to omit any provision not required to be included. Amendments are required when any changes are made in the articles of organization. The amendment form is available at the Secretary of State's web site at www.sos.state.mn.us/business/forms.html or by fax from the Fax Forms library at (651) 296-2803 or by mail from the Secretary of State's office.

Articles of organization may be amended by submitting the amendment to the members at a regular or special meeting called with proper notice. Proper notice means that information on the time, location and meeting agenda and a brief description of the amendment is mailed to each member at least ten days before the meeting, unless other laws or the articles or by-laws permit a shorter time for notice. The amendment must be approved by a majority of the voting power of the members unless the articles require a larger majority or the amendment will increase a majority already required in the articles of a closely held limited liability company. If this larger majority is to be adopted, the amendment must be approved by this higher majority.

The articles of amendment must include the following provisions: the name of the limited liability company as it appears in the records of the Secretary of State; the text of the amendment; and a statement that the amendment was adopted pursuant to Minnesota Statutes Chapter 322B. There is a $35 filing fee.

A limited liability company also may restate its articles of organization in their entirety. In addition to stating the name of the limited liability company and reciting that the restatement was approved pursuant to Minnesota Statutes Chapter 322B, all articles are presented in the language which the limited liability company now wishes to use. In other words, all changes are combined in one document. A restatement that includes substantive amendments must be approved by the members in the same way as any other amendment is approved. If the restatement is only to combine all previous changes into one document, only the board of governors need approve.

Articles of amendment must be signed by a person who has been authorized by the limited liability company to sign such documents.

Change of Registered Office or Registered Agent

Every time a limited liability company moves or changes its registered agent, it must report the new information to the Secretary of State on a change of address/agent form which is available at the Secretary of State's web site at www.sos.state.mn.us/business/forms.html or by fax from the Fax Forms library at (651) 296-2803 or by mail from the Secretary of State's office. The form states the name of the limited liability company, the new address of the registered office, the name of the new registered agent, if one is being appointed, and that the change was approved by the board of governors.

If a registered agent is appointed, the registered agent must be physically located at the registered office address. The statement must be signed by an authorized representative of the limited liability company. There is a filing fee.

The registered office address and agent information can also be changed using the amendment procedure described above.

POST-ORGANIZATION ISSUES

General Considerations

After the limited liability company is formed, it must perform certain start-up tasks, such as obtaining federal and state tax identification numbers, obtaining an unemployment compensation identification number, setting up and maintaining the books and records of the business, calling and conducting the initial meeting of the board of governors or members, and taking other actions. All actions taken and decisions made by the limited liability company through its governors, managers and members must conform with the articles of organization, operating agreement, and applicable law. All actions and decisions should be recorded in the company's minute book. Specific guidance on post-organization issues may be obtained from the company's legal and tax advisors.

Annual Registration

Both Minnesota and non-Minnesota limited liability companies must register with the Secretary of State once every year. The Secretary of State's office will send a registration form to the limited liability company at its registered office. The form is also available at the Secretary of State's web site at www.sos.state.mn.us/business/forms.html or by fax from the Fax Forms library at (651) 296-2803 or by mail from the Secretary of State's office. The registration is due before the end of the calendar year. Failure to file will result in administrative termination. Reinstatement may occur within one year of the date of the administrative termination by filing the registration form and paying a $25 reinstatement fee.

FOREIGN LIMITED LIABILITY COMPANIES DOING BUSINESS IN MINNESOTA

A limited liability company that is organized under the laws of a state other than Minnesota that transacts business in Minnesota must obtain a certificate of authority before doing business in Minnesota. The requirements for obtaining the certificate of authority are specified by Minnesota Statutes §§ 322B.90 to 322B.955, and are set forth on forms available from the Secretary of State's web site at www.sos.state.mn.us/business/forms.html or by fax from the Fax Forms library at (651) 296-2803 or by mail from the Secretary of State's office. A certificate of status or certificate of good standing from the state or province of organization must accompany the registration form.

The term "transacting business" is not clearly defined in the law, but the standard used in making the determination is the "minimum contacts" standard used in determining jurisdiction. Under this standard the facts are analyzed by the limited liability company to determine whether the business or its local agents have conducted a continuous course of business in Minnesota or with Minnesotans sufficient to justify being governed by Minnesota law.

Neither the Secretary of State's office nor any other state agency will make a determination as to whether a particular limited liability company should register as a foreign limited liability company. As a general rule, doubts should be resolved in favor of registering the organization.

Minnesota Statutes § 322B.945 establishes certain activities as exceptions to the registration requirement. Limited liability companies organized under the laws of a state other than Minnesota should consult with their legal counsel to determine whether any of the exceptions apply.

In addition to obtaining the certificate of authority, a foreign limited liability company must obtain a Minnesota tax identification number from the Department of Revenue. If the company will have employees in Minnesota, it also must complete the Department of Revenue's withholding tax forms and arrange for workers' compensation insurance. The procedure for obtaining these numbers and forms is described in the section of this Guide on business taxes and the Checklist for Hiring an Employee.

If the foreign limited liability company changes the name or address of its registered agent or other statements made in the application for the certificate of authority become inaccurate, the foreign limited liability company must file an amended certificate of authority with the Secretary of State. A foreign limited liability company also must obtain any state and local business licenses necessary to conduct business operations. Information on business license requirements may be obtained from the Minnesota Small Business Assistance Office at the address and telephone number provided in the Resource Directory section of this Guide.

SPECIAL TYPES OF BUSINESS ORGANIZATIONS

S CORPORATIONS

Both "S" and "C" corporations are created by filing articles of incorporation with the Secretary of State, after which the shareholders must decide whether to treat the corporation as an S corporation or as a C corporation for tax purposes. An S corporation is a corporation which meets Internal Revenue Service criteria for tax treatment as an S corporation rather than as a C corporation, and whose shareholders unanimously choose to be so treated. An S corporation is taxed under Subchapter S of the Internal Revenue Code, whereas C corporations are taxed under Subchapter C of the Internal Revenue Code. A corporation that has a valid election to be taxed as an S corporation for federal purposes is also an S corporation for Minnesota tax purposes.

The S corporation is taxed in much the same manner as a partnership, i.e., the S corporation files an information tax return, Form 1120S, to report its income and expenses, but it is not separately taxed. Income (including, if certain requirements are met, capital gains) and expenses of the S corporation flow through to the shareholders in proportion to their shareholdings, and profits are taxed to the shareholders at the shareholders' individual tax rates. For Minnesota purposes, the S corporation also pays a minimum fee, based on its Minnesota-sourced property, payroll and sales. See the Tax Rates section of this Guide.

By contrast, the C corporation is a separate taxable entity. The C corporation reports its income and expenses on a corporation income tax return and is taxed on its profits at corporation income tax rates. Profits are taxed to the C corporation before dividends are paid. Dividends, when paid, are taxed to shareholders who then report them as income. This results in double taxation of profits which are paid as dividends. By choosing S corporation status, this double taxation of corporate profits can be avoided.

An S corporation is defined by statute as a domestic corporation (i.e., a corporation organized under the law of one of the states of the United States) which:

- Does not have more than 75 shareholders;
- Does not have any non-individual shareholders (other than estates, certain trusts, and certain tax exempt entities);
- Does not have a nonresident alien as a shareholder, and
- Does not have more than one class of stock.

Certain corporations by statute are ineligible for S corporation status. If the corporation qualifies for S corporation status, the shareholders must formally choose to be so treated for tax purposes. This is accomplished by filing Form 2553 with the Internal Revenue Service on which all shareholders consent in writing to have the corporation treated as an S corporation. The election must be made in a timely manner, as prescribed by the Internal Revenue Service.

The election is valid for the taxable year for which it is made, and for all succeeding taxable years of the corporation, until the election is terminated. Statutory procedures determine how the termination is accomplished. In general, S corporation status is terminated when it is revoked by vote of the shareholders, or when the corporation no longer meets the statutory criteria for S corporation status. S corporation status also may be terminated when passive investment income (income from interest, rents, royalties, dividends and the like) exceeds a certain statutorily defined threshold.

Because of the possibility that S corporation status may be inadvertently terminated, persons planning to establish an S corporation are strongly encouraged to consult in advance with legal and tax counsel in order to properly structure the corporation and its capitalization. In some cases, formation of a limited liability company, rather than an S corporation, may better suit the owners' business and tax objectives. See the discussion of limited liability companies in the sections of this Guide titled Choosing the Form of Business Organization and Forming a Minnesota Limited Liability Company.

PROFESSIONAL ENTITIES

The Minnesota Professional Firms Act, Minnesota Statutes, Chapter 319B, was enacted in 1997 and authorizes practitioners of certain licensed professions to elect to be professional firms under any one of three different forms of organization: corporations (either for-profit or non-profit); limited liability companies; and limited liability partnerships. In the absence of the Minnesota Professional Firms Act and its predecessors, members of such professions would not be able to practice under these forms of organization because the ethics rules of their respective licensing boards prohibit organizing in a way that limits the professional practitioner's professional liability towards clients. The Minnesota Professional Firms Act does not affect a practitioner's liability for her or his own malpractice or other wrongful conduct directly arising from the rendering of professional services, but permits the professional to have limited liability for debts or obligations of the business itself to the extent that the generally applicable governing law for the chosen form of organization permits.

Professional firms are subject to the law under which the entity has been formed as well as the Professional Firms Act which contains additional restrictions; where the two conflict, the Professional Firms Act will control. Members of the professional firm are also subject to the laws, regulations and licensing requirements of their respective licensing boards.

In order to practice a profession in any form other than sole proprietorship or general partnership, professionals must comply with the Professional Firms Act, except as the rules of the respective licensing board provide otherwise.

Members of the following professions may elect to be professional firms: medicine and surgery, chiropractic, registered nursing; optometry; psychology; social work; dentistry and dental hygiene; pharmacy; podiatric medicine; veterinary medicine; physician's assistants; architecture; engineering; surveying; landscape architecture; geoscience; certified interior design; accountancy; and law.

In order to operate as a professional firm, a Minnesota entity must first be formed under the chosen statute: the Minnesota Business Corporation Act (Minnesota Statutes, Chapter 302A); the Minnesota Nonprofit Corporation Act (Minnesota Statutes, Chapter 317A); the Minnesota Limited Liability Company Act (Minnesota Statutes, Chapter 322B); or the Minnesota Limited Liability Partnership Act (Minnesota Statutes, Chapter 323A). An existing non-Minnesota entity wishing to practice a profession in Minnesota should register under the Minnesota Foreign Corporation Act (Minnesota Statutes, Chapter 303) or the foreign registration provisions of the Limited Liability Company or Limited Liability Partnership Acts.

Then, either as an addendum to the original documents of formation for the entity or as a later amendment or update to those documents, the firm must file with the Secretary of State language stating:

- that the firm elects to be covered by the Minnesota Professional Firms Act (Minnesota Statutes, sections 319B.01 to 319B.012);
- that the firm acknowledges that it is subject to those sections; and
- specifying from the list of professions set forth above the profession or professions to be practiced by the firm.

A non-Minnesota firm must state in addition to the above that to the extent that its generally applicable governing law differs from or conflicts with Minnesota Statutes, sections 319B.01 to 319B.12, that it has made the necessary changes to the agreements and other documents controlling its structure, governance, operations and internal affairs so as to comply with those sections.

Such a filing constitutes an election to be a professional firm. These entities may rescind such elections, may again elect professional status, and may change the designated practiced profession freely, subject to the regulations of the appropriate governing board(s).

Health professionals (including medicine and surgery; chiropractic; registered nursing; optometry; psychology; dentistry and dental hygiene; pharmacy and podiatric medicine) are specifically authorized to practice in the same professional firm; others should consult their licensing boards for further information on whether joint practices are permitted. Where they are not, a professional firm can provide only those professional services listed in the election described above.

The name of a professional firm which is a corporation must include one of the following designations or abbreviations; Professional Corporation, Professional Service Corporation, Service Corporation, Professional Association, Chartered, Limited, P.C., P.S.C., S.C., P.A., or Ltd.

The name of a professional firm which is an LLC must include Professional Limited Liability Company, Limited Liability Company, P.L.L.C., P.L.C., or L.L.C.

The name of a professional firm which is an LLP must include Professional Limited Liability Partnership, Limited Liability Partnership, P.L.L.P. or L.L.P.

The internal governance of professional firms is governed by the same statutes that apply to non-professional firms. For example, a professional LLP and a non-professional LLP are bound in virtually all respects by the same statutes. The only difference is that the professional LLP may provide professional services as listed above and the non-professional LLP may not.

NONPROFIT CORPORATIONS

A Minnesota nonprofit corporation is defined by statute as a corporation which:

- Is formed for a purpose not involving pecuniary gain to its members (other than members that are nonprofit organizations or governmental units), and
- Pays no dividends or other pecuniary remuneration, directly or indirectly, to its members as such (other than to members that are nonprofit organizations or governmental units).

Thus, a business corporation (regardless of whether it actually makes a profit) cannot be a nonprofit corporation because a primary purpose of every business corporation is to remunerate its shareholders.

A nonprofit corporation may be formed under the Minnesota Nonprofit Corporation Act, Minnesota Statutes Chapter 317A, for any lawful purpose, unless another statute requires incorporation for a different or specific purpose. The nonprofit corporation is managed by a board of directors, which must consist of at least three individuals. The nonprofit corporation must have at least two officers, a president and a treasurer. One person may perform both of these functions. The Minnesota Nonprofit Corporation Act does not apply to cooperative associations, public cemetery corporations and associations, and private cemeteries. Religious corporations may be formed under the Minnesota Nonprofit Corporation Act or under the Minnesota religious corporation statute, Minnesota Statutes Chapter 315. Nonprofit corporations are required to file an annual registration with the Secretary of State once each calendar year, on a registration form mailed to the corporation's registered office address. Failure to file in a calendar year will result in statutory dissolution, but non-profit corporations may be reinstated at any time upon filing the annual registration. Note that beginning on July 1, 2002, the registered office address may be updated without charge.

A nonprofit corporation may qualify for tax exempt status for some or all of its income, for federal or state tax purposes, or both. Donors to the tax exempt organization may qualify for a tax deduction on their contributions to the organization. Application for tax exempt status must be made with the Internal Revenue Service and the exemption must subsequently be established with the Minnesota Department of Revenue. Additional specific language may be required in the articles of incorporation by the Internal Revenue Service before an application will be granted. Annual federal and state informational filings also are required, and if the organization solicits funds in Minnesota, it also must register with the Charities Division of the Minnesota Attorney General's office. The formation and tax treatment of nonprofit corporations are highly technical areas which should not be attempted without competent advice from qualified professionals.

Forms for non-profit corporation filings are available at the Secretary of State's web site at www.sos.state.mn.us/business/forms.html or by fax from the Fax Forms library at (651) 296-2803 or by mail from the Secretary of State's office.

COOPERATIVES

A cooperative is a form of business organization in which the business is owned and controlled by those who use its services. A cooperative may be organized as a legal entity or it may be an unincorporated association. Cooperative associations are organized as legal entities under and governed by Minnesota Statutes Chapter 308A. Non-Minnesota cooperatives that wish to do business in Minnesota register under Chapter 303.

Cooperatives are organized primarily for the purpose of providing service to their user-owners, rather than to generate profit for investors. Although cooperatives had their origins in Minnesota in the agricultural sector, in recent years many consumer cooperatives have been established. Some of the more common purposes for which cooperatives are formed are:

- To supply members with agricultural production components such as fuels, fertilizers, feed and chemicals;
- To provide members with an organizational structure for jointly handling and marketing their products;
- To provide services to members, like housing, electricity, telephone, insurance, and health care.

Cooperatives have several features that distinguish them from for-profit business corporations. These include control of the cooperative by user-owners, services provided at cost, and limited return on equity capital.

Starting in 2001, cooperatives will be required to file a periodic registration in every odd-numbered year. Failure to file this registration will result in dissolution. The cooperative will have one year to reinstate by filing the registration and paying a $25 fee.

User-owner Control

Cooperatives are owned and controlled by their members. By statute in Minnesota, members each have one vote, rather than multiple votes based on their capital investment in the cooperative. In some other states, proportional voting based on a member's volume of business with the cooperative is allowed. Operations generally are conducted by a board of directors elected by members, and by management hired and supervised by the board.

Service at Cost

Cooperatives stress providing services to members at the lowest responsible cost. After setting aside reserves to protect the cooperative's financial security and growth, any remaining net margin is distributed to members as a patronage refund, according to the business volume each has done with the cooperative during the year.

Limited Return on Equity Investment

Cooperatives are designed primarily to provide services to members, rather than to produce a profit for investors. Accordingly, the return on investment in the form of dividends is limited. Minnesota statutes permit, but do not require, the payment of dividends on capital stock. Dividends may be paid only when the net income of the cooperative for the previous fiscal year is sufficient, and dividends may not be cumulative.

FRANCHISES[1]

A franchise is an agreement or contract between two or more persons by which the franchisor, for a fee, gives the franchisee the right to engage in the business of offering or distributing goods or services using the franchisor's trade name, trademark, service mark, logotype, advertising, or other commercial symbol. Both the franchisor and the franchisee must have a community of interest in the marketing of the goods or services.

Franchising is a method of distributing and marketing goods or services. It is not a separate form of business organization. The franchisor's business and the franchisee's business each will take one of the forms of organization previously discussed.

Franchises are regulated in Minnesota by the Department of Commerce, and anyone contemplating the sale of a franchise should check with that office for registration and filing requirements and exemptions that may apply. Regulatory requirements applicable to franchises are discussed further in the section of this Guide on Franchise Registration.

---

[1] For more information about Franchises, see *An Introduction to Franchising*, available without charge from the Minnesota Small Business Assistance Office, 500 Metro Square, 121 7th Place East, St. Paul, MN 55101, telephone (651) 296-3871 or (800) 657-3858 (ask for Small Business), or available from the website www.dted.state.mn.us

FILING DOCUMENTS WITH THE SECRETARY OF STATE

DRAFTING THE DOCUMENT

Standard forms are available without charge from the Secretary of State's web site at www.sos.state.mn.us/business/forms.html or by fax from the Fax Forms library at (651) 296-2803 or by mail from the Secretary of State's office. While these forms are designed to meet minimum requirements of the law, they are not intended to address every possible situation. Consultation with an attorney can help the business owner draft a document that reflects the needs and desires of the parties and understand the legal effects of the filing.

Documents must be legible. The Secretary of State's office permanently records all documents; this process demands a legible copy. Thus, documents that are illegible are not accepted for filing. Copies and legible fax transmissions are acceptable. Original signatures are acceptable if legible, but are not required; in most cases a copy will suffice.

The proper fee must accompany the document. A current fee schedule appears at the end of this section.

FILING THE DOCUMENT

Documents may be mailed or brought in person to the Secretary of State's office. An expedited fee is charged for immediate handling of documents brought in person to the Secretary of State's office. The address of the Secretary of State's office is provided in the Resource Directory section of this Guide. The address also is printed on standard forms provided by the Secretary of State.

Documents that do not require a fee may be faxed to (651) 297-5844. Documents requiring a fee may be faxed to that number if a payment is to be made by automated clearing house (ACH). For information on establishing an ACH account call (651) 296-2803. Forms are available at the Secretary of State's web site at www.sos.state.mn.us/business/forms.html or by fax from the Fax Forms library at (651) 296-2803 or by mail from the Secretary of State's office.

TIME REQUIRED FOR FILING AND PROCESSING DOCUMENTS

Documents are usually reviewed the day they are received by the Secretary of State's office. In cases of complex documents or heavy seasonal workloads, review may take place the day following receipt. Non-expedited drop-offs are reviewed the business day following drop off.

COMMON REASONS WHY DOCUMENTS ARE NOT ACCEPTED FOR FILING

A document may be returned unapproved and not accepted for filing by the Secretary of State's office for a number of reasons. Some of these include:

- An incomplete address is submitted. Documents must state the full street address, city or town and zip code number.
- The filing fee submitted is not correct.
- The signatures of the required parties are incorrect or incomplete. All incorporators of a corporation or organizers of a limited liability company must sign the original articles. Other filings must be signed by a person who is authorized by the business entity to sign those documents. The business entity's attorney can assist in determining who is authorized to sign documents.
- The name submitted for a corporation, limited liability company or limited liability partnership is not distinguishable from an existing corporate or assumed name, trademark or service mark, limited liability company, limited partnership or limited liability partnership name.
- The name referred to in an amendment or subsequent filing is incorrect. In submitting amendments or any other subsequent filings the name of the corporation or other business entity must be identical (in spelling and punctuation) to the legal name on file with the Secretary of State.

SECRETARY OF STATE FEE SCHEDULE

The following fees are effective as of the date this Guide was printed. Questions may be directed to the Secretary of State's office at the address and telephone number provided in the Resource Directory section of this Guide.

Assumed Names (Minnesota Statutes Chapter 333)	**FEES**
Registration	$ 25
Amendments	$ 25
Renewal	$ 25
Cancellation	No fee
Minnesota Business, Professional, Financial and Insurance Corporations (Minnesota Statutes Chapters 302A, 300, 319B)	
Incorporation	$ 135
Amendments	$ 35
Dissolution Filings	$ 35 each (two are usually required)
Merger	$ 60
Name Reservation	$ 35
Annual Registration	No fee, unless delinquent, then $25
Minnesota Limited Liability Companies (Minnesota Statutes Chapter 322B)	
Articles of Organization	$ 135
Amendments	$ 35
Merger	$ 60
Reinstatement	$ 50
Termination	$ 35
Name Reservation	$ 35
Annual Registration	No fee, unless delinquent, then $25
Foreign Corporations and Foreign Cooperatives (Minnesota Statutes Chapter 303)	
Certificate of Authority	$ 200
Amendments	$ 50
Merger (per each qualified corporation)	$ 50
Non-Profit Certificate	$ 50
Reinstatement (only for foreign cooperatives)	$ 300
Annual Registration	$ 115
Withdrawal	$ 50
Foreign Limited Liability Companies (Minnesota Statutes Chapter 322B)	
Certificate of Authority	$185
Amendments	$ 35
Merger (per each qualified corporation)	$ 35
Withdrawal	$ 35
Annual Registration	No fee, unless delinquent, then $25
Foreign Limited Partnerships (Minnesota Statutes 322A.70)	
Registration	$ 85
Amendments	$ 50
Cancellation	$ 50
Minnesota and Foreign Limited Liability Partnerships (Minnesota Statutes Chapter 323A)	
All filings	$ 135

Limited Partnerships (Minnesota Statutes Chapter 322A)

Registration	$ 100
Amendments	$ 50
Cancellation	$ 50

Partnership Statements

All partnership statements, amendments, and cancellations of statements	$135 each

Minnesota Cooperatives (Minnesota Statutes Chapter 308A)

Incorporation	$ 60
Amendments	$ 35
Merger	$ 60
Periodic Registrations (Odd Numbered Years)	No fee, unless delinquent, then $25

Non-Profit Corporations (Minnesota Statutes Chapter 317A)

Incorporation	$ 70
Amendments*	$ 35
Dissolution Filings	$ 35 each (two are usually required)
Merger	$ 35
Reinstatement	$ 25
Name Reservation	$ 35
Annual Registration	No fee, unless delinquent, then $25

Business Trusts (Minnesota Statutes Chapter 318)

Declaration of Trust	$ 150
Business Trust Amendments	$ 50

Legal Newspapers	$ 25
Consent	$ 35

Trademarks and Service Marks (Minnesota Statutes Chapter 333)

Registration	$ 50
Assignment	$ 15
Renewal	$ 25
Cancellation	No fee

Service of Process

Minnesota Corporations	$ 35
Non-Minnesota Corporations	$ 50

Articles of Correction	$ 35

Certificates

Certificates (each)	$ 5
Certified copies (per certification plus the photocopying fee)	$ 5

Photocopies

Assumed name (per name; entire file or part thereof)	$ 3
Corporations, limited partnerships, trademarks and service marks:	
Original filing	$ 3
All amendments for that entity	$ 3
Other Non-UCC Documents (per page)	$ 1

Expedited Fee

For immediate processing of all over-the-counter, non-UCC transactions filed in the Office of the Secretary of State	$ 20

*Note that beginning July 1, 2002, a nonprofit corporation may change its registered office's address without charge.

REGULATORY CONSIDERATIONS

SECURITIES REGISTRATION

Broadly defined, a security is an interest in, or an obligation of, the business entity that issues the security. Examples of securities are corporate stock, interests in a limited partnership, and corporate bonds and debentures. Note that the label assigned to an interest in a business is not necessarily determinative, and that the definition of a security is a very broad one; note that many seemingly innocent activities, such as the use of a website can constitute the "offer" of securities. **A business owner who is giving or selling ownership interests in a business to other persons, even to friends and family members, is strongly advised to seek the advice of counsel.** This is true whether the ownership interests are transferred when the business is organized or later in its life. In general, securities must be registered with the federal Securities and Exchange Commission and the Minnesota Department of Commerce before they legally can be advertised or sold to investors unless the security or transaction qualifies for an exemption under state or federal laws. A security or transaction may qualify for a federal exemption but not a state exemption or vice versa. Again, given the highly technical laws, regulations, and judicial decisions in this area, as well as guidance from the SEC (such as that issued on the use of electronic media), the advice of counsel is very important.

The basic purpose of both state and federal securities laws is to protect the investor. Therefore, sales in violation of these laws, even if done through inadvertence or in good faith reliance, can create civil and criminal penalties on both the state and the federal level. If interstate sales are involved, civil and criminal penalties in multiple states may apply. The anti-fraud provisions of these laws apply even if the securities or the transaction are exempt from registration.

Securities registration is a sophisticated area requiring the services of experienced professionals. In some cases these professionals may be able to assist in structuring the offering and sale to qualify for an exemption. In other cases their services may be necessary to register and to sell the securities. In all cases involving the offer or sale of securities, discussing the matter with legal counsel is the best starting point.

Some of the common exemptions to the registration requirements of the federal and state laws are discussed below. Readers should be aware that this is not a comprehensive list of the exemptions. Minor changes in fact circumstances may result in the loss of the exemption. Also, both the Securities and Exchange Commission and the Minnesota Department of Commerce periodically amend their regulations in a way that may affect available exemptions. The business person contemplating the offer and sale of securities should consult with experienced professionals to determine the availability of any exemptions.

Further information on federal securities registration requirements and a pamphlet may be obtained from the publications office of the United States Securities and Exchange Commission.

Information on state regulations may be obtained from the Minnesota Department of Commerce Registration and Analysis Division. Also, a copy of "Raising Capital: Securities Law and other Considerations – An Entrepreneur's Guide" is available at no charge from the Minnesota Small Business Assistance Office. The addresses and telephone numbers of these agencies are provided in the Resource Directory section of this Guide.

FEDERAL EXEMPTIONS (15 UNITED STATES CODE § 77)

The Intrastate Exemption

The intrastate exemption applies to securities offerings which are confined to a single state and which are purely local in nature. The scope of the intrastate exemption is extremely narrow, and even though the offering is exempt from federal regulation, it is subject to state law requirements. To qualify for the intrastate exemption, the securities must be part of an issue that is offered and sold only to residents of a single state. The issuer must be a resident of the same state and must have its principal place of business there. If the issuer is a corporation it also must be incorporated in that state. There are restrictions on subsequent sales of the securities, and the issuer must take certain precautions against interstate offers and sales.

Small Offerings – Regulation A Exemption

Regulation A (17 Code of Federal Regulations § 230.251 to § 230.262) permits the offering of up to $5 million of securities in a year without complying with all registration and disclosure requirements. If the Regulation A exemption is available, a shorter form of federal registration is permitted. Full state registration may be required, however.

A simplified disclosure form may be used. Although the federal securities laws generally do not permit advertising prior to registration, recent amendments to Regulation A allow small companies to test investor interest through a written solicitation of interest document before proceeding with a full, and costly, registration.

Private Placements – Regulation D Exemption

The Regulation D exemptions (17 Code of Federal Regulations § 230.501 to § 230.508) authorize the offer and sale of securities through certain private placement transactions. There are restrictions on the number and amount of sales, and on publicity, advertising or solicitation, and resale. Notice of Regulation D offerings must be filed with the Securities and Exchange Commission, but the full registration and disclosure requirements of a public offering need not be met.

LIMITED OFFERINGS IN MINNESOTA

Companies attempting to raise capital by the sale of securities subject to Minnesota securities law should consider the use of one of the following exemptions.

Isolated Sales

Isolated sales, whether or not affected through a broker-dealer, are exempt from registration. No person may make more than ten sales in Minnesota of securities of the same company during any period of twelve consecutive months pursuant to this exemption. In the case of sales by a company (except sales of securities registered under the Securities Act or exempted by Section 3(b) of the Securities Act), the seller must reasonably believe that all buyers are purchasing for investment and the securities must not be advertised for sale to the general public in newspapers or other publications of general circulation or otherwise, or by radio, television, electronic means, or similar communications media, or through a program of general solicitation by means of mail or telephone.

Institutional Investors

Chapter 80A provides an exemption for any offer or sale to a bank, savings institution, trust company, insurance company, investment company, pension or profit sharing trust, or other financial institution or institutional buyer, or to a broker-dealer, whether the purchaser is acting for itself or in some fiduciary capacity.

The term "financial institution or institutional buyer" includes, but is not limited to, a corporation with a class of equity securities registered under Section 12(g) of the Exchange Act and a person or entity considered to be an accredited investor.

Limited Offerings

Sales by a company to no more than 25 persons in Minnesota are exempt under the following circumstances:

(1) The company reasonably believes all the buyers in this state (other than those designated as institutional investors) are purchasing for investment.

(2) No commission or other remuneration is paid or given directly or indirectly for soliciting any prospective buyer in this state (other than those designated as institutional investors), except reasonable and customary commissions paid by the company to a broker-dealer licensed under Chapter 80A.

(3) The company has, ten days prior to any sale under this exemption, filed with Minnesota a statement of the issuer on the form prescribed.

Rule 505 or 506 Offerings

Offers and sales by an issuer by a company are exempt under Minnesota law if made in reliance on the exemptions provided by Rule 505 or 506 of Regulation D and if certain other conditions and limitations are met, such as:

- A notice on Form D must also be filed with Minnesota.

- No remuneration may be paid for soliciting a prospective purchaser unless the recipient is registered (or exempt from registration) in Minnesota as a holder-dealer.

- The exemption is not available if certain people associated with the offerings have been found within the last five years to have violated certain securities laws.

Sales to Existing Security Holders

Any transaction pursuant to an offer to existing security holders of the company, including persons who are holders of convertible securities, nontransferable warrants or transferrable warrants excercisable within not more than 90 days of their issuance, is exempt from registration under the following circumstances:

- no commission or other remuneration (other than a stand-by commission) is paid or given directly or indirectly for soliciting any security holder in the state; and

- the commissioner has been furnished, no less than ten days prior to the transaction, with a general description of the transaction, and with such other information as the commissioner may by rule prescribe.

SCOR (SMALL CORPORATE OFFERING REGISTRATION)

The Small Corporate Offering Registration (SCOR) is a simplified procedure for registering stock offerings which enables small, start-up companies to raise up to $1 million in a 12-month period.

SCOR: Access to Capital for Small Businesses

Increased Access to Capital

A SCOR offering is a tool for small businesses to raise capital without the prohibitive costs involved in traditional stock offerings.

Regulatory Relief and Streamlining

Because the offering is registered solely with the state, multiple reporting requirements are eliminated. In addition, the enhanced form U-7 disclosure document is simply formatted into 50 detailed questions designed to satisfy the necessary disclosures without burdensome requirements.

Reduced Legal Fees and Transaction Costs

The "Question and Answer" format of the Form U-7 may allow an entrepreneur to prepare the initial draft of a securities prospectus.

Expanded Pool of Potential Investors

The SCOR method provides a larger pool of initial investors over and above the traditional "friend and family" method. SCOR allows a company to offer securities to the public through advertisement and other alternative forms of solicitation, which are typically not allowed in traditional private placements.

Increased Investment Opportunities

SCOR provides early-stage investment opportunities for those investors who want these types of potentially more risky opportunities.

Lower Minimum Investment Amounts

Because SCOR is a public registration process, there are no numerical limits on the number of "unaccredited" investors allowed in an offering. This allows entrepreneurs to offer lower "minimum investments" than are typically available from traditional stock offerings.

Local Investing

Since many of the SCOR offerings are local in nature, many investors will become aware of local investment opportunities.

Federal and State Securities Law

Registration is the process of filing and getting approval of a company's offering from the SEC or the state regulator. The traditional registration process costs a corporation anywhere from $100,000 to $200,000.

Federal securities laws offer an exemption under Regulation D. Under Regulation D, companies do not need to register certain small offerings, private offerings and offerings to accredited investors. The SCOR program provides a simplified registration process for offerings that are exempt under Rule 504 of Regulation D. Using SCOR reduces administrative burdens by eliminating multiple reporting requirements.

SCOR and Regulation D only simplify the registration requirements of the statute. No one is ever exempt from the securities law anti-fraud provisions, including the requirements to disclose all material information.

Completing the Form U-7

The process of completing a SCOR offering is centered around the form U-7. The Form U-7 is less complex than traditional stock prospectuses. The Form U-7 consists of 50 detailed questions designed to provide the state and the investor with important information regarding the company's operations. The questions in the U-7 form consist of items such as the company's history; its business and properties; risk factors facing the company; use of the offering proceeds; description of the securities being offered; dividend history; key personnel; principal stockholders; and pending or threatened litigation.

Answering the Form U-7 questions adequately and completely will satisfy the required disclosures in law.

Once the Form U-7 is completed, it is submitted, along with reviewed or audited financial reports, and the required fee to the State of Minnesota Department of Commerce Registration Division. The Department reviews and provides comments on the documents. So long as no stop order is in effect and no proceeding is pending under Minnesota Statutes section 80A.13 a SCOR registration statement becomes effective automatically at 5:00 p.m. on the twentieth full business day after the filing of the registration statement, or the last amendment of it, or at some earlier time determined (by order) by the Commissioner of the Department of Commerce.

An issuer can raise up to $1 million in a 12 month period, and offerings must sell for at least $1 per share. Minnesota is the 45th state to adopt the SCOR program.

FRANCHISE REGISTRATION*

DEFINITION OF FRANCHISING

Franchising is a method of marketing and distributing goods and services. Franchises are offered and sold for many types of businesses, including services, retail trade, finance, real estate, transportation, and communications.

A franchise is broadly defined as a contract or agreement between two or more persons by which the franchisor (the seller), for a fee, gives the franchisee (the buyer) the right to engage in the business of offering or distributing goods or services using the franchisor's trade name, trademark, service mark, logotype, advertising or other commercial symbol. Both the franchisor and the franchisee must have a community of interest in the marketing of the goods or services.

Under the Minnesota franchising statute, a franchise also includes business opportunities in which the seller sells or leases products or services to the purchaser **and** represents that the seller will find or assist in finding locations; or represents that the seller will purchase the products made; or guarantees that the purchaser will make a profit.

Note that the 2000 Legislature enacted new laws adding significant requirements for franchises for the sale of motor fuel (see Minnesota Statutes Section 80F.01, *et. seq.)* Note also that in October 1999 the U.S. Federal Trade Commission issued proposed amendments to its FTC Franchise and Business Opportunities Rule. As of the time this Guide went to press, those proposed amendments had not been finalized.

*A comprehensive discussion of franchise and business opportunities issues is provided in the publication *An Introduction to Franchising*, available from the Minnesota Small Business Assistance Office, 500 Metro Square, 121 7th Place East, St. Paul, MN 55101-2146 (or from its website at www.dted.state.mn.us)

FRANCHISE REGISTRATION AND REGULATION

Any proposed offer or sale of a franchise that meets the above definition may be subject to the registration and other requirements of the Minnesota Franchise Act (Minnesota Statutes Chapter 80C) and rules of the Department of Commerce, Minnesota Rules 2860.0100-2860.9930. Unless there is a specific statutory exemption, a proposed franchise must be registered with the Department of Commerce and must be effective before any offers or sales are made.

The Minnesota Franchise Act and rules define franchises and exemptions; establish registration criteria, procedures, and fees; set requirements for public offering statements; define unfair and prohibited practices; mandate the keeping of books and records; establish enforcement standards, and provide for imposition of civil liability for violations. The Act and rules also address issues like temination and notice periods for non-renewal of franchises, liquidated damages, termination penalties, arbitration, security deposits and governing law.

Minnesota accepts franchise applications which comply with the Uniform Franchise Offering Circular (UFOC) Guidelines of the North American Securities Administrators Association. The UFOC Guidelines prescribe disclosures that a franchisor must make available to prospective franchisees, and require that franchisors supply prospective franchisees with audited financial statements and copies of all proposed contracts and agreements pertaining to the proposed franchise relationship.

COMMERCE DEPARTMENT ENFORCEMENT ACTIONS

The Enforcement Division of the Minnesota Department of Commerce investigates complaints against companies selling franchises and business opportunities. Action can be taken only when a violation of the Minnesota Franchise Law (Minnesota Statutes Chapter 80C) has occurred. To check on a specific company or to inquire about filing a complaint, individuals may call (651) 296-2488 or (800) 657-3602.

OTHER ENFORCEMENT AND INFORMATION ASSISTANCE

In addition to the regulation done by the State of Minnesota, the United States Federal Trade Commission (FTC) has regulatory authority over the sellers of franchises and business opportunities. Pursuant to Section 5 of the Federal Trade Commission Act, the FTC has issued its Franchise and Business Opportunity Rule, which imposes certain obligations on the sellers of franchises or business opportunities. Note that in the past two years, the FTC has issued a number of pronouncements relating to the future revision of that Rule. Anyone with questions about the FTC's regulation of franchises and business opportunities is strongly advised to seek the advice of counsel. While the FTC does not have the authority to resolve individual disputes between the seller and buyer of a franchise or a business opportunity, it does have the authority to take action against such sellers that participate in a pattern of possible violations of the law. One group that works with the FTC in this area is the National Fraud Information Center (NFIC) (telephone (800) 876-7060), a private, nonprofit organization that operates a consumer hotline to provide service and assistance in filing complaints about franchises and business opportunities. The NFIC assists the FTC and state Attorneys General by entering complaints into a computerized database to help track and identify operators of frauds.

Along with its enforcement activities, the FTC issues a number of publications designed to educate potential buyers and sellers of franchises and business opportunities. Examples are: *Franchise and Business Opportunities,* a discussion of a buyer's rights under the Franchise and Business Opportunity Rule, along with suggestions on where to complain about a seller of a franchise or business opportunity; *A Consumer Guide to Buying a Franchise; Business Opportunities: Avoiding Vending Machine and Display Rack Scams; Guide to the FTC Franchise Rule;* and *Work-at-Home Schemes.* Many of the FTC's publications are available on its web site, at www.ftc.gov. Also available there is a *Summary of Recent Enforcement Cases,* a list of the lawsuits the FTC has initiated, including the names of the parties against which the FTC has filed a legal complaint and the docket number of each case.

EXEMPTIONS

There are eight registration exemptions available under Minnesota Statutes § 80C.03. These include sale of a franchise by a franchisee-owner; sales by an executor, administrator, sheriff, trustee in bankruptcy, guardian or conservator; sales to a bank or insurance company; sales of registered securities; a single isolated sale of a franchise under specified conditions; the sale of a franchise to a franchisee with specified experience in the business and who derives 80 percent or more of its sales from other sources; sale of a foreign franchise to a nonresident of Minnesota under specified conditions; and sales exempted by order of the Commissioner of Commerce. It is strongly recommended that anyone considering the offer or sale of a franchise consult a knowledgeable attorney before relying on an exemption.

FRANCHISING IN OTHER STATES

Although many states regulate franchises in a manner similar to Minnesota, each state's laws are different. Accordingly, franchisors who plan to offer or sell franchises in other states should check with appropriate officials in those states regarding their franchising laws and requirements.

INTERPRETIVE OPINIONS

Under Minnesota Statutes § 80C.18, subd. 2, a company may request an interpretive opinion from the Department of Commerce on whether a business being offered is a franchise, whether registration is required, and whether an exemption is available. An opinion fee is required.

FEES

Fees charged by the Department of Commerce for franchise-related transactions are: initial application fee, $400; annual report (renewal) fee, $200; amendment fee, $100; and opinion fee, $50.

QUESTIONS AND FURTHER INFORMATION

Questions concerning franchise registration should be directed to the Minnesota Department of Commerce at the address and telephone number provided in the Resource Directory section of this Guide.

Copies of the Minnesota Franchise Act, rules of the Department of Commerce, and the UFOC Guidelines may be purchased from the State of Minnesota Bookstore at the address and telephone number provided in the Resource Directory section of this Guide.

EVALUATING A BUSINESS OPPORTUNITY

SOME GENERAL CONSIDERATIONS

When buying an existing business, investing in a franchise, or beginning a new business, the entrepreneur should thoroughly evaluate the business opportunity he or she is considering. This step is very important but often overlooked; many times, a person's hopes for a business cloud his or her judgment. It is not uncommon for an entrepreneur to invest a substantial sum in a business without analyzing whether the business opportunity is a viable one. In addition, it is not uncommon for an unscrupulous business promoter to take advantage of such an entrepreneur.

Although there are no foolproof steps to take in evaluating a business, this section of this Guide will offer guidance on the types of questions to ask, and sources of information to review, before investing in a new business (whether or not it is a franchise) or buying an existing business. Assuming that after evaluating the opportunity the entrepreneur still wants to proceed, the sections of this Guide on Accounting for the New Business – Income Forecasting Techniques, and on Business Plans, should be consulted.

It is worth emphasizing here that an entrepreneur's analysis and evaluation should occur before he or she makes any kind of commitment (even oral), whether contractual or financial, to the business, or makes any payment, of any size, in connection with the business. In any event, a potential entrepreneur should carefully avoid obligating himself or herself to participating in any business opportunity, in any way, without first evaluating that opportunity.

USING PROFESSIONAL ADVISORS

Even before beginning that evaluation, the entrepreneur often will decide whether to perform that evaluation himself or herself, or engage an accountant or attorney to assist him or her. Professional advisors, such as attorneys and accountants, can greatly enhance an entrepreneur's review of a potential business. This is true for at least two reasons. First, those professionals will have no emotional attachment or stake in that review process; their objectivity may serve as an important counterbalance to an entrepreneur's enthusiasm. Second, those professionals should be able to provide thorough review of financial or intellectual property information provided, and should be knowledgeable of any potential obstacles to the success of the business (such as the need for licenses or permits). For instance, it is important that someone thoroughly evaluate financial information supplied by a seller or offeror, or pro forma information prepared by the entrepreneur, and in many cases a professional is best suited to that task.

SOURCES OF INFORMATION

One source of information is the Minnesota Attorney General's office, at (651) 296-3353, and the Better Business Bureau, at (651) 699-1111, to determine if any complaints have been filed in connection with that business. Also, the National Fraud Information Center (NFIC) is a private, nonprofit organization that operates a consumer hotline to provide service and assistance in filing complaints against unscrupulous business operators. The NFIC helps the FTC and state Attorneys General by entering complaints into a computerized database to help track and identify operators of business frauds. Contact the NFIC at (800) 876-7060, 9:00 a.m. to 5:30 p.m., EST, Monday through Friday. These are prudent, but not foolproof, steps in evaluating any business opportunity.

Note that the FTC is another potential source of information about the offeror. The FTC's Internet site (www.ftc.gov) contains a summary of each of the FTC's legal actions against offerors of franchises and business opportunities, along with information on specific types of fraudulent business opportunities that the FTC has become familiar with. Also, that Internet site contains a copy of the FTC's brochure, *Franchise and Business Opportunities,* which summarizes the types of protections provided to entrepreneurs by the FTC's Rule on Franchising and Business Opportunity Ventures, 16 C.F.R. section 436 (the FTC Rule). Remember that, as discussed in more detail in the Franchise Registration section of this Guide, the Minnesota Department of Commerce also will have copies of the registration statement made by the offeror of any franchise or business opportunity that is a franchise within the meaning of the Minnesota Franchise Act, Minnesota Statutes Chapter 80C.

SPECIFIC INFORMATION TO SEEK FROM THE OFFEROR

If the franchise or business opportunity is a franchise under the Minnesota Franchise Act, the offeror is required to make certain filings, including the Uniform Franchise Offering Circular (UFOC) with the Minnesota Department of Commerce, before offering that franchise or business opportunity to anyone. See the section of this Guide on Franchise Registrations. Note that although the UFOC will contain certain detailed information on the business opportunity or franchise, including audited financial statements, it is not the job of the Minnesota Department of Commerce, or any other government agency, to assess the merits, completeness, or even accuracy of any of the information contained in a UFOC. That work is for the entrepreneur.

Similarly, if a franchise or business opportunity does not meet the definition of a "franchise" for Minnesota state law purposes, it nevertheless may be subject to the FTC Rule. Similar to the Minnesota regulation of franchises and business opportunities, the offeror of a business venture covered by the FTC Rule must provide certain information to the prospective offeree. Also, and again similar to the Minnesota system of regulation, it is not the job of the FTC to assess the merits, completeness, or even accuracy of the information mandated by the FTC Rule.

Even for ventures not regulated by the Minnesota Department of Commerce or the FTC, the FTC in its *Franchise and Business Opportunities* brochure recommends that an entrepreneur seek the following information before investing or committing to a franchise or business opportunity:

- Talk to any persons named as owners or investors in the opportunity. Don't rely on persons listed as "references", unless it is clear that they are truly owners or investors. Although it is possible that those persons have been hired by the offeror to say only positive things about the business, it is also possible that those persons will have valuable insights into how operating the business differs from the description provided by the offeror.

- Carefully and thoroughly investigate any claims made about potential earnings. Seek written information on this topic, not just oral statements, and seek the most detailed information available (i.e., do not rely on broad claims such as "we are a ten billion dollar industry"). Independently analyze, if possible, the written basis for those claims. For example, the entrepreneur could hire his or her own CPA to independently audit that information.

- Seek similar information from the business competitors of the offeror. For instance, seek the UFOCs from other offerors of similar franchises or business opportunities.

- Be aware of high pressure sales tactics, and consider why they are being used; if the offeror does not have any other way to sell the franchise or business opportunity, do you really want it? Be wary of any oral statement that differs from any statement made in writing. Also be wary of any presentation that promises "easy money". Successful entrepreneurs almost always agree that there is no "easy money", and that owning one's own business, while rewarding, takes a great deal of time and energy.

BUSINESS LICENSES AND PERMITS

IN GENERAL

The startup, operation or expansion of a business in Minnesota may involve securing one or more business, occupational or environmental licenses or permits. Those licenses and permits fall into a number of categorical groupings according to purpose:

- Licenses and permits to ensure the competency of practitioners of a business, trade or profession.

- Licenses and permits to ensure the safety and efficacy of a product or process.

- Licenses and permits to prevent fraud or ensure the financial solvency of parties to a business transaction.

- Licenses and permits to control access to markets or to encourage or restrict competition in a specific industry.

- Licenses and permits to regulate activities in pursuit of broad social goals like clean air, clean water.
- Licenses and permits to ensure the appropriate and responsible use of natural resources, particularly non-renewable natural resources.
- Licenses and permits to control the development and implementation of new technology.
- Licenses and permits to authorize a business to serve as the state's agent for collection of revenue.

The Bureau of Business Licenses provides information about federal, state and local licenses and assistance in securing them. The Bureau also publishes, free of charge, the State of Minnesota Directory of Licenses and Permits which contains a complete list of regulated activities, licenses and permits, and the appropriate state agency contact. It is reprinted at the end of this Guide.

The Bureau, together with the Small Business Assistance Office makes recommendations to state departments and the Legislature for eliminating, consolidating, simplifying, expediting, or otherwise improving licensing and regulatory practices affecting business undertakings.

A list of state regulated business activities, required licenses and permits and state agency contacts appears in the Directory of Licenses and Permits section of this publication. A list of licenses and permits with more extensive information on requirements, schedules, fees and the like appears on the Department of Trade and Economic Development web site at www.dted.state.mn.us.

LOCAL LICENSURE

In addition to the licensing requirements imposed by the state, some local governments also require certain kinds of business activity to be licensed on the local level. In some cases this local licensure may take the form of a general business license involving no more than registration and payment of a fee. In other cases it may involve compliance with local ordinances specific to a particular type of business. For example, current state law imposes no license requirements on commercial building contractors. Many municipalities, however, require registration and bonding of these contractors before the municipalities will issue necessary building permits or conduct necessary inspections.

Larger cities like Minneapolis and St. Paul have regular licensing departments. Smaller municipalities usually rely on the city clerk to direct licensing activities. A call to either of these early in your business planning will help avoid confusion and delay later. In addition, the city clerk can in most cases give you information on local zoning requirements. Municipal offices are usually listed in the blue pages of the telephone book under the name of the municipality.

LOCAL ZONING

Zoning is the process by which a local community enacts ordinances to regulate and control the uses of privately owned land and structures within the community. In practice this process involves the creation of districts or zones within the community and restriction on the use of land, and the use, height and area of buildings within these districts. Zoning serves to promote and conserve the health, safety, convenience and general welfare of the community.

The local zoning board or planning commission should be contacted early in your business planning to determine the regulations regarding any space in which you plan to operate your business. This is true especially if you plan to operate your business out of your home. The zoning ordinances of each local community detail the procedure for establishment of zones and the procedures for petition for variances.

Note that the Legislature enacted modifications to certain statutes that, speaking generally, prohibit counties and municipalities from using "amortization" to eliminate or terminate a particular use of land. In this context, the term "amortization" occurs when a local government asserts that a once-lawful use of land is no longer allowed, so that the unit of government can take or condemn that land under the theory that it has no value.

BONDING

A bond is a contract, similar to an insurance policy, between a bonding company (called a "surety") and the business that purchases the bond. The bond runs in favor of a third person to protect that person against financial loss caused by the act or default of the business. Surety bonds guarantee the performance of various types of obligations assumed by contract or imposed by law. Fidelity bonds guarantee against loss due to the dishonesty of employees.

A surety bond often is required of a business which is licensed by the state of Minnesota or by a unit of local government. Businesses that contract to provide goods or services to the state or other public agencies within the state generally must be bonded. These bonding requirements are established by statute. A private firm may by contract require bonding as well. Such bonds are most common in the construction industry.

Bonds are obtained through insurance agents or through a bonding company. The cost of a bond is a portion of the face amount of the bond, and will depend in part on the risk to the bonding company in covering the potential loss.

The Minnesota Bonding Program

The Minnesota Bonding Program (MBP) provides individual fidelity bonds to employers for job applicants who may be denied coverage.

The Fidelity Bond insurance is issued as a policy of McLaughlin Company. The Minnesota Department of Economic Security is an authorized agency for the issuance of bonds to cover persons who make application for seeking employment at Minnesota WorkForce Centers. Either the job applicant or the prospective employer (on the applicant's behalf) may make the initial contact with a local WorkForce Center to apply for the issuance of bond insurance coverage.

Bond coverage becomes effective when the WorkForce Center certifies the bond (usually the day the job offer is made) to take effect the day that the applicant begins work. MBP coverage is provided at no cost to the employer or the job applicant.

A listing of WorkForce Centers can be found in the Resource Directory section of this guide.

ENVIRONMENTAL PROTECTION PROGRAMS

The Legislature has declared in statute that each person in Minnesota has a right to the protection, preservation and enhancement of air, water, land and other natural resources, and that each person also has the responsibility to contribute to the protection, preservation and enhancement of those resources. To secure and advance that right a number of state agencies have responsibility and authority for policy development, standard setting, permitting and enforcement in environmental areas. These agencies include the Minnesota Environmental Quality Board, the Minnesota Pollution Control Agency, the Minnesota Department of Natural Resources, the Minnesota Department of Agriculture, the Minnesota Department of Health, and others. The Directory of Licenses and Permits at the back of this book lists the appropriate regulatory agency by regulated activity.

ENVIRONMENTAL REVIEW

Certain projects (for example, the construction or expansion of commercial or industrial facilities) can trigger specialized environmental review intended to prevent damage to environmental resources as a result of private or public development projects. This preventive planning approach helps identify and mitigate possible environmental problems while the project is still in the planning stages before permits are issued and construction or operation begins.

Those reviews are conducted by a legally defined "responsible governmental unit" and are of two types: an Environmental Assessment Worksheet and an Environmental Impact Statement. An Environmental Assessment Worksheet is a preliminary review to evaluate the potential for significant environmental effects from a project. An Environmental Impact Statement is a more comprehensive environmental review. The size and nature of certain projects trigger a mandatory Environmental Worksheet and/or an Environmental Impact Statement while in other cases the nature of review is at the discretion of the responsible governmental unit. For more information, contact the Minnesota Environmental Quality Board or the Minnesota Pollution Control Agency at the address and telephone numbers listed in the Resource Directory section of this Guide.

THE MINNESOTA POLLUTION CONTROL AGENCY

As noted above, several state agencies have responsibilities for environmental protection. The Minnesota Pollution Control Agency (MPCA) is the agency specifically charged with efforts to eliminate, reduce or control the levels of pollution in the environment. It is the principal agency for permitting associated with air quality and water quality, for the management of hazardous and solid waste, and for the enforcement of pollution control statutes and regulations.

Permit requirements, application procedures, schedules and other procedural requirements vary with the facility or activity involved. Most permits require a 30-day public notice. If members of the public object to issuance of the permit, and/or ask for a public hearing before a state administrative law judge, there may be further evaluation of the application and delay in issuance of the permit. The MPCA always has the option of denying a permit if the proposed facility or activity may result in some significant potential for pollution that cannot be corrected.

Non-compliance with MPCA rules or permit requirements could result in MPCA enforcement action involving administrative penalties, stipulated damages, civil or criminal legal action, and revocation of the MPCA permit. As a practical matter, MPCA permit holders should ensure that they have adequate and appropriate operating practices and qualified personnel in place to meet permit requirements and avoid enforcement action.

HAZARDOUS WASTE

Minnesota has an extensive program for the "cradle-to-grave" management of hazardous waste. Every business in Minnesota is responsible for determining if the waste it produces is hazardous. Many types of businesses, organizations, non-profit groups and governments generate hazardous waste in the course of providing their products or services, including but not limited to the following: cleaning and maintenance; chemical manufacturing and formulating; construction; equipment repair; health care providers; furniture manufacturing and refinishing; wood preservation; laboratories; laundries and dry cleaning; metal manufacturing; electroplating; transportation; electronics; textile, plastics, and leather manufacturing; pesticide manufacture and application; printing and photography; schools and colleges; vehicle repair and auto body shops; and utilities.

Wastes may be hazardous by either exhibiting a hazardous-waste characteristic or by being listed as a hazardous waste.

Characteristic wastes include:

Ignitable waste. A liquid is ignitable if it has a flash point less than 140 degrees Fahrenheit. Check the product's label or Material Safety Data Sheet (MSDS) for this information. A solid waste is ignitable if, at a standard temperature and pressure it can cause a fire through friction, absorption of moisture, or spontaneous chemical changes, and burns so persistently that it creates a hazard.

Oxidizing waste. An oxidizer adds oxygen to a reaction or fire in the absence of air. Oxidizing wastes often have chemical names beginning with "per..." or ending with "...oxide" or "...ate" (for example: persulfate and chlorate). Many oxidizing wastes also contain nitrogen or halogens such as fluoride, chlorine, bromine, and iodine.

Corrosive waste. Any water-based waste having a pH of 2 or less (an acid) or 12.5 or more (a base) is corrosive. Check the product's label or MSDS for this information. A corrosive waste may also be a liquid that is able to corrode greater than one-fourth of an inch of steel per year at 130 degrees Fahrenheit.

Reactive waste. Unstable or explosive wastes, wastes that react violently when brought in contact with water, and wastes that release toxic vapors (such as hydrogen cyanide or hydrogen sulfide) are considered reactive and hazardous (example of reactive waste: unspent lithium batteries greater than 9 volts).

Lethal waste. Lethal wastes exhibit oral or dermal values (LD50) or inhalation values (LC) below a certain lethal threshold. If the health hazard data on the MSDS or other information leads you to suspect a waste may be lethal, contact your metropolitan county (Anoka, Carver, Dakota, Hennepin, Ramsey, Scott or Washington) or MPCA district office hazardous waste staff for assistance.

Toxic waste. Wastes are considered toxic if using The Toxicity Characteristic Leaching Procedure (TCLP), they leach metals or organics at or above certain threshold values. A list of T.C. chemicals and their maximum allowable concentrations is available on the MPCA website at www.pca.state.mn.us under Waste/Publications for Businesses/#2.04, characteristic wastes.

Listed hazardous wastes are printed in Minnesota Rules 7045.0135 and include the following:

- Many spent chlorinated solvents used for degreasing (carbon tetrachloride, methylene chloride, trichloroethane, trichloroethylene, and others);
- Many other waste solvents, cleaners and strippers (acetone, butyl alcohol, carbon disulfide, cresol, ethyl acetate, methyl ethyl ketone (MEK), methyl isobutyl ketone (MIBK), methyl or wood alcohol, toluene, xylene, and others);
- Certain wastes derived from products containing ten percent or more of the above solvents;
- Residues from distillation units (or other similar systems) used to recover the above solvents;
- Most wastes from electroplating operations (cleaning and stripping tank solutions, plating bath solutions and sludges, and sludges from pre-treatment of wastewater);
- Certain wastes from the heat treatment of metals;
- Wastes produced during specific manufacturing processes (certain chemicals, explosives, inks, and pigments), petroleum refining and steel finishing (pickle liquor);
- Many unusable or off-specification commercial products: aniline, certain antibiotics, arsenic compounds, benzenes, chloroform, creosote, cyanide compounds, formaldehyde, hydrofluoric acid, hydrogen sulfide, lead compounds, mercury compounds, naphthalene, many nitrogen compounds, many pesticides, and pentachlorophenol (penta);

- Phenols and pyradine; and
- Polychlorinated biphenyls (PCBs) at concentrations greater than 50 parts per million.

The four lists of hazardous waste (F, K, P and U) are available on the MPCA website at www.pca.state.mn.us under Waste/Publications for Businesses/#'s 2.00, 2.01, 2.02 and 2.03.

Hazardous waste must be managed in accordance with Minnesota hazardous-waste rules. The generator requirements are summarized as follows:

- An EPA identification number must be obtained (at no cost) by filling out the Notification of Hazardous-waste Activity (Form #8700-12) and sending it to the EPA regional office in Chicago. This form, instructions, and assistance for completing the form may be obtained from the MPCA or the appropriate metropolitan county hazardous-waste program.
- Next, a company must apply for a hazardous-waste generator license from the MPCA (for businesses located in greater Minnesota) or from the appropriate metropolitan county (for businesses located in the seven-county metropolitan area).
- Hazardous-waste containers must be properly marked and labeled. As soon as a waste is put in a container, it must be marked with the words "hazardous waste," an accumulation start date, and an easily understood description of the waste.
- Prior to off-site shipment, most hazardous wastes must be placed in specific Minnesota Department of Transportation (DOT) containers and labeled with a DOT hazard label and hazardous-waste label. For more information, request MPCA fact sheet #1.04 or contact your metropolitan county office.
- Store hazardous waste properly and restrict its accumulation time and amounts to specified limits as noted below.

Indoor storage of hazardous waste is regulated by fire prevention and building codes, in addition to hazardous-waste rules. Containers must be stored closed, with adequate aisle space between them for easy access and inspection. Floor drains must not allow waste to escape.

Hazardous waste stored outdoors must be in an area where access is restricted. The waste must be stored on a curbed, impermeable surface, and, if ignitable, must also be protected from direct sunlight.

If less than 220 pounds (or 100 kilograms) of hazardous waste is generated each month, the generator can accumulate up to 2,200 pounds (1,000 kg) indefinitely. Once this amount (about four drums of liquid) has accumulated, the generator has 180 days to have it transported off-site to a storage, treatment, or disposal facility within 200 miles. If the designated facility is farther away than 200 miles, the generator has an additional 90 days to ship the waste.

If between 220 and 2,200 pounds (or 100 to 1,000 kilograms) of hazardous waste is generated each month, the generator must ship the waste to a storage, treatment, or disposal facility within 180 days of the accumulation start date, provided the receiving facility is within 200 miles. If the facility is farther away than 200 miles, the generator has 270 days to ship the waste.

If more than 2,200 pounds (1,000 kg) of hazardous waste is generated each month, the generator must ship all accumulated hazardous waste off-site to a storage, treatment, or disposal facility within 90 days of the accumulation start date. If the 90-day deadline is not met, the generator must obtain a hazardous-waste storage facility permit.

Licenses must be renewed annually and fees are based on the amount of hazardous waste generated and the disposal method. Permit fees are also assessed if generators need an MPCA permit for their waste treatment, storage or disposal activities. For more information contact the MPCA or the metropolitan county hazardous-waste office.

It is the generator's responsibility to know the rules that apply to the management of a particular hazardous waste. Copies of the hazardous-waste rules can be obtained from the Minnesota Bookstore at the address and telephone number listed in the Resource Directory section of this Guide.

STORAGE TANKS

Tank owners are required to register their tanks with the MPCA. Owners of regulated underground storage tanks (USTs) and above ground storage tanks (ASTs) must report information such as tank age, size, and contents within 30 days after installation of a new tank, or within 30 days after any changes in tank ownership, use, or contents. The agency provides forms for this purpose. Septic tanks and some pipeline facilities do not have to meet this requirement.

The MPCA must receive 10 days advance notice, in writing, prior to the installation, removal, or upgrade of regulated USTs. Only MPCA certified contractors can perform UST installation and removal projects. The agency provides a list of these certified contractors. Contractors are not required to be certified or provide advance notice for installation, removal, or upgrade of ASTs or non-regulated USTs. However, individuals and companies doing AST work must follow applicable standards outlined in Minnesota Rules, Chapter 7151. MPCA does not regulate USTs with a capacity of 110 gallons or less, residential or farm USTs storing 1,100 gallons or less of motor fuel (used for non-commercial purposes), and USTs storing 1,100 gallons or less of heating oil (used to heat the property where the tank is located).

According to Minnesota Rules, Chapter 7150, most new and existing regulated USTs must have spill, overfill, and corrosion protection. USTs that do not have these safeguards must immediately be taken out of service until they are upgraded, replaced, removed, or abandoned-in-place with fire marshal approval. Regulated USTs were required to have leak detection on or before 1993 based on the age of the tank. Regulated USTs that need only corrosion protection include waste oil tanks receiving no more than 25 gallons of product at a time.

With a few exceptions, all new and existing AST facilities with a total storage capacity of less than one million gallons must have corrosion protection, overfill protection, secondary containment, and substance transfer area protection according to Minnesota Rules, Chapter 7151. Monitoring and leak detection requirements also exist for these ASTs. A general permit is no longer required for these regulated AST facilities. Some tanks excluded from these regulations include farm ASTs, ASTs with a capacity of 500 gallons or less, residential ASTs storing 1,100 gallons or less of motor fuel (used for non commercial purposes), and ASTs storing 1,100 gallons or less of heating oil (used to heat the property where the tank is located). A reimbursement program for bulk plant operators exists for the upgrade or installation of required AST safeguards. Money is available for work completed between June 1, 1998, and November 1, 2003.

If an AST holds more than 10,000 gallons, a spill response plan is required. This plan describes the steps the tank owner will take if there is a spill or another type of accident. Call the MPCA at the telephone number listed in the Resource Directory of this Guide for the content requirements of a spill response plan.

AST facilities with total storage capacity of greater than or equal to one million gallons must obtain an individual permit for their tanks. The individual permit addresses tank inspection and maintenance, spill containment, tank gauging, overfill protection, corrosion protection, and tank upgrades. Permits are issued for up to five years. To obtain an individual site permit for your facility, please call the MPCA's AST program.

Tank owners and operators can participate in an environmental audit program. This program allows tank owners to make improvements to their site before fines or violation notices are issued or enforcement action is taken. The environmental audit cannot be used at facilities where serious and repeat violations have occurred.

More information about tanks is available by calling the Tank Hot Line or by exploring the MPCA web site at www.pca.state.mn.us. Click on programs and select "Aboveground Storage Tank Systems" or the "Storage Tank Compliance and Assistance Program".

WATER QUALITY REQUIREMENTS

Businesses may need a permit or certificate from the MPCA if they:

1. Discharge any wastewater into surface waters (including storm sewers);
2. Operate an agricultural feedlot;
3. Operate a disposal system which land-applies wastewater, or by product;
4. Operate a large on-site drain field; or
5. Operate any one of a class of categorical industries.

Businesses requiring an extension of a sanitary sewer system will be affected by the MPCA requirement that any municipality must have a Sewer Extension Permit before extending its sanitary sewer lines. Application must be made 60 days before the planned commencement of construction. There is a $240 sewer extension permit application fee.

6. Discharge storm-water from an industrial or construction site.
7. Plan to dredge, fill, inundate or drain a wetland to the extent that a United States Army Corps of Engineers permit would be required. The MPCA must then certify that permit.

Feedlot Permits

Feedlot permits are required for any livestock or poultry facility with more than 50 animal units (for example, one unit equals one slaughter steer or horse, ten sheep or 100 chickens). Virtually all livestock and poultry facilities (except pastures) fall under these rules. Very large feedlots (more than 1,000 animal units) may require National Pollutant Discharge Elimination System (NPDES) permits.

Information on feedlot permits, regulations and related issues is available from the MPCA at the address and telephone number listed in the Resource Directory section of this Guide.

National Pollutant Discharge Elimination System (NPDES) Permits

NPDES permits are required for any discharge of wastewater into surface waters, including non-contact cooling water and air-conditioning or heat-pump water. NPDES permits are not required if the discharge is to a publicly-owned sanitary sewer system. However, local permits may be required – check with your local municipality.

NPDES permits are required for feedlots of more than 700 dairy cows, 2,500 swine, 1,000 beef or equivalent other animals discharging directly into surface waters, in lieu of feedlot permits.

Permit applications are available from the MPCA at the address and telephone number listed in the Resource Directory section of this Guide. Applications must be submitted 180 days before the planned activity commences. There is an $85 application fee. A typical small industry discharging to a surface water can expect a permit annual fee of $1,230. Except for the categorical industries listed below, there are no such fees if the discharge goes to a sanitary sewer. Applicants should be prepared to provide information on the location, quantity and quality of the proposed discharge. NPDES permits are issued for a period of up to five years.

Storm-water Discharge Permits

Certain types of industrial facilities must apply for a storm-water discharge permit from the MPCA. In addition, storm-water permits may be required for certain construction activities. Minnesota's storm-water permitting program is designed to help improve the quality of the state's waters by reducing or eliminating the chemicals and sediments carried into surface waters with storm-water runoff.

All required industrial facilities must apply for a general storm-water discharge permit from the MPCA. In addition, an industry-specific permit may be required depending on the environmental risk of storm-water runoff from the facility. Construction projects disturbing five or more acres must apply for a general NPDES storm-water permit from the MPCA. Storm-water permits may require the preparation of a plan for managing storm-water runoff, potentially including construction of holding basins or diversion structures.

The program is changing due to new federal regulations, so, if you have potential discharges find out if your industrial facility requires a storm-water permit, by contacting the MPCA's storm-water permitting program at the address and telephone number listed in the Resource

Directory section of this Guide. In addition, the MPCA and EPA will have web sites with information on Phase II of the storm water permit programs. Check the MPCA home page and EPA storm-water page for new information.

State Disposal System Permits

State disposal system permits are required for disposal of wastewater other than to surface waters, including large septic tank and drainfield systems and spray irrigation of wastewater. Any industry or business that operates a disposal system would need an SDS permit. The need for an SDS permit may be satisfied by certain construction or operating practices; these must be evaluated on a case-by-case basis. Only domestic sewage should be discharged to drainfields.

Process wastewater, washwater and other wastewater should be discharged to a city sewer system. This may be a major consideration when siting a new industry.

Application forms are available from the MPCA at the address and telephone number listed in the Resource Directory section of this Guide. Applications should be submitted 180 days ahead of the anticipated beginning of construction. SDS permits are issued for a period of up to five years. There is an $85 application fee and a $500 to $1,300 annual fee, depending on the size of the facility.

Permits for Categorical Industries

Certain types of industries are required to be regulated under the Clean Water Act even if they discharge their wastewater to a municipal sanitary system. Examples of these industries are: pulp and paper mills; most food processing plants; textile mills; chemical manufacturing plants; electroplating companies; plastics and other synthetics manufacturers; fertilizer plants; metal manufacturing plants; steam power plants; companies producing leather, glass, asbestos, rubber, and timber products.

Requirements for categorical industries are set by the U.S. Environmental Protection Agency. In most cases, a prospective permit holder cannot contest these requirements. Categorical industries are subject to U.S. EPA pretreatment regulations.

A number of large sanitary districts and cities have been delegated authority to issue categorical-industry permits. These include the Metropolitan Council, Environmental Services, the Western Lake Superior Sanitary District, Winona, Rochester, Albert Lea, Owatonna, St. Cloud and Mankato.

Categorical-industry permits are issued for other cities by the MPCA for a period of up to five years. Application forms may be obtained from the MPCA. There is an $85 application fee and a $1,230 annual fee for categorical industry permits. Permit applications should be submitted 180 days ahead of the commencement of the proposed activity. Questions about water quality permits should be directed to the MPCA. Addresses and telephone numbers are listed in the Resource Directory section of this Guide.

Underground Disposal Control

Disposal of industrial wastewater in underground sewage treatment systems is strictly regulated in Minnesota. The regulations and policies regarding underground disposal affect many businesses, such as vehicle-maintenance shops and car washes and large septic systems. The MPCA has free information and assistance for those interested in finding out more.

AIR POLLUTION CONTROL REQUIREMENTS

Minnesota businesses must comply with MPCA rules to protect air quality. Some rules apply even though the business will not have air emissions requiring permits.

Motor Vehicle Emission Controls

Owners of businesses that operate motor vehicle fleets should be aware that it is contrary to state rules and federal regulations to remove or disable the air pollution control equipment on motor vehicles, and it is illegal to operate motor vehicles unless the pollution control equipment is in place and is in operating condition.

Notification of Emergency Air Releases

The MPCA must be notified immediately of any releases to the air that might endanger human health, damage property or create a public nuisance. The business must take the steps necessary to prevent such releases.

Indirect Source Permits

Any facility that will attract a large volume of traffic that results in carbon-monoxide emissions, such as airports and highways; retail, commercial and industrial facilities; parking facilities; office and government buildings; apartment and condominium buildings; education facilities; and recreation, amusement sports and entertainment facilities may need an Indirect Source permit (ISP) before beginning construction. For indirect sources other than airports and highways, the need for an ISP is based on the number of parking spaces to be built. A new project needs an ISP if it will have 2,000 or more parking spaces. A permit is required if 1,000 parking spaces or more are added to an existing development, or if the additional number of parking spaces will increase the total number of spaces to 2,000 or more. Adding 500 spaces to an existing parking facility or developing 1,000 new spaces under certain conditions may require an ISP. Projects with less than 500 parking spaces are exempt.

Business owners or developers uncertain as to whether they need to apply for permits, and those that need permits for airport and highway projects, should call the MPCA. At least 180 days should be allowed for processing the permit, depending upon the size of the proposed project. Information about the ISP Program and the ISP Rule, can be found at www.pca.state.mn.us/air/isp/html.

Air Emissions Facility Permits

An air-emissions facility permit will be required if the business has the potential to emit more than the following airborne pollutants in a single year (in tons/year): lead 0.5; fine particulate matter < 10 microns, 25; single hazardous air pollutant 10; two or more hazardous air pollutants 25; sulfur dioxide 50; nitrous oxides, 100; carbon monoxide 100; volatile organic compounds 100. Under certain circumstances, local health and welfare problems have to be addressed through an air emission facility permit even though the business would otherwise be exempt under Minnesota rules. This may be because of toxic air emissions or dust from the proposed business.

Although not all will require air-emissions permits, business operators who should be aware of MPCA air quality rules are those whose businesses include the use of boilers, incinerators, electrical generators and solvent-borne coatings. Other businesses whose operations fall under air quality rules are those that create emissions such as dust, including grain elevators, concrete batch plants, sand and gravel operations and building demolition operations.

Permit applications should be submitted at least 180 days before construction is to begin. Applicants will need to know the characteristics of the exhaust gas stream before and after, any emission control equipment, type and design of emission control equipment, the relation of emission points to nearby structures and other information. The permitting process may be delayed if information is inadequate, if the facility is proposed in an area where the air quality is already below standards, or if public demands result in scheduling public hearings.

Business operators in doubt about the need for a permit should call the MPCA. Businesses that have less than 100 employees and are independently owned and operated may call the MPCA's Small Business Assistance Program at the telephone number listed in the Resource Directory section of this Guide.

Asbestos Removal

Prior to any renovation or demolition work in a commercial space, a survey for the presence of asbestos is required. This survey must be conducted by an inspector that is certified by the Minnesota Department of Health. An asbestos abatement contractor licensed by the Minnesota Department of Health may be required for removal depending on the type and quantity of asbestos affected by the project. Notifications must be submitted to the MPCA prior to all demolition and most asbestos abatement projects. Business owners should be aware that asbestos removal is also regulated by the Asbestos and Lead Compliance Unit of the Minnesota Department of Health and the Occupational Safety and Health Division of the Minnesota Department of Labor and Industry. The respective addresses and telephone numbers for information on these requirements is listed in the Resource Directory section of this Guide. For further information, contact the MPCA Asbestos Unit.

SOLID WASTE MANAGEMENT

County Waste-Management Plans

The Minnesota Legislature gave primary responsibility for solid-waste management to the state's 87 counties. Contact the county solid-waste officer for details about the county waste-management plan, which outlines waste disposal options for businesses and for information about relevant ordinances. This plan, developed by the county and approved by the state's Office of Environmental Assistance, may have specific business-related requirements. Cities may also have local solid-waste ordinances, and those plans should be reviewed as well.

The Legislature also gave direction to counties about the most preferred methods of waste management, a hierarchy from the most to the least environmentally beneficial. Since waste generation has increased one to two percent each year for more than 30 years, it pays for government and businesses to reduce wastes as much as possible, thereby reducing garbage bills, specific business solid-waste fees, and the percentage of taxes going toward waste-disposal costs.

The waste management hierarchy is:

- **Reduce and reuse** – the best waste is, of course, none at all, so it is prudent to reduce waste by wise purchasing, good inventory management, and reuse of waste products.
- **Recycling** – by separating out those wastes with intrinsic value, disposal costs will be reduced. Among wastes local governments may collect (or you may decide to collect and recycle yourself): glass, aluminum, tin, some plastics, white office paper, mixed paper, cardboard, paperboard, Tyvek envelopes, newsprint, printer cartridges, and more. Also, by establishing business policies that promote recycling, such as separating white office paper, and purchasing recycled paper and packing, markets are created for those materials that otherwise might be discarded.
- **Composting** – yard wastes and some food products can be composted into beneficial soil amendments.
- **Incineration** – a waste-to-energy incinerator consumes solid waste and produces energy, but has possible air-quality impacts, costs more than landfilling and produces its own waste – ash.
- **Landfilling** – shipping wastes to a permitted landfill safely isolates wastes, but does not normally produce any side benefit (except in rare cases where methane is recovered for energy use) or reduce solid-waste volume.

Counties' integrated waste-management systems use a combination of these waste-management techniques. By considering these various options along with the county's plan, a business can demonstrate concern for community needs and enhance its reputation as a business that cares about the environment.

Solid-Waste Fees for Business Wastes

Businesses pay different solid-waste fees than households in the same area. Recent changes in solid waste management taxes and fees have created a price-based tax: 9.75 percent on residential garbage service and 17 percent on commercial garbage service. Businesses that produce construction, demolition debris, medical waste, or nonhazardous industrial waste will also pay a tax on that of 60 cents per cubic yard of collection capacity. The Department of Revenue collects the taxes, which are used to support cleanup of old landfills and grants for waste-reduction and recycling programs.

Solid-Waste Permits and Enforcement

The Minnesota Pollution Control Agency permits and regulates solid-waste facilities, including landfills (mixed municipal solid waste, demolition debris, and industrial types), transfer stations, incinerators, composting facilities and more. In addition to state permits, local units of government (such as counties, cities or townships) may also have ordinances or licenses required for certain activities or facility types. These requirements attempt to assure that any solid wastes disposed of in Minnesota facilities will not become a source of liability later. If your wastes go to other states, it makes sense to find out whether you could be held liable for cleanup of those wastes later.

The MPCA has permit application processes to build or operate a solid-waste facility as part of a business, or to dispose of nonhazardous industrial wastes by land application (lime residues applied to agricultural land, for example). Concerns about illegal dumping of solid waste on a property can be directed to the county solid waste officer, the MPCA or the Minnesota Department of Natural Resources, all of which have certain authorities that may be of assistance.

Specific Materials Banned From the Waste Stream or Requiring Specific Disposal

Some wastes are banned or must be disposed of according to state laws or MPCA rules. Among those things that are banned from normal disposal are: waste tires; yard and tree waste; motor oil and filters, as well as other vehicle fluids; lead-acid batteries; nickel-cadmium batteries or other rechargeable or nonremovable battery packs; major appliances, including removal of items containing polychlorinated biphenyls (PCBs), such as old transformers; computer monitors; telephone books; all mercury including fluorescent and high-intensity discharge lamps and mercury switches (building, automotive); lead paint waste; chlorofluorocarbon (CFC) refrigerants; and petroleum-based sweeping compound. To find out more about disposal or recycling options for these materials, contact your solid-waste officer, call the MPCA or visit the MPCA web site at the address listed in the Resource Directory Section of this Guide, to look at a copy of the Minnesota solid waste rules.

Heavy Metals in Products

Minnesota law limits the use of heavy metals (lead, cadmium, mercury and hexavalent chromium) in all packaging and certain products. If the business produces a product or packaging using these metals, contact the MPCA to determine whether the business is in compliance with regulations. Certain legal products containing mercury, such as thermometers, thermostats, and automobile switches, are among the materials with restricted distribution or disposal. Contact the MPCA if you have questions about heavy metals in products or packaging.

Buying Recycled Products

Businesses that buy recycled products help to create better markets for recyclables. Through wise purchasing of recycled products or those using less toxic constituents or less packaging, a business makes a statement about its commitment to the environment, can reduce solid-waste fees and makes its collected recyclables increase in value.

Recycling Space Requirements for Building Owners

Minnesota state law requires buildings of 1,000 square feet or more to provide "suitable space" for the separation, collection, and temporary storage of recyclable materials (Minn.Stat. 16B.61). The law applies to new or significantly remodeled commercial structures.

In addition to the requirements of state law, specific numeric standards for recycling space have been adopted in the Minnesota Uniform Building Code (UBC). The UBC requires a certain percentage of space to be set aside for recycling, depending on how the space is used.

Labeling and Purchasing Recycled Products

The recycling logo is one way to signal that the business produces a product that contains recycled materials or is packaged in recycled materials to the consumer. While there are no specific regulations governing use of the recycling logo, the preferred practice is to use the logo, percent of recycled content, and percent of recycled content made up of postconsumer waste (i.e., materials recycled by consumers).

Food Wastes

The OEA, MPCA and several other organizations currently are forming a strategy for businesses seeking to reduce, recycle or compost food wastes. If the business produces food wastes, there are several cost-saving and environmentally sound methods of reuse or disposal. Contact OEA or MPCA for more information.

COMPLIANCE ASSISTANCE

MPCA Publications

The MPCA offers more than 800 free fact sheets to assist the regulated community with specific aspects of air quality issues and water quality issues and of solid/hazardous-waste management. For a list of available fact sheets, contact the MPCA or access it on the MPCA website at www.pca.state.mn.us under Publications within the program pages. In addition, in 1999 MPCA published "Environmental Guide for Small Business in Minnesota," created to give small manufacturers a user-friendly guide to Minnesota's environmental regulations. That publication addresses air quality, hazardous waste, water quality, emergency response, storage tanks, cleanup and remediation, pollution prevention, OSHA, and agriculture issues. Copies are available by contacting the MPCA's Small Business Assistance Program at the address and telephone number listed in the Resource Directory section of the Guide. Copies are also available on the internet at www.pca.state.mn/industry/sbeg.

Minnesota Technical Assistance Program (MnTAP)

This University of Minnesota business assistance program helps industrial-waste generators improve process efficiency while minimizing their impact on human health and the environment. MnTAP is a nonregulatory program that offers free, confidential assistance to help business comply with environmental regulations by evaluating pollution prevention strategies before offering other waste management suggestions. For more information, contact MnTAP at the telephone number listed in the State Government section of the Resource Directory section of this Guide.

Superfund and Voluntary Investigation and Cleanup (VIC)

The federal and state Superfund programs deal with old hazardous-waste sites where contamination threatens public health and the environment. The Minnesota Environmental Response and Liability Act (MERLA), Minnesota's Superfund law, gives the MPCA the authority to require those responsible for the contamination to undertake investigation and cleanup.

The Voluntary Investigation and Cleanup program provides guidance and technical assistance to parties who want to voluntarily clean up a property contaminated with hazardous substances. For more information about the state or federal Superfund programs or the VIC program, call the numbers listed in the Resource Directory under Minnesota Pollution Control Agency.

Small Business Assistance Program/Environmental Rules and Regulations

Small businesses with limited resources can get help understanding Minnesota's environmental rules and regulations through the Small Business Assistance Program at the MPCA. The purpose of this program is to help small businesses understand the environmental rules and regulations that may apply to their business; determine if they need an air emission permit; assist in completing permit applications; inform the business of their rights and responsibilities regarding environmental rules and regulations; and provide assistance so that the business may comply with environmental rules and regulations even when a permit is not required.

Businesses requesting this service should contact the MPCA's Small Business Assistance Program at the address and telephone number listed in the Resource Directory section of this Guide.

Small Business Ombudsman

The Small Business Ombudsman serves as a representative, or a liaison, for small businesses in their interactions with the MPCA. The Ombudsman offers the following services: confidential assistance to small businesses involving regulations and compliance; resolution of complaints or disputes involving regulations and small businesses; help in identifying funding sources; and coordination of small-business input during rule development. The Ombudsman also solicits feedback from small businesses and trade associations for the development of assistance activities tailored to small-business needs.

The ombudsman is located at the MPCA at the address and telephone number listed in the Resource Directory section of this Guide.

The Small Business Environmental Improvement Loan Program

The Small Business Environmental Improvement Loan Program offers low interest loans of up to $50,000 for financing environmental projects such as equipment or process upgrades and costs associated with the investigation and clean-up of hazardous materials. More information and an application are available by calling the Small Business Ombudsman at PCA at the address and telephone number listed in the Resource Directory section of this Guide.

Potential Environmental Problems with Property

Real-estate transactions have consequences for property buyers, sellers, developers, lenders, insurance companies, landlords and tenants. These parties have an interest in limiting the potential liability involved with the transfer of land that has been affected by hazardous substances, pollutants or contaminants. As a result, the MPCA receives requests from many businesses for assistance with evaluating and dealing with known or suspected land contamination.

The state has a range of services to assist those involved in land transfers in dealing with potential problems. In most cases, potential land buyers or developers will request or be willing to perform an environmental assessment of the property before sale. If contamination is discovered, then decisions need to be made about who will pay for further investigation or cleanup, how health or environmental risks will be minimized or eliminated, and what liability remains. The following programs can be helpful to those involved with land transactions, including environmental consulting firms hired to help businesses access or clean up property.

Properties Where Environmental Assessments Have Not Been Completed

Over the past few years, it has become standard practice for those involved in land transfers to perform an environmental assessment of the property before sale. Buying or developing land, particularly in former or current industrial-use areas, can pose problems if all parties involved do not know whether the property has been affected by its former use. Past disposal practices did not take into account what we now know are the problems posed by hazardous substances. It pays to follow the general rule "buyer beware."

The first step in performing an assessment is usually hiring an environmental consulting firm with the expertise to evaluate the property. While the MPCA does not recommend specific consulting firms, the agency does have lists of consultants who can be hired to assess property. The agency's Voluntary Investigation and Cleanup (VIC) Program also has a series of fact sheets which outline the features of a good environmental assessment. If, following the assessment, the business performing the assessment wants legal assurances that the property is clean or poses no or limited liability, the business can sign up for the VIC Program. The VIC staff will oversee the environmental investigation and cleanup, if needed, and work to provide the necessary assurances. Voluntary parties pay the cost of MPCA review, oversight and preparation of assurances of the assessment.

If petroleum chemicals are the contaminants most likely to be found on site, the MPCA Voluntary Petroleum Investigation and Cleanup (VPIC) Program can assist with review and oversight. If agricultural chemicals are involved, the Minnesota Department of Agriculture provides similar review and oversight services.

The assessment involves seeking existing information about the property, its past uses, and its enforcement or permitting history, if any. It also includes an inspection of the site, noting areas where further testing is needed. The MPCA Property Transfer File Evaluation Program provides a search of the agency's files and databases and provides a report of findings. This service can be very helpful to consultants performing phase I assessments.

The environmental investigation involves actual testing of soil, ground water, surface water, tank contents or other possible contamination areas. The results of the testing may indicate another round of testing or may be sufficient to make a determination about whether the site is contaminated and, if so, where and with what substances at what levels. If the assessment indicates site contamination above health limits, the business and/or consultant performing the assessment has the duty to notify the MPCA, no matter whether the land transfer takes place or not. The land owner also has the responsibility of filing an affidavit with the county where the property is located prior to a transfer of ownership. However, the business discovering environmental problems is not necessarily the party who is required to perform further work to clean up the site.

"Brownfields" Sites

"Brownfield" is a term for abandoned, urban industrial properties that are prime candidates for redevelopment but sit idle due to actual or suspected contamination. Cities, development agencies, counties and other groups have identified land that would be attractive to developers if information about environmental status of these sites were available. For sites where no voluntary party has come forward, the state and federal governments have developed several initiatives that will allow interested parties to obtain environmental information about sites. The Department of Trade and Economic Development (DTED), the U.S. Environmental Protection Agency, and the MPCA all are involved in various efforts (including grant and loan programs) to assess and, if needed, clean up brownfield sites. Contact the MPCA or DTED to find out more information about brownfields initiatives.

Voluntary Investigation and Cleanup

Many old industrial sites, located in strategic areas near available workforces, transportation and suppliers, have merits that make their development particularly attractive. A contamination problem doesn't change that. A limited or even major environmental problem can be dealt with effectively in many ways, but the state's preferred method is voluntary investigation and cleanup. A voluntary party often decides that investing in further site cleanup will pay off in the long run.

If the voluntary party decides to undertake further investigation, risk reduction or cleanup activities, the VIC or VPIC Programs will oversee those activities and provide liability assurances after work is completed. These assurances, which can be provided for all or part of a site, provide financial backers of development projects (such as bankers, insurers or others) with the necessary comfort that the site's liabilities will not pose problems later. More than 1,500 sites have been enrolled in the VIC Program since the passage of the Land Recycling Act of 1994, and substantial amounts of contaminated land have been "recycled" into productive use. Contact the MPCA to find out more about the VIC or VPIC Programs.

Even sites that have been listed on the state's Superfund list, the Permanent List of Priorities, can opt for a voluntary approach to investigation and cleanup. By working cooperatively with the MPCA, businesses can achieve results faster and with less legal involvement.

Superfund: Sites Posing Imminent Risks, Abandoned Sites, and Enforcement Approaches

There are certain sites that aren't good candidates for voluntary approaches, and the state and federal Superfund programs are designed to handle these problem sites. Among the types of sites most appropriate for Superfund:

- Sites that pose an imminent risk to public health or the environment, where the state must act quickly to assure that the public or environment is protected;
- Sites that pose risks, but are abandoned and have no responsible parties that can fund investigation and cleanup activities; and
- Sites where responsible parties are known, but are unable or unwilling to undertake necessary investigation and cleanup actions.

Under Superfund law, responsible parties are defined as site owners, facility operators who handled wastes on the site, transporters who brought wastes to the site, and generators whose wastes end up on the site. If an imminent risk requires fast action or no responsible parties have been identified, a site can be assessed by the MPCA and placed on the state Superfund list. Listed sites are eligible for use of the "funds" appropriated for site investigations and cleanups under the state Superfund law. The MPCA can also utilize these funds to perform removal work or emergency actions if an immenent risk to public health or the environment does exist.

If responsible parties are known but refuse to undertake cleanup, both state and federal laws can be used to enforce action. Usually, this non-cooperative approach is more expensive, time-consuming and difficult for both the regulatory agency and the responsible party. The MPCA can assess a site, add it to a national database of potentially contaminated sites, add it to the Superfund list, formally identify parties responsible for the contamination and request response actions.

Other Land Contamination Programs

The state has other special programs or laws dealing with contaminated land, a few of which are listed below:

- Contamination Tax: The Minnesota Legislature has established a contamination tax on properties affected by hazardous substances. This law is designed to discourage landowners with contaminated land from seeking property tax reductions based on claims that their land was worthless because of environmental contamination. Instead, the law provides a tax incentive to landowners who clean up contaminated property. Contact the Minnesota Department of Revenue for more information.
- Contamination Cleanup Grants: The Legislature provides money for Contamination Cleanup Grants for cities, housing and redevelopment authorities, economic development authorities and port authorities. To qualify for a grant, the applicant must provide the Commissioner of DTED with a site description, approved response action plan, detailed estimate of cleanup costs, appraisal of the market value of the property, description of planned land use, and explanation of how the applicant plans to pay for its share of the project. The applicant must be willing to pay at least 50 percent of the project cost. Contact DTED for more information.
- Drycleaner Legislation: A special fund has been established to deal with land contamination from former dry-cleaning operations. Funds for investigation and cleanup activities come from fees on drycleaning services. Contact the MPCA for more information.
- Orphan Share Initiatives: At some Superfund sites, many responsible parties have been bankrupt or have no funds to initiate investigation and cleanup. This leaves the other viable responsible parties to pay for the "orphan share," forcing them to carry the undue burden of another business's liability. The U.S. EPA and MPCA have developed approaches to dealing with orphan share situations. Contact the MPCA for more information.
- Guidance Documents and Technical Assistance: The MPCA provides guidance documents for investigation and cleanup of contaminated land, fact sheets on state and federal Superfund programs, site-specific fact sheets on some sites, and other brochures and newsletters on contaminated property issues. Contact the MPCA for more information.

Environmental Audit Program

Environmental auditing is a process of examining a facility to determine how well its operations are complying with local, state and federal environmental regulations. This four-year pilot program was begun at the MPCA in 1995, and made "permanent' by the legislature in 1999, encouraging businesses and other organizations to conduct their own environmental audits and correct any problems they may discover. The intent of the program is to focus on the goal of achieving greater environmental compliance, rather than fines or other penalties. In addition to involving more people in helping to protect the environment, the program also allows businesses to discover and correct minor problems before they become major liabilities, and, in most cases, to avoid enforcement penalties that might otherwise be assessed.

Any business or governmental unit that is regulated by an environmental law or rule in Minnesota can conduct an environmental audit, using either on-site personnel or an outside firm if desired. The MPCA provides free audit checklists to assist organizations in conducting their audits. After the audit, the organization must submit a report that includes a summary of the results, a schedule for any corrective actions that must be taken (subject to MPCA approval if greater than 90 days), and either a statement that pollution-prevention opportunities have been examined (for smaller facilities) or a certification that pollution-prevention requirements have been met (for larger facilities).

Generally, participants in the audit program are then given protection from enforcement fines or other penalties for any violations found, unless they are repeat violations or involve either criminal activities or activities that cause serious harm to the environment or public health. Audit forms need not be submitted to the MPCA (although they may be requested by the agency if there is probable cause to believe that a crime occurred), but participants should be aware that their summary reports are considered public documents and will be placed in the agency's files, subject to public review under Minnesota's Data Practices Act.

The Environmental Audit Program is designed to help both business and government work actively and cooperatively in protecting our environment. When a participant successfully meets the requirements of the program, that facility can display a "Minnesota Green Star" award for a period of two years after completing the audit and any required corrective or cleanup work. For more information and/or copies of fact sheets and checklists, call the MPCA or check the agency's website at www.pca.state.mn.us and look under Waste/Waste Prevention/ Environmental Auditing Project, or Programs/Environmental Audit Program.

ACCESS TO THE REGULATORY PROCESS

The Legislature delegates to state administrative agencies, commissions and boards, the authority to make rules to implement the laws administered and enforced by the agencies commissions and boards. (Note that the Governor has the power to veto all or part of a rule. To do so, the Governor must submit a notice of veto to the State Register within 14 days of receiving a copy of the final rule from the Secretary of State or Agency. The veto is effective when the notice is submitted to the State Register.) The process by which these rules are adopted is governed by the Minnesota Administrative Procedure Act (MnAPA). This process includes broad public access to information about proposed regulations and opportunities for public participation in the rulemaking process.

Before publication of a notice of intent to adopt a rule, or a notice of public hearing on a proposed rule, agencies are required to solicit comments from the public on the subject of the rule under consideration. That solicitation must be published in the weekly *State Register* and must include a description of the subject matter of the proposal, the types of groups and individuals to be affected, the procedures for comment, and how drafts of any proposal may be obtained.

By the time notice of a rulemaking hearing is published and mailed, the agency must prepare, review and make available for public review a statement of need and reasonableness (SONAR) regarding the rule under consideration. That SONAR must contain a description of the classes of persons likely to be affected; the probable costs to the agency of implementation and enforcement of the rule; a determination of whether there are less costly or intrusive means of accomplishing the purpose of the proposed rule; a description of any alternatives considered together with the reasons for their rejection; the probable costs of compliance; and an assessment of any differences between the proposed rule and existing federal regulations and a specific analysis of the need for and reasonableness of each difference.

The SONAR must describe how the agency considered and implemented the legislative policy supporting performance-based regulatory systems when developing rules. The policy requires agencies to develop rules and regulatory programs that emphasize superior achievement in meeting the agency's regulatory objectives and maximum flexibility for the regulated party and the agency in meeting those goals. In addition, the SONAR must describe the agency's efforts to notify persons or classes of persons who may be affected by the proposed rule or they must explain why these efforts were not made.

Over the course of the entire rulemaking process, agencies are required to maintain the official rulemaking record for every rule adopted under the MnAPA. This record constitutes the official and exclusive agency rulemaking record with respect to agency action on or judicial review of the rule. The official rulemaking record contains: copies of all publications in the *State Register* pertaining to the rule; all written petitions, requests, submissions, or comments received by the agency or the administrative law judge pertaining to the rule; the SONAR for the rule; the official transcript of the hearing if one was held; or the tape recording of the hearing if a transcript was not prepared; the report of the administrative law judge, if any; the rule as submitted to the administrative law judge; the administrative law judge's written statement of required modifications, if any; other documents required by applicable rules of the office of administrative hearings; the agency's order adopting the rule; the revisor's certificate approving the form of the rule; and a copy of the adopted rule as filed with the Secretary of State. The official rulemaking record is available for public review.

Agencies are also required to maintain a current, public rulemaking docket and have the docket available for the public. The public rulemaking docket must contain a listing of each rule currently under active consideration by the agency for proposal and include the following: the subject matter of the proposed rule; a citation to all published notices relating to the proceeding; where comments may be inspected; the time during which comments may be made; the names of persons requesting a hearing; where those requests may be inspected and the time and location of any hearing; the current status of the proposed rule; the timetable for agency decisions or other action; the date of the rule's adoption and the date of filing with the Secretary of State; and the date the rule will become effective.

Agencies may withdraw a portion of a rule before it takes effect.

During the 2001 Regular Session of the legislature, there were a number of changes to the administrative rulemaking process. Among the changes are the creation of a new process relating to variances from agency rules, authority for legislative committees to delay the effective date of proposed rules, establishment of a new process that agencies may use to repeal obsolete rules and creation of a new process for a person to challenge agency attempts to enforce policies without going through rulemaking. Chapter 106 contains minor changes, the more significant changes can be found in Chapter 179.

Any person may submit a written petition (contents are specified) to an agency for relief from a rule adopted by that agency. Such variances can be either discretionary or mandatory, and must be granted or denied in writing within sixty days of the receipt of the completed petition (unless the requestor grants a later date). Mandatory variances are granted if the agency finds that the application of the rule, as applied to the petitioner, would not serve any of the purposes of the rule. Discretionary variances are granted if the agency finds that: (1) application of the rule would result in hardship or injustice; (2) variance would be consistent with public interest; and (3) variance would not prejudice substantial legal of economic rights of any person. Failure of an agency to act within that sixty-day time (unless the requestor agreed to a later date) period results in automatic approval of that petition. Note also that these changes require that in addition to any notice required by other law, an agency is required to make "reasonable efforts to ensure that persons or entities who maybe affected by the variance have timely notice of the request for the variance. The agency may require the petitioner to serve notice to any other person or entity in the manner specified by the agency." Also, agencies are authorized to issue rules setting forth general standards under which an agency will grant mandatory or discretionary variances from its rules. These changes are effective July 1, 2002 (rules described in the previous sentence may be issued beginning May 26, 2001).

With respect to the opportunity to receive relief from what is referred to as an "unadopted rule," persons may petition the Office of Administrative Hearings for an order of an administrative law judge "determining that an agency is enforcing or attempting to enforce a policy, guideline, bulletin, criterion, manual standard or similar pronouncement as though it were a duly adopted rule." Note also that "an agency determination is not considered an unadopted rule when the agency enforces a law or rule by applying the law or rule to specific facts on a case-by-case basis." An agency has ten working days to respond to such a petition. In some circumstances the agency will be responsible for the costs of the Office of Administration Hearings associated with the petition. These changes are effective July 1, 2002.

PROTECTING INTELLECTUAL PROPERTY: PATENTS, TRADEMARKS, AND COPYRIGHTS [1]

OVERVIEW

Intellectual property law stimulates progress in the useful arts by providing a legal framework within which people who make their creative works available to the public may, for a limited time, prevent others from taking unfair commercial advantage of their creative efforts. Our government grants these exclusive rights only in exchange for information provided to the general public. In the case of patents, the inventor discloses the best way known for making and using the invention; in exchange, the patent owner receives exclusive rights for a limited period of time. Patents expire 20 years after the date the application is filed. Design patents expire 14 years after the date of issuance. In the case of trademarks, there is no limitation of time on trademark ownership-rights exist so long as the mark is used to identify the owner's goods or services. Copyright enables authors and artists to prevent others from reproducing their works without authorization, making derivative works based on the author's works, and selling or renting copies of the work, while allowing the free exchange of ideas. Copyright protection continues for a specific period ranging from 70 to more than 120 years, depending upon when the work was created and whether the author was a natural person or an organization.

PATENTS

The U.S. Constitution gives Congress the power "to promote science and the useful arts" and, as a result, Congress created our patent system. A patent is a grant by the government to an inventor. In return for this grant the inventor must provide a full description of how to make and use the invention so that anyone of ordinary skill in the field who wishes to make or use the patented invention may do so after the patent expires. The patent gives the patent owner the right to take legal action against any patent infringer. Whoever makes, uses, sells, offers, or imports the invention without the patent owner's consent during the time the patent is in force infringes the patent. In other words, a patent owner has the right to sue a patent infringer in U.S. district court. Patent rights may be sold or licensed to others.

[1] This material is reprinted with the permission of the Minnesota State Bar Association. This material is not intended as legal advice regarding an individual's conduct of intellectual property affairs. Patent, trademark and copyright laws change constantly. For advice on these subjects, for interpretation of the law and for guidance, a lawyer trained in these areas should be consulted. The publications, ***A Guide to Intellectual Property Protection*** **,** ***A Legal Guide for the Software Developer,*** **and** ***A Legal Guide to the Internet*** which deal with these subjects in greater detail, are available without charge from the Minnesota Small Business Assistance Office, 500 Metro Square, 121 7th Place East, St. Paul, MN 55101-2146, telephone (651) 296-3871 or 1-800-657-3858 (ask for Small Business Assistance or at www.dted.state.mn.us).

There are three kinds of patents in the United States. First are utility patents that cover mechanical, electrical, chemical, and business processes, machines, articles of manufacture, compositions of matter, and/or any new and useful improvements thereon. Second are design patents that cover only ornamental designs applied to useful articles. Third are plant patents that cover new plants that are sexually propagated. The term of both utility patents and plant patents expires at the end of 20 years from the date the application is filed. Patents granted from applications filed before June 8, 1995 are issued for a term of 17 years from the date the patent issues, or 20 years from filing, whichever is longer. The term of a design patent is 14 years from the date it issues. Patents cannot normally be renewed or extended without a special act of Congress. Exceptions to this general rule are sometimes available if interference or appeals procedures within the U.S. Patent and Trademark Office (P.T.O.) have delayed patent issuance and in cases where the FDA has delayed approving the sale of patented pharmaceutical products.

WHAT PROTECTION DOES A PATENT GIVE?

A patent gives the owner the right to exclude others from making, using, selling, importing, or offering to sell the claimed invention for the term of the patent. If necessary, a patent owner can enforce patent rights by bringing an action in federal district court. There is no "protection" given the inventor before a patent issues from the P.T.O., and the inventor cannot prevent manufacture, use or sale of the invention until the patent has issued. When a patent issues, the patented product or the packaging should be clearly labeled with the patent number. An acceptable form of notice is "U.S. Patent No. 1,234,567." If a product is not properly marked, there may be a reduction in the amount of damages recoverable by the patent owner in a patent infringement lawsuit.

The words "Patent Pending" or "Patent Applied For" have no legal effect in enabling the inventor to stop others from copying the invention. However, this form of notice can be valuable because it provides notice that the inventor claims rights in the invention, has applied for a patent on that invention, and has not abandoned the application. It is not lawful to use the notation "Patent Pending" or "Patent Applied For" unless a patent application has been filed and is pending in the P.T.O. Including notice that a patent is pending on a product or packaging may deter other suppliers from developing a comparable product.

HOW IS A PATENT OBTAINED?

In the U.S., patents are awarded to the first person to "invent" something. This is in contrast to many foreign countries where the patent protection is awarded to the first person to file a patent application. Therefore, the ability to prove your date of invention may be important if other inventors file patent applications before you do. If you can prove that you invented first, you will get the available patent rights in your invention.

An inventor applies for a patent by filing an application in the P.T.O. and paying the required fees. The application must be filed in the name of the true inventor or inventors. The application usually comprises four major parts: (1) an abstract, which is a brief summary of the application; (2) a specification which is a detailed description of the best mode of practicing the invention, concluding with one or more claims defining what the inventor considers to be the invention; (3) drawings of the invention; and (4) a signed oath or declaration in which the inventor states that she believes she is the first to invent the claimed invention. The application remains secret and can be withdrawn by the inventor at anytime. However, new legislation (effective November 29, 2000) causes applications to be published after eighteen months. Publication of a patent application provides advantages, such as the potential to recover damages from infringing activities that occurs during the pendency of the application. The inventor can request that an application not be published so long as the inventor is not going to apply for a patent in any foreign countries that require publication after eighteen months. This publication statute does not apply to provisional applications and design patents.

Patent attorneys usually recommend a preliminary search of the prior art (public domain materials, such as patents and other printed publications) to determine whether the same invention or an obvious variation of the invention has been patented or otherwise publicly disclosed by someone else in the U.S. The search may reveal unexpected obstacles or limits to the scope of protection available for the invention. Even when positive, the search results are only an indication of novelty, or newness, and should never be taken as a guarantee of patentability.

While an inventor may prepare and prosecute his or her own application, it is discouraged by the P.T.O. and it is exceedingly difficult for an inexperienced person to obtain claims that fully protect their invention. Patent law changes continually, not only with the enactment of new legislation, but also with announcement of new court decisions. Accordingly, considerable care and attention are necessary to design a patent application which provides thorough and comprehensive protection. This is particularly true in drafting the patent claims, which define the metes and bounds of all patent rights. Moreover, other parts of the patent application affect the viability and strength of the claims. In short, the best application reflects a high level of legal craftsmanship.

Dates are critically important in patent law, particularly application filing dates. Any public use, offer for sale, or sale of the invention in this country, or disclosure in a printed publication in this or a foreign country more than one year prior to filing a patent application, prohibits issuance of a valid U.S. patent. In other words, after the first public disclosure of or offer to sell an invention, the inventor has only one year to file a U.S. patent application for that invention. Unfortunately, most foreign countries prohibit filing a patent application after any public disclosure of the invention. Thus, to obtain international patent rights, the inventor must file a patent application before publicly disclosing the invention. Because of the criticality of these dates and the care and attention necessary to build an effective patent application, prudent inventors will act to protect their inventions as soon after conception of their inventions as they can.

In 1995, the U.S. created a provisional patent application which has a smaller government filing fee than regular, or non-provisional patent applications. A provisional application differs from a regular, or non-provisional patent application in at least two important ways. First, provisional applications are not subject to some of the formal requirements of regular applications. Most notably, the provisional application need not follow any particular format, nor include patent claims. This means that company documents sometimes can be filed "as is" or with some modifications as provisional applications. However, whatever is filed as a provisional application must meet the basic disclosure requirements of patent law: enablement and best mode. Second, provisional applications expire one year after filing and cannot mature into enforceable patent rights without later filing a full patent application. In fact, provisional applications are never even examined by the P.T.O. Provisional applications merely serve the purpose of establishing a filing date for the invention in the P.T.O. In essence, a provisional holds an inventor's place in line at the P.T.O., allowing the inventor to satisfy filing date requirements, that is, to avoid loss of rights because of untimely filing.

HOW CAN THE INVENTOR PROVE THE DATE OF INVENTION BEFORE A PATENT APPLICATION IS FILED?

An inventor should promptly make, or have made, a carefully written and dated description of the invention and what he or she thinks it will do. A dated drawing or even a rough sketch showing and describing the invention is usually necessary. The invention should also be explained to one or more trustworthy people who would be available to testify at a trial if the need arises. They should sign the written description and drawing with a statement that they understand the invention, and note on the description the date the invention was explained to them. A copy of this description and drawing may then be discussed with a patent attorney for advice as to any further course of action. If an inventor cannot prepare a suitable drawing or description, a patent attorney can help. After a record of the date of invention is made, the inventor should promptly complete the invention either by building and successfully operating a full-scale working model, or by filing a patent application covering the invention.

The P.T.O. has a Disclosure Document Program, which is preferable to the questionable and relatively ineffective practice engaged in by some inventors of sending disclosures to themselves by registered mail, to be opened for evidence when required. To be effective, a disclosure document should be prepared according to the recommendations of the P.T.O., and its value depends on the care taken to draft it. It should disclose everything that the inventor expects to include in any priority claim of inventorship. When the P.T.O. receives the disclosure document, it will be given a filing date and a serial number which may be noted in a patent application filed within two years of that date. The program is not a substitute for the conventional process of maintaining a written record of the invention which is reviewed, witnessed and signed. It is simply one more step the inventor can take to establish credible evidence for a date of invention.

While proof of date of invention can be helpful in gaining a patent, it is equally important that the inventor is diligent. Diligence is the process of continuously working on the invention, culminating with an application at the P.T.O. If an inventor chooses not to work on an invention and does not file a patent application he will "lose" his date of invention priority. A second inventor who is diligent and then files with the P.T.O. can get the patent.

DOES A PATENT GIVE THE RIGHT TO MARKET THE INVENTION?

No. A patent grants the patent owner exclusive rights, not permissive rights. Several situations can arise in which even the patent owner may not market the patented invention. Once a patent issues from the P.T.O., the inventor or other patent owner has the right to prevent anyone from making, using, selling, importing, or offering to sell the patented invention in the U.S. without permission. A patent owner may enforce those exclusive rights and halt infringing activities by bringing a lawsuit in United States District Court. However, "infringement" and "patentability" are two completely different issues. For example, an inventor may obtain a patent for an invention which is an improvement on something covered by a prior unexpired patent. If the newer patented improvement falls within the claims of the prior patent, the patented improvement infringes the prior patent. The owner of the later improvement patent cannot make or sell the patented improvement if it infringes the claims of the prior patent, and the owner of the prior patent cannot make the specific improvement covered by the claims of the later patent. If either wishes to make, use, sell, import, or offer the invention of the other, the two patent owners must mutually agree to do so.

On the other hand, the fact that the P.T.O. refuses to issue a patent does not necessarily indicate that an inventor would infringe the patent of someone else simply by making, using, or selling the invention. The refusal merely indicates that one patent examiner does not believe that the invention meets the standards for patentability established by law. For example, an inventor could be refused a U.S. patent if the invention had been described in a Ukrainian patent application that was published more than one year before the inventor applied for a U.S. patent. (Foreign patents cannot be enforced in the U.S. and U.S. patents cannot be enforced in foreign countries).

CAN THE EMPLOYED INVENTOR OBTAIN A PATENT OF HIS OR HER OWN?

A technical employee who is employed primarily to invent will typically have an obligation in an employment contract and invention assignment agreement to keep the employer fully apprised of inventions. The decision to file the patent application, however, rests with the employer, since the employer is the owner of the employee's inventions. If the employee is not employed to invent but uses company shop facilities and materials in making an invention, the employee may own the invention but the company may own "shop rights," which are rights to make, use and sell the invention without being required to pay royalties to the inventor. The employee who is not employed to invent and who does not use company time or facilities in making his or her inventions usually retains ownership and is entitled to seek his or her own patents, unless the contract of employment makes other provisions. In case of doubt, it is wise to review the employment contract with the guidance of independent legal counsel. In some cases in which the employer has rights to, but no interest in, the employee's invention, the employer may give a release so that the employee may seek his or her own patent.

Owners of small businesses should take steps to ensure the protection of valuable technical information, including inventions, developed by employees. Foremost among these steps is a written agreement with each employee, under which the employee agrees not to disclose or misuse information which the company considers confidential. The written agreement also should include the employee's commitment to promptly disclose inventions, and to cooperate with the company in the company's efforts to secure patent protection for such inventions. Minnesota law limits a company's rights in employee inventions; the limitations depend on factors such as whether the inventions are developed on the employee's own time, with his or own equipment, and whether the invention reasonably relates to the company's business. Minnesota law also limits the scope and duration of employee "non-compete" agreements. It may be helpful to consult an attorney before becoming a party to a non-compete agreement.

FOREIGN PATENT PROTECTION

U.S. inventors who want to obtain international patent protection may choose among several readily available methods for obtaining patent rights in foreign countries. First, a U.S. inventor may file applications in the desired countries, subject to certain restrictions on technology exports that may be contrary to the national interest. Second, a U.S. inventor may base an application for a patent in a foreign country on his or her U.S. application covering the same invention. Many foreign countries will grant an application (that is based on a U.S. patent application) an effective filing date that is the same as the U.S. filing date, so long as the foreign application is filed within one year of the U.S. application filing date.

An alternative to filing applications country by country is to file a single application for those countries belonging to a regional patent convention such as the European Patent Convention (E.P.C.). Most European countries belong to the E.P.C. Another alternative is to file an application under the Patent Cooperation Treaty (P.C.T.), naming the countries in which protection is desired. A P.C.T. application may be based on a pending U.S. application if it is filed within one year after the original U.S. application. Applications filed under the P.C.T. are subject to a deadline for filing national patent applications in each of the countries named in the P.C.T. application. These alternatives have different advantages and disadvantages, and a patent attorney should be consulted to determine an optimal approach for any particular situation. In contrast to the current U.S. practice which allows the inventor to apply for a patent up to one year after the invention is first used in public or offered for sale, many foreign countries require that a patent application covering the invention be filed prior to the public disclosure of the invention anywhere in the world. Therefore, to preserve an option to obtain international patent rights, one should generally file a U.S. provisional or non-provisional patent application.

TRADEMARKS

WHAT IS A TRADEMARK?

A trademark is the "brand name" by which we identify goods of a particular manufacturer. For example, "KODAK" identifies film made by a particular manufacturer. A trademark may take any form, such as: a word, words, an emblem, symbol, slogan or other device; as long as it serves to identify the goods of a particular source. The value of a trademark to its owner lies in the "goodwill" attached to it - customers ask for "KODAK" film or another product with the expectation of receiving the same quality of product which they formerly purchased under that name. The principles of trademark law apply also to service marks that are presented or displayed when services are purchased or delivered and used to identify the providers of those services. "Visa" and "MasterCard" are examples of service marks presented in connection with the provision of credit services.

A trademark should not describe the goods with which it is associated. For example, the mark "Leakproof Tires" is a poor choice of trademark for a line of tires which cannot leak because it merely describes the product: if one manufacturer of a product could prevent others from using the words that describe the products offered for sale, desirable competition would be unfairly eliminated. In this example, it would be possible to give the product a mark such as "Goodyear" brand leakproof tires. Any other fanciful, arbitrary or suggestive (of the type of product) marks could also be used. An example of a suggestive mark is "Fritos" brand corn chips. "Fritos" is a construction of the Spanish word for "fried" and therefore suggests that the contents of a package bearing such a mark might be fried.

The underlying goal of trademark law is to identify the source of goods or the provider of services in order to prevent customers and potential customers from being confused. Trademark law also protects the goodwill and reputation of the trademark owner. The owner of a trademark may bring a lawsuit to stop others from using a similar trademark on similar goods. In addition, the owner of a federally registered trademark may obtain the assistance of U.S. Customs inspectors to prevent misbranded or counterfeit goods from being imported into this country.

A variety of legal requirements must be met when choosing and protecting trademarks. Since the long-term investment in the development and protection of a trademark is likely to be quite high in any successful enterprise, it is normally desirable to consult an attorney experienced in the law of trademarks before adopting any mark.

HOW IS A TRADEMARK OBTAINED?

Trademark rights, in contrast to patent rights, are not granted by the United States government; trademark rights are created under common law by use of the mark in commerce. However, a person cannot acquire rights in a trademark through use if the trademark is confusingly similar or identical to a trademark already owned by another and used for similar goods. Federal registration strengthens the property rights established through use, gives national notice of the registrant's claim to those rights, and makes it easier to enforce the trademark owner's rights. To receive full benefit of the registration the owner should mark the goods "Trademark Registered, U.S. Patent and Trademark Office," or "Reg. U.S. Pat. and T.M. Office," or simply ®. The registration must be renewed at prescribed intervals and may continue so long as the mark is used and the renewals are properly made. The indicia of a trademark registration identified above may be used only if registration process has been completed. The owner of an unregistered mark can and should use the symbol "TM" or "SM" to identify the trademark or service mark. Some marks, by their very nature, are denied federal registration. For example, marks which are merely descriptive, deceptively misdescriptive, or immoral may not be granted federal registration. Applications for registration of a trademark in the P.T.O. may be filed after goods bearing the mark have been shipped or sold in interstate or international commerce. It is possible to file the application for registration before the mark has been used if the applicant has a *bona fide* intention to use the mark in interstate or international commerce. However, registration will not become final until the mark has actually been used in commerce of a type that Congress can regulate.

A trademark may lose its proprietary significance if its owner allows the mark to be used by the public as the common name for an article. Examples of lost trademarks include the words "aspirin," "cellophane," "milk of magnesia," and "escalator." In order to guard against loss of trademark rights, it is advisable to use the generic name of the product along with the trademark (e.g., "Scotch" brand adhesive tape). The trademark should always be used as an adjective and not as a noun or verb.

These comments regarding trademarks apply equally to marks used to designate the origin of services. These marks are generally known as "service marks." An example of a service mark is "MCI Communications."

TRADEMARK REGISTRATION

In addition to federal registration of marks discussed above, Minnesota and most other states provide for registration of trade and service marks used within a state. A trademark may be registered in some or all states and/or the P.T.O., depending on the geographic range in which the goods or services will be offered. The Minnesota and federal standards for registration of trademarks, service marks, and collective marks are quite similar and reasonably uniform rules for acceptance or rejection are applied. Generally speaking, a trademark or service mark will not be registered if:

- It is merely descriptive or misdescriptive of the product or service. A term such as Vacuum Cleaner would not be registrable as a trademark for an actual vacuum cleaner product; or

- It is a surname or geographic name, unless that name has become distinctive of the applicant's services or goods which can be shown, for example, by the use of the name for the five years preceding the application for the mark. A name such as "Dayton's" would be registrable under this exception while other names might not; or

- It is a generic name. Gasoline is a generic name, but "SuperAmerica", "Holiday", "Coke" and "Xerox" are not; or

- The same or a confusingly similar name is already being used as a corporate name, an assumed name, or as the mark of others for similar goods or services.

The same name, mark, or other word may be used by several different trademark owners without the multiple use being confusing to consumers - but only when the goods sharing the mark belong to different classifications. For example, there is little danger that consumers would be deceived by the use of the mark "Pioneer" for sale of seed corn by one manufacturer and also for sale of electronic audio-visual equipment by another manufacturer.

Once a trademark has become established, the owner generally has exclusive use of that mark for his or her trademark. There are over 40 different classifications of goods and services in which trademarks can be registered. A trademark may be established without registration using traditional common law methods (i.e., using the mark in commerce for a specified length of time, with that use beginning before others start to use the mark). Registration of the mark with the appropriate governmental body will usually confer greater rights on the owner of the mark than would be available without registration. Federal registration carries a presumption of trademark validity and registrant's ownership. Registration usually makes enforcement of trademark rights easier by simplifying proof of ownership of the mark and the exact mark in which rights are claimed. Registration of a trademark usually will prevent anyone else from forming a corporation with a name that is similar or identical. However, the registration of a corporation does not create any trademark rights in that name and does not grant the right to use a corporate name if it infringes someone else's trademark.

A Minnesota trademark registration is effective for ten years and may be renewed for successive ten year periods. The Minnesota Secretary of State currently charges a fee of $50 for trademark registration and $25 for trademark renewal. A Minnesota registration only gives the right to exclude others from using the trademark within the state.

A federal trademark registration is effective for ten years and may be renewed for successive ten year periods. The P.T.O. currently charges a fee of $325 for trademark registration and $400 for trademark renewal. A federal registration gives the right to exclude others from using the trademark in a way which may cause a likelihood of confusion anywhere in the country and acts as nationwide constructive notice of trademark ownership. A federal registration will also prevent anyone else from registering the same mark for the same type of good or service either federally or in state registrations.

COPYRIGHTS

WHAT IS A COPYRIGHT?

A copyright protects the expression of an idea. It does not extend protection to the idea itself. The United States Copyright Act of 1976 gives the copyright owner the exclusive right to prevent others from reproducing works of authorship for a limited period of time, usually the author's life plus 70 years. Copyright on "works for hire" made by employees lasts for 95 years from the date of publication or 120 years from the date of creation, whichever is less. Copyright protection exists in original works of authorship fixed in any tangible medium of expression. Copyrighted works include books (a term which includes leaflets and single sheets); periodicals and contributions to periodicals; lectures, sermons or addresses prepared for oral delivery; dramatic or dramatico-musical compositions; musical compositions; maps; works of art; models or designs for works of art; reproductions of works of art; drawings or plastic works of a scientific or technical character; photographs, prints or labels used for articles of merchandise; motion pictures; sound recordings; and computer programs. The owner of a copyrighted work has the exclusive right to: reproduce copies of the work, prepare derivative works, distribute copies of the work, perform the work publicly, and display the work publically.

HOW IS A COPYRIGHT OBTAINED?

An author automatically obtains a copyright at the instant the work is fixed (recorded) in some tangible form (manuscript, sound recording, etc.) which can be understood by humans with or without the aid of machines. Copyright protection exists regardless of whether the copyright is registered with the Copyright Office. However, registration is required for filing an infringement action. It is highly advisable, but not mandatory in the U.S., to use a proper copyright notice showing the year of publication and the name of the copyright owner on every copy of published work. Since the United States is a member of the Berne Convention, the General Agreement on Tariffs and Trade (GATT) Treaty and the Universal Copyright Convention, a U.S. citizen can, if certain rules are followed, obtain simultaneous copyright protection in well over 60 countries. The Universal Copyright Convention requires a copyright notice in the following form:

© 1995 Jane Doe

(Use the year in which the work was first published and the name of the author).

Although copyright registration is usually relatively inexpensive, it can provide several potentially valuable benefits. If an application to register a copyright is made within three months after the initial publication of a work, the copyright owner may recover from an infringer statutory damages (money) which are unavailable if registration is delayed until a later date. A suit to enforce copyrights can be brought against an infringer only after the copyrighted material is registered. Registration is made by an application addressed to the Register of Copyrights, Library of Congress, Washington, D.C. 20559. Copies of the work (usually two) together with a small fee (currently $30) must be submitted with the application.

TRADE SECRETS

Minnesota, Wisconsin, Iowa and thirty-five other states have adopted the Uniform Trade Secrets Act (UTSA). The protection of trade secrets is governed by state law, in contrast to copyrights and patents which are governed by federal law and trademarks which are governed by both state and federal law.

Trade secret law can provide protection for competitively significant information that does not meet the patenting requirements and/or cannot be copyrighted. Trade secret law can protect ideas, in contrast to copyright law which only protects the expression of an idea.

One may maintain a trade secret indefinitely, so long as one takes proper steps. Therefore, the holder of a properly maintained trade secret can enjoy a competitive advantage for longer than the 20 year term of a patent or the life plus 70 year term provided by copyright registration. Because trade secret law provides protection which can be broader and longer lasting than either patent or copyright law, trade secret protection can be the best choice, if not the only choice, for protecting certain types of information. However care must be taken because if the secrecy of a trade secret is not maintained, the trade secret is gone.

A trade secret is "information." Examples include: formulas (for chemicals, food, etc.); methods of doing business; customer lists; tables of data (e.g., special pricing or cost data); information on manufacturing techniques; marketing analyses and plans; and computer software. The information must be secret i.e., not generally known by others.

The information must not be readily ascertainable by proper means. Another person can acquire trade secret information through proper means without violating trade secret law. Proper means for obtaining a trade secret include: disclosure of the information in published literature; reverse engineering the information from a publicly available product; public use or display of a product in a manner that discloses the trade secret information; and the trade secret information may be independently invented. If the information is easy to obtain or figure out, then it cannot be effectively protected by trade secret.

The trade secret owner must make reasonable efforts to maintain the secrecy of the information. The proper maintenance of a trade secret must be tailored to the specific circumstances surrounding the secret. Examples of possible means of controlling trade secrets, often used in combination, include: educating employees and others about the sensitive nature of the information and the company's intent to keep it secret; nondisclosure or confidentiality agreements; physical security measures (e.g., locked or secured areas, separate secured storage of secret information, limited visitor access and physically covering ongoing work); document handling policies (e.g., shredding, copy machine control, and marking documents as "confidential"); nondisclosure agreements with outside consultants, vendors or subcontractors; and exit interviews upon employee termination.

The information must derive economic value from its secrecy. The secret information must provide its owner with some commercial advantage or economic value. For example, information has such value when, if kept secret, it would be useful to a competitor and require cost, time and effort to duplicate.

If someone misappropriates a trade secret by acquiring secret information through improper means, disclosing secret information that they have a duty to keep secret or using secret information without permission, the remedy is to sue them for damages and/or an injunction to prevent further disclosure.

DIFFERENCES AMONG PATENTS, TRADEMARKS, COPYRIGHTS AND TRADE SECRETS

Patent, trademark, and copyright laws differ fundamentally in what they protect, the duration of protection, the extent of their enforceable rights, the manner their rights are acquired, and the formalities of securing those rights. Patents prohibit anyone from making, using, selling, importing, or offering to sell the invention described in the patent claims without the patent owner's permission. A utility patent is granted by the federal government to an inventor of a new and useful machine, process, article of manufacture, or composition of matter. Utility and plant patents expire 20 years after the application filing date; design patents expire 14 years after the design patent issue date. In order to obtain a patent, the inventor must give a detailed explanation and necessary drawing to enable others skilled in the field of the invention to make and use the invention in the best way known to the inventor when the patent application was filed.

Patents are generally the most difficult and most expensive of intellectual property protections to acquire. Federal statutes (35 U.S.C.) create stringent requirements that must be met before a patent is issued. The process of acquiring a patent, called patent prosecution, often takes more than a year and is very difficult without the aid of a patent agent or patent attorney (who are specially certified to practice before the P.T.O.). The fees and other costs, such as prior art searches, are not insubstantial. However, in return the inventor gains a limited monopoly to prevent others from making, using or selling his or her invention for a number of years.

Patents have the power to protect "useful" inventions or ideas, which trademarks and copyrights cannot do. Patent protection also extends to equivalents of the invention. This prevents another from creating an invention that differs from the patented invention by only an inconsequential change.

A trademark, service mark, or collective mark is obtained by adoption and use; these marks are brand names which identify the goods or services or origin of the goods and services by manufacturer or distributor. It is important to realize that a trademark does not tell the customer who is the manufacturer of a product by name. The trademark identifies that all goods bearing that mark will have the same origin and same level of quality. For example, there are several different types of detergent with the trademark "Tide". The name does not convey the manufacturer's name, Proctor and Gamble, but consumers know that all detergents labeled "Tide" are made by the same manufacturer with the same quality level. Trademarks prevent purchasers of goods and services from being confused about the source of the goods or services.

A trademark cannot be "patented"or "copyrighted," and a trademark is not a "patented name" or "copyrighted name."

Copyright gives authors of original creative works of a literary or artistic nature the right to prevent others from making copies of their works. It is often stated that "copyright protects the expression, not the idea." It is obviously impossible for an author to prevent the ideas expressed in an original work from being incorporated into the minds of those who read or view or otherwise perceive the work.

In some instances, an article may be covered by three types of legal protection. For example, a loaf of bread may bear on its wrapper a trademark which indicates to the purchasing public a particular bakery. The wrapper might also bear a patent number, indicating that a patent has been granted on improvements in the wrapper or in the composition of the bread. The wrapper might also bear a copyright notice showing that the writings or artistic matter printed on the wrapper are protected by copyright.

In contrast to patents, trademarks and copyrights, trade secrets are unregisterable forms of intellectual property. A trade secret is maintained, as its name indicates, by keeping the information secret. Trade secret maintenance is clearly just not possible for many items. For example, publishing a book or having a trademark are incompatible with secrecy. But for some information, such as client profile information, trade secrecy is an effective method of protection. Trade secrets are protected and governed by your own actions to keep the information secret and the contractual relationships you have with the people with whom you share the secret.

FURTHER INFORMATION

For patent and trademark information, visit the P.T.O at www.uspto.gov. A sampling of information available includes: forms, fees, frequently asked questions, contact information and lists of patent and trademark attorneys.

The following publications may be obtained from the Superintendent of Documents, U.S. Government Printing Office, Washington, D.C. 20402: *Patents and Inventions, an Information Aid for Inventors, General Information Concerning Patents, Obtaining Information from Patents, Questions and Answers About Patents, Questions and Answers About Plant Patents, Disclosure Document Program, General Information About Trademarks, Questions and Answers About Trademarks.* These documents are also available from the P.T.O.

For information about copyrights, write to the Register of Copyrights, Copyright Office, Library of Congress, Washington, D.C. 20559 or write to the Consumer Information Center, Pueblo, Colorado 81009, and request: *New Copyright Registration Procedures.* Information is also available at http:// lcweb.loc.gov/copyright.

PATENT DEPOSITORY LIBRARY

The Minneapolis Public Library[1] has a complete file of U.S. patents from 1790 to the present; it is the only patent depository library in Minnesota. The collection was established in 1981 and is located in the Technology/Science/Government Documents Department of the library at the address and telephone number listed in the Resource Directory Section of the Guide under Government Document Depository Libraries and Inventors.

The collection contains:

- Utility Patents, 1790 - date. These are housed on cassette microfilm in order of issuance.

- Design Patents, 1842 - date. This is a complete file, also on cassette microfilm in order of issuance.

- Plant Patents, 1931 - date. This is a complete file in paper copy, many with color illustrations, filed in order of issuance.

- Reissue Patents, 1832 - 1972. These are republication of defective patents on microfilm.

- CDR file, 1973 - date. This contains corrections, disclosures and the continuation of the reissue file, on microfilm.

- Official Gazette, Vol. 1, 1872 - date. This is a weekly publication listing patents granted and official notices of the U.S. Patent and Trademark Office. The library has the paper volumes from the first to the most current volumes, and in microfilm from vol. 1 date and vol. 990 (1980) - date.

Patent Classification and Search Materials:

- **Index to the U.S. Patent Classification.** This is a one volume annual alphabetical index to patents that lists patent classes and subclasses.

- **Manual of Classifications.** A "family tree" of patent classifications, arranged by class and showing interrelationships between subclasses. Three volumes.

- **U.S. Patent Classification Definitions.** Expands on the Manual of Classification by defining both classes and subclasses for utility patents. Microfiche.

[1] Note: The Minneapolis Public Library plans to begin the demolition of its current building, and the construction of a new building on the same site, in 2002. At the time this Guide went to press, the Library was still studying possible sites for an interim library for use during that project.

- **CASSIS CD-Rom.** This regularly updated multi-disk set is useful for prelimininary prior art patent searching. Categories for searching include: inventors, assignees, class/subclasses of art, patent titles, and abstract summaries. Search results list patents by number. The full text of the patent is on microfiche.

- **Trademarks are also searchable on CASSIS.** Two bimonthly updated disks include registered and pending works.

- **Automated Patent System (APS).** A fee based online computer search system containing the full text, minus the drawings, of most U.S. Patents back to 1971.

The patent collection and accompanying resources are available for self-service use during regular library hours. Library staff will provide assistance in the use of the materials. An introductory lecture on how to do a preliminary patent search is offered on alternative Fridays. Contact the library for more information.

Note also that limited patent searching is available on the U.S. Patent and Trademark Office's website, at www.uspto.gov.

BUSINESS PLAN

One of the first steps in a new venture is the development of a business plan. The business plan describes the business: its product or service, market, people and financing needs. A well-prepared business plan serves several purposes:

- For the new business, it helps the owner determine the feasibility and desirability of pursuing the steps necessary to start a business.
- For the company seeking financing, it is an important sales tool for raising capital from outside investors.
- For an existing company, the business plan forms the basis of a more detailed operational plan and thus becomes an important management tool for monitoring the growth of the firm and charting future directions.

This outline represents a generalized approach. Business plans always should be tailored to the specific circumstances of the business and should emphasize the strengths of the proposed venture and address the potential problems and challenges to be faced. Although it is possible to prepare a business plan by merely "filling in the blanks" from a template (such as those available on the Internet), the likelihood of achieving desired results from doing so is small (i.e., how often do you respond to form letters?). Business plans prepared in connection with a loan application or for the purpose of obtaining venture capital financing will emphasize financial data and characteristics of the management team. The business plan should comply with the format requirements of the lender or venture capitalist.

Several organizations offer assistance in preparing business plans. These include Small Business Development Centers, SCORE organizations, Small Business Management programs and others described in the section of this Guide titled "Sources of Information and Assistance." Addresses and telephone numbers of these organizations are provided in the Resource Directory section of this Guide.

SAMPLE BUSINESS PLAN FORMAT

Summary

The summary should concisely describe the key elements of the business plan. For the firm seeking capital, the summary should convince the lender or venture capitalist that it is worthwhile to review the plan in detail. The summary should briefly cover at least the following items:

- Name of the business.
- Business location and plan description.

- Discussion of the product, market, and competition.
- Expertise of the management team.
- Summary of financial projections.
- Amount of financial assistance requested (if applicable).
- Form of and purpose for the financial assistance (if applicable).
- Purpose for undertaking the project (if financial assistance is sought).
- Business goals.

The Company

This section provides background information on the company. It commonly includes a general description of the business, including the product or service and may describe the historical development of the business, legal structure, significant changes in ownership, organizational structure, products or lines, acquisitions, subsidiaries and degree of ownership, and the principals and the roles they played in the formation of the company.

The Product or Service

This is a detailed description of product or service lines, including the relative importance of each product or service to the company. Include sales projections if possible. If available, include product evaluations, comparison to competitors' products or product lines, competitive advantages over other producers, and the elasticity or inelasticity of demand for this product (i.e., does demand respond to factors other than price?). Possible sources of information for this section include competitor's web sites, business directories and census data like that published in the *U.S. Industrial Outlook.*

The Project

If financing is sought for a specific project, describe the project, the purpose for which it is undertaken, its cost, and the amount, form and use of the financial assistance.

Management

Discuss the firm's management. Provide an organizational chart. Discuss key management and supervisory personnel having special value to the organization. Describe their responsibilities and provide resumes describing their skills and experience as they relate to activities of the business. State their present salaries, including other compensation such as stock options and bonuses. Discuss planned staff additions. Describe other employees, including the number of employees at year end, total payroll expenses for each of the previous five years (break down by wages, benefits, etc.), method of compensation, and the departmental or divisional breakdown of the work force.

Ownership

Provide names, addresses, and business affiliations of principal holders of the firm's common stock and other types of equity securities. Discuss the degree to which principal holders are involved in management. Describe principal non-management owners. Provide the names of the board of directors, areas of expertise, and the role of the board. Specify the amount of stock currently authorized and issued.

Marketing Strategy/Market Analysis

Describe the industry and the industry outlook. Identify the principal markets (commercial/industrial, consumer, government, international). Include industry size currently as well as its anticipated size in the next ten years. Explain the sources of your projections. Describe major characteristics of the industry and the effects of major social, economic, technological or regulatory trends on the industry.

Describe major customers, including names, locations, products or services sold to each, percentage of annual sales volume for each customer over previous five years, duration and condition of contracts in place.

Describe the market and its major segments. Describe principal market participants and their performance. Identify the firm's target market. For each customer, include the requirements of each and the current ways of filling these requirements. Also include information on the buying habits of the customers and the impact on the customer of using the product or service.

Describe the companies with which the business competes and how the business compares with these competitive companies. This is a more detailed narrative than that contained in the description of the product or service, above.

Describe prospective customers and their reaction to the firm and any of the firm's products or services they have seen or tested.

Describe the firm's marketing strategy, including overall strategy; pricing policy; method of selling, distributing and servicing the product; geographic penetration, field/product support, advertising, public relations and promotion; and priorities among these activities.

Describe how the firm will identify prospective customers and how and in what order the firm will contact the relevant decision-makers. Also, describe the sales effort the firm will have (e.g., sales channels and terms, number of salespersons, number of sales contacts, anticipated time, initial order size) and estimated sales and market share.

Sources of information include census data (on both industries and on consumer demographics), business directories, specific industry reports (either from government or private sources), and competitors' web sites.

Technology

Describe the technical status of your product (i.e., idea stage, development stage, prototype stage, etc.) and the relevant activities, milestones, and other steps necessary to bring the product into production. Discuss the firm's patent or copyright position. Include how much is patented and how much can be patented (i.e., how comprehensive and effective the patents or copyrights will be). Include a list of patents, copyrights, licenses or statements of proprietary interest in the product or product line.

Describe new technologies that may become practical in the next five years which may affect the product. Also describe new products the firm plans to develop to meet changing market needs. Describe regulatory or approval requirements and status, and discuss any other technical and legal considerations that may be relevant to the technological development of the product. Include a discussion of research and development efforts and future plans for research and development.

Production/Operating Plan

Explain how the firm will perform production or deliver its service. Describe capacity and status in terms of physical facilities: are they owned or leased; size and location; sales volume and unit capacity; expansion capabilities; capital equipment. Include a facilities plan and description of planned capital improvements and a timetable for those improvements.

Describe suppliers including name and location of principal suppliers; length of lead time required; usual terms of purchase; amounts, duration and conditions of contracts; and subcontractors. Also describe the current and planned labor supply, including number of employees; unionization; stability (seasonal or cyclical); and fringe benefits (insurance, profit sharing, pension, etc.).

Provide a profile of key patents and describe technologies and skills required to develop and manufacture the products. Provide a cost breakdown for material, labor, and manufacturing overhead for each product, plus cost vs. volume curves for each product. Provide block and workflow diagrams of the manufacturing process where appropriate, and provide a schedule of work for the next one to two years. Describe the production or operating advantages of the firm. Discuss whether they are expected to continue.

Financial/Administrative

Provide name and address of key advisors, including auditor, legal counsel, and banker.

Describe financial controls including the cost system and budgets used. Describe cash requirements, now and over the next five years, and how these funds will be used. Specify financial needs to be raised from debt and from equity. Discuss plans to "go public." Relate this to future value and liquidity of investments.

Provide financial statements and projections for next five years. These should include profit and loss or income statements by month at least until breakeven and then by quarter; balance sheets as of the end of each year; cash budgets and cash flow projections; capital budgets for equipment and other capital acquisitions; include key assumptions you have made in your *pro formas* and how these assumptions reflect industry performance.

If financing is sought, most lenders and venture capitalists will require a funding request indicating the desired financing, capitalization, use of funds, and future financing; a financial statement for the past three years; current financial statements; monthly cash flow financial projections including the proposed financing for two years, and projected balance sheets, income statement, and statement of changes in financial position for two years including the proposed financing.

ACCOUNTING FOR THE NEW BUSINESS

BASIC ACCOUNTING PRINCIPLES

Accounting is the process of collecting, organizing, maintaining, reporting and interpreting financial data about a business.

That financial information is useful both to the business owners and managers in operating a business in a profitable and efficient way, and to outsiders like investors or creditors who require a picture of the business' financial position and performance. In both cases the information is intended to make decision making easier: decisions inside the business about the use of resources and structuring transactions for the lowest tax liability, and decisions by outsiders about subjects like the granting or continuing of credit to the business.

The information collection, organization and maintenance parts of accounting are called bookkeeping. The reporting and interpreting parts are called statement preparation. The complexity and sophistication of bookkeeping and statement preparation depend on the size and nature of a business and the size and nature of its markets and are beyond the scope of this publication. It is valuable here, however, to understand the way in which any accounting system, small or large, handles financial information.

Accounting is the formal process performed according to a set of generally accepted accounting principles. In many cases the business can choose the principles to be used as long as they are consistently applied and any changes in the principles used are disclosed to users of the business' financial statements. Certain industries have specialized accounting principles specific to businesses in those industries.

Because both internal and external users will rely on accounting information, accounting systems contain definitional concepts and principles which both define and limit the nature and use of the information they contain.

The business entity concept provides that for accounting purposes every business is separate and distinct from both its owners and from other businesses. Defining the business entity that way prevents distortion of the financial position of the business which might occur if information on the business owners or other related businesses were included.

The going concern concept assumes that a business on which accounting information is being prepared will continue in existence and is not about to be liquidated. As a result the financial information provided offers only a snapshot of the business based on historical data and ongoing reporting rather than reflecting current market values.

The stable dollar concept requires reporting of accounting information in dollar units which remain stable in value with no adjustment for inflation or the purchasing power of money.

The accounting period concept requires that financial reports showing changes in financial position be produced at fixed annual reporting periods.

The cost principle requires that all costs be recorded at the actual acquisition cost regardless of what the asset acquired might be perceived as being "worth." The cost recorded is the actual exchange price.

The objectivity principle requires that costs be objectively established and verifiable: guesses or estimates are not acceptable.

The revenue recognition principle requires that revenue be entered in the accounting records only at the time it is earned and not before.

The matching principle requires that expenses be matched with the revenue they produced.

The full disclosure principle requires that no significant information be omitted or concealed and that statements be prepared in accordance with generally accepted accounting principles.

The materiality principle provides for an exception from full disclosure for transactions with insignificant economic effect.

The consistency principle requires that the same accounting principles be followed from period to period to allow for comparison of financial performance.

The conservative principle requires that in presenting financial information, accounting procedures should be used which present the least favorable view of the firm's owners' equity.

These concepts and principles taken together produce a periodic picture of the financial position of the business expressed in constant dollars. While all the information which goes into the system is "real," the accounting principles used can change the way transactions are structured and reported and the effects – like tax consequences – of the transaction.

In addition, an accounting system imposes a set of internal controls on the business to ensure appropriate and consistent control of financial operations.

As noted above, the substance of any accounting system will vary with the size, complexity and sophistication of the business. The choice of an accounting system, the use of bookkeeping services or broader accounting services, and the use of mechanical or computerized systems or recordkeeping aids are best discussed with an accounting professional.

INCOME FORECASTING TECHNIQUES

One of the most important steps in the construction of a written plan for your proposed business is the development of meaningful financial projections or *pro formas.* No business enterprise should be undertaken without a clear plan of profit potential and an understanding of the sales volume needed to achieve this profit. Experienced entrepreneurs recognize such projections as necessary for the success of any new business, and potential investment and lending sources will insist upon reviewing your financial projections before any serious discussion can take place. To be of maximum value in the planning process, your projections should accurately reflect the potential of your business and must not be influenced by wishful thinking.

Maintaining a high level of objectivity while researching the potential for a new business can be difficult. The difficulty results from the fact that many prospective business owners select the type of business to enter for a variety of quite personal reasons. They may choose a type of operation because the very nature of the work involved appeals to them. Others may work for someone else in a similar business and now would like to be their own boss. Some may have spent time acquiring the necessary technical skills or may have simply observed that a particular enterprise appears enjoyable or profitable. When combining any of these personal reasons for entering business with the complex task of analyzing the market, it is not uncommon for a prospective business owner to start up an operation with unrealistic expectations of the potential returns.

It is suggested that in your planning efforts you use the desired income approach to help determine the feasibility of your idea. This approach recognizes that, for the investment of time and effort and the assumption of risk, you are entitled to a fair monetary return. If this business were not started, your money could be invested to earn a return elsewhere and your time and effort could be devoted to working for someone else. The desired income approach allows you to select the minimum desired return and build on this to determine the level of sales required to achieve this return. If this sales level cannot be reasonably supported by market analysis, you would probably be better off working for someone else or investigating a different business opportunity.

To begin, you must first ascertain the minimum acceptable level of profit. To do this, it is necessary to explore the uses of profit. Profit can be used to support personal living needs, to pay back borrowed funds, or to reinvest in the company. Since we are attempting to determine the minimum level of profit, we will not be concerned with reinvestment which involves a use of profit over this minimum.

To determine personal living requirements, you must consider the minimum amount you will need to withdraw from the proposed business. If there is substantial personal income available from other sources, the amount required from the proposed business may be reduced. If there is no other source for personal income, then the proposed business should be recognized as the sole source for providing a living. Obviously, this desired draw will vary by individual needs and must be arrived at by thoughtful personal planning.

If it is necessary to borrow funds to begin the proposed enterprise, it must be realized that these borrowed dollars will have to be repaid from earnings of the business. This is of special importance to prospective lenders. It is the reason why a presentation of a projected income statement is required when seeking outside financing for a business. To determine the level of profit necessary to repay a loan, you need to determine the dollar amount to be borrowed, the term of the loan and the percentage of interest likely to be charged.

The loan amount usually is the total amount of money needed to begin the business less the amount supplied by you in the form of equity. The term of the loan is based on the use of the proceeds and the percent of interest reflects the general risk involved. It is advisable to speak with lenders and those offering business advice to help determine realistic terms and current interest rates for your situation.

For our example, we will use $30,000 as the amount of the loan requested and a term of five years at 15 percent annual interest rate.

The calculation of the annual payment is as follows:

$30,000 over five years at 15 percent
$30,000 / .023790* = $713.70/month
$713.70 x 12 months = $8,564.40/year

*(.023790 comes from loan amortization tables which are available at local book stores or in most finance textbooks.)

This $8,564.40 represents the total interest and principal repaid on the loan the first year of operation. If we round this figure to $8,600 and estimate personal living expenses to be withdrawn from this business at $15,000, we have a total of $23,600 which must be generated to sustain our personal needs and keep current with the lender.

The next step is to determine the level of sales necessary to earn the $23,600. From industry statistics, we can ascertain average performance data for various types of business operations. One of the most commonly used sources for this information is ***Annual Statement Studies***, published by Robert Morris Associates, Philadelphia National Bank Building, Philadelphia, PA 19107. Other sources can be found in the library and include Dun and Bradstreet, the Bank of America and local and national trade associations. Be sure to determine that the industry standard being applied includes the owner's draw as a part of profit. If it does not, this withdrawal amount will have been deducted as a salary expense in the operating statement and will have to be added to the stated profit to get an accurate indication of the total percent of sales available as profit to the business owner. For our example we will assume the industry sources show that, for the type of business under consideration, the average profit, including the owner's draw or salary, is 11 percent of sales.

To determine required annual sales volume:

$23,600 is 11 percent of X
X = minimum required annual sales
.11 X = $23,600
X = $214,500

We have now determined that, if our proposed business is assumed to be average, we will need to sell $214,500 of our products or services to cover expenses, keep our loan current through the first year and withdraw the desired $15,000. This in no way implies that we will sell $214,500, but this dollar amount serves as a goal that must be met. We now have available a minimum target sales figure to test and verify through the techniques of market analysis. For some, it will be readily apparent that the required sales target is not realistic. For others, careful market research will be necessary before any conclusion can be drawn.

The desired income approach of determining required sales can help us answer the question of whether we would start a particular business, begin the business as we have it conceptualized or whether the idea we have is likely not to grant the desired return. It gives a benchmark that must be met. It provides a realistic financial goal that must be achieved. If our research shows that this goal is attainable and that estimated sales are likely to meet or surpass this level, we can enter business with that much more confidence. If our market investigation does not thoroughly support the minimum required sales level, we can rethink our position. We can consider changes to our business plan which will make the concept more realistic or we can search for another, potentially more profitable business opportunity. The desired income approach allows us to start up a business operation with knowledge of what must be achieved and the level of return we can expect for our efforts.

To verify whether your target minimum sales are attainable, it is necessary to thoroughly investigate your potential market. Market research is an imprecise science, but basic research can be performed by most prospective entrepreneurs. Stated simply, market research is the orderly and objective gathering of facts about your market. It involves finding out how things are, not how you think they are or would like them to be. Much raw data already exists, but before this data will be of use to you, it is necessary to develop some basic definitions regarding your proposed business.

The first of these definitions involves describing in detail the business you wish to establish and the industry it will operate within. Concerns here relate to the image you wish to project and the products and services to be offered. Your business image is the single most important factor in achieving target sales. Be careful to design an image that addresses a perceived market need, and do not select an image that appeals solely to you. Industry influences are also important and involve an assessment of firms currently operating within your industry and major historical trends. In addition, you should examine and define significant outside influences on your business such as government regulation, energy concerns, inflation and other economic factors. Many of these forces will be beyond your control, but they must be recognized and planned for.

A full and complete analysis of your production capabilities should be developed. Your ability to satisfy market demand will be directly limited by your ability to produce, finance, sell and service. It is of little value to determine from the market that potential revenues can meet or exceed your target minimum sales volume if your production cannot match this needed output. Similarly, sales revenues are limited by the availability of working capital and by your ability to negotiate sufficient sales transactions. Indeed, you may determine that a substantial market potential exists, but you will need to consider the restricting impact of these internal factors.

Next, you will need to define the actual market segment you wish to enter. Attempt to describe in detail the target customer most likely to be interested in your product or service. There is a definable portion of the population to whom the output of your business will be of special interest. This is your target customer and the focus of your market analysis. Target customers can be defined in terms of some demographic descriptor. Examples could include income level, home ownership, sex, marital status, age, occupation, education or any of a host of market related characteristics. You will need to spend considerable time researching and defining a target customer profile, but this process is critical to further market analysis.

Once you have arrived at a definite category of customer, you can begin investigating where your potential customers are and in what numbers. Basic demographic data outlining population size, density, distribution and other vital statistics is readily available from a variety of sources. A list of such sources would include the following: U.S. Bureau of Census, Chambers of Commerce, colleges and universities, James J. Hill Reference Library (St. Paul, MN), and your local library, which contains sources for locating trade journals, directories and local and national trade associations. You will also need to develop a trade area based on geographic considerations. Defining your trade area involves making a determination of how far you can reasonably and profitably take your product or service out into the marketplace or how far you can expect to draw customers to your place of business. This trade area is related to the type of business you are investigating and can range from a segment of a community to international dimensions. Within this trade area you will need to examine the population data you have researched to determine how many target customers are available. Of course, not all these potential customers will do business with you. The market deals with people and their constantly changing likes and dislikes which are affected by hundreds of influences.

Competition within and adjacent to your trade area should be thoroughly examined. Attempt to describe who your competitors are and compare strengths and weaknesses with the business you want to operate. Become familiar with your competitors' pricing policies and overall method of operation. You will be competing head-on for the limited number of opportunities within your selected trade area and you must have as much knowledge of your competition as possible. Do not neglect to analyze future competition. Market dynamics are not static and freely allow others to enter your market and to change and improve on products or services you will be offering.

Keep in mind throughout all of your research efforts that verification of your target minimum sales is your goal. Ask basic questions about your business. How much does the average customer spend in a typical sales transaction? How many sales transactions are required to meet your target minimum sales? Does your knowledge of the market indicate that there is a sufficient customer base to generate the needed sales revenue? As mentioned previously, market research is an inexact process, but, with a desired income as your target and an orderly approach to gathering data, you can become aware of the magnitude of market opportunities. This knowledge will then assist you in making rational and intelligent decisions regarding your proposed business.

BUSINESS LOANS

Funding for a business usually comes in two forms: debt and equity. Debt is obtained from borrowing and must be repaid from cash flow. Equity is contributed by owners or investors (including venture capitalists and sale of stock) and is not repaid from operations. Equity investors receive a return from their investment in the form of dividends based on a percentage of their stock ownership.

Retail and service businesses are difficult to finance. Funding for these enterprises is usually used for working capital, inventory and fixtures. These forms of collateral in most instances do not meet the lender's resale recovery criteria. As such, retail and service operations are often 100 percent equity financed.

Historically, it is extremely difficult to start a business with 100 percent debt. Private lenders and government loan programs often require 20 to 50 percent equity participation by the owner. The exact percentage depends on the project, the financial resources of the owners, the type of industry, the use of funds, and the financial institution's general loan policy.

Most traditional lenders prefer manufacturing or industrial operations where funds will be used to purchase fixed assets, i.e., land, building, or production equipment. These items offer the type of collateral often required to secure the debt.

Possible sources of debt financing include banks, credit corporations, savings and loans, federal, state and local government loan programs, personal friends, credit cards, and venture capital companies.

Possible sources of equity include personal savings, private investors, venture capital firms, and sale of stock.

Private investors and venture capital companies can offer a broad range of opportunities for existing and new businesses. Unlike banks, private investors and venture capital operations can take an equity position in a company. And, depending on their percentage of ownership, they often participate in the selection of management and board of directors.

As the earlier section of this Guide on securities registration shows, the raising of equity capital through sale of stock is a complex and highly regulated matter requiring consultation with legal counsel. Raising debt capital and other sources of equity is less complicated. Private and government lenders require detailed information from the prospective borrower. A complete loan package should contain the following information:

- A summary of the business: describes the business, its financial history, key management, financial needs, uses and payback.
- Description of the company and the industry.

- Products (or services) and markets: a description of products, markets served, marketing strategy and plan, including competition, advertising media, current and future new product development.
- Production and manufacturing: raw materials categories and costs, suppliers, inventory, physical facilities, employees, utilities.
- Finance and accounting: audited statements for three, five or ten years, and latest unaudited statements, listing and status of receivables and payables.
- Management and ownership: organizational chart, resumes of key management, names/background of officers and directors, legal structure, stock information.
- Legal and administrative: articles of incorporation and by-laws, legal agreements/actions pending or contemplated, patents, trademarks, etc., insurance, stocks/shares, names of bankers, attorneys, consultants, etc.

Even in those cases where such comprehensive information may not be required, you generally will be expected to supply the following information to the banker or other source of financing you elect to approach:

- Current financial statement (both business and personal) listing all assets and liabilities.
- Profit and Loss Statement (earnings statement) for the last three years (on an existing business).
- List of collateral being offered as security with an estimate of the current market value of each item.
- Amount of loan being requested and exact purpose(s) for which proceeds are to be used.
- *Pro forma* (income and expense for the current operation).
- If this is a new business:
    - Description of the type of business, experience and management capabilities of the owners.
    - Estimate of the amount you (or others) will invest in the business.
    - Current financial statement (balance sheet) listing all personal assets and all liabilities.
    - Detailed projection of earnings for the first year of operation.

U.S. SMALL BUSINESS ADMINISTRATION (SBA)

Small Business Administration (SBA)
210-C Butler Square Building
100 North Sixth Street
Minneapolis, MN 55403
(612) 370-2324
www.sba.gov

The Small Business Administration (SBA) has financial assistance programs which provide access to debt and equity primarily from banks or other private sources. The various types of SBA financing programs are briefly explained below. The qualifications for these programs change from time to time, and it is recommended that you check with SBA for the most recent criteria.

SBA evaluates each loan application on two levels. The first is for eligibility which varies by industry and SBA program. The second evaluation is based on the credit merits of the application. Note that the SBA once used (before October 1, 2000) SIC Codes to determine if a particular business was eligible as a "small business", the definition of which varies, depending on industry and SBA program. The SBA now uses the North American Industry Classification System (NAICS) instead of SIC codes for this purpose. For information about the NAICS and tables converting SIC Codes to NAICS, see the SBA's website.

Eligibility

Eligible Applicants. Standards for eligibility are based on the average number of employees for the preceding twelve months or on sales volume averaged over a three year period. General ranges are presented below; there are some exceptions.

- Manufacturing – Number of employees may range up to 1,500.
- Wholesale – Number of employees may range up to 100.
- Service – Annual receipts not exceeding $5 million to $18.5 million.
- Retail – Annual sales or receipts not exceeding $5 million to $18.5 million.
- General construction – Annual sales or receipts not exceeding $9.5 million to $17 million.
- Special trade construction – Average annual receipts not exceeding $7 million for three most recently completed fiscal years.
- Agriculture – Annual receipts not exceeding $500,000 (with some exceptions).

Ineligible Applicants. Most small businesses in Minnesota are eligible for SBA financial assistance, provided they are independently owned and operated, are not dominant in their field (size), and can show that they are unable to obtain private financing on reasonable terms without SBA assistance. The Small Business Act, however, does exclude certain businesses, namely the following:

- Nonprofit enterprises, except for sheltered workshops.
- Floor planning.
- Gambling.
- Speculation in any kind of property, real or personal, tangible or intangible.
- Real property held primarily for sale or investment.
- Illegal activities.
- Applications may not be accepted from persons currently incarcerated, or on probation or parole.
- Persons who have caused a financial loss to the Federal government through its various loan programs.

Credit Merits

The SBA places its primary emphasis for loan consideration on the demonstrated ability of the business to repay all business-related debt, including the new loan obligation. Additionally, a reasonable "at stake" equity injection by the applicant is required. Each application is individually considered based on earnings potential, collateral, track record and/or projections, management, and the type of businesses in the same field. While SBA's standards are designed to be more relaxed than those of commercial lenders (banks), the SBA will not approve loans to businesses with unsatisfactory profit history, inadequate equity investment, or unsupported projections.

SBA Loan Programs

SBA's four basic loan programs are as follows:

- Guaranteed Loans
  - Regular Guaranteed Loans
    - International Trade
    - Low-Doc
  - Short Term Guaranteed Loans
    - Contract Loan Program
    - Seasonal Line of Credit
    - Export Working Capital Program
    - Asset Based
- Certified Development Company Loans or 504 Loan Program
- Small Business Investment Companies
- Micro Loans

Guaranteed Loans

Regular Guaranteed Loans

This is SBA's most frequently used loan program. A guaranteed loan is one made by a commercial lending institution (bank) to a small business customer. The SBA provides the bank with a guarantee that will pay the bank a portion of the unpaid balance on loans that are not paid in full by the customer. Every bank has its own internal credit standard and policy for approval of its loans. The SBA's guarantee permits a bank to broaden its own criteria to accommodate additional lending because of the federally-backed assurances. While the guaranty extends the range of credit available through commercial lenders, it will not cover unsubstantiated repayment, poor collateralization, or improperly documented requests. Therefore, it is incumbent on the applicant to find out if the request has a chance and then work with the bank to submit all required documentation first, so that the bank may evaluate the proposal and make its decision. Under this program, the bank analyzes the credit and makes one of three decisions: to approve it entirely by itself; to approve subject to an SBA guaranty; or to decline the loan. Should the second method be chosen, the bank will submit the application to SBA on behalf of both the borrower and itself. Keep in mind that the applicant is the bank's customer and the bank is SBA's customer.

General Information. Under the guaranty program, the lender provides all of the money. The SBA can guarantee loans up to $1,000,000; the guarantee is 75 percent of a loan over $150,000 and 80 percent of a loan up to $150,000. A small business may have more than one SBA loan, but the SBA's share cannot exceed $1,000,000. The SBA charges a two percent to 3.5 percent fee on the guaranteed portion of the loan based on the dollar amount borrowed.

Terms of Loan. The bank and its client (small business) negotiate the terms within the parameters described in the following paragraphs.

Interest Rate: There are two rate structures available on SBA guaranty loans: fixed and variable. Variable rate loans can be adjusted monthly, quarterly, semi-annually, annually, and float with the prime rate. Fixed rate loans do not change during the life of the loan. The maximum allowable rate for both types of loans is 2.75 percent over prime for loans of seven years and longer, and 2.25 percent over the prime rate for loans up to seven years. This prime rate is the minimum New York prime rate as published in *The Wall Street Journal.* Loans under $50,000 may have a higher rate.

Maturity: The length of a loan is determined by the use of the loan proceeds. Working capital loans are generally limited to seven years. Machinery and equipment loans are based on the life of the machinery and equipment, but not to exceed ten years. Real estate loans have maximum maturity of 25 years. These are the maximum terms. The bank may request shorter terms.

Use of Proceeds: A business may borrow for anything on the balance sheet such as inventory, receivables, land, buildings, machinery, equipment, furniture, fixtures, autos, trucks, accounts payable. Funds may be used to purchase a business. Generally funds may not be used to effect a change of ownership among family members. If part of the funds are to be used to pay debts owing to the participating bank, additional collateral may be required from the bank.

Collateral: Collateral are those assets which secure a loan in the event of a default. Collateral can consist of the following: land, buildings, machinery, equipment, furniture, fixtures, autos, trucks, inventory, accounts receivable, mortgages on fixed assets held personally, or an assignment of the interest in a contract for deed. SBA can take a second position, if necessary. The collateral offered should be reasonably adequate to secure the loan.

Equity: An applicant must have an adequate capital investment in its own business. Typically, a new applicant should inject 33 percent of the total funds needed to start a new business. For existing businesses, SBA uses the business ratios provided by Dun and Bradstreet and Robert Morris Associates. The SBA considers all credit factors before making a decision.

Repayment: SBA and the bank expect a loan to be paid out of the profits of the business. The bottom line of any credit decision is whether a business can repay the loan and other obligations from earnings. This is determined by analyzing all the facts presented in an application; primarily, management ability, equity invested, financial statements of owners, and detailed justification of projected earnings.

International Trade Loans. This program operates under the Guaranteed Loan Program and utilizes the same credit criteria and conditions. SBA may guarantee 85 percent to a maximum of $1 million for fixed asset acquisition and 85 percent to a maximum of $250,000 for working capital. No consolidation of existing debt or refinancing is allowed.

The applicant must establish that the loan proceeds significantly expand existing exports, develop new export markets or show substantial adverse impact by imports.

Low-Doc. Under this program, the SBA will guarantee up to 85 percent of a loan of $150,000 or less. The Low-Doc program focuses on the strength of the character and credit of the applicants. No pre-determined percentage of equity is required, and lack of adequate collateral is not by itself a determining factor.

In order to be eligible for the Low-Doc program, the borrower's average annual receipts may not exceed $5 million, and the borrower must not have more than 100 employees. Additionally, under the Low-Doc program the total outstanding balance of all SBA loans to the borrower must not exceed $150,000; all loans exceeding that limit are processed under the SBA's regular loan guaranty program.

For this program, the SBA uses the same interest rate structures as those under the SBA's regular guaranty program. Personal guarantees are required of each person who owns 20 percent or more of the business. Maximum loan maturities are 7 years for loans for working capital, 10 years for equipment and 25 years for loans used for real estate. If there is a default, the lender must liquidate the pledged assets before the SBA can pay on its guarantee of the loan, and only interest accruing 120 days or more after the date of default will be paid under the program.

Under this program, a modified application is completed, along with the lender's internal loan report (including cash flow analysis and *pro forma* balance sheet), income tax returns for the last three years (either Schedule C or the front page of the corporate tax return, whichever is applicable), and personal financial statements of all obligors and guarantors, if any.

In order for a lender to participate in the Low-Doc program, the lender and the SBA must have entered into a valid 750 agreement, and the lender must supply the SBA with a Low-Doc program lender's registration. Low-Doc applications are processed at SBA's Low-Doc Loan Processing Center, in Hazard, Kentucky.

Other General Information. The guaranteed portion of a loan may be sold on the secondary market and the bank will receive a fee for servicing the portion that was sold. The guaranteed portion does not count against the bank's risk to asset ratio or legal lending limit.

Short Term Guaranteed Loans

Contract Loan Program. The purpose of this program is to provide working capital needed to handle short term contracts. A business must have been in operation for 12 months preceding the date of application. Any small business which constructs, manufactures, or provides a service under an assignable contract is eligible. An application must be filed for each contract. More than one contract may be outstanding at any one time. All disbursements must be supported by invoices and/or time sheets. Maturity is generally not more than 12 months. Applicant's ability to cost the work, bid, and perform is a prime requisite. Cash flow projections are mandatory. SBA requires an acknowledged assignment of the contract proceeds as collateral, however, the lender is expected to take such additional collateral as prudent lending practices dictate. Proceeds or an agreed upon percentage must be applied to the loan balance. The percentage must be set forth in the loan authorization and note. If bonding is necessary and the surety requires an assignment of the contract SBA will consider only other collateral that is worthwhile. The guarantee fee is one quarter of 1 percent of the guaranteed portion of the loan.

Seasonal Line of Credit. The Seasonal Line of Credit program is used to finance working capital needs arising from the seasonal upswing of a business. Typical uses are to build up inventory and to pay for increased labor costs. Loans are repaid from the cash flow of the business. This program may have a limited revolving feature and is only available under the bank guarantee program. To be eligible, a small business must have been in operation for the previous twelve months and have a definite pattern of seasonal activity. Only one seasonal line of credit may be outstanding at one time and followed by an out of debt (SBA) period of at least 30 days. The applicant must be current on payroll taxes and have in operation a depository plan for payroll taxes. A cash flow projection showing the business' ability to provide for its needs is required. Maturity may not exceed twelve months. As a minimum, collateral will consist of inventory and accounts receivable. The guaranty fee is one quarter of one percent. These loans may not be sold on the secondary market.

Export Working Capital Program. Under this program, the SBA guarantees short-term working capital loans made by participating lenders to exporters. Proceeds of loans guaranteed under this program may not be used to purchase fixed assets, but can be used to finance the acquisition and production of goods and services being exported, or the accounts receivable of export sales.

Proceeds guaranteed under this program can be used for single or multiple export sales, and the underlying loan can be a revolving one. The maximum maturity is one year. Eligibility requirements with respect to the size of the borrower, the amount of the guarantee and the loan are the same as for the SBA's regular guaranty program. The borrower must have been in business for at least 12 continuous months before filing an application.

Asset Based. This program provides a guarantee of a short-term revolving line of credit, based upon the value of the borrower's accounts receivable and inventory.

The maximum term of an Asset Based loan is five years, and the balance of the line of credit can revolve, in that it can be drawn upon and repaid as the borrower's cash cycle dictates, so long as the outstanding balance does not exceed the approved amount of the Asset Based account. Under this program, the SBA can guarantee up to $1,000,000 of the line of credit, and the SBA's guarantee cannot exceed 75 percent of the total line of credit. Generally, any business eligible under the SBA's regular guaranty program will be eligible.

The SBA uses the same interest rate structures as under its regular guaranty program. Unlike the regular guaranty program, under the Asset Based program no lender's fee restrictions apply, although the lender must disclose all fees charged in connection with the loan through its final payout. Personal guarantees are required of each person who owns twenty percent or more of the borrowing business.

Participating lending banks must have reached a 750 agreement with the SBA and completed a lender's registration (different from the Low-Doc registration) with the SBA. The lender must conduct field examinations of borrowers, both initially and at least semi-annually during the term of the line of credit, including an analysis of accounts receivable, inventory, accounts payable, and financial statements and accounts. The lender, however, can hire a third party server.

In the event of default, the SBA will pay on the guaranty after the pledged assets have been liquidated, but the SBA will pay only the interest that has accrued more than 120 days after the date of default.

Certified Development Company Loans or 504 Loan Program

Offered through the Small Business Administration, the 504 loan program makes joint federal and private sector financing available to small businesses. The purpose of the program is to stimulate growth and expansion of small businesses within cities, regions and states having an SBA approved Certified Development Company, thereby creating more jobs, increasing the local tax base, and expanding business ownership opportunities.

This program provides long-term fixed asset financing for small businesses. This type of loan is made by a Certified Development Company (CDC) in conjunction with a second loan from a commercial lender (bank) in order to meet a majority of the total financing requirements of a specific project. An eligible project's purpose is to assist small businesses with financing plant acquisition, construction, conversion or expansion including acquisition of land, existing buildings and leasehold improvements for an identifiable small business, and machinery and equipment with a minimum ten year economic life. Loan proceeds cannot be used for working capital or debt repayment. Financing for the 504 program is provided jointly by the federal government and the private sector. The CDC loan amount will vary between 30 and 40 percent of the total project, not to exceed $1,300,000, with the balance coming from non-governmental sources. Usually, 50 percent is lent directly by a bank and 10 to 20 percent originates from the applicants themselves. The CDC obtains its funds from the sale of a debenture, which is fully guaranteed by the SBA, and then again lends these funds to the borrower. Maturities of debentures are for ten and twenty year periods. The useful life of the asset determines the term of the debenture. The interest rate is set at the time of the sale of the debenture. The benefits of this program are a favorable interest rate mix and a longer pay back period.

This program has certain unique requirements such as a measure of economic impact through the job generation potential of each project, so it is recommended that any interested party discuss the application directly with the 504 company serving its area.

A list of Certified Development Companies is available from the Minnesota Center for Community Economic Development or the Office of Marketing and Business Development of the Minnesota Department of Trade and Economic Development. Both addresses and telephone numbers can be found in the Resource Directory section of this Guide.

Small Business Investment Companies

The SBA licenses, regulates and provides financial assistance to privately owned and operated Small Business Investment Companies (SBICs) whose major function is to make venture investments by supplying equity capital and extending unsecured loans and loans not fully collateralized to small enterprises which meet their investment criteria. SBICs are privately capitalized and obtain financial leverage from the SBA. The administration of the SBIC program is handled by the SBA Central Office in Washington, D.C. A list of the Minnesota SBICs can be found in the Resource Directory section of this Guide.

Microloans

The purpose of the SBA's Microloan program is to assist women, low income individuals, minority entrepreneurs and business owners, and other individuals possessing the capability to operate successful business concerns and to assist small business concerns in those areas suffering from a lack of credit due to economic downturns.

The SBA is authorized under this program to make direct loans to eligible and qualified intermediary lenders who will use those loan proceeds to make short-term, fixed interest rate loans to start-up, newly established and growing small business concerns. The loans can range in amount from a few hundred dollars to as much as $35,000. Further, the SBA may make grants to the eligible and qualified intermediary lenders to be used to provide intensive marketing, management, and technical assistance to their borrowers.

In Minnesota, four intermediaries have been approved and can be contacted regarding the details of their respective programs. The name, address, telephone number, and service areas of each such intermediary is listed in the Resource Directory section of this Guide.

Program for Investment in Micro entrepreneurs (PRIME) Act

The Program for investment in Micro entrepreneurs Act (PRIME) created by Title VII of the Gramm-Leach Bliley Act authorizes the SBA to make grants to "qualified organizations" to fund training and technical assistance for disadvantaged Micro entrepreneurs. It also authorizes SBA to make grants to increase the training and technical assistance capacities of Micro enterprise Development Organizations (MDOs). Further, it authorizes funding for grants for research and development, and other undertakings consistent with the purpose of the Act. The PRIME program requires that grants made by the SBA be matched by grantees from non-Federal sources. Four categories of technical assistance grants are targeted to these purposes ("Capacity Building," "Discretionary," "Research and Development," and "Technical Assistance.")

Grants made either for the purpose of providing technical assistance to disadvantaged Micro entrepreneurs or for capacity building purposes initially will be awarded, on a competitive basis, in amounts not less than $50,000. These grants may be renewable, annually, for up to four additional years.

Grants for research and development will also be awarded on a competitive basis, though not subject to a minimum award. These grants may also be renewed.

Qualified organizations can apply for PRIME grant awards in response to Program Announcements issued by the SBA which specify the terms, conditions and evaluation criteria for each potential set of awards.

The final regulations issued by the SBA can be found in the May 29, 2001 edition of the *Federal Register.*

USDA RURAL DEVELOPMENT

Rural Business-Cooperative Service
410 Agri Bank Building
375 Jackson Street
St. Paul, Minnesota 55101-1853
(651) 602-7811

A list of USDA Rural Development Regional offices can be found in the Resource Directory section of this Guide.

Business and Industry Guaranteed Loans

Type of Assistance: These loan guarantees are for purchase and expansion of land, equipment, buildings, and working capital, aquaculture, commercial nurseries, tourist and recreation facilities, hotels, motels, community facility-type projects, housing development sites, apartment buildings and the purchase of stock in a start-up cooperative where commodities are being produced by the members for processing by the cooperative. Ineligible purposes include lines of credit, gambling, golf courses, or agricultural production over $1 million or more than 50% of a project and when not part of an integrated agriculture processing.

Program Description: These are loan guarantees only. The cost is a one-time, up-front fee of 2% of the amount guaranteed. A reduced fee may be obtained for a high impact business in a persistently poor community. Most traditional lenders are eligible. Non-traditional lenders may be considered for eligibility based upon experience and expertise. A Certified Lender Program is available for pre-approved eligible lenders to expedite the loan guarantee process.

Maximum Amounts: The maximum guarantee is generally 80% for loans up to $5 million, 70% for $5 million to $10 million, and 60% for $10 million to $25 million.

Eligibility Requirements: Loans are made to businesses which save or create jobs in rural areas (under 50,000 in population). Borrowers may be an individual, partnership, cooperative, for-profit or non-profit corporation, Indian tribe or public body. Refinance is eligible if necessary to improve cash flow, better rates and terms are offered by the lender and the refinance is less than 50% of the total loan. Annual financial statements prepared in accordance with Generally Accepted Accounting Principles (GAAP) are required. A minimum of 20% tangible balance sheet equity in accordance with GAAP is required for a new business, and 10% for an existing business. The guaranteed portion of the loan does not count against a financial institution's lending limit. All or part of the guaranteed portion may be sold on the secondary market.

Interest Rate: Interest rates are negotiated between the lender and business. They may be fixed or variable.

Terms: The term is typically 12-15 years for real estate, 7 years for machinery and equipment (depending on useful life), and 5-7 years for working capital.

Collateral: The lender will ensure collateral is sufficient. All collateral must secure the entire loan. Personal and corporate guarantees are required. Real property will be appraised in accordance with the Federal Institutions Reform, Recovery and Enforcement Act (FIRREA). Chattels will be evaluated in accordance with normal banking practices.

Contact: Applications are made by the lender and business at the Rural Development State Office.

Business and Industry Direct Loans

Type of Assistance: The purposes of this direct loan program include purchase and expansion of land, equipment, buildings, and working capital. Loans to public bodies can be used to finance community facilities and construct and equip industrial plants for lease to private businesses. Ineligible purposes include hotels, motels, tourist activities, convention centers, line of credit and agricultural production. Agricultural processing is eligible.

Program Description: The purpose of the Business and Industry Direct Loan Program is to improve, develop or finance business, industry and employment and improve the economic and environmental climate in rural communities.

Maximum Amounts: A borrower's total outstanding direct loan balance cannot exceed $10 million.

Eligibility Requirements: Loans are made to individuals, partnerships, for-profit and non-profit businesses, cooperatives, Indian tribes and public bodies who are unable to obtain conventional credit at reasonable rates and terms. Loan guarantees must be considered prior to a direct loan. Priorities are creating or saving jobs in rural areas (under 50,000 in population), assisting areas of high out-migration and Champion Communities and Empowerment Zones and Economic Community (EZ/EC) areas (targeted assistance areas). Annual audits are required for loans over $1 million. A minimum of 20% tangible equity is needed for a new business and 10% for an existing business.

Interest Rate: Interest rates are as prescribed by the Agency, but usually equal the prime rate. This rate is fixed at the time of loan approval or closing.

Terms: The term for real estate loans is limited to 30 years. Machinery and equipment loans are limited to the useful life of the collateral, not exceeding 15 years. Working capital loans are limited to 7 years. Loans for community facility purposes may have a term up to 40 years.

Collateral: Eighty percent of market value is allowed on real estate, 100% of appraised value on machinery and equipment, and 60% of book value on accounts receivable and inventory. Appraisals are required.

Contact: Applications are made at the Rural Development State Office.

Rural Economic Development Loans and Grants

Program Description: The purpose of this program is to develop projects that will result in a sustainable increase in economic productivity, job creation, and incomes in rural areas. Projects may include business start-ups and expansion, community development, incubator projects, medical and training projects, and feasibility studies. Ineligible purposes are those which directly benefit the borrower, conflicts of interest, and costs incurred prior to the application.

Eligibility Requirements: Applicants are current or pre-paid Rural Utility Service (RUS) electric and telephone borrowers. The project does not have to be within their service area. The majority of the beneficiaries must be in a rural area of under 2,500 in population.

Fund Availability and Maximum Amounts: Funding is either a zero-interest loan or a grant to the borrower, which in turn is re-lent as a zero-interest loan. The maximum amount available varies each year. In fiscal year 1998, the maximum was $750,000 for a loan and $330,000 for a grant. The minimum is $10,000. Loan money is appropriated by Congress. Grant money comes from Cushion-of-Credit accounts – (advance payments made by borrowers on their loans.)

Terms: For a zero-interest loan, the borrower will sign a promissory note with a term not to exceed 10 years. Principal may be deferred up to two years. All loans will be secured. The borrower must have a specific recipient at the time of application. All loans to this recipient will be at zero interest. Repayment by the recipient will ordinarily equal the term of the loan to the borrower.

Grant funds must be matched 20% up-front by the borrower. These accounts will be used as zero-interest (initially) revolving loans for: community development for public bodies and non-profits; business incubators owned by non-profits; or facilities and equipment for education, training, or medical care of rural residents. Funds from other sources must at least equal 20% of the loan or grant amount.

Contact: Applications are made at the Rural Development State Office. Funding selections are made in Washington, D.C.

Rural Business Enterprise Grants

Type of Assistance: There is no maximum dollar limit for any one project. Funds can be in the form of a grant (but not a pass-through grant) or for a revolving loan program.

Program Description: These are grants for financing and developing small and emerging private businesses with less than $1 million in revenues and which will have fewer than 50 new employees.

Eligibility Requirements: Applicants are public bodies, non-profit associations, and Indian tribes. Projects must be in areas of less than 50,000 in population, where the unemployment rate exceeds the State rate, which have a median household income less than the State's total median household income by the 1990 Census, where the applicant has substantial experience in administering such programs, and where a specific industry is committed to locate on the site.

Contact: Applications are made at these Rural Development Area Offices: Waite Park, Willmar and Alexandria.

Intermediary Relending Program

Type of Assistance: To finance business facilities and community development projects in rural areas, innovative projects, land, building construction or repair, equipment, working capital, interest, feasibility studies, and professional services.

Program Description: Intermediaries (or borrowers) are private non-profit corporations, any state or local government, an Indian tribe, or a cooperative. Intermediary Relending Program money is lent to the above, which in turn is re-lent by the intermediary to ultimate recipients. The ultimate recipient must be unable to obtain credit elsewhere at reasonable rates and terms.

Eligibility Requirements: Service area must be under 25,000 in population.

Maximum Amounts: Maximum Rural Development funding is $15 million per intermediary. Applicants should not exceed the amount expected to be re-lent in 12 months. Maximum loan to any ultimate recipient is $250,000.

Interest Rate: The interest rate to an intermediary is 1%. Rates to ultimate recipients will be negotiated, with lower rates encouraged.

Term: The maximum term is 30 years.

Collateral: Collateral can be real or personal property or pledged securities of intermediary or ultimate recipient.

Contact: Applications are made at the Rural Development State Office. Funding selections are made in Washington, DC.

PUBLIC SOURCES OF FINANCING – STATE PROGRAMS

Note: In 1999, the Minnesota legislature modified the Minnesota Statutes concerning the reporting of (and, in some cases, notice to the public of) business subsidies, a term broadly defined in the legislation making those modifications. Under that legislation (Chapter 243, Article 12, codified as Minn. Stat. sections 116J.993 to 116J.995), the term "business subsidies" includes many types of financial assistance provided to businesses by state or local governments, and by certain entities created or authorized by a local government. When this legislation applies, in many cases the business receiving a "business subsidy" will be required, among other things, to enter into a "business subsidy agreement" that will include goals for wages and jobs to be offered and paid by that business. If those goals are not met within a certain period of time, in almost all cases the business will be required to repay the amount of the subsidy, plus interest.

MINNESOTA DEPARTMENT OF TRADE AND ECONOMIC DEVELOPMENT

Minnesota Department of Trade
and Economic Development
500 Metro Square
121 7th Place East
St. Paul, MN 55101-2146

Minnesota Investment Fund (651) 297-1391

Contact: Office of Business Development and Finance, Business and Community Development Division, Minnesota Department of Trade and Economic Development.

The purpose of the Minnesota Investment Fund is to assist expanding businesses in creating and retaining high quality jobs, with an emphasis on manufacturing, technology and professional services employment. Through this program, administered by the Business and Community Development division of DTED, funds are awarded to local units of government to help them create quality employment opportunities and assist with business expansions. Businesses receiving assistance under this program are required to meet job creation and wage goals.

Funds for the Minnesota Investment Fund originate from two sources. The first source is a portion of the federally-funded Small Cities Development Program; the second source of funds is the state's Minnesota Investment Fund appropriation, authorized by the Minnesota legislature.

The purposes of the Minnesota Investment Fund are to create or retain jobs and to stimulate new private investment in order to expand, maintain, or start a business. This program is not intended to substitute for conventional business financing techniques, nor should it be used in place of programs, such as the Challenge Grant Program and the Small Business Administration programs described elsewhere in this Guide, which may be better suited to meet specific project needs. Instead, funds from this program are intended to be used in situations in which a funding gap exists and alternative sources of public and private financing are not adequate.

Grants are awarded to local governments which, in turn, make loans for specific business projects. Those loans may be used to finance building construction or renovation, property acquisition or equipment or infrastructure improvements necessary to support businesses located or intending to locate in Minnesota. A local unit of government may receive up to $500,000 in economic development grants per state fiscal year.

Application Process: The first step in accessing a Minnesota Investment Fund grant is for the local unit of government to submit a Business and Community Development application to DTED. Upon review, the applicant and the business will be invited to a meeting at DTED to further discuss the proposal. If the project meets the program criteria, a Part Two forms package is given to the local unit of government to complete. Some of the items that must be included in the final application are:

- A project description and cost breakdown along with a description of the use of funds and jobs to be created.
- For an existing firm, financial statements for the previous three years plus three years of financial projections.
- For a proposed business, three years of financial projections.
- Resumes and personal financial statements of all principals of the business.
- Marketing and management plan.
- Sources of equity and other private financing. (Generally there must be $3 or $4 of private financing for every $1 of state assistance requested.)
- Letters of commitment from all financial participants.
- Resolution of application from the local unit of government.
- Public hearing minutes.

Applications may be submitted anytime.

Loan Repayment: Loan repayment terms are negotiated between the applicant and the business and are approved by DTED. If state funds are used, the unit of government may keep the first $100,000 of principal repayment and all accrued interest to reuse on future economic development projects. Where federal money is the source of the grant, all repayment proceeds may be kept by the unit of government for use in future economic development activities.

Microenterprise Assistance Grants Program

Under this program, DTED reimburses nonprofit business development organizations for the qualified expenses incurred by those organizations while providing technical assistance and financial support to entrepreneurs starting a business, or to existing businesses looking to expand. For a business to qualify, it must be a "microenterprise," which is defined as a business that employs fewer than five people (in addition to the owner), and requires less than $35,000.

Small Business Development Loan Program

The Minnesota Agricultural and Economic Development Board (MAEBD) makes small business loans, the funds for which come from industrial development bonds issued by the Board. Eligible businesses are those manufacturing and industrial businesses located or intending to locate in Minnesota and which meet the small business size standards of the U.S. Small Business Administration; eligible purposes of loan proceeds include the acquisition of land, building, machinery or equipment; building construction or renovations. Loan proceeds may not be used to meet working capital or refinancing needs. Loans are made in amounts ranging from $500,000 to $6 million.

For information on either program, contact the Minnesota Department of Trade and Economic Development at (651) 297-1391.

WorkForce Development Division

This unit of the Department of Trade and Economic Development is charged with helping businesses by supporting a flexible, skilled workforce, and with helping individuals by assisting them find well-paying jobs with the potential for growth. This unit is comprised of two parts, the Dislocated Workers Program and the Minnesota Jobs Skills Partnership Board.

The Minnesota Job Skills Partnership Board administers a number of programs, described in the following paragraphs.

Minnesota Job Skills Partnership Program

The purpose of this program is to serve as a catalyst between business and education in developing cooperative training programs that provide training for new jobs, or to retrain existing employees. Under this program, grants are awarded to educational institutions to finance educational infrastructure improvements necessary to meet the training needs of a business located, or intending to locate, in Minnesota. An eligible project must involve at least one educational institution and one business, which must work together. The business must match program funds in cash, or in-kind, on at least a dollar-for-dollar basis. Other requirements must be met. For more information, contact the Minnesota Job Skills Partnership at (651) 296-0388.

Minnesota Pathways Program

This program is very similar to the Minnesota Job Skills Partnership Program in that funds are provided for educational infrastructure improvements to support business's training needs, and many of the requirements are the same. In addition, the projects qualifying for this program are ones that provide training, new jobs and career paths for individuals making the transition from public assistance to the work force. For more information, contact the Minnesota Job Skills Partnership at (651) 296-0388.

Health Care and Human Services Training Program

Grants are awarded under this program to consortiums of employers in the health and human services industries, WorkForce Centers, Minnesota counties, and higher education institutions so that such consortiums can provide training to alleviate worker shortages in the health care and human services industries, and to increase opportunities for advanced employment for employees in those industries. Other requirements apply. For more information, contact the Minnesota Job Skills Partnership at (651) 296-0388.

Distance-Work Grants

An educational institution in partnership with at least one business may apply for a grant under this program in order to promote distance-work training projects that involve implementing technology in rural areas, so that workers can tele-work from their homes or rural satellite offices. Other requirements apply. For more information, contact the Minnesota Job Skills Partnership at (651) 296-0388.

Hire Education Loan Program (HELP)

Loans are awarded to Minnesota businesses that contract with training institutions to train new or existing employees. The maximum amount of a loan under this program is $250,000; loans are interest-free and must be for a term of five years or less. Other requirements apply. For more information, contact the Minnesota Job Skills Partnership at (651) 296-0388.

Rural Initiatives

Regional Revolving Loan Program
(651) 297-1170

The Department of Trade & Economic Development has established partnerships with six regional rural Minnesota organizations. State appropriations (also known as "challenge grants") totaling $6 million are matched by each regional organization with private support.

Businesses seeking assistance in start-up or expansion may apply directly to the regional organizations in their region. Referrals to the regional organization may also be made through the Business and Community Development application process. Eligible business enterprises include technologically innovative industries, value-added manufacturing, agri-processing, information industries, agricultural marketing, and tourism.

The following criteria apply to loans made under the Challenge Grant Program:

- Loans must be made to businesses that are not likely to undertake a project for which loans are sought, without assistance from the program.
- A loan must be used for a project designed principally to benefit low-income persons through the creation of job opportunities for them.
- The minimum loan is $1,000 and the maximum is $200,000.
- All loans must be matched by at least an equal amount of new private investment.
- A loan may be used for microenterprises, including retail businesses, but state participation is limited to $10,000. Businesses that are directly competitive with other enterprises in an area are generally not eligible.
- A business applying for a loan must obtain a sponsorship resolution from the governing body of the local government in whose jurisdiction the project is located.

Each regional organization can provide detailed information on eligibility requirements. To learn which regional organization serves a particular part of the state, see the listing of Rural Initiative regional organizations in the Resource Directory section of this Guide.

Urban Initiative Program

(651) 297-1170

The Urban Initiative Board has established partnerships with local and neighborhood organizations in the Twin Cities to provide loans to new and expanding businesses in St. Paul, Minneapolis, and eight suburbs (South St. Paul, West St. Paul, Hopkins, Columbia Heights, Hilltop, Lauderdale, Mendota, St. Anthony). State funds ("challenge grants") will be matched by non-state funds, making a total of $12 million available.

Loans are in the range of $1000 to $150,000. The program will focus on minority business enterprises, defined by statute to include minority and women owned and operated enterprises and other businesses creating jobs for minority and other persons in low income areas.

Eligible enterprises include start up and expanding businesses, particularly manufacturing enterprises and others which create quality wages for their employees. Loan funds may be used for normal business expenses such as machinery and equipment, inventory and receivables, new construction, working capital, renovation and site acquisition. Funds cannot be used to refinance existing debt.

Community partners of the Urban Initiative Program are also connected to management training and other sources of assistance available to businesses. Contact the Urban Initiative Program at the number above to identify the group or groups which might best suit your needs.

Tourism Loan Program
(651) 296-6858

The tourism loan program accesses a low interest revolving loan fund which provides loans or loan participations to resorts, campgrounds and other tourism related businesses that provide overnight accommodations.

To receive a loan under this program, the borrower must be an existing business entity engaged in a tourism-related business defined by the standard industrial classification codes 7011 or 7033. Loans cannot be used for refinancing, working capital, purchase of an existing business, or for new business start-ups. An eligible borrower must remain as a tourism-related business during the term of the loan. A borrower may only receive a loan under this program once every three years. Funds may be used for either tourism construction and renovation purposes, or to finance septic system replacement or upgrade.

Capital Access Program
(651) 296-6858

The Capital Access Program is designed to provide credit enhancement to encourage financial institutions to make loans which may be more risky than traditional bank loans to small and medium sized businesses. The program works by setting up a "reserve fund" which is an administrative account maintained by the Commissioner of Trade and Economic Development to cover losses sustained by a lender on enrolled loans. The reserve fund is funded by premium charges determined by the lender and matched by the state. The premium paid by the borrower will be between one and one-half percent and three and one-half percent of the amount of the loan. The premium paid by the lender is equal to the amount paid by the borrower and may be recovered from the borrower in any manner in which the lender and borrower agree.

Eligible loans. Eligible loans may include loans made for industrial, commercial, or agricultural purposes; refinancing of loans made for these purposes; or lines of credit agreements established between the lender and borrower which are used for these purposes. Loans that are used for housing or to refinance passive real estate ownership are not eligible. The borrower may be a corporation, partnership, joint venture, sole proprietorship, cooperative, or other entity, whether profit or nonprofit, which is authorized to conduct business in the state.

Loan applications. Loan applications are made directly to the financial institution. The interest rate and loan terms are negotiated between the lender and the borrower. The financial institution enrolls all or part of the loan in the Capital Access Program by filing a completed loan enrollment form with the Commissioner within ten business days after the lender makes the loan.

Community Development Venture Capital Fund. Chapter 153, effective May 22, 2001 permits the Department of Trade and Economic Development to invest funds from the Capital Access Fund "to make equity investments in community development venture capital funds for the purpose of providing capital for small and emerging businesses. The community development venture capital fund must have experience in equity investments in small businesses and the ability to raise private capital." For these purposes, a "community development capital fund" is defined as "a regional or local venture capital fund that makes equity investments in small or emerging companies and has a financial as well as a social mission."

ENVIRONMENTAL FINANCIAL ASSISTANCE PROGRAMS

Office of Environmental Assistance
520 Lafayette Road, 2nd Floor
St. Paul, MN 55155-4100
(651) 296-3417 or (800) 657-3843

The Office of Environmental Assistance (OEA) offers environmental assistance grants and loans to help organizations move toward environmentally sustainable projects. Projects must focus on pollution and waste prevention, recycling market development, environmental education, sustainable community development and/or resource recovery.

Eligible Projects and Costs. Projects that lead to source reduction, reuse or recycling of waste materials, develop markets for recyclables or compost, or result in better processing of waste materials are eligible for environmental assistance loans and grants. Also eligible are projects or practices that prevent or reduce toxic pollutants or hazardous substances, or that implement resource conservation or environmental education. In addition, projects that leverage grant funds to obtain loans, or to reduce interest payments on loans from financial institutions for environmental assistance projects or practices are eligible for grants.

Grant funds are available for the development and/or implementation of specific project activities not already underway within organizations. In general, the costs of researching, developing, or implementing eligible projects qualify for environmental assistance grants. State agencies are not eligible to apply for OEA grants. Costs incurred before the execution of a grant agreement and the costs of purchasing real property are not eligible for funding.

Priority projects or targets for funding may be accentuated in individual funding "rounds." Priority projects will be identified in a Request for Proposals (RFP) issued at the onset of each competitive funding cycle and published in the *State Register.* The RFP may also identify additional restrictions on eligible costs or applicants that relate to specific funding priorities. Please contact the OEA for additional information at the address and telepone number listed in the Resource Directory section of this Guide.

SMALL BUSINESS ENVIRONMENTAL IMPROVEMENT LOAN PROGRAM

Minnesota Pollution Control Agency
Small Business Ombudsman
520 Lafayette Road
St. Paul, MN 55155-4100
(651) 297-8615
(800) 985-4247

This program provides assistance to help small businesses conduct environmental projects such as equipment or process upgrades and costs associated with the investigation and clean-up of hazardous materials. Special businesses may be considered special targets by the MPCA, including: sources subject to Clean Air Act Standards; businesses undergoing site investigation and cleanup; businesses doing a facility-wide environmental compliance and pollution-prevention project; or industry sectors that are MPCA outreach priorities.

Eligibility: To be eligible for the program, a borrower must be making an equipment purchase or process upgrade that meets or exceeds environmental standards, or doing a site investigation and cleanup; be a small business corporation, sole proprietorship, partnership or association; have less than 50 full-time employees; have an after-tax profit of less than $500,000; and have a net worth of less than $1,000,000.

Terms: The conditions of the loans available through the program are: loan amounts of not less than $1,000 and not more than $50,000; an interest rate of four percent or one-half the prime rate, whichever is greater; and a repayment term of not more than seven years.

This program is funded through a revolving account with loan applications reviewed on a quarterly cycle. The number of loans awarded during an individual cycle is based on the amount of funds in the account.

PUBLIC SOURCES OF FINANCING – LOCAL PROGRAMS

Various governmental units at different levels are currently providing some form of assistance to entrepreneurs. This assistance may be in the form of financial services and loan packaging or technical assistance, tax credits, and the like. To learn more about the variety of programs, contact the planning or business services unit of the county, municipality or township where the proposed business will be located.

In Duluth, contact TEAM Duluth, 118 East Superior Street, Duluth, MN 55802, telephone (218) 722-5501 for assistance with project packaging, site location and workforce assistance. Additionally, in Duluth (Northeast Minnesota), contact the University of Minnesota Duluth, Center for Economic Development, 11 E. Superior Street, Suite 210, Duluth, MN 55802, or on the web site address listed in the Resource Directory section of this Guide. Request: *Northeast Minnesota Small Business Resources Directory 1995.* (Note that as of the time this Guide went to press, the 1995 edition was the most current.)

In Minneapolis, contact the Minneapolis Community Development Agency, Business Finance Unit, Crown Roller Mill, Suite 200, 105 Fifth Ave. S., Minneapolis, MN 55401, telephone (612) 673-5095. Request: *Helping Small Business Grow.*

In St. Paul, contact the Business Resource Center, 25 West Fourth Street, St. Paul, MN 55102, telephone (651) 266-6600. The Business Resource Center is the city of St. Paul's single point of contact for business information and resources, including financial, management and technical assistance.

Note that the Resource Directory section of this Guide contains information on other sources of local, public financing.

PRIVATE SOURCES OF FUNDS

VENTURE CAPITAL FIRMS

Venture capital firms provide equity capital to emerging and growth oriented businesses that have high market potential. Their major function is to assess management ability, determine market potential and fund the capital needs for businesses that might not be able to obtain funding from other sources. The major venture capital firms in Minnesota are listed in the Resource Directory section of this Guide.

MINNESOTA INITIATIVE FUNDS

Minnesota initiative funds are charitable, private non-profit organizations funded with a McKnight Foundation allocation supplemented with funds from various public and private sources. Funds are distributed in grants and loans for human services, economic and business development, education, leadership development, health, community services and administration. The six initiative funds are separate entities and each has its own programs, funding levels and guidelines. Three of the six initiative funds (Northwest, Northeast, and Southwest) now refer to themselves as Foundations, which they feel more accurately describe their functions. Initiative funds, the counties they serve, and the office addresses are provided in the Resource Directory section of this Guide.

COMMUNITY/ECONOMIC DEVELOPMENT CORPORATIONS

Community Development Corporations (CDCs) are privately owned community development agencies serving a predefined geographic area. CDCs are usually organized as non-profit corporations in order to obtain funds from sources interested in economic development such as federal or state governments. CDCs address the development needs of a geographically defined area and investment emphasis will vary by locality. The one requirement for a CDC investment is that the venture be located in the community being served. Examples of programs operated by CDCs include economic and business development programs, including programs that provide financial and other assistance to start, expand, or locate businesses in or near the areas served so as to provide employment and ownership opportunities for residents of such areas; community development and housing activities that create new training, employment and ownership opportunities and which contribute to improved living conditions; and manpower training programs. Most CDCs can assist new or expanding businesses in developing a business plan, management or financial plans including assistance in qualifying for a loan, putting the paperwork together and presenting a proposal to a financial institution.

Information on Community Development Corporations can be obtained from the Office of Rural Initiatives, Minnesota Department of Trade and Economic Development. Addresses and telephone numbers for both are listed in the Resource Directory section of this Guide.

WILLIAM C. NORRIS INSTITUTE

A unit of the University of St. Thomas Graduate School of Business, the Institute provides seed capital investments and assistance to stimulate the startup of industrial and technology-based companies in Minnesota. Preference is given to entrepreneurs with links to the University of St. Thomas and to those who locate their companies in economically depressed areas of Minnesota. Contact the program director at the address and telephone number listed in the Resource Directory section of this Guide.

NORTHEAST ENTREPRENEUR FUND, INC.

The Northeast Entrepreneur Fund, Inc., is a private, nonprofit organization that helps people start or expand businesses in Northeastern Minnesota. The Northeast Entrepreneur Fund, Inc., makes loans to small businesses in Aitkin, Carlton, Cook, Itasca, Koochiching, Lake or St. Louis counties; other criteria also apply. The fund also offers certain consulting services. Contact the Fund at the addresses and telephone numbers listed in the Resource Directory of this Guide.

INSURANCE

Before you begin your business, you should thoroughly investigate your business insurance needs. The insurance industry today can tailor an insurance package to meet the general and specialized needs of almost every business.

Within each of these broad classes, various kinds of protection are offered under separate contracts. Because the insurance problems and needs of each business differ, no general insurance program can be outlined to fit every business. To be completely satisfactory, it should be tailored to fit the individual needs of each business. You should consult with an experienced insurance agent or broker.

TYPES OF INSURANCE

Business insurance is a matter of good business judgment. It is difficult to conceive of a sound business not carrying insurance custom-tailored to its individual needs. Among the basic kinds of coverage you should consider are:

Property Insurance

This protects the owner of the property (or the mortgagee) against loss caused by the actual destruction of a part or all of the property by fire, windstorm, explosion, falling aircraft, riot and other perils.

Business Interruption Insurance (and Other Time Element Coverages)

These protect a business against loss of earnings resulting from an interruption caused by damage to or destruction of the physical property. Business interruption insurance will pay you approximately what you normally would have earned. The premiums, especially when part of a complete insurance package, are low. There is also similar insurance which provides coverage if you are hospitalized and have to shut down business.

Liability Insurance (Including Business Automobile)

This protects a business against loss arising out of legal liability for death, injury or damage to the person or property of others caused by negligence. Included are obligations to pay medical, hospital, surgical and disability benefits to injured persons, and funeral and death benefits to dependents, beneficiaries or personal representatives of persons who are killed, irrespective of legal liability.

Bonds

Fidelity bonds guarantee against loss due to the dishonesty of employees. Surety bonds guarantee the performance of various types of obligations assumed by contract or imposed by law. Surety bonds are most often used in the construction industry and are often required on public construction projects.

Information on the Minnesota Bonding Program which provides individual fidelity bonds to employers for job applicants who may be denied coverage can be found earlier in this Guide in the section Business Licenses and Permits.

Workers' Compensation Insurance

This provides for payment of compensation benefits, as established by state law, to injured employees of a business. See the section in this Guide on Workers' Compensation for additional information.

Group Insurance for Employees

Group life insurance and group health insurance provided as employee benefits must conform to standards established by state and federal statute. These requirements are described in greater detail in the section of this Guide on Employee Benefits.

Product Liability

This refers to insurance coverage for any product manufactured by the insured. Coverage applies to the product once it leaves the manufacturer's hands and covers the manufacturer in case the ultimate user of the product sues for bodily injury or property damage.

E-INSURANCE FOR COMPANIES WITH AN ONLINE PRESENCE

With the growth of the Internet and e-commerce, the law regarding business insurance is evolving as coverage is being extended to new areas. Both the insurance industry and the courts are starting to sort out which risks need to be covered and which may be covered by existing forms of insurance.

Businesses that operate on the Internet face the possibility that their activities may subject them to liability in other jurisdictions. Since the Internet transcends geographical boundaries, one may be subject to a lawsuit in another state or even another country. It is fair to say that any company doing business on the Internet should consider that it is essentially a global business that might be sued in any court and in any territory where its business presence becomes known.

Companies with operations on the Internet are in the business of information publishing, vulnerable to liabilities that typically plague media companies such as defamation, invasion of privacy and intellectual property infringement claims. While these causes of action are not new, an Internet company's assets are more vulnerable to theft or business interruption. Damages associated with intangible assets, such as data theft or loss of business capability, pose risks unique to Internet companies.

As with all insurance, a business must make sure of what is and is not covered by their current insurance before investigating the variety of Internet-specific policies.

HELP FOR BUSINESSES UNABLE TO OBTAIN LIABILITY INSURANCE

The availability and cost of business insurance, particularly professional liability and general commercial liability coverage, have attracted substantial recent attention. To help remedy this problem, two state programs assist businesses that are experiencing difficulty in obtaining liability insurance. These programs are the Joint Underwriting Association (JUA) and the Minnesota Market Assistance Plan (MMAP) program.

The JUA was created to provide liability insurance coverage only to persons or entities unable to obtain insurance through ordinary methods if the insurance is required by statute, ordinance or otherwise required by law, or is necessary to earn a livelihood or conduct a business and serves a public purpose. The legislature specifically authorized the JUA to provide insurance coverage to day care providers, foster parents, foster homes, developmental achievement centers, group homes, sheltered workshops for mentally, emotionally, or physically disabled persons and certain citizen participation groups. The eligibility of other classes of business for JUA coverage is determined on a class by class basis.

The JUA is specifically prohibited by statute from issuing either product liability coverage or environmental impairment coverage. Further, the JUA cannot issue coverage to any business which is conducted substantially outside the state of Minnesota unless the insurance is required by statute, ordinance, or otherwise required by law. The JUA may reject high risk clients and risks it deems hazardous.

After having been unable to find an insurer willing to write the coverage sought, application may be made to the JUA. A copy of each application is forwarded to the Minnesota Market Assistance Program. MMAP has 30 business days to produce a quote for an applicant before the JUA can extend coverage. Upon receipt of an application, the JUA will make a determination whether the risk falls within a class for which the Association has already been activated to provide assistance. The Commissioner of the Minnesota Department of Commerce may publish notices of activation of the JUA for specified new classes of business each week in the *State Register.* The JUA has the authority to insure classes of business for 180 days from the time the notice is published. A public hearing may be held with each notice of activation in order to receive testimony from a class of business to determine whether statutory requirements for JUA coverage have been met.

The actual time frame for issuing a policy is dependent on several factors including whether:

- The appropriate policy form has been approved for use by the JUA Board of Directors;
- A rate schedule has been adopted for that class;
- The class or particular applicant requires committee or Board review prior to quoting;
- The 30-day MMAP period has expired and no quote for coverage has been offered;
- The applicant's current coverage has expired;
- The MMAP has reported to the JUA that no market can be found; or
- The applicant is quoted by MMAP at a premium rate ten percent or more in excess of the JUA's rates for similar coverage.

Addresses and telephone numbers for the Joint Underwriting Association and the Minnesota Market Assistance Program can be found in the Resource Directory section of this Guide.

ISSUES FOR EMPLOYERS*

WHO IS AN EMPLOYEE?

IN GENERAL

Many laws affecting the worker/employment relationship will require the business owner to first determine whether an individual who performs services for the business is an "employee" for purposes of the particular law. **Business owners who use "independent contractors" may think they do not have employees and, therefore, employment laws do not apply to them. An individual's status as an independent contractor, however, is not determined by agreement or by what he or she is called; the individual's status is determined by what he or she does.** The relationship between the business and the individual may be that of:

- A common law employee.
- A statutory employee.
- An independent contractor.

If the individual is a common law employee, the business by law must obtain workers' compensation coverage, withhold FICA (Social Security and Medicare) and income taxes, pay the employer's share of the FICA tax and pay federal and state unemployment taxes. Fair labor standards laws, occupational safety and health requirements and a variety of other federal and state laws also may apply.

If the individual is a statutory employee, the business does not withhold federal or state income tax. The employer should consult with an attorney or other competent tax advisor with respect to withholding Social Security and Medicare taxes and paying unemployment tax. Fair labor standards laws will probably apply.

An independent contractor is himself or herself a sole proprietor of a business, and not an employee. The tax requirements for sole proprietorships are discussed in the "Choosing the Form of Business Organization – Tax and Non-Tax Considerations"section of this Guide.

The question of whether a worker is an independent contractor or an employee may be determined by common law rules (definitions fashioned by the courts based on specific cases)

*A comprehensive discussion of employment issues is provided in the publication ***An Employer's Guide to Employment Law Issues in Minnesota***, available without charge from the Minnesota Small Business Assistance Office, 500 Metro Square, 121 7th Place East, St. Paul, MN 55101-2146. Two other employment-related publications are also available from the Minnesota Small Business Assistance Office: ***An Employer's Guide to Employee Handbooks in Minnesota***, and; ***An Employer's Guide to Employee Benefits.*** Note also that the text of each of those publications can be found at www.dted.state.mn.us.

or by statute. A person may be an employee for certain purposes but not for others. If a question arises, the employer is strongly urged to seek professional advice.

COMMON LAW EMPLOYEES

Under common law rules, courts balance a number of factors to determine whether an employer-employee relationship exists. The employer's right to control the manner and means of performing the work is the most important factor distinguishing an employer-employee relationship. It does not matter that the employer gives the employee substantial discretion and freedom to act, so long as the employer has the legal right to control both the method and result of the service.

Some of the other factors examined by the courts in determining whether an employment relationship exists include:

- **Mode of payment**. Workers who are paid on a regular basis, e.g., hourly or bi-weekly, are more likely to be considered employees than are persons who are paid a fixed amount for a specific service. Withholding for taxes and providing fringe benefits such as medical insurance are considered typical of an employer-employee relationship.
- **Materials and tools**. A person who furnishes his or her own materials and tools in connection with providing the service is less likely to be considered an employee than is a person who uses tools and materials furnished by the hiring entity.
- **Control of the premises.** An employer-employee relationship is more likely to be found where the hiring entity owns or controls the premises where the work is performed. Premises controlled by the service provider or by a third person are considered more characteristic of an independent contractor relationship.
- **Right of discharge.** The ability of the hiring entity to discharge the worker and the conditions under which the worker may be discharged also are factors examined in determining whether an employment relationship exists.

It is important to note, however, that none of the above factors, standing alone, will determine whether an employment relationship exists. The most important factor is the hiring entity's right to control the manner and means of the work. Doubtful situations generally are resolved by examining the facts of the specific case in light of all relevant factors.

If an employment relationship exists, the legal requirements placed on employers will apply regardless of what the parties call the worker, regardless of how payments are measured or made, and regardless of whether the person works part time or full time, unless a statutory exception applies to the situation.

In some cases, an employment relationship may exist between the employee and more than one employer, creating a situation of joint employment. A common example of this is when businesses obtain employees on contract from a temporary employment agency. It is important for employers to know that when they are in a situation of joint employment, both employers are jointly responsible to ensure that the employee is paid in accordance with the federal Fair Labor Standards Act as described in the Labor Standards section of this chapter. Note also that the Equal Employment Opportunity Commission (EEOC) has issued guidance on the application of Title VII of the Civil Rights Act of 1964 (Title VII), the Age Discrimination in Employment Act (ADEA), the Americans with Disabilities Act (ADA) and the Equal Pay Act (EPA) to individuals placed in job assignments by temporary employment agencies and other staffing firms (the EEOC refers to such individuals as "contingent workers"). In that Guidance, the EEOC states that either the staffing firm or the client (i.e. the business to which the contingent workers have been supplied), or both, may properly be considered an employer. If either or both has "control" over the contingent worker's work, that party will be an employer under Title VII, the ADA, the ADEA, and the EPA. Also, even if either lacks such "control", it will be considered an employer of that contingent worker, if it has enough other employees so as to be subject to those laws.

STATUTORY EMPLOYEES

Even if a worker is not an employee under common law rules, he or she may be considered an employee for certain statutory purposes, such as FICA (Social Security and Medicare) tax, federal and state unemployment compensation taxes, workers' compensation, Fair Labor Standards Act compliance, occupational safety and health requirements, and other statutory programs. Likewise, a federal or state statute may exempt certain employers or employees from its application.

Because both federal and state statutes define employees covered by their respective laws, both sources must be consulted before concluding a legal requirement is not applicable to a specific situation. Special rules apply to certain occupations, such as salespersons, and to special situations such as family owned businesses that employ family members.

The definition of "employee" often involves a legal determination. For this reason, particularly before concluding an individual is not an employee, it is important in doubtful cases to consult an attorney.

INDEPENDENT CONTRACTORS

Persons who follow an independent trade, business or profession in which they offer their services to the general public usually are considered independent contractors and not employees. Examples are self-employed lawyers, accountants, doctors, contractors, and subcontractors. However, whether such persons are employees or independent contractors depends on the law and facts applicable to each case. For example, Minnesota law considers nonresidents who perform personal or professional services in Minnesota to be employees for certain purposes, such as income tax withholding. This is true even though under federal law they would be considered self-employed independent contractors. Similarly, certain individuals such as direct sellers and real estate agents are by statute considered independent contractors for federal tax purposes if certain conditions are met.

In general, the individual will be considered an independent contractor if the business entity obtaining the person's services has the legal right to control the result of the work but does not have the legal right to control the manner and means of accomplishing the result.

Independent contractors offer their services to the public through the exercise of an independent business enterprise. An independent contractor is responsible for making his or her own estimated tax payments and paying self employment (Social Security and Medicare) tax. The business that obtains the independent contractor's services generally is not required to obtain workers' compensation insurance, withhold taxes or pay employment taxes on behalf of the independent contractor. Independent contractors generally do not receive benefits such as paid holidays, health insurance or sick pay from the business that obtains their services.

CONSTRUCTION CONTRACTORS

By state statute, an independent contractor doing commercial or residential building construction, or improvements in the public or private sector, is considered an employee of any employer under the workers' compensation statutes and for whom the independent contractor is performing services. In other words, those independent contractors are treated the same as employees for purposes of workers compensation.

That legislation does provide a safe harbor from such inclusion. Such an independent contractor will not be considered an employee if that person meets all of the nine requirements listed in the legislation (see Minnesota Statutes section 176.042 (worker's compensation)). Generally, the independent contractor must: maintain a separate business with his or her own office and equipment; have a federal employer identification number; operate under contracts under which the independent contractor maintains control; incur the main expenses related to the work he or she does; be responsible for satisfactory completion of the work, and liable for failure to complete the work; receive compensation on only a commission, per-job, or competitive bid basis; have the potential to realize a profit or suffer a loss under such contracts; have continuing or recurring business liabilities or obligations; and have the success or failure of his or her business depend on the relationship of business receipts to expenditures. Any business interested in this safe harbor is strongly advised to examine the legislation and, if necessary, seek the advice of counsel.

FURTHER INFORMATION

In addition to consulting a professional advisor, more detailed information on "Who is an Employee" for various purposes may be obtained from the following sources, at the addresses and telephone numbers listed in the Resource Directory section of this Guide. See also the section of this Guide titled "Checklist for Hiring an Employee."

- **Federal income, withholding and FICA (Social Security and Medicare) tax:** ***Publication 15 – Circular E, Employer's Tax Guide; Publication 15A, Employer's Supplemental Tax Guide; Publication 1779 – Employee or Independent Contractor;*** and ***Form SS-8, Determination of Employee Work Status for Purposes of Federal Employment Taxes and Income Tax Withholding,*** available from the Internal Revenue Service.
- **Minnesota income tax:** ***Minnesota Income Tax Withholding Instructions and Tax Tables,*** available from the Minnesota Department of Revenue.
- **Minnesota unemployment tax:** ***Publication MDES-130, Minnesota Employers' Unemployment Handbook,*** available from the Minnesota Department of Economic Security.

- **Workers' Compensation:** ***Employer's Quick Reference Guide to the Minnesota Workers' Compensation System,*** available from the Minnesota Department of Labor and Industry, Research and Education Unit. The Department of Labor and Industry has adopted rules addressing the conditions under which workers will be considered employees or independent contractors for workers' compensation purposes. These rules can be found at *Minnesota Rules* Chapter 5224. *Minnesota Rules* is available at law libraries and many public libraries. A general information sheet on independent contractor/employee questions is available from the Department of Labor and Industry's Legal Services Unit and many public libraries.
- **Federal Fair Labor Standards Act:** U.S. Department of Labor, Employment Standards Administration.
- **Minnesota Fair Labor Standards Act:** Minnesota Department of Labor and Industry, Labor Standards Division.
- **Human Rights:** Minnesota Department of Human Rights.

EMPLOYMENT AGREEMENTS

EMPLOYMENT AT WILL

The doctrine of employment at will generally states that an employment relationship may be terminated at any time by either party. In the absence of a collective bargaining agreement or other contract, the employer may discharge an employee at any time for any legal reason, or for no reason, with or without notice. Likewise, the employee may resign at any time for any reason, with or without notice. Minnesota follows this general rule.

The employment at will relationship can be contrasted with a contractual relationship, in which the rights and duties of the parties are governed by specific contractual provisions. The courts in recent years have identified several situations in which an employment at will relationship is changed to a contractual relationship, or where for public policy reasons the employment at will rule will be disregarded. These situations are discussed in the section on Employment Contracts, below.

EMPLOYMENT CONTRACTS

Employment contracts may be written or oral. Employment contracts may be provided to employees who would not otherwise accept employment without the security of a contract, or in cases where the employer wishes to secure certain protections, such as the protection of confidential information or trade secrets. Employment contracts typically set forth the term or length of employment, compensation and benefits, job duties, and circumstances for termination. Some contracts also may include provisions relating to confidentiality, assignment of intellectual property rights like patents or copyrights, and non-compete agreements.

In recent years, Minnesota courts have used contract-based theories to carve out exceptions to the employment at will doctrine for public policy reasons. For example, the courts have found a contract to exist where the employee provides something of value, in addition to performing the job, in exchange for a promise of continued employment. A contract also has been found where the employee, in reliance on an offer of employment, gave up another job to accept employment. Most recently, Minnesota courts have determined that statements in a personnel handbook may create an enforceable contract if the terms are sufficiently definite, are communicated to the employee, and the employee accepts the terms and provides value by continuing to work. Implied contracts may be found to exist in other situations.

In cases where employees are represented by a union, the employer and the collective bargaining agent negotiate a contract which governs the relationship of the parties throughout its term.

PROTECTION OF CONFIDENTIAL INFORMATION

Minnesota law protects employers' confidential information and trade secrets in several ways. First, an employee has a generally recognized duty of loyalty to not disclose trade secrets or proprietary information of the employer. Second, the statutory Uniform Trade Secrets Act, adopted by Minnesota, prohibits misappropriation of trade secrets. And third, employers may require employees to execute nondisclosure agreements to prevent release of trade secrets or confidential information during or after their employment.

To be protected as a trade secret under the Uniform Trade Secrets Act, the information must not be generally known or readily ascertainable by the general public, it must provide economic value to the employer, and the employer must make reasonable efforts to maintain its secrecy.

Confidentiality agreements must be supported by "adequate consideration," i.e., the employee must be given something of value in exchange for the promise not to disclose the information. Examples of adequate consideration vary from case to case but might include the initial hiring of the employee in exchange for the agreement, promotions, salary increases or cash payments. Continued employment, without more, generally is not recognized as adequate consideration to support a confidentiality agreement.

ASSIGNMENT OF PATENTS AND INVENTIONS

An employer may require an employee, as a condition of employment, to assign the employee's rights in certain inventions to the employer. Under state law, such an assignment must exclude inventions for which no equipment, supplies, facilities or trade secret information of the employer were used, and which were developed entirely on the employee's own time, and which do not relate directly to the employer's business or its actual or demonstrably anticipated research or development, or which do not result from any work performed by the employee for the employer. (See also the section of this Guide "Can the Employed Inventor Obtain a Patent of His or Her Own?")

NON-COMPETE AGREEMENTS

An employer may require, as a condition of employment, that an applicant or employee sign an agreement agreeing not to work for a competitor or to start a competing business during employment and for a limited time following termination of employment. Non-compete agreements generally are enforceable so long as they protect a legitimate interest of the employer, are supported by adequate consideration, and are reasonably limited in scope and time. Where a court determines the restrictions are too broad or unreasonable, it may fashion a more limited agreement or refuse to enforce the agreement.

LABOR STANDARDS

GENERAL INFORMATION

Wages, overtime pay and record keeping requirements are regulated at the federal level by the Fair Labor Standards Act, 29 United States Code 201 *et seq.* (federal act) and at the state level by the Minnesota Fair Labor Standards Act, Minnesota Statutes Chapter 177 (Minnesota act). Each act specifies the employers and employees to which it applies, but where the Minnesota act and the federal act are different, the law providing more protection for the employee or setting the higher standard applies. **Employers should assume that they are covered by the federal act (for reasons discussed below) unless they are told otherwise by legal counsel.**

This section discusses provisions of the federal act and the Minnesota act pertaining to persons covered, minimum wage and overtime requirements, prevailing wage requirements, and wage records.

Further information on the federal act may be obtained from the U.S. Department of Labor, Employment Standards Administration, Wage and Hour Division. Information on the Minnesota act may be obtained from the Minnesota Department of Labor and Industry, Labor Standards Unit. Addresses and telephone numbers are provided in the Resource Directory section of this Guide.

PERSONS COVERED

Federal Act

The federal act covers all workers employed by: 1) hospitals and residential care facilities; 2) preschools, elementary or secondary schools, and institutions of higher education; 3) enterprises with annual gross sales of $500,000, or more, whose workers are engaged in interstate commerce, produce goods for interstate commerce , or handle, sell, or otherwise work on goods or materials that have been moved in or produced for interstate commerce; 4) public agencies; and

Other employees will be covered by the federal act if they are individually engaged in interstate commerce, the production of goods for interstate commerce, or in any closely related process or occupation directly essential to such production. Such employees include those who: work in communication and transportation; handle, ship or receive goods moving in interstate commerce; regularly use the mails, telephone, fax, or e-mail for interstate communication or who keep records on interstate transactions; regularly cross state lines in the course of their work; and perform clerical, custodial, maintenance or other work for firms engaged in interstate commerce or in the production of goods for interstate commerce. Due to the broad nature of this category, an employer that wishes to assert that its employees are not involved in interstate commerce should seek the advice of counsel.

Exceptions to the federal act are discussed in the section on "Federal Act Exemptions" below.

The federal Fair Labor Standards Act (and other federal employment laws, such as the Occupational Safety and Health Act, unemployment insurance, and anti-discrimination laws) apply to working welfare recipients in the same manner as it applies to other workers. The welfare law does not exempt welfare recipients from these laws. Welfare recipients would probably be considered covered employees in many, if not most, of the work activities under the welfare law, and in "workfare" arrangements. Exceptions are most likely to include individuals engaged in activities such as vocational education, job search assistance, and secondary school attendance, because these programs are not ordinarily considered employment under the federal act.

Further information on the federal act may be obtained by contacting the United States Department of Labor, Wage and Hour Division at the local address and telephone number provided in the Resource Directory section of this Guide. If you have a question about the federal act and welfare recipients, a Wage and Hour publication entitled "How Workplace Laws Apply to Welfare Recipients" is available through the Wage and Hour Division, and can be found in the compliance information section of the Wage and Hour Division website.

Minnesota Act

The Minnesota act generally applies to all employers and employees in Minnesota who are not covered by the federal act. Also, the Minnesota Act will apply to employers and employees subject to the federal act when the Minnesota Act would provide more protection to the employee or would set a higher standard. Exceptions to the Minnesota act are discussed in the section on "Minnesota Act Exemptions" below.

EXEMPTIONS

Federal Act Exemptions

The federal act exempts some employees from federal minimum wage or overtime requirements, or both. These exemptions are narrowly defined and applied on a workweek by workweek basis. A business that wishes to pay a worker as an exempt employee should carefully check the exact requirements to make sure the exemption is applicable. The fact that an employee is paid a salary or commission rather than an hourly wage does not by itself determine that an employee is exempt from overtime or minimum wage requirements. A job title is also insufficient for determining exempt or non-exempt status. All of the specific requirements for the exemption must be met in order for the employee to be classified as exempt.

Exemptions from Federal Minimum Wage and Overtime Requirements. In general, the following are exempt from both the minimum wage and overtime requirements of the federal act: executive, administrative and professional employees and outside sales persons (as defined in regulations of the U.S. Department of Labor), employees engaged in fishing operations, and farm workers employed by anyone who used no more than 500 work-days of farm labor in any calendar quarter of the preceding calendar year. Casual babysitters, and persons employed as companions to the elderly or infirm in a private residence may also be exempt from the minimum wage and overtime requirements.

Exemptions from Federal Overtime Pay Requirements Only. The following may be exempt from overtime pay provisions of the federal act, but are not exempt from the minimum wage requirements:

- Certain highly paid commission employees of retail or service establishments; auto, truck, trailer, farm implement, boat or aircraft sales workers, or parts workers and mechanics servicing autos, trucks or farm implements, and who are employed by nonmanufacturing establishments primarily engaged in selling these items to ultimate purchasers.
- Employees of railroads and air carriers, taxi drivers, certain employees of motor carriers, seamen on American vessels, and local delivery employees paid on approved trip rate plans.
- Announcers, news editors, chief engineers of certain nonmetropolitan broadcasting stations, and employees of motion picture theaters.
- Domestic service workers residing in the employer's residence, and farm workers.

Minnesota Act Exemptions

Like the federal act, the Minnesota act exempts certain workers from its coverage. A business that wishes to rely on any of the exemptions should check the law carefully to be sure that the exemption is applicable to the firm's situation.

Exemptions from Minnesota Minimum Wage and Overtime Requirements. The Minnesota act covers all employees of an employer unless there is a specific statutory exemption. The following are some of the more common exemptions for for-profit employers.

- Individuals employed in a *bona fide* executive, administrative, or professional capacity, or a sales person who conducts no more than 20 percent of sales on the premises of the employer. This exemption is discussed more fully under "Exemptions from Minnesota Overtime Pay Provisions" below.
- Taxicab drivers.
- Individual babysitters.

- Some salaried farm employees and farm employees under age 18 except corn detasselers and hand field workers when one or both of the minor's parents or physical custodians also are hand field workers. (Corn detasselers under age 18 are exempt from the state minimum wage provision, but must be paid for overtime.)

Other exemptions apply to certain employees of governmental units, nonprofit organizations and religious groups. Information on these exemptions may be obtained from the Labor Standards Division of the Department of Labor and Industry.

Exemptions from Minnesota Overtime Pay Requirements. The requirement for employers to pay employees premium pay for overtime is determined by whether the worker is an exempt or nonexempt employee. The fact that an employee is paid a salary or commission rather than an hourly wage does not by itself determine whether overtime pay is required. The specific requirements of the law must be met. Four types of workers are exempt from overtime pay requirements. They are: executive, administrative, professional, and outside sales workers.

- **Executive:** An employee who is paid no less than $250 a week in salary may qualify for exemption from overtime if: (1) the work consists mainly of the management of the business or management of a department or some other division of the company, and (2) if the employee regularly supervises and directs the work of at least two employees in the department or division (working foreman do not qualify.)
- **Administrative:** An employee who is paid no less than $250 a week in salary may qualify for exemption from overtime if: (1) the work performed is office or nonmanual work directly involved in management policy or the general operations of the company or its customers, and (2) if the work calls for use of discretion and independent judgment. An employee must have enough authority to make policy decisions.
- **Professional:** An employee who is paid no less than $250 a week in salary may qualify as an exempt employee if: (1) the majority of the work is in performance of tasks which assume a knowledge in an advanced field of learning, teaching or science, with consistent use of discretion and judgment; or (2) if the work performed is in a field of artistic endeavor, such as invention or use of imagination or talent. Generally, an advanced degree is a requirement of the job.
- **Outside Sales Worker:** This person is hired for, and is usually away from the place of business for, the purpose of making service calls or obtaining orders and contracts for products or services provided by the employer. The working hours require spending at least 80 percent of the workweek outside the employer's premises. In addition the outside work may not be conducted at any one fixed place, even if not owned by the employer.

Employees earning less than the amounts specified in each category above may still qualify as exempt, but they must fulfill work requirements more detailed than indicated above.

Other employees subject to the Minnesota act but exempt from overtime requirements are:

- Seasonal employees of a carnival, circus, fair, or ski resort.
- Construction workers of on-farm silos or installers of appurtenant equipment who are paid on a unit or piece rate.

- Salesperson, parts person, or mechanic paid on a commission or incentive basis if employed by a non-manufacturing establishment primarily engaged in selling automobiles, trailers, trucks or farm implements to ultimate purchasers.
- Employees of a retail or service establishment if the regular rate of pay is in excess of one and one half times the minimum wage and more than half the compensation represents commissions on goods or services.

MINIMUM WAGE REQUIREMENTS

Federal Minimum Wage Requirements

The federal act requires that covered non-exempt employees receive a minimum wage of at least $5.15 per hour.

Some employees are excluded from the federal act's minimum wage provisions under specific exemptions provided in the law. Because these exemptions are generally narrowly defined, employers should check them carefully with the Wage and Hour Division of the U.S. Department of Labor before concluding that a lower minimum wage is applicable.

There is also an exception which permits employers to pay workers under 20 years of age not less than $4.25 per hour during their first 90 consecutive calendar days of employment. Employers who use this youth subminimum wage are prohibited from taking any action to displace employees in order to hire employees at the youth minimum wage.

Minnesota Minimum Wage Requirements

Minnesota employers with more than $500,000 in annual revenues must pay a minimum wage of at least $5.15 per hour. Employers with less than $500,000 in annual revenues must pay a minimum wage of at least $4.90 an hour. However, any Minnesota employer may during the first 90 consecutive days of employment pay an employee under age 20 a wage of $4.25 per hour. An employer wishing to pay the lower $4.25 wage may not, however, take any action to displace any employee, including a partial displacement through a reduction in hours, wages, or benefits, in order to hire an employee at the $4.25 wage.

The Minnesota act does not provide for a tip credit. The minimum wage for tipped employees is the same as for all other employees.

The Minnesota act provides for a subminimum wage for disabled workers when a permit is obtained from the Labor Standards Unit of the Minnesota Department of Labor and Industry.

The Minnesota act also permits a credit against the minimum wage for meals and lodging furnished by the employer. A meal credit is equal to 60 percent of the adult minimum wage rate for one hour, per meal accepted. A lodging credit is equal to 75 percent of the adult minimum wage rate for one hour, per day of lodging.

OVERTIME PAY REQUIREMENTS

Federal Overtime Pay Requirements

The Federal act requires that covered non-exempt employee receive overtime pay at a rate of one and one-half times their regular rate of pay after 40 hours of work in a workweek. Exemptions from the federal overtime pay requirements are addressed above.

A workweek is a period of 168 hours during seven consecutive 24-hour periods. It may begin on any day of the week and any hour of the day established by the employer, but the established workweek must remain consistent. For purposes of computing overtime pay, each workweek stands alone; there can be no averaging of two or more workweeks (except for hospital or nursing home employees on an "8 and 80").

Overtime pay must be based on the regular rate. Generally, the regular rate includes all payments made by the employer to or on behalf of the employee (i.e., non-discretionary bonuses, incentive pay, shift differentials), although some statutory exceptions may apply. To calculate the regular rate, divide all pay received by all hours worked in the work week.

Overtime compensation must be paid in cash wages. There is an exception for public sector employees who can accrue hours worked over 40 as compensatory time to be paid out at a rate of time and one-half, in lieu of cash wages.

Minnesota Overtime Pay Requirements (Minnesota Statutes § 177.25)

As a general rule, employers covered by the Minnesota act are required to pay nonexempt employees time and a half for all time worked in excess of 48 hours in one workweek. Each workweek stands by itself. The employer may not average the worker's hours over the two weeks. A special overtime law, Minnesota Statutes § 177.25, Subd. 2, applies to hospitals and the health care field.

Exemptions from the Minnesota overtime pay requirements are addressed earlier in this section. An exception to the 48 hour rule for payment of overtime appears at Minnesota Statutes §§ 177.41-177.44. This statute, the Minnesota Prevailing Wage Law, requires that employees who work on state-funded construction projects be paid time-and-one-half for all time worked in excess of eight hours per day and 40 hours per week.

Premium pay need not be made for a period when no work is performed, such as sick days, holidays, and vacations. Overtime applies only after 48 hours of actual work, not hours paid.

PREVAILING WAGE LAWS

Both the federal government and the State of Minnesota by law require contractors who are awarded government funds for public works projects to pay their employees the prevailing wage for the locality in which the project is located. In 1990, the Minnesota Legislature extended the provisions of its prevailing wage law to recipients of state funds for certain economic development projects. The law applies to three forms of state financial assistance:

- Economic development grants where a single business receives $200,000 or more of the grant proceeds;
- Loans made by a state agency for economic development purposes where the loan recipient receives $500,000 or more of the loan proceeds, and
- Sales tax reductions or abatements made for economic development purposes in certain geographic areas.

Economic development is defined as financial assistance provided to a person directly or to a local unit of government or nonprofit organization on behalf of a person who is engaged in the manufacture or sale of goods and services, except for financial assistance provided for certain housing projects.

The law requires the person receiving or benefiting from the financial assistance, as a condition of receiving the assistance, to certify to the Commissioner of Labor and Industry that laborers and mechanics assigned to the project will be paid the prevailing wage rate for the area. The prevailing wage rate is determined periodically by the Department of Labor and Industry.

The federal government enforces the Davis-Bacon and Related Acts, which require the payment of prevailing wage rates and fringe benefits on federally-financed or assisted construction, and the Service Contract Act, which requires the payment of prevailing wage rates and fringe benefits on contracts to provide services to the federal government.

The prevailing wage rate is defined as the hourly basic rate of pay plus the employer's contribution for health and welfare, vacation, pension, and other economic benefits paid to the largest number of workers engaged in the same class of labor in the area. Area is defined as the county or other locality from which labor for any project normally is secured.

RECORD KEEPING REQUIREMENTS

Federal Record Keeping Requirements

Federal employer record keeping requirements are specified by regulation of the U.S. Department of Labor. Most of the information is of the kind generally maintained by employers in ordinary business practice and in compliance with other laws and regulations. The records do not have to be kept in any particular form and time clocks need not be used. The following records must be kept on all employees subject to the minimum wage and overtime provisions of the federal act.

- Employee name, home address, occupation, sex and date of birth (if under age 19);
- Hour and day when workweek begins;
- Total hours worked each workday and each workweek;
- Total daily or weekly straight-time earnings;
- Regular hourly pay rate for any week when overtime is worked;
- Total overtime pay for the workweek;

- Deductions from or additions to wages;
- Total wages paid each pay period;
- Date of payment and pay period covered.

Records required for exempt employees differ from those for nonexempt workers and special information is required on employees working under uncommon pay arrangements or to whom lodging or other facilities are furnished. Firms that employ industrial home workers must keep records in handbooks supplied by the Department of Labor.

In addition to the record keeping requirements imposed for records relating to employee compensation, a number of federal statutes impose record retention requirements on documents associated with employee recruitment and selection. These records include job postings and advertisements, test papers, interview records, lists of applicants, applicant resumes, ranking and valuative criteria and other records. Requirements range from six months to five year retention. Each year a comprehensive update of federal record retention requirements is published in the *Federal Register.* A business or government reference librarian can direct employers to the latest compilation.

Minnesota Record Keeping Requirements (Minnesota Statutes § 177.30)

Employers covered by the Minnesota act are required to make and retain for at least three years the following records for every worker:

- Employee's name and home address;
- Occupation and rate of pay;
- Amount paid each pay period to each employee;
- Hours worked each day and each workweek, including starting and ending hours each day, with both morning and afternoon designations.

The above records must be available for inspection by a representative of the Department of Labor and Industry or must be submitted to the Commissioner on request. The employer is subject to a penalty of up to $1,000.00 issued by the Commissioner and may also be subject to a civil action for each failure to submit or deliver records or failure to post a summary of the Minnesota Act or failure to maintain records.

ADDITIONAL MINNESOTA REQUIREMENTS

Statement of Wages

At the end of each pay period, the employer must give each employee a written earnings statement covering that pay period. The earnings statement may be in any form determined by the employer, but must include all of the following:

- The employee's name.

- Hourly rate of pay (if applicable; not applicable if the employee is paid on a basis other than hourly).
- Total number of hours worked by the employee, unless the employee is exempt from Minnesota Statutes Chapter 177 (e.g., *bona fide* executive, administrative, professional or outside sales person).
- Gross pay earned by the employee during the pay period.
- List of deductions made from the employee's pay.
- Net amount of pay after all deductions are made.
- The date on which the pay period ends.
- The legal name of the employer and the operating names of the employer if different from the legal name.

One can institute a civil action for failure to provide a proper written earnings statement.

Payment of Wages

General Rule. All employers are required by statute to pay all wages due an employee at least once every 31 days on a regular pay day designated in advance by the employer. Wages earned during the first half of the first 31 day period become due on the first regular payday following the first day of work.

Discharged Employees. When an employer discharges an employee, wages and commissions earned and unpaid at the time of discharge become immediately due and payable at the demand of the employee. If the employee is not paid within 24 hours following the demand, the employer may be liable to the employee for an additional sum equal to the employee's average daily earnings, for every day up to 15 days that payment is not made.

Employees Who Quit or Resign. An employee who quits or resigns and who did not have a contract for a definite period of service must be paid in full not later than the next regularly-scheduled payday after his or her last day of work. If that payday is fewer than five days after the employees' last day of employment, the wages may be paid at the next regularly-scheduled payday, as long as that payday is no more than twenty days after the last day of employment. Wages not paid during this time period are immediately due upon the employee's request, and if not paid upon that demand the employer is liable to the employee for an amount equal to the employee's average daily wage for each day the wages are unpaid, up to fifteen days.

An exception is made for migrant workers; they must be paid within five days after they quit or resign. Also, an employee subject to a collective bargaining agreement will be subject to terms of payment contained in that agreement.

Penalties Relating to Payment of Wages

Chapter 386 provides penalties for violations of many Minnesota statutes relating to the payment of wages by employers to employees. First, the penalties for an employer's failure to submit or deliver the employment records required by Minnesota Statutes section 177.27, subdivision 2, is $1,000. Second, the Commissioner of the Department of Labor and Industry (Commissioner) has the power to issue compliance orders in connection with additional Minnesota Statutes that speak to the payment of wages.

In terms of the Commissioner's enforcement powers, the Commissioner may issue cease and desist orders with respect to violations of any of the statutes listed in Minnesota statutes section 177.27, subdivision 4, or of the rules adopted under Minnesota statutes section 177.28. Also, with respect to the same violations, the Commissioner may take whatever steps he or she determines necessary to effectuate the purposes of the rule or statute violated, and also order the employer to pay the employee back pay, gratuities, compensatory damages (net of any amounts already paid to the employee), and liquidated damages. Repeated or willful violations are subject to a civil penalty of up to $1,000 per violation per employee; Chapter 386 contains factors to be used by the Commissioner in determining the amount of that penalty. Finally, in some instances, an employer can be required to pay the litigation and hearing costs incurred by the Attorney General's office and the Department of Labor and Industry.

Chapter 386 also allows employees to sue directly in district court (without first exhausting administrative remedies) for violations of many of the Minnesota statutes relating to the payment of wages. Employers found to have violated such statutes are also liable for an employee's reasonable costs, disbursements, witness fees, and attorneys' fees.

Deductions from Wages

In General. By Minnesota statute, employers may only deduct certain items from an employee's wages. The employee must authorize the deduction in writing. Deductions authorized by law include deductions for union dues, life insurance premiums, hospitalization and surgical insurance, group accident and health insurance, group term life insurance, group annuities, contributions to credit unions or a community chest fund, contributions to a local arts council, local science council or Minnesota benefit association, contributions to a federally or state registered political action committee, and contributions to an employee stock purchase plan or savings plan. Minnesota Statutes § 181.06, subd. 2.

Uniforms and Equipment. Minnesota law limits the deductions directly or indirectly that may be made for uniforms, equipment and consumable supplies used on the job, and travel expenses. No deductions may be made for these items if the deduction would reduce the employee's wages below minimum wage. Deductions for uniforms or equipment may not exceed $50, and when employment is terminated, the employer must reimburse the full amount deducted. The employer may require the employee to surrender items for which reimbursement is made, but may not hold the employee's last check for failure to return the items. Minnesota Statutes §§ 177.24, subd. 4 and 5; 181.79.

Lost or Damaged Property. An employer may not deduct from wages any amount for lost, stolen or damaged property, or recover any claimed amount owed by the employee to the employer, unless the employee voluntarily authorizes the employer in writing to make the deduction after the loss has occurred, or unless the employee is found liable by a court for the loss or indebtedness. There are specific statutory limits on the amount which may be deducted in each pay period.

Child Support or Spousal Maintenance and Medical Support Obligations. The Minnesota Department of Human Services is directed to have employers participate in a centralized work reporting system for child support enforcement purposes. Employers are required to report certain information on newly-hired employees, and on independent contractors, within fifteen days of hiring or engaging that person.

Employers also must ask all new employees whether they have court-ordered medical support or dependent health or dental insurance obligations that must be withheld from income, and the terms of any court order. If medical support must be withheld, the employer must do the appropriate withholding. If the employee is required to obtain dependent insurance the employer must tell the employee about the application process and enroll the employee and dependents in the plan. An employer who willfully fails to comply is liable for the health or dental expenses incurred by dependents during the time they were eligible to be enrolled. The law also requires a court to order the parent with the better health care insurance plan to provide it for the children, if the plan is paid for by the employer or union.

Garnishment of Wages. An employer may be required to garnish and pay over money an employee owes to third persons. Certain statutory requirements must be met, and there is a limit on the amount of wages that may be garnished. These requirements and limitations are provided in the garnishment notice. An employer is prohibited by law from retaliating against an employee due to garnishment. An employer may charge the employee $3 for each written response the employer must provide for purposes of administering the garnishment of wages.

Access to Personnel Records (Other Than Employee Assistance Records)

Employers who employ one or more employees must allow those workers to review their personnel records and to obtain a copy under certain circumstances.

A worker must request the right to review his or her personnel file in writing, and can only do so once in a six month period. An employee who separates from service may review the file once within a year of separation. After the employee makes the request, the employer must comply within seven working days if the personnel record is in Minnesota, and within 14 days if the record is outside the state.

The file must be made available for review during the employer's normal hours of operation, but need not be made available during the employee's working hours. For separated employees, this requirement is met if the employee is given a copy of the file. The employer may require that the review be done in the presence of the employer or the employer's designee. After the review and upon the employee's written request, the employer must provide a copy of the record to the employee. The employer may not charge a fee for the copy. A request to review the record may be denied if the employer determines it is not made in good faith.

The law specifies a procedure for removal or revision of information that is disputed by the employee. If the employer and employee cannot agree on removal of disputed information, the employee may submit a written statement of up to five pages specifically identifying the disputed information and explaining the employee's position. The employee's statement must be included along with the disputed information for as long as the information is maintained in the employee's personnel record. A copy of the employee's statement must be provided to any person who receives a copy of the disputed information.

Communication of information obtained through a review of the employee's personnel record cannot be the basis of a defamation action, unless the employer refuses to follow the dispute resolution procedure. The law specifies conditions under which a defamation action may be maintained.

The law specifically prohibits retaliation against an employee for asserting his or her rights under the law. An employee may bring a civil action against an employer for violation of the law. Generally, the employee may recover actual damages and costs. If the employer is found to have unlawfully retaliated against the employee, the employee also may recover back pay, reinstatement or other equitable relief, and reasonable attorneys fees. The Minnesota Department of Labor and Industry may also assess a fine of up to $5000 for violations of the law.

Access to Personnel Records Relating to Employee Assistance Programs

When employees avail themselves of an employer's employee assistance program, Minnesota Statutes section 181.980 governs what must be done with the resulting records. An employee assistance provider must give, upon written request of a person who has received such services (or the parent or guardian of a minor person who has received such services), that person an opportunity to review and obtain copies of that person's employee assistance records. No fee may be charged for copies of records, and the employee assistance provider must comply with such a request no later than seven working days after receipt of such request, if the records are located in Minnesota, or fourteen working days if the records are elsewhere. Also, that statute mandates that such records "must be maintained separate from personnel records and must not become part of an employee's personnel file." The statute also prohibits disclosure of such records, or the fact of the participation in such a program, to a third person, including the employer or its representative, absent the prior written authorization of the person receiving the services, or his or her legal representative. There are some exceptions to that prohibition. The statute also provides that its rights and obligations "are in addition to rights or obligations created under a contract or other law governing access to records." Finally, the statute provides that "[i]n addition to other remedies provided by law, the recipient of employee assistance services may bring a civil action to compel compliance with this section and to recover damages, plus costs and reasonable attorney fees

Indemnification of Employees

Minnesota employers are required by state statute to indemnify their employees for civil damages, fines and penalties arising out of their employment. To receive indemnification, employees must have acted within the scope of their duties and not have engaged in intentional misconduct, willful neglect of duty, or bad faith. Exceptions apply when another law or private agreement provides for indemnification.

REST BREAKS AND LEAVE TIME

Unless a collective bargaining agreement provides otherwise, employers generally are free to establish their own policies regarding rest breaks and leave time. This section discusses several exceptions to the general rule.

REST BREAKS

Minnesota law establishes two mandatory rest breaks. Employers must permit each employee who works eight or more consecutive hours sufficient time to eat a meal. The employer is not required to pay the employee during the meal break as long as the employee is completely relieved of their duties for 20 minutes or longer (30 minutes under Federal rules). An employer also must allow each employee adequate time within each four consecutive hours of work to utilize the nearest convenient restroom. A collective bargaining agreement may establish different rest and meal breaks.

Accommodation for Nursing Mothers

Minnesota Statutes § 181.939 requires employers to provide "reasonable unpaid break time each day to an employee who needs to express breast milk for her infant child," unless to do so would "unduly disrupt the operations of the employer." The statute also provides that the break time must, if possible, run concurrently with any break time already provided to the employee. Additionally, the employer must make "reasonable efforts" to provide a room or other location, in close proximity to the work area (other than a toilet stall), where the employee can express her milk in private. (Editors note: An amendment to Minn. Stat. § 617.23 makes clear that it is not a violation of the state "indecent exposure" law for a woman to breast feed.)

LEAVE TIME

Vacation, Holiday, and Sick Leave

Minnesota employers are not required by law to provide vacation, holiday or sick time for their employees. Most employers do provide such leave, however. Employers should provide employees with notice of their vacation, holiday and sick leave policies in an employee handbook, or otherwise communicate these policies to employees in writing. These policies should address whether vacation or sick leave can be carried over from year to year, or whether it is forfeited if unused by the end of the year. The policies also should address whether the employee will be paid for unused leave.

Family Leave

Family and Medical Leave (Federal Law). The federal Family and Medical Leave Act (FMLA) requires employers engaged in commerce or in an industry affecting commerce, of 50 or more employees in 20 or more weeks in the current or prior calendar year to provide up to 12 weeks of unpaid leave or accrued paid leave to eligible employees for certain family and medical reasons. Employees are eligible if they have worked for a covered employer for at least 12 months, and for 1250 hours over the previous 12 months immediately preceding the need for FMLA leave, and are employed at a worksite where the employer employs at least 50 people within 75 miles.[1]

In determining if the business meets the 50 or more criteria, the employer should include those people whose names appear on the employer's payroll, including part-time employees, those currently on approved leaves of absence or disciplinary suspensions and jointly owned (e.g. leased) employees. Employees on long term or indefinite layoff are not counted. Employees whose worksites are outside the United States, its territories or possessions are not covered for purposes of determining employer coverage nor are they protected by FMLA.

Employers must grant leave to employees in connection with the birth, placement or adoption of a child, to care for a spouse, minor or incompetent child or parent who has a serious health condition, or for their own serious health condition that makes them unable to perform their job. A serious health condition according to Regulations promulgated by the U.S. Department of Labor, includes an illness, injury, impairment, or physical or mental condition that involves either hospital care; absence plus continuing treatment; pregnancy; a chronic condition requiring treatment; permanent long-term supervision; or multiple treatments (non-chronic conditions). Note that many courts, including the Eighth Circuit Court of Appeals, have been asked to interpret those Regulations; as those courts have reached varying conclusions, anyone with questions in this area is urged to seek the advice of counsel. Employees may be required to provide advance notice of the leave and medical certification as established by the FMLA and Regulations of the U.S. Department of Labor.

The FMLA requires all covered employers to comply with notification requirements, including posting information on the FMLA in a general location where all employees would have an opportunity to see it, providing general written information regarding employee rights under the FMLA to all employees, either in an employee handbook or as a handout, and providing all employees requesting or on FMLA leave with written notice detailing the specific obligations and expectations of the employee, and the consequences of failing to meet such obligations.

Although the law does not require the employer to provide paid leave, in some cases certain kinds of paid leave may run concurrently with FMLA leave. During the leave, employers must maintain group medical insurance coverage under conditions the employer would have provided coverage had the employee continued working. (Employers may in some cases recover premiums paid for maintaining health coverage from employees who do not return to work following the leave.) Upon return from FMLA leave, employees must be restored to their original or an equivalent position with equivalent pay, benefits and other employment terms. The FMLA allows employers to deny job restoration to "key employees" (employees who are paid on a salary basis and are among the highest paid ten percent of the workforce) if reinstatement of the employee would cause "substantial and grievous economic harm to the

[1] The U.S. Department of Labor's Regulations on the FMLA are at 29 CFR Chapter 825.

employer, and if the employer has provided the specific notification as required by the FMLA for "key employees".

The law does not supersede any state or local law which provides greater family or medical leave rights, nor does it affect greater leave rights provided under a collective bargaining agreement. Also, employers may adopt policies more generous than those required by the FMLA. Employers must post a notice, available from the U.S. Department of Labor, explaining employee rights and responsibilities under the law. This notice obligation also includes posting notices in languages necessary to accommodate the employer's workforce.

In January, 1995, the U.S. Department of Labor issued final Regulations under the FMLA. Employers should familiarize themselves with those Regulations, especially as those Regulations give detailed guidance on several aspects of the FMLA. In addition, as those Regulations have been the subject of much litigation (*see e.g., Ragsdale v. Wolverine Worldwide, Inc.* No. 99-3319, July 11, 2000, in which the Eighth Circuit Court of Appeals struck down a portion of those Regulations), employers are urged to seek the advice of counsel when dealing with those Regulations.

Parenting Leave (Minnesota Law). A Minnesota employer must grant an unpaid leave of absence to certain employees in conjunction with the birth or adoption of a child. The law applies to employers who have more than 20 employees. The employee must have been employed by the employer for 12 consecutive months immediately preceding the request, on at least a half-time basis.

The length of the leave may not exceed six weeks, unless otherwise agreed to by the employer, and must begin at a time requested by the employee. The employer may adopt reasonable policies governing the timing of requests for unpaid leave. The length of leave may be reduced by any period of paid parental or disability leave, but not accrued sick leave, provided by the employer so that the total leave does not exceed six weeks unless otherwise agreed by the employer. The employer may provide additional parental leave benefits.

The employer must not retaliate against an employee for requesting or obtaining a leave of absence, and must continue to make group insurance or health care coverage available to the employee during the leave. The employer is not required to pay the cost of the insurance or health care coverage while the employee is on leave of absence.

An employee returning from a leave of absence is entitled to return to employment in the former position or in a position of comparable duties, number of hours, and pay. Certain exceptions apply to situations where the employer experiences a layoff that would have affected the employee and to collective bargaining situations.

Upon return to work, the employee is entitled to the rate of pay the employee was receiving at the time of the leave, plus any automatic adjustments in the employee's pay scale that occurred during the leave period. The employee retains all accrued preleave benefits of employment and seniority.

An employee who is injured by a violation of this law may sue for damages and to recover attorneys fees, and may seek an injunction or other equitable relief from the courts.

Employers or employees with questions about the interaction of federal and state parenting or family leave laws should seek professional advice.

Sick Child Leave (Minnesota Law). Employers with more than 20 employees must allow employees to use personal sick leave benefits for absences due to illness or injury of their children, for reasonable periods of time, on the same terms as the employees are able to use sick leave benefits for their own illness. The child must be under age 18 or under age 20 if he or she is attending secondary school. To qualify for sick child leave, an employee must have worked for the employer for 12 consecutive months immediately preceding the request on at least a half-time basis. Salary continuation and disability payments are not included in determining benefits available for sick child leave. This section applies only to sick leave benefits paid from the employer's general assets, and (presumably) does not apply to sick leave benefits paid by a third-party insurer.

School Leave

Employers with one or more employees must grant leave of up to 16 hours during the school year to enable a parent to attend a child's school conferences or school-related activities and day care or kindergarten activities if those conferences or activities cannot be scheduled during nonwork hours. Employees are eligible for school leave if they work on at least a half-time basis. Employees need not be paid for school leave, but they may use accrued paid vacation leave or other appropriate leave for this purpose. Where the need for school leave is foreseeable, the employee must give the employer reasonable prior notice and must make a reasonable effort to schedule the leave so as not to unduly disrupt operations.

Bone Marrow Donations

Employers with 20 or more employees must grant paid leaves of absence of up to 40 work hours to an employee who seeks to undergo a medical procedure to donate bone marrow. The employer may not retaliate against the employee for requesting or obtaining the leave. The employer may require a doctor's statement verifying the purpose and length of the leave. If there is a medical determination that the employee does not qualify as a bone marrow donor, paid leave granted prior to the medical determination is not forfeited. There is no requirement that the employee be employed by the employer for a certain period of time before becoming eligible for the leave.

Military Leave

Employers must allow regular employees who are members of the Military Reserve or National Guard or Civil Air Patrol unpaid time off for military duty and training. The employee generally must be reinstated to a position of like seniority, status and pay following discharge or release from active duty.

Jury Service

Under Minnesota law an employer cannot deprive an employee of employment, or threaten or coerce an employee with respect to his or her employment, because the employee is called for, or responds to, a summons for jury service. An employer who violates the statute may be found guilty of criminal contempt and fined up to $700 or imprisoned up to six months or both.

If the employer discharges an employee because he or she is called for or responds to a summons for jury service, the employee may bring a civil action for recovery of lost wages and reinstatement. The civil action must be brought within 30 days of the discharge. Recoverable damages cannot exceed lost wages for six weeks. An employee who prevails in the civil action may be allowed reasonable attorney fees. Minnesota law does not require an employer to pay the employee during the period of jury service unless salaried.

Election Judge

An employee must be given paid time off to serve as an election judge. The employee must give 20 days written notice. The employer may reduce the pay by the amount paid to the election judge by the appointing authority. The paid time off requirement applies to all state elections unless otherwise provided by law.

Time Off to Vote

Employers must allow their employees who are eligible to vote at a regularly scheduled state primary or general election; an election to fill a vacancy in the office of United States senator or United States representative; and a presidential primary election to be absent from work for the purpose of voting during the morning of election day, without penalty or deduction from salary or wages because of the absence.

Political Convention Leave

An employee who is a member of the state central committee or executive committee of a major political party, or who is a delegate to a political convention, is entitled to an unpaid leave to attend a meeting of the committee or attend the convention. Employees must provide ten day's written notice to the employer.

EMPLOYEE TESTING AND BACKGROUND CHECKS

PRE-EMPLOYMENT TESTING

A Minnesota employer may require an applicant to take a pre-employment test (other than a physical exam or alcohol or drug test) so long as the test is not given for the purpose of discriminating against any member of any protected class. (Protected classes are discussed in the section of this Guide on Human Rights.)

The test must measure only essential job related abilities and must be required of all applicants for the same position, regardless of disability (except for tests authorized under the workers' compensation law). The test must accurately measure the applicant's aptitude, achievement level or other relevant factors and it may not reflect the applicant's impaired sensory, manual or speaking skills except when those skills are what are being legitimately tested.

Employers who employ at least 15 employees during each of 20 or more calendar weeks in the current or preceding calendar year also must comply with the federal Equal Employment Opportunity Commission (EEOC) guidelines for pre-employment tests. Under those guidelines, an employer may be required to prove that its test has no adverse impact on any member of any protected group. Employers who must comply with the EEOC guidelines are advised to seek the advice of counsel.

An employer conducting a pre-employment test should be able to demonstrate that the test truly measures essential job-related abilities. If a facially neutral test or other business practice has a statistically significant, disparate impact within a protected class, such as sex or race, an employer may need to show the practice is job related and, if so, that no comparable, effective practice exists which has a significantly lesser adverse impact. Unless the test is obviously job-related, such as a typing test for an applicant for a typing job, the employer may want to consult an expert to be sure the requirements of the law are met.

PRE-EMPLOYMENT PHYSICAL EXAMINATIONS

A Minnesota employer at their own cost, may require an applicant, as a condition of hire, to submit to a pre-employment physical examination, which may include a medical history, if the applicant has first received an offer of employment contingent only upon passing the physical exam; the exam tests only for essential job-related abilities; and the exam is required of all persons conditionally offered employment for the same position, regardless of disability (except for exams authorized under the workers' compensation law).

An employer may not refuse to employ an applicant due to physical inability to perform the job unless the applicant is unable to perform the essential requirements of the job. If it appears, pursuant to competent medical advice, that the applicant may not be able to perform the essential duties of the job, certain employers have an obligation to "reasonably accommodate" the applicant, unless the employer can demonstrate that the accommodation would impose undue hardship on the company. Reasonable accommodation means taking steps to accommodate the known physical or mental limitations of a qualified disabled person. The reasonable accommodation requirement applies to those employers with 15 or more employees. See the section of this Guide entitled "Issues for Employers – Human Rights."

EMPLOYEE DRUG TESTING

By statute, an employer may not require an employee or job applicant to undergo drug testing unless testing is done pursuant to a written drug testing policy that meets statutory criteria, and testing is conducted by an approved laboratory. The statute applies to both alcohol and drug testing.

An employer may not discipline, discharge, discriminate against or require rehabilitation of an employee on the basis of a positive test unless the test is verified by a confirmatory test. An employee or job applicant who is damaged by violation of the statute may bring a civil action against the employer or laboratory. An action for an injunction or equitable relief such as reinstatement with back pay also may be brought, and attorneys fees may be awarded.

Employers with at least one employee required to hold a commercial driver's license are urged to seek the advice of counsel regarding the potential applicability of federal regulations requiring drug testing.

POLYGRAPH TESTING

State and federal laws prohibit employers from using the results of a polygraph or lie detector test to take adverse employment action against an employee or prospective employee. The federal law requires employers to inform employees of their rights under the law by posting a notice available from the U.S. Department of Labor. The Minnesota law is enforced by the Department of Labor and Industry, and the federal law is enforced by the U.S. Department of Labor. In addition to enforcement actions brought by the government agencies, an employee who is injured by a violation of the law may bring a private civil action against the employer.

GENETIC TESTING

State law prohibits an employer or employment agency from, as a condition of employment, directly or indirectly administering a genetic test or requesting or requiring protected genetic information; that law also prohibits an employer or employment agency from affecting the terms or conditions of employment, or terminating the employment of any person, based on protected genetic information. Likewise, the state law provides that no person shall provide or interpret for any employer or employment agency protected genetic information on a current or prospective employee. Any person aggrieved by a violation of this law may bring a civil action and the court may award up to three times the actual damage suffered due to the violation, plus punitive damages, reasonable costs, attorneys' fees and injunctive or other equitable relief.

USE OF CONSUMER REPORTS FOR EMPLOYMENT PURPOSES

Employers who wish to obtain a consumer report for employment purposes should be aware of notice and consent requirements on employers who seek to obtain credit reports for use in connection with the hiring or promotion process. (A consumer report is a report prepared by a consumer reporting agency bearing on a person's credit worthiness, credit standing, credit capacity, character, general reputation, personal character or mode of living that is used in connection with employment, or eligibility for credit or insurance). Prior to obtaining a report, an employer must fulfill notice and consent requirements. First, the employer must provide notices to the applicant, in "clear and conspicuous" language contained in a separate written disclosure form that discusses only the notice, that a report may be obtained for employment purposes. Second, the employer must obtain the applicant's written authorization to obtain the report. Third, the employer must certify to the reporting service that it has properly notified the applicant; that a copy of the report and summary of consumer rights will be provided to the applicant if any adverse action is taken based on the report; and that information from the report will not be used in violation of any applicable Federal or State equal employment opportunity law or regulation. Finally, before taking any adverse action based on information in the report, the employer must provide the applicant with a copy of the report and a summary of consumer rights. (Editor's note: Employers who obtain credit reports for job applicants, whether potential or current employees, should develop disclosure and consent documents. The Federal Trade Commission, which implements and enforces the Federal Fair Credit and Reporting Act for most industries, has issued sample notices which are available at http://www.ftc.gov. See also 15 U.S.C. 1681b).

TESTING RECORD KEEPING

The federal Age Discrimination in Employment Act requires retention for one year from date of personnel action of the results of employment and physical testing or examinations. Federal regulations on testing for the use of alcohol or controlled substances impose various record keeping requirements of from one to five years. Each year a comprehensive update of federal record retention requirements is published in the *Federal Register.* A business or government reference librarian can direct employers to the latest compilation.

BACKGROUND CHECKS

When hiring persons to perform certain jobs, employers are required by statute to perform a background check. For example, employers hiring security guards are required to check their backgrounds with the Minnesota Board of Criminal Apprehension; employers hiring certain counselors are required to check their references for evidence of sexual contact with patients or former patients. Also, other Minnesota laws require rental property owners to request background information from the Minnesota Bureau of Criminal Apprehension before hiring property managers. Likewise, employees, contractors and volunteers of a home health care provider or hospice are subject to background checks.

Employers in other instances may be interested in preforming background check of potential employees. Those employers are strongly urged to seek the advice of counsel before performing those background checks. That is for many reasons, including but not limited to avoid any claims of discriminatory use of background checks and to ensure compliance with the Americans with Disabilities Act, the Minnesota Human Rights Act, the Fair Credit Reporting Act and the Minnesota Access to Consumer Reports law.

EMPLOYMENT OF MINORS

Minnesota employers generally are covered by the Minnesota Child Labor Standards Act. Federal child labor laws apply if the employer is under the jurisdiction of the federal Fair Labor Standards Act and the federal act would provide more protection or set a higher standard. Information on federal child labor laws may be obtained from the United States Department of Labor.[1] Information on state child labor laws may be obtained from the Minnesota Department of Labor and Industry. Addresses and telephone numbers for both are listed in the Resource Directory section of this Guide.

FEDERAL CHILD LABOR STANDARDS

The child labor provisions of the federal act are designed to protect the educational opportunities of minors and prohibit their employment in jobs and under conditions detrimental to their health or well-being. The provisions include lists of hazardous occupation orders for both farm and nonfarm jobs declared by the Secretary of Labor as being too dangerous for minors to perform.

Regulations governing youth employment in nonfarm jobs differ somewhat from those pertaining to agricultural employment. In nonfarm work, the permissible kinds and hours of work, by age, are:

- 18 years or older: any job, whether hazardous or not, for unlimited hours.
- 16 and 17 years old: any nonhazardous job, for unlimited hours. (However, the State requirements do not allow 16 and 17 year olds to work after 11 p.m. on the night before a school day, or before 5 a.m. on a school day, subject to some exceptions.)
- 14 and 15 years old: outside of school hours in various nonmanufacturing, nonmining, nonhazardous jobs, under these conditions: no more than three hours on a school day, 18 hours in a school week, eight hours on a nonschool day or 40 hours in a nonschool week. Also, work may not begin before 7 a.m. nor end after 7 p.m., except from June 1 through Labor Day, when evening hours are extended to 9 p.m.
- Under a special provision 14 and 15-year-olds enrolled in an approved Work Experience and Career Exploration Program (WECEP) may be employed for up to 23 hours in school weeks and three hours on school days (including during school hours).
- 14 is the minimum age for most nonfarm work. However, at any age, youths may deliver newspapers, perform in radio, television, movie or theatrical productions, work for parents in their solely owned nonfarm business (except in manufacturing or on hazardous jobs), gather evergreens and make evergreen wreaths.

Hazardous occupations which are not permitted for any minor under age 18 are: working with explosives and radioactive materials; operating certain power-driven woodworking, metalworking, bakery, meat processing, and paper products machinery; operating various

[1] The U.S. Department of Labor has issued various Regulations on the Federal Child Labor Laws. These can be found in various Chapters in 29 CFR (including Chapters 570, 575 and 579).

types of power-driven saws and guillotine shears; operating most power-driven hoisting apparatus such as non-automatic elevators, fork lifts, and cranes; most jobs in slaughtering and meat packing establishments; most jobs in excavation, logging and sawmilling; roofing, wrecking, demolition, and shipbreaking; operating motor vehicles or working as outside helpers on motor vehicles; and most jobs in the manufacturing of bricks, tiles, and similar products. Note that in November 1999, the Department of Labor issued Proposed Regulations (which as of November 2001 have not yet been finalized) that, if adopted, would, among other things, impose new rules regarding the types of cooking activities fourteen and fifteen year olds could legally engage in. Exemptions from some of the Department of Labor's hazardous occupation orders apply for apprentices and students in vocational education programs.

In addition to the above-listed hazardous occupations for minors aged 18 and under, minors who are 14 and 15 years old may not work in the following jobs: manufacturing, mining, most processing work, and all occupations declared hazardous by the Secretary of Labor; operating or tending most power-driven machinery; public messenger service; and work connected with warehousing, storage, transportation, communications, public utilities, and construction (except office and sales jobs when not performed on transportation vehicles or on construction sites).

The Child Labor provisions do not apply to children under 16 years of age employed by their parents in occupations other than manufacturing or mining or occupations declared hazardous by the Secretary of Labor. However, this exception only applies when the parent is the sole employer of the minor.

Although an employer is not required by federal law to obtain an age certificate or work permit in order to hire minors, Minnesota law does require an employer to have proof of age of any employee or applicant who is a minor. Employers may, however protect themselves from unintentional violations of the child labor laws by keeping on file an age certificate or work permit for each minor employed. Employers who are found to have violated the federal child labor laws may be fined up to $10,000 for each violation.

MINNESOTA CHILD LABOR STANDARDS

Under the Minnesota Child Labor Standards Act, a minor under 14 may not be employed, except:

- If at least 11 years old, as a newspaper carrier.
- If at least 12 years old, in agricultural operations with parents' or guardian's permission.
- As an actor or model with approval from the Minnesota Department of Labor and Industry.

A minor under 16 may not work:

- Before 7 a.m. or after 9 p.m. except as a newspaper carrier.
- More than 40 hours a week or eight hours in a 24-hour period except in an agricultural operation.
- On school days during school hours, unless an Employment Certificate is issued by the appropriate school officials and kept on file by the employer.

Sixteen and 17 year old high school students may not work:

- After 11 p.m. on evenings before school days (11:30 p.m. with written permission of a parent or guardian) or
- Before 5 a.m. on school days (4:30 a.m. with written permission of a parent or guardian).

A minor may not be employed in an occupation found by the Commissioner of Labor and Industry to be particularly hazardous or detrimental to the well being of minors. The list of occupations is extensive. Some of the types of occupations that are prohibited for minors include those where the minor may be exposed to hazardous substances; those involving power-driven machinery and equipment; those which involve operation of amusement rides; jobs in processing plants, and jobs in establishments where intoxicating liquors are served. Questions concerning whether a particular occupation is prohibited for minors should be directed to the Labor Standards Unit of the Department of Labor and Industry at the address and telephone number provided in the Resource Directory section of this Guide.

The following are exceptions to the general rule prohibiting employment of minors in hazardous occupations:

- A minor may be employed at tasks away from or outside of the area of hazardous operation, equipment or materials.
- The law does not apply to a minor employed to do home chores or to babysit or to a minor employed by his or her parents. Home chore work is that which is usual to the home of the employer. Work performed in connection with or as part of the business, trade, or profession of the employer is not a home chore. Home chores are all those variable tasks normal to the running of a household and include but are not limited to mowing lawns, raking leaves, removing snow, light housekeeping, washing clothes or dishes, vacuuming, yard cleaning and food preparation.
- The prohibitions do not apply to a minor training in a state-approved apprenticeship program or a program approved by the Division of Vocational Technical Education, Minnesota Department of Children, Families & Learning.
- The prohibitions do not apply to 17-year-old high school graduates.
- The prohibitions do not apply if the corporation the minor works for is totally owned by, and its daily business is supervised by, one or both parents. If the minor's parent is a member of the family farm corporation where the minor works, the prohibitions also do not apply.

Every employer in Minnesota is required to have proof of age of any employee or applicant who is a minor. (Minnesota Statutes § 181A.06.) This must be secured from the minor in the form of an age certificate, a copy of the minor's birth certificate, a copy of the minor's drivers license, or a United Stated Department of Justice Immigration and Naturalization Service Employment Eligibility Verification Form I-9.

The Commissioner of the Department of Labor and Industry may impose a fine of up to $5000 for each child labor law violation. Misdemeanor and gross misdemeanor charges also may be brought.

PROTECTION OF EMPLOYEES WHO REPORT VIOLATIONS OF LAW

"WHISTLEBLOWERS"

A Minnesota employer cannot discharge, discipline, threaten, otherwise discriminate against, or penalize an employee regarding the employee's compensation, terms, conditions, location, or privileges of employment because:

- The employee, or a person acting on behalf of an employee, in good faith, reports a violation or suspected violation of any federal or state law or rule adopted pursuant to law to an employer or to any government body or law enforcement official;
- The employee is requested by a public body or office to participate in an investigation, hearing or inquiry; or
- The employee refuses an employer's order to perform an action that the employee has an objective basis in fact to believe violates any state or federal law or rule or regulation adopted pursuant to law, and the employee informs the employer that the order is being refused for that reason.

An employee whose employment is involuntarily terminated may, within five working days following termination, request in writing that the employer provide the reason for the termination. The employer must provide the truthful reason for the termination in writing within five working days following receipt of the request. If the employee was terminated for "whistleblowing" activities, and the employer fails to provide the written reason for termination within the time period specified by law, the employer may be subject to a civil penalty of $25 per day per injured employee, up to a maximum of $750 per injured employee. Communication of the statement furnished by the employer cannot be the subject of a defamation action by the employee against the employer.

The identity of an employee making a report or providing information must be kept confidential by the public official or law enforcement officer unless the employee consents to identification or the investigator determines that disclosure is necessary for prosecution. If disclosure is necessary for prosecution, the employee must be informed prior to the disclosure. The law does not permit an employee to make statements or disclosures knowing they are false or that they are in reckless disregard of the truth. The law also does not permit disclosures that would violate federal or state law or diminish or impair the rights of any person to the continued protection of confidentiality of communications provided by common law.

Employers must notify employees of their rights by posting a summary of the law. A summary is included on the minimum wage poster available from the Minnesota Department of Labor and Industry.

OTHER STATUTORY PROTECTIONS

In addition to the protections of the "whistleblower" law discussed above, other Minnesota laws prohibit employers from discriminating, retaliating, or taking adverse action against employees for exercising their legal rights. Some of these laws include the Minnesota Human Rights Act, the federal Age Discrimination in Employment Act, the Americans with Disabilities Act, the state and federal Fair Labor Standards Acts, the Occupational Safety and Health Act, Workers' Compensation laws, the Employee Retirement Income Security Act, and the Minnesota Parenting Leave law. Employers also may not take adverse employment action against employees whose wages are subject to garnishment, employees who are required to report child abuse and who do so, employees who participate in a strike, employees who are called to jury duty or who are summoned to court, and employees who request access to their personnel files as permitted by state law.

HUMAN RIGHTS

FEDERAL LAWS PROHIBITING DISCRIMINATION

Under Title VII of the U.S. Civil Rights Act of 1964, it is unlawful for any employer of 15 or more employees to refuse to hire, to discharge, or to treat employees differently in any way because of their race, color, religion, sex or national origin. Employers may not limit, segregate, or classify employees in any manner so as to deprive them of employment opportunities or adversely affect a worker's employment status because of race, color, religion, sex or national origin. Note that the U.S. Supreme Court, the U.S. EEOC and many lower courts have in the past few years issued a number of decisions (and in the EEOC's case, guidance) on sexual harassment. Anyone with questions about this topic is strongly advised to seek the advice of counsel.

The Age Discrimination in Employment Act (ADEA) protects persons age 40 or older from discrimination by employers of 20 or more employees. Under that law, employers also must provide the same level of health care benefits to persons over the age of 65 as offered to younger employees. Note that the EEOC has issued guidance on, and many courts have decided cases involving, the type of waivers of claims under the ADEA that employers may lawfully obtain from their employees.

Minnesota law protects persons age 18 or older from age discrimination in employment.

The Rehabilitation Act of 1973 prohibits discrimination because of physical or mental disability and applies to any employer who receives federal financial assistance or is a federal contractor. This law is enforced by the Office of Civil Rights, in the U.S. Department of Health and Human Services, Chicago, Illinois and the U.S. Department of Labor. Any employer with a federal contract of $2,500 or more must comply with an affirmative requirement to employ disabled persons. Alleged violations of this part of the Act are handled by the U.S. Office of Federal Contract Compliance.

The Americans With Disabilities Act prohibits discrimination on the basis of disability. The employment provisions of this Act are substantially similar to those in the Rehabilitation Act of

1973. The employment provisions of the Act apply to employers of 15 or more employees. To assist businesses in making structural modifications necessary to make their facilities accessible to disabled persons, both the Internal Revenue Code and Minnesota Statutes allow some or all of these expenses to be deducted in computing income tax.

The "Uniformed Services Employment and Reemployment Rights Act of 1994", prohibits employers from discriminating with respect to the employment, promotion or employee benefits of persons who serve, or apply to serve, in the uniformed services. As that Act is written in broad terms, employers are urged to seek the advice of counsel in this area.

STATE LAW PROHIBITING DISCRIMINATION

The Minnesota law prohibiting illegal discrimination (including reprisals against persons who sought relief against discrimination) is the Minnesota Human Rights Act, Minnesota Statutes Chapter 363. Generally, it has wider application than the federal anti-discrimination laws. It applies to all employers in the state who have one or more employees, as well as to employment agencies, labor organizations and temporary help agencies.

The state law makes it an unfair employment practice, except when based on a limited, statutory exception or a *bona fide* occupational qualification, for an employer to refuse to hire, to discharge, or otherwise to treat a person differently with respect to hire, tenure, compensation, terms, upgrading, conditions, facilities or privileges of employment, because of race, color, creed, religion, national origin, sex, marital status, status with regard to public assistance, disability, age, or sexual orientation; or in reprisal for objecting to, or participating in the investigation or litigation of, alleged discrimination or for associating with a disabled person or persons of a different race, color, creed, religion, sexual orientation or national origin. Employers may not use these protected characteristics as a factor in making any employment decision. In rare instances, certain jobs may require persons to be chosen on the basis of one of these characteristics, but there is a strict burden of proof on the employer to show that the discrimination was demanded by the job in that all or virtually all persons excluded on the basis of the protected characteristic could not perform the job or that some other compelling business reason exists that justifies the action.

Before hiring, an employer may not require or request from applicants, or from any source, information which pertains to a protected characteristic, including on an application form or in an interview. An employer may, however, seek information to determine whether a person can safely and efficiently perform the duties of the position at issue. This may include requiring or requesting a physical examination, if the requirements of the law are met (see the section of this Guide on pre-employment testing). In general, employers also may, with the consent of the employee, after employment has commenced, obtain additional medical information to assess continuing ability to perform the job or to assess employee health insurance eligibility; for purposes mandated by law; for purposes of assessing the need to reasonably accommodate an employee; or pursuant to the state drug testing law; or other legitimate business reasons not otherwise prohibited by law. With limited exceptions, medical documentation must be collected and maintained on separate forms and kept confidential.

Under the state law, businesses with 15 or more full-time or part-time employees must provide reasonable accommodation for their employees' and job applicants' known disabilities, unless the business can demonstrate that the accommodation would impose an undue hardship on the business. This requirement is similar to that required by the federal Americans with Disabilities Act. "Reasonable accommodation" under the state law generally means making facilities readily accessible to the disabled person, or initiating practices like job restructuring, work schedule modifications, reassignment to a vacant position, acquisition or modification of equipment or devices, or providing aides on a temporary or periodic basis. "Undue hardship" is determined by evaluating a number of factors, including the size of the business, the type of operation, work force size and composition, the nature and cost of the needed accommodation, the employer's ability to finance the accommodation, and good faith efforts to explore less restrictive or less expensive alternatives with the employee and individuals or organizations knowledgeable about the needs of disabled persons.

The state law provides that whenever health care records or medical information adversely influence any hiring, firing or promotional decision about an applicant or employee, the employer must notify that person of that fact within 10 days of the final decision. There is no requirement in the state law that the employee must first request the information from the employer.

The Act also makes it a discriminatory practice for an employer not to treat women who are pregnant, or who have pregnancy-related disabilities, the same as other persons who are not so affected, but who are similar in their ability or inability to work. An employer's duty to make reasonable accommodation, as discussed above, also applies to women disabled by pregnancy, childbirth or related disabilities.

The Human Rights Act prohibits a business from refusing to do business with a woman based on her use of her current or former surname; and a business may not intentionally refuse to do business with or contract with, or discriminate in the basic terms of the contract because of a person's race, national origin, color, sex, sexual orientation or disability, unless it is for a legitimate business purpose.

Businesses are also prohibited from discriminating in the extension of personal or commercial credit, because of race, color, creed, religion, disability, national origin, sex, sexual orientation, marital status, or receipt of public assistance, including medical or rental assistance.

Another Minnesota law (Minnesota Statutes section 181.938) prohibits an employer from retaliating against an employee or prospective employee who engages in the lawful use of food, alcoholic beverages, or tobacco during non-working hours. Exceptions apply for *bona fide* occupational requirements or to avoid a conflict of interest, and in certain other circumstances.

Valid, voluntary or required affirmative action programs are not prohibited by the Human Rights Act. Obtaining otherwise prohibited information from applicants is allowed for affirmative action purposes, but it must be kept separate and apart from other job application information and not be provided to or considered by any person involved in the selection of an employee, except when an effort is being made to make a hiring decision from among candidates in an underutilized protected group, pursuant to a bona fide affirmative action plan.

The Human Rights Act prohibits advertisements for employment that state a preference for applicants based on any of the protected characteristics, such as race, color, creed, religion, sex, age, sexual orientation, or marital status. Employers should avoid using terms which convey a preference for persons of a particular age or gender, e.g., "girl friday," or "maintenance man."

As a place of public accommodation, a business is prohibited from discriminating against the public on the basis of race, color, creed, religion, disability, national origin, marital status, sexual orientation, or sex. Thus, a business must make reasonable accommodation, including removal of physical barriers and modification of policies, for a person with a disability, unless such access would pose a direct threat. A properly identified service animal, accompanying a person with a disability, must be allowed in a public place, provided the animal is properly leashed.

CHARGES OF DISCRIMINATION

An employee or applicant who feels discriminated against because of his or her age, race, sex, religion or other protected characteristic may file a charge with the Minnesota Department of Human Rights within one year of the occurrence of the discriminatory practice. The Department, after determining jurisdiction and accepting a charge for filing, will gather facts relevant to the charge and weigh the evidence provided by both sides. While parties to a charge may be represented by legal counsel, every effort is made to keep the procedure simple enough so that neither side will necessarily have to retain an attorney. Both sides are encouraged to settle the matter at any time in the process. In Minnesota, aggrieved parties may bypass the Human Rights Department and go directly to state district court to bring suit against the employer.

If the evidence does not support the charge, the Department will issue a "no probable cause" finding on the merits of the charge. Note also that whether or not the Department concludes that the evidence supports the charging party's allegations, the Department has the discretion to "dismiss" charges for a variety of non-substantive reasons, such as not warranting the resources of that Department or a failure of the charging party to submit a rebuttal to the responding party's answer to the change. Note that both a finding of "no probable cause" and a "dismissal" may be appealed (although there are different time periods for each appeal). Note again that a charging party, no matter what the Department concludes, may file a private lawsuit in district court. If the charge of discrimination is supported by the evidence, action is taken to stop the discriminatory act or practice and relief is sought for the person who was discriminated against. If relief is not obtained through this conciliation, the Department or the charging party may take the matter to court or to a public hearing.

Relief in employment discrimination cases may include the hiring, reinstatement, or upgrading of a person; up to three times back pay, including compensation for fringe benefits and interest accrued; and adoption of policies or participation in a training program. Relief could also include other compensatory damages, punitive damages, and damages for mental anguish. Violators of the law also may be assessed a civil penalty payable to the state. A person who violates the laws regarding public accommodations and discrimination on the basis of a disability is guilty of a misdemeanor.

Minnesota Rules 5000.2250 requires that an employer charged with discrimination must retain all charge-related documents, under its control, until the Department informs the employer that the charge has been resolved. All job applicant and employment records must be retained by an employer for at least one year after they are made, whether or not a charge has been filed.

In addition, a number of federal statutes govern the retention of records regarding employees' charges of discrimination, including disability discrimination, improper termination, or violation of civil rights. These impose retention requirements of from one year to final disposition of charges, whichever is later. Each year a comprehensive update of federal record keeping requirements is published in the *Federal Register.* A business or government reference librarian can direct employers to the latest compilation.

GUIDELINES FOR PREVENTING DISCRIMINATION IN HIRING

When interviewing prospective job applicants, the employer should only ask questions which reasonably relate to the job in question. The burden of proof is on the employer to demonstrate that questions are not used to discriminate. Asking an applicant to supply information that is not job-related or that might reveal an applicant's protected status could lead to charges of discrimination. Inquiries that may improperly request protected status information include those about age, date of birth, marital status (including identity or situation of spouse), sexual orientation, sex, race, creed, color, religion, national origin, and disabilities.

The employer may ask questions that help assess the applicant's ability to do the job, and which are asked of all applicants for the job. Inquiries that elicit information about the applicant's education, experience, abilities, licenses and certifications that are job related generally are permissible, as are inquiries about willingness to travel, salary expectations, references, and the applicant's interest in the job. It generally is permissible to talk about job duties and responsibilities, the business itself, career growth potential, and opportunities for advancement, so long as these topics are relevant to the job and are presented consistently to applicants, regardless of their individual status within a protected class.

An employer may not use prohibited information obtained from any source for the purpose of making a hiring or job decision. Employers should examine job restrictions to ensure that they are not based on assumptions or stereotypes that are unrelated to job performance. Employers with questions in this area may contact the Minnesota Department of Human Rights at the address and telephone number provided in the Resource Directory section of this Guide.

AMERICANS WITH DISABILITIES ACT (ADA)

The ADA is a complex piece of federal legislation that has three components. Title I prohibits job discrimination against qualified disabled individuals. Title II applies the laws on both hiring and access to local, state, and federal government agencies and public transportation. Title III regulates public accommodation and access in existing, new and remodeled public buildings, such as restaurants, hotels, convention centers and theaters. (Note that in July 1999, Proposed Regulations were issued applying the ADA to recreational facilities. As of the time this Guide went to press, there had been no further developments on these Proposed Regulations).

The ADA is applicable to employers who have 15 or more employees. While the ADA is concerned with several types of discrimination against disabled persons, employers will be primarily concerned about discrimination in the workplace.

Basically, the ADA prohibits employment discrimination against a qualified individual with a disability who is qualified to perform the "essential" activities of the job. This prohibition applies to job application procedures, hiring, job advancement, termination, (note that in 2001, two U.S. Courts of Appeal found that, like Title VII, under the ADA a disabled person has a cause of action for asserting harassment in the workplace) compensation, job training, and any other condition of employment. More specifically, the ADA contains several basic requirements: the law states that persons with disabilities should not be disqualified from consideration because of an inability to perform nonessential or marginal functions of the job; any selection criteria that could tend to screen out or eliminate people with disabilities must be job related and consistent with business needs; and employers are required to provide individuals with a reasonable accommodation to enable them to meet legitimate job criteria.

An individual has a disability for purposes of the ADA if he or she has a physical or mental impairment that substantially limits a major life activity; has a record of such an impairment; or is regarded as having such an impairment. Note that the U.S. Supreme Court has recently spoken as to whether a person meets the ADA's definition of the term "disability" if there are measures (such as eyeglasses or medications) that mitigate the effects of a person's impairment. In those cases, *Sutton v. United Air Lines, Inc.* (527 U.S. 471 1999), and *Murphy v. United Parcel Service, Inc.* (527 U.S. 516 1999), the Court ruled that such mitigating measures may be taken into account in determining whether a person is disabled within the meaning of the ADA. In other words, for ADA purposes a person's impairment must be considered in its corrected state, taking into account the effect of measures such as eyeglasses or prosthetic limbs.

Moreover, the Court has held any correction a person's own body makes must also be taken into account. The Court, in considering the disability claim of a person who was blind in one eye but whose body has developed subconscious mechanisms for compensating for that blindness, wrote, "[w]e see no principled basis for distinguishing between measures undertaken with artificial aids, like medications and devices, and measures undertaken, whether consciously or not, with the body's own systems." (See *Albertsons, Inc. v. Kirkingburg,* (527 U.S. 555 1999).

Finally, note also that the U.S. Supreme Court has issued a decision in a case involving simultaneous claims for disability benefits under Social Security laws and a claim alleging disability discrimination under the ADA. (That plaintiff was simultaneously claiming that she could not work,and should be treated as "disabled" for Social Security purposes, yet was also able to perform the essential functions of her job, a required element of an ADA claim.) The Court found that there was no presumption that making a claim under the Social Security benefit system precludes making an ADA claim. See *Cleveland v. Policy Management Systems Corp.* (526 U.S. 795 (1999).

A qualified individual with a disability is a disabled person who, with or without reasonable accommodation, can perform the essential functions of the job that he or she holds or desires.

Essential functions are tasks that are fundamental to the position, not marginal or incidental. Consideration is given to the employer's judgement as to what job functions are essential and a business necessity.

The term reasonable accommodation means modifications or adjustments to a job application process that enables qualified applicants with a disability to be considered for the position he or she desires; modifications or adjustments to the work environment, or to the manner or circumstances under which the position held or desired is customarily performed, that enable a qualified individual with a disability to perform the essential functions of that position; or modifications or adjustments that enable a covered employer's employee with a disability to enjoy benefits and privileges of employment equal to those enjoyed by other similarly situated employees without disabilities. Reasonable accommodation may include such things as job restructuring, a leave of absence, modifying work schedules or equipment. Note that in March, 1999, the EEOC issued a lengthy Enforcement Guidance on reasonable accommodations and undue hardship under the ADA. Because of the length and scope of that Enforcement Guidance, and its potential for controversy (as some persons believe that it contradicts judicial opinions), anyone with questions on this topic is strongly urged to seek the advice of counsel.

Employers do not have to make accommodations if doing so would impose an undue hardship on the employer. Undue hardship is generally defined as an action requiring significant difficulty or expense to accomplish. The factors to be considered in making the undue hardship determination include the nature and cost of the accommodation, the overall financial resources of the employer; the overall size of the business and the nature of its operations and the impact of the accommodation upon the operation of the facility.

The prohibition against discrimination also includes medical examinations and inquiries.

The Equal Employment Opportunity Commission administers and enforces ADA's employment aspects. Material that explains the federal regulations, compliance and enforcement is available from the EEOC Office of Communications and Legislative Affairs at the address listed in the Resource Directory section of this Guide.

Of particular use to small businesses are the guidelines on the kinds of questions which can be asked of applicants before an offer is made. Those guidelines appear in "ADA Enforcement Guidance: Preemployment Disability-Related Questions and Medical Examinations," published after section 902 of the "EEOC Compliance Manual, Vol. II."

It is also highly recommended that employers consult with persons familiar with this area when making individual determinations.

AFFIRMATIVE ACTION REQUIREMENTS FOR GOVERNMENT CONTRACTORS

Businesses that contract with the government may be subject to affirmative action requirements. Federal, state and local laws each have different criteria to determine if a business must comply with their respective affirmative action or equal employment opportunity requirements.

Under Executive Order 11246 ("Non-Discrimination in Employment by Government Contractors and Subcontractors"), as amended, and its implementing Regulations issued on November 13, 2000, by the U.S. Department of Labor's Office of Federal Contract compliance Programs (OFCCP), a business with 50 or more employees that has a non-construction contract (or subcontract) with the federal government of $50,000 or more, or a business receiving in excess of $10,000 for a federally assisted construction project, must develop an affirmative action plan. Note that those Regulations, according to the OFCCP, refocus compliance emphasis from the development of a written affirmative action plan to the implementation of such a plan into the overall management of the contracting or subcontracting business. Note also that those

Regulations place greater emphasis on (and give OFCCP greater/monitoring powers over) whether such businesses are discriminating with respect to employee pay. Compliance with the Executive Order is monitored by the Office of Federal Contract Compliance Programs.

Under Minnesota Statutes § 363.073, a business that either bids on or submits a proposal for a contract or agreement, executes any contract or agreement or receives construction or non-construction contracts with the State of Minnesota in excess of $100,000 and that employed over 40 full-time employees within Minnesota on a single working day during the past 12 months is required to have an affirmative action plan for the employment of minority persons, women and persons with disabilities. The plan must be approved by the Commissioner of Human Rights, who then issues a Certificate of Compliance. Before bidding on such a contract, a business must submit to the Minnesota Department of Human Rights an affirmative action plan. Likewise before such a contract can be executed, a business must have a Certificate of Compliance. The Department of Human Rights is responsible for enforcing compliance with this statute.

The cities of Minneapolis and St. Paul have city ordinances which require compliance with their specific affirmative action requirements. The Minneapolis Department of Civil Rights and the St. Paul Department of Human Rights are the agencies which enforce the respective city ordinances. Other cities or counties in Minnesota also may have affirmative action or equal employment opportunity requirements for businesses who contract with them. The entity awarding the contract should be able to inform the business of its affirmative action requirements.

IMMIGRATION LAW COMPLIANCE

The federal Immigration and Nationality Act (18 U.S.C § 1324a) requires employers to verify that all persons they hire are legally authorized to work in the United States. The law also prohibits employers from knowingly hiring or continuing to employ persons not authorized to work in the United States as well as knowingly contracting for work by someone not authorized to work in the United States. The law applies to all employers, regardless of the number of employees they have, and to all individuals hired after November 6, 1986. Note that merely because a person holds a visa authorizing entrance into the United States, that person does not necessarily have authorization to be employed in the United States. It is the employer's responsibility to determine whether a person has that authorization to work in the United States.

Employment verification is documented on Form I-9, available from the United States Immigration and Naturalization Service. The law requires the employer to ensure that every employee completes Section 1 of Form I-9 at the time the employee begins work. The law also requires the employer, within three days of hire, to review the documents establishing the employee's identity and eligibility to work and to properly complete Section 2 of Form I-9. The documents that satisfy the verification requirements are listed on Form I-9.

A self employed person who is a sole proprietor need not complete a Form I-9 on himself or herself. If, however, the business owner is an employee of the business entity (i.e., an employee of a corporation), a Form I-9 is required.

Employers must keep the verification forms on file for three years from the date of hire or for one year following the employee's separation from service, whichever is later. The forms may be inspected by the Immigration and Naturalization Service and the United States Department of Labor, and the Office of Special Counsel for Immigration Related Unfair Employment Practices.

Sanctions for failure to comply with the law include warnings, cease and desist orders, and civil penalties ranging from $100 to $10,000 per violation. Total fines may exceed these amounts. Criminal penalties may be imposed for a pattern and practice of violations.

The Immigration Reform and Control Act (IRCA) and Title VII of the Civil Rights Act of 1964 prohibit employment discrimination. Employers with four or more employees may not discriminate in the hiring, firing, or recruitment or referral for a fee of employees on the basis of the employee's national origin or citizenship status. In practice, this means that employers must treat all employees the same when completing Form I-9. Employers cannot set different employment eligibility verification standards or require that different documents be presented by different groups of employees. Employees can choose which documents they want to present from the lists of acceptable documents. An employer cannot request that an employee present more or different documents than are required or refuse to honor documents which on their face reasonably appear to be genuine and to relate to the person presenting them. An employer also cannot refuse to accept a document or refuse to hire an individual, because a document has a future expiration date. Penalties may be imposed upon violators. To minimize charges of discrimination, employers are encouraged to make hiring decisions irrespective of the national origin or citizenship status of applicants authorized to work in the United States. Questions like "What is your national origin?" and "Are you a United States citizen?" may be considered discriminatory. It is permissible, however, to ask whether an applicant is legally authorized to work in this country.

Detailed information on the requirements of the law is provided on Form M-274, "Handbook for Employers with Instructions for Completing Form I-9." This material may be obtained from the Immigration and Naturalization Service at the address and telephone number provided in the Resource Directory section of this Guide.

OCCUPATIONAL SAFETY AND HEALTH

GENERAL INFORMATION

The Occupational Safety and Health Division of the Minnesota Department of Labor and Industry administers the Minnesota Occupational Safety and Health Act. The express legislative purpose of this Act is "to assure so far as possible every working man and woman in the State of Minnesota safe and healthful working conditions and to preserve our human resources."

The Minnesota Occupational Safety and Health Rules and Regulations adopt by reference the federal Occupational Safety and Health Standards. In addition, Minnesota has adopted some localized standards that apply to hazards not covered by the federal OSHA standards. Minnesota OSHA standards apply to all places of employment in the state with the exception of those under the exclusive jurisdiction of the federal government.

All places of employment are subject to inspection to ascertain compliance with published Minnesota Occupational Safety and Health Rules and Regulations. Inspections are scheduled following the guidelines of an administrative inspection scheduling plan approved by the federal Occupational Safety and Health Administration and in accordance with established priorities. Those priorities are: (1) imminent danger conditions; (2) catastrophes/fatalities/ serious injuries; (3) employee complaints; (4) target industry inspections; and (5) follow-up inspections. If violations are found, a citation will be issued specifying abatement dates for all violations. A monetary penalty may also be assessed. Criminal penalties including imprisonment and fines also may be assessed for knowing or willful violations.

EMPLOYER RIGHTS AND RESPONSIBILITIES

An employer's rights and responsibilities under the Act include, but are not limited to, the following:

- An employer must furnish to employees conditions of employment that are free from recognized hazards that are causing or are likely to cause death or serious injury.
- Employers are entitled to participate in the development, revision or revocation of OSHA standards by commenting on proposed standards, participating in hearings concerning standards, or by requesting the development of a new standard.
- An employer may request a variance from the requirements of a particular OSHA standard if the employer is unable to meet the mandates of that standard and wishes to use alternative means of compliance.
- Employers are entitled to protection of trade secrets or other legally privileged communications.
- Employers must post the "Safety and Health Protection on the Job" poster in their places of employment. Posters may be obtained from the Department of Labor and Industry at the address and telephone number provided in the Resource Directory section of this Guide or downloaded from that Department's website, www.doli.state.mn.us.
- Employers must provide to their employees all necessary protective equipment required by OSHA standards at no cost to the employee.
- An employer who receives a citation and/or proposed monetary penalty following an OSHA inspection may contest the citation or penalty by submitting a Notice of Contest to the Commissioner of the Department of Labor and Industry.
- Employers may obtain technical assistance from OSHA by writing or calling any of the area offices listed in the Resource Directory section of this Guide or by accessing the Minnesota Department of Labor and Industry or federal OSHA on the internet.

RECORDKEEPING

Employers must maintain a log of injuries and illnesses as prescribed in the Minnesota OSHA rules and must post an annual summary of those injuries. The OSHA 200 Form, which is used for this purpose, includes information and instructions for completing the form and is available from the OSHA office of the Department of Labor and Industry. This injury and illness information must also be made available to an OSHA investigator should an inspection be conducted at the place of employment.

In addition, the Occupational Safety and Health Act imposes record retention requirements on documents relating to employee exposure to toxic substances. These documents include the above noted OSHA Form 200, records of medical examinations, records of exposure monitoring, records of injury from or adverse reaction to toxic substances and other records. The Act provides for retention of such records for periods of from five to thirty years. Each year a comprehensive update of federal record retention requirements is published in the *Federal Register.* A business or government reference librarian can direct employers to the latest compilation.

REPORTING WORK-RELATED FATALITIES

Employers must report work-related fatalities that result in the death of at least one employee, or incidents that result in the in-patient hospitalization of at least three employees, to Minnesota OSHA within eight hours after the death or hospitalization. Such a report must be made orally, in person or by telephone, to one of the area offices listed in the Resource Directory section of this Guide. After normal business hours, the report can be made by telephoning (800) 321-OSHA.

WORKPLACE SAFETY PLAN

Employers in certain industries must develop and implement a written workplace accident and injury reduction program to promote safe and healthful working conditions. Industries where a plan is required are identified by the Commissioner of Labor and Industry by Standard Industrial Classification, based on the industry segment's Bureau of Labor Statistics' injury and illness record. The list is updated every two years and is published in Minnesota Rules section 5208.1500.

An employer who is in a designated industry must develop its written plan within six months following the date the standard industrial classification (SIC) for the industry is placed on the list. The program must have clearly stated goals and objectives, and must describe responsibility for implementing the program; management participation; methods used to identify, analyze, and control new or existing hazards, conditions and operations; communication of the plan to affected employees; investigation of workplace accidents and corrective action; and enforcement of safe work practices. The employer must conduct and document a review of the workplace accident and injury reduction program at least annually and document how procedures described in the program are met.

EMPLOYEE RIGHTS AND RESPONSIBILITIES

Although the primary responsibility for compliance with the law rests with the employer, employees are obliged to comply with OSHA standards and regulations which are applicable to their own actions and conduct. Employees cannot be cited or fined for noncompliance;

employers must set up their own disciplinary procedures for employees who violate standards or regulations. Employee rights include, but are not limited to, the following:

- Employees have the right to request an OSHA inspection by filing a written complaint with the Minnesota Occupational Safety and Health Division describing the hazardous conditions that exist at the work facility. The complaint must be filed by a current employee or an authorized employee representative and must be signed. A complainant's name is not revealed nor is it part of any inspection record made available for review.
- Employees may participate in standards development activities.
- Employees must be notified of a variance request filed by their employer; employees may petition for a hearing on the variance request.
- Employee representatives may participate in the opening conference, walk-around inspection and closing conference conducted as part of an OSHA inspection; employees who exercise this right must be paid their usual wage.
- Employees may not be discriminated against because they exercised any right afforded them under the Minnesota OSHA Act. In addition, note that when an employee sues, alleging discrimination or discharge due to his or her assertion of rights under that Act, any communication between that employee and attorneys representing the Minnesota Department of Labor and Industry is, per Minnesota Statutes section 182.669, subdivision 1, "privileged as would be communications between an attorney and a client."

EMPLOYEE RIGHT-TO-KNOW ACT

The Minnesota Employee Right-to-Know Act is intended to ensure that employees are aware of the dangers associated with hazardous substances, harmful physical agents, or infectious agents that they may be exposed to in their workplaces. The Act requires employers to evaluate their workplaces for the presence of hazardous substances, harmful physical agents, and infectious agents and to provide training to employees concerning those substances or agents to which employees may be exposed. Written information on hazardous substances, harmful physical agents or infectious agents must be readily accessible to employees or their representatives. Labeling requirements for containers of hazardous substances and equipment or work areas that generate harmful physical agents are also included.

The Employee Right-to-Know Act applies to all Minnesota employers regardless of size. Special provisions apply to certain technically qualified individuals as defined in the standard, farming operations, and waste service employers regulated by the federal Resource Conservation and Recovery Act.

Employers should conduct an inventory of their workplaces to determine what hazardous substances, harmful physical agents or infectious agents are present and which employees are at risk of exposure. Once the survey is completed, the employer must obtain, and have accessible to employees, written information on those substances or agents. This written information on hazardous substances is usually in the form of a material safety data sheet (MSDS) which can be obtained from the manufacturer of the substance. Material safety data sheets will provide the basic information that must be presented in the oral training program.

The Employee Right-to-Know Standard is being enforced as part of the Minnesota Occupational Safety and Health program. The standard provides guidelines concerning the type of information that must be included in the written training program, how often training must be provided, requirements for documentation and maintenance of training records, and labeling of hazardous substance containers and equipment that generates a harmful physical agent or infectious agents. The standard also includes lists of hazardous substances, harmful physical agents and infectious agents to assist employers in evaluating their workplaces. A copy of the Employee Right-to-Know Standard may be obtained by contacting the Minnesota Bookstore at the address and telephone number provided in the Resource Directory section of this Guide or through the agency's website at www.doli.state.mn.us. Questions concerning the Employee Right-to-Know Act may be directed to one of the Occupational Safety and Health Division offices, also listed in the Resource Directory section of this Guide.

WORKPLACE SAFETY CONSULTATION

The Department of Labor and Industry's Workplace Safety Consultation (WSC) unit offers a number of programs, including a grant program, to employers to identify potential hazards at their work sites and improve their safety management systems. For more information on these topics, see www.doli.state.mn.us/wsc.html.

Safety Consultation

WSC offers free, confidential assistance, on request, to help employers improve their safety and health record, lower the cost of accidents and reduce OSHA-issue citations and penalties. This program targets small, high-hazard businesses. No citations or penalties are issued as a result of using these services, although any problems identified by a WSC consultant that are not corrected by the employer can be reported to MN OSHA Compliance staff for further investigation.

WSC consultants will help employers recognize hazards, make recommendations for solving problems and suggest other sources of help that may be available. In order to receive these services, the employer must commit to the timely correction of any serious safety or health hazard that may be found during the site visit by WSC consultants. Once an employer makes that commitment, the WCS consultant conducts a site visit and issues a report containing recommendations.

Minnesota Safety and Health Achievement Recognition Program (MNSHARP)

MNSHARP is a voluntary, consultation-based program that assists small, high-hazard employers in achieving safety and health improvements and recognizes them for doing so. Eligibility is limited to employers with up to 500 workers at the work site; priority is given to employers with fewer than 100 employees. Participating employers receive a comprehensive safety and health consultation survey that results in a one-year action plan. During that year, participating employers must correct identified hazards and develop and implement an effective safety and health program; all employees must participate in these efforts. When the participating employer has met the requirements of the preceding sentence, and its lost-workday injury and illness rate falls below the national average for their industry, that employer is awarded with a MNSHARP Certificate of Recognition and for the next year that employer is exempted from programmed inspections from MNOSHA. Participating employers can enjoy renewed Certificates, as well as a continuance of their exemption from those programmed exemptions, if an on-site safety and health survey by WSC confirms that the employer is continuing to meet the requirements of MSHARP.

MNSTAR Program

This program is a voluntary one, available to any employer in Minnesota, including small employers who previously successfully participated in MNSHARP. MNSTAR relies mainly on self-assessment by the employer, using the federal Voluntary Protection Program (see OSHA Instruction TED 8.1A, *Revised Voluntary Protection Programs (VPP) Policies and Procedures Manual*). Participating in MNSTAR requires the employer to commit to completing an extensive application, which will include providing WSC with copies of all the written policies and programs of the employer that WSC requests. In addition, the employer's lost workday injury and illness rate must be below state and national levels for its industry.

Labor-Management Safety and Health Committees

All employers with at least twenty-five employees are required to have a safety and health committee comprised of representatives from labor and management. Also, any other employer is likewise required to have such a committee if: that employer has a lost workday cases incidence rate in the top ten percent of all rates for employers in the same industry; or the workers' compensation premium classification assigned to the greatest portion of the payroll for that employer has a pure premium rate, as reported by the workers' compensation rating association, in the top 25 percent of premium rates for all classes. If both the labor and management representatives request it, WSC is available to help interpret OSHA standards, offer training in self-inspection techniques, and prepare and assist in the preparation and implementation of educational and training programs.

Loggers Safety Education Program

This program provides safety training through eight-hour seminars offered throughout the state. Attendance at these seminars is one of the requirements for a logging employer to receive workers' compensation premium rebates from the Targeted Industry Fund.

Safety and Health Education Outreach Program

WSC offers workshops to help educate employers and employees about workplace safety and health hazards and the OSHA standards that address them. The goal of these workshops is to lower injury and illness rates, and reduce workplace injury costs, by helping employers implement and maintain effective safety and health programs.

WSC, in partnership with thirteen organizations throughout the state, offers a series of one-day safety and health seminars. Specific topics change each calendar quarter. In addition, upon request WSC will offer safety and health training to individual companies or organizations, by means of either an informal training session accompanied by an on-site consultation, or a formal training session.

Safety Grants Program

The Safety Grant program awards up to $10,000 to qualifying employers for the cost of projects designed to reduce the risk of injury and illness to their employees. To qualify, an employer must be under MNOSHA's jurisdiction; a qualified safety professional must have conducted an on-site safety inspection and issued a written report with recommendations based on that inspection; the project must be consistent with the recommendations of that inspection, it must reduce the risk of injury or disease, and it must be feasible; the employer must be committed to the project's implementation, including an ability to provide funds to match the awarded grant amount, as well as be able to cover all estimated project costs by available funds, and; the project must comply with all federal, state and local laws and regulations. Priority for funds is given first to manufacturing businesses, then to workplaces that have had jobs lost due to safety issues, and then, finally, to all other projects.

WORKPLACE VIOLENCE PROTECTION

Due to the degree to which workplace violence occurs, and is increasing, employers must affirmatively ensure that their own employees are free from job related violence, not only to create a safe working environment for their employees but also to reduce the likelihood of costly litigation and/or compliance settlements arising out of workplace violence issues.

While there is currently no standard that regulates violence in the workplace, OSHA's "general duty clause" (a clause designed to cover hazards where no specific standard exists) is available to place an affirmative duty upon employers to investigate and evaluate workplace hazards, and to develop and implement preventive programs to curb violence and protect employees. The general duty clause could serve as the basis for a MNOSHA citation related to workplace violence. In addition, federal OSHA has developed guidelines concerning job-related violence in late-night retail establishments, health care and social service industries, and for taxi drivers.

WSC helps employers and employees reduce the incidence of violence in workplaces by providing on-site consultation, telephone assistance, education and training seminars, and a resource center. These efforts are targeted towards workplaces at high risk of violence, such as convenience stores, service stations, taxi and transit operations, restaurants and bars, motels, guard services, patient care facilities, schools, social service industries, residential care facilities and correctional institutions.

WHAT IS WORKERS' COMPENSATION?

Workers' compensation insurance provides compensation to employees who have a work-related injury or disease. Compensation includes partial wage replacement and full payment of medical and vocational rehabilitation costs. In case of death, workers' compensation benefits are paid to the employee's dependents. Workers' compensation insurance companies and self-insured employers pay these benefits and collect the premiums. The Minnesota workers' compensation law was designed to standardize benefits, reduce litigation, and encourage early rehabilitation intervention, good employee/employer relationships and return-to-work programs.

WHO IS REQUIRED TO HAVE WORKERS' COMPENSATION?

Generally all employers are required to have workers' compensation insurance and display the name of their insurer in a conspicuous place on a poster provided by the Department of Labor and Industry. If, however, all of the employees/workers of a small business are owners or spouses, or parents or children of the owner, the business may be exempt from coverage. A farm operation is required to carry workers' compensation if it has employees. A family farm operation is exempt from coverage if it paid less than $8,000 in total wages in the previous calendar year or less than the statewide average yearly wage in total salaries (approximately $33,366) and carries a farm liability policy covering farm laborers with $300,000 in liability coverage and $5,000 in medical coverage.

Employers who do not obtain the required insurance face serious consequences including penalties of up to $1,000 per employee per week and an order prohibiting the employer from employing any person. In addition, the employer of any nonresidential construction, repair, or remodeling project that fails to provide workers' compensation coverage for employees may be sued for damages by any losing bidder on the project. The losing bidder may be entitled to recover the amount of profit the winning contractor expected to make on the project, as well as costs and attorney fees.

WHO IS COVERED UNDER WORKERS' COMPENSATION?

Employees of profit-making organizations, such as corporations, partnerships and individual proprietorships; of charitable organizations; and of state, county and local governmental agencies are covered by workers' compensation insurance.

WHAT INJURIES AND DISEASES ARE COVERED?

Workers' compensation insurance covers injuries and diseases that arise out of and in the course and scope of the employment. A work-related injury or disease is generally a physical condition that is caused, aggravated, precipitated or accelerated by the work or the work environment. Covered injuries can occur at the work place or outside the work place if the employee is on an assignment or is in transit between different work sites.

EMPLOYEES WHO ARE INJURED OUT OF STATE

Employees who are hired in Minnesota by a Minnesota employer or generally work here and also work out of state are covered by the Minnesota workers' compensation law. If a worker is employed in another state but is injured on the job in Minnesota, he or she can choose to be covered by the Minnesota workers' compensation law or by the law in his or her resident state.

WHAT TO DO WHEN AN EMPLOYEE IS INJURED

When an employee is injured, it is the employer's responsibility – not the employee's – to complete a First Report of Injury form. The employer must give the employee the "Minnesota Workers' Compensation System Employee Information Sheet" at the time the employee is given a copy of the First Report of Injury Form. This form must be sent to the employer's workers' compensation insurance company so that it is received no later than 10 days after knowledge of the injury. The insurance company in turn must send the report to the Department of Labor and Industry so that it is received no later than 14 days after the injury if the injured worker is disabled more than three days. If the report is not filed within these deadlines, the employer or insurance company can be fined by the department. Self-insured employers have 14 days in which to file the report with the department.

It is important that the report is filed promptly so the insurance company will have adequate time to investigate the claim. If the work-related injury is serious or results in a fatality, the Department of Labor and Industry must be notified by telephone within 48 hours. The First Report of Injury form also must be filed.

Completing a First Report of Injury form does not mean that the employer accepts liability for the injury. The insurance company will pay on the claim only after it has been investigated and determined that it is most likely compensable.

RETURNING AN EMPLOYEE TO WORK

Employers are strongly encouraged to bring their injured workers back to work as soon as they can. In cases of serious injuries, this might mean reasonably accommodating employees as they improve or modifying jobs they had before they were injured. Employers are encouraged to establish disability management programs to plan for these cases. The employer's workers' compensation insurer can assist in establishing such a program.

If the employee requests it or if the employee remains (or is expected to remain) off work more than 90 days and a valid request for waiver of rehabilitation services is not filed by the employer/insurer, the employee is entitled to receive a vocational rehabilitation consultation to determine whether the employee is qualified to receive vocational services. A rehabilitation consultation is provided at the request of the employer, the insurer, the employee, or the

Department of Labor and Industry and must be conducted by a qualified rehabilitation consultant registered with the Department.

It is important to coordinate these return-to-work programs with the employee's union, if there is one, to see that a return-to-work program does not conflict with seniority provisions in union contracts.

For employers of more than fifteen full-time employees, Minnesota law provides a civil penalty for an employer's refusal without reasonable cause to offer continued employment to an employee when continued employment is available within the employee's physical limitations. That penalty is one year's wages for the employee, up to $15,000.

MAKING A SUITABLE JOB OFFER

A suitable job offer is the offer of a job that is within the injured employee's medical restrictions and that returns the employee as close as possible to the economic status he or she enjoyed before the injury. Economic status includes not only wages, but also opportunities for promotion and advancement. Employee fringe benefits also may be considered in determining economic status. For example, if the employee had a minor injury, the only appropriate suitable job would be his or her old job or one similar to it. Any job, even a job with another employer, can qualify as a suitable job if it meets the tests of medical appropriateness and economic status, and takes into account the employee's former employment age, education, previous work history, interests and skills.

DISPUTE RESOLUTION

The majority of workers' compensation claims are administered without disputes arising.

The Minnesota Department of Labor and Industry "must make efforts to settle problems of employees and employers by contacting third parties, including attorneys, insurers, and health care providers, on behalf of employers and employees and using the department's persuasion to settle issues quickly and cooperatively." (Minnesota Statute § 176.261).

For this purpose, the Department has workers' compensation specialists and attorneys available to the public either by telephone or on a walk-in basis. The addresses and telephone numbers for both the St. Paul and Duluth offices can be found in the Resource Directory section of this Guide.

If informal methods are unable to resolve the problem, the Department and the Office of Administrative Hearings offer administrative conferences and mediation sessions.

The Department offers administrative conferences to try to resolve medical and rehabilitation benefit issues. The judges at the Office of Administrative Hearings conduct conferences to determine if the workers' compensation insurers are to be granted their request to discontinue disability benefits to an injured worker. The holder of an administrative conference will attempt to help the parties reach acceptable resolutions of the issues, but if this is not possible, the Department will issue a decision and order, which is appealable.

Administrative conferences are designed to be fast, informal proceedings to resolve workers' compensation disputes. Attorneys may represent the parties but are not mandatory.

Mediation sessions are also used as a method to expedite the handling of disputed workers' compensation claims. The Department will conduct a mediation session at the request of the parties. All parties must be agreeable to the mediation. Unlike other types of dispute resolution proceedings, the presiding official does not issue a decision. The mediator assists the parties in their efforts to work towards solutions and makes sure the agreements are in conformity with the workers' compensation laws. If the parties are successful in reaching resolutions, the mediator will prepare the mediation award and arrange for it to be properly signed, awarded, served and filed. As with administrative conferences, attorneys may represent the parties, but are not mandatory.

Other dispute resolution services offered at the Office of Administrative Hearings are settlement conferences, small claims court, special terms hearings, attorney fees and cost hearings, and formal hearings on workers' compensation issues. Some decisions are appealable to the Worker's Compensation Court of Appeals and the Minnesota Supreme Court.

REDUCING WORKERS' COMPENSATION COSTS

Workers' compensation insurance rates are set within broad limitations by the insurance company. Rates are adjusted by payroll risk classifications and by the employer's experience rating, which is the history of injuries in the business.

It is difficult to control the payroll risk classification because it is determined by the nature of the business and the type of work employees do. However, there are a number of ways to control the cost of workers' compensation premiums for the future. Employers who have accident prevention programs generally will have lower workers' compensation costs. The employer can take an active role in lowering workers' compensation costs by:

- Developing wellness programs that incorporate physical fitness and health education.
- Providing employee education on proper lifting techniques and appropriate body mechanics.
- Initiating return-to-work policies that include reasonable accommodation.
- Contacting Workplace Safety Consultation at the Department of Labor and Industry, which provides a free, nonenforcement service to assist small private-sector employers in high hazard industries in their voluntary efforts to improve workplace safety and health. The Workplace Safety Consultation Division can be reached at the address and telephone number provided in the Resource Directory section of this Guide.

Under state law, all high hazard employers and those with more than 25 employees must establish a joint labor-management safety committee to address workers' compensation and workplace safety issues.

The employer's insurance company or agent can provide more information about accident prevention, safety and health programs and return-to-work programs.

BUYING WORKERS' COMPENSATION INSURANCE

There are several thousand licensed insurance agents who sell workers' compensation insurance in Minnesota. It is best to contact several agents to review the business and to quote prices for the insurance. In Minnesota, workers' compensation insurance is sold through open competition, which means insurance companies establish rates and compete for business. All workers' compensation policies provide coverage mandated by law; therefore, only the price and quality of service varies, and shopping for insurance can save money. Other factors to consider in choosing a carrier are claims servicing, safety counseling, and the carrier's reputation.

Options other than insurance may be available to cover an employer's workers' compensation liability. For example, some large employers or groups of employers are approved by the Department of Commerce to self-insure, which allows them to directly manage their workers' compensation claims and contain their costs. Many large employers who are approved to self-insure their risk hire a claims administration company.

Occasionally, an employer is unable to obtain workers' compensation insurance on the open market because the business is too small to justify the expense of selling and servicing the account or because of the nature of the risk involved in the business. In this case, the employer would buy the insurance through the Assigned Risk Pool. Additional information about this type of plan can be obtained from an insurance agent.

SEMINARS ON WORKERS' COMPENSATION

The Minnesota Department of Labor and Industry provides speakers and sponsors seminars and programs for employers on controlling workers' compensation costs. Information about workers' compensation seminars may be obtained from the Department of Labor and Industry at the address and telephone number provided in the Resource Directory section of this Guide, or at its website, www.doli.state.mn.us.

FURTHER INFORMATION

Additional information on workers' compensation may be obtained by calling the Workers' Compensation Division at the address and telephone numbers provided in the Resource Directory section of this Guide.

EMPLOYEE BENEFITS*

Employers commonly provide some form of health care, life insurance and retirement benefits for their employees. Although employers are not required to provide these plans, if the plans are provided they must comply with federal and state laws.

FEDERAL EMPLOYEE RETIREMENT INCOME SECURITY ACT

At the federal level, the Employee Retirement Income Security Act (ERISA), 29 United States Code §§ 1001-1461, governs pension plans and medical, surgical, sickness, disability and death benefit plans sponsored by employers who are engaged in interstate commerce or in other activities affecting interstate commerce. ERISA establishes standards governing information to be provided participants, eligibility for participation, benefit rights and benefit accrual, vesting, employer and employee contributions, payment of benefits, plan termination and mergers, and survivor benefits. Federal agencies charged with enforcing ERISA include the Department of Labor, the Treasury Department, the Internal Revenue Service, and the Pension Benefit Guaranty Fund. Information on ERISA may be obtained from the Department of Labor's Office of Pension, Welfare, and Benefit Programs at the address and telephone number provided in the Resource Directory section of this Guide.

ERISA is an extremely complex and technical law. Historically it has been amended frequently by Congress, and been the subject of a great deal of litigation. Failure to conform to its requirements can create civil liability for the employer, and can cause the employer to lose a tax deduction for amounts contributed to the benefit plan. For these reasons, employers who are contemplating benefit plans covered by ERISA should obtain the advice of experts in this field before setting up the plan.

MINNESOTA REQUIREMENTS FOR GROUP HEALTH AND LIFE INSURANCE

Minnesota employers who offer group health insurance, health maintenance (HMO) coverage, or group life insurance must comply with Minnesota statutes and regulations of the Minnesota Department of Commerce concerning those products. In addition, HMO coverage is also regulated by Minnesota statutes and regulations of the Minnesota Department of Health. This is the case regardless of whether the employer is also covered by ERISA, although in some situations ERISA may preempt state law.

The state statutes and regulations establish minimum standards and requirements in areas like filing and obtaining approval of policy forms and certificates, minimum coverage requirements, content requirements for insurance certificates, limitations on cancellation and conversion procedures on termination of employment.

* A comprehensive discussion of employment issues is provided in the publication, *An Employer's Guide to Employee Benefits*, available without charge from the Minnesota Small Business Assistance Office, 500 Metro Square, 121 7th Place East, St. Paul, MN 55101-2146 or on its website at www.dted.state.mn.us.

As with ERISA, the state requirements governing these plans are technical and complex. Expert advice should be sought before establishing any of these plans.

Insurance is regulated in Minnesota by the Minnesota Department of Commerce and, in the case of HMO coverage, by the Minnesota Department of Health. The departments can be contacted at the address and telephone number provided in the Resource Directory section of this Guide.

RECORD KEEPING

Both federal and state laws impose record keeping requirements on documents relating to employee benefit plans. These include plan descriptions, participants' elections, worksheets and other documents. Retention periods range from six years to duration of the plan plus one year. Each year a comprehensive update of federal record retention requirements is published in the *Federal Register.* A business or government reference librarian can direct employers to the latest compilation.

COBRA NOTIFICATION

Health Insurance

The federal Consolidated Omnibus Budget Reconciliation Act of 1985 (COBRA) requires employers who sponsor group health plans to offer covered individuals the right to elect continuation of the group coverage under certain circumstances. Minnesota law imposes additional requirements on employers whose health plans are funded through insurance contracts.

Employers who offer these types of benefits must provide employees (and, if covered, their spouses and dependents) with notice of their continuation rights when an event occurs that would otherwise cause a loss of coverage. The covered individual may elect to obtain for a limited period of time continuation of the coverage they had before the event. The individual may be required to pay up to 102 percent of the cost of the premium for their coverage.

COBRA requirements are complex. Firms that offer group health insurance to their employees should consult with legal counsel to assure that their notice procedures conform to federal and state law.

Life Insurance

There is no right under federal law to continue employer-provided life insurance coverage after employment terminates. Under Minnesota law, however, group term life insurance policies issued within the state must permit covered employees who are voluntarily or involuntarily terminated, incur a reduction in hours to the point where they are no longer eligible for coverage, or are laid off, to elect continuation of the coverage for themselves and their dependents. Coverage ends after 18 months or on the date on which coverage is obtained under another group policy, whichever occurs first. As with health insurance continuation coverage, the employee can be required to pay the cost of the life insurance continuation.

HIPAA NOTIFICATION

Employer group health plans are also subject to the Health Insurance Portability and Accountability Act of 1996 (HIPAA). HIPAA prohibits certain forms of discrimination based on health status and grants certain health plan enrollment rights to employees. The main purpose of HIPAA, however, is to ensure that workers who change jobs will not lose health insurance coverage due to exclusions for pre-existing conditions. Under HIPAA, group health plans may not exclude coverage for pre-existing conditions for longer than 12 months (18 months for late enrollees). In addition, any exclusion period is reduced by an employee's period of coverage under a prior employer's group health plan. To implement these requirements, group health plans must provide "certificates of creditable coverage" to employees who lose coverage, and accept such certificates from other plans.

Insurance companies will often take responsibility for complying with HIPAA's notice and administrative requirements, but employers with insured plans should verify that their insurer is complying with HIPAA. Employers that maintain self-funded health plans are on their own, and should seek assistance from legal counsel to develop the appropriate notices and forms (or contract with a third party administrator for HIPAA compliance services). HIPAA also made changes to COBRA and cafeteria plans, and employers should review related forms and plan documents with the assistance of legal counsel.

PLANT CLOSINGS

FEDERAL LAW

The federal Worker Adjustment and Retraining Notification Act (WARN) applies to employers of 100 or more full time employees. Employers with fewer employees are encouraged to comply with the spirit of the law, although they are not bound by it.

The federal law requires employers to provide 60 days' notice to several entities before ordering a plant closing or massive layoff. These entities include affected employees or their collective bargaining representative, the state dislocated worker unit (in Minnesota, the Department of Trade and Economic Development and its Rapid Response Team, listed in the Resource Directory section of this Guide), and the chief elected official of the unit of local government in which the business is located. If the firm is situated in more than one locality, notice must be given to the local governmental unit to which the employer pays the highest taxes.

Employers who violate the law may be liable to employees for back pay and benefits for which they would have been eligible under an employee benefit plan. An employer who fails to notify the local governmental unit of the plant closing may be liable for a civil penalty of up to $500 per day of violation.

MINNESOTA LAW

Minnesota law requires all employers who must provide notice under WARN to notify the Department of Trade and Economic Development (specifically, its Rapid Response Team) of the names, addresses and occupations of the employees whose jobs will be terminated. The law encourages, but does not mandate, businesses that are considering a plant closing, substantial layoff or relocation of operations outside Minnesota to give early notice of that decision to the Department of Trade and Economic Development, the employees of the affected establishment, any collective bargaining agent representing the employees, and the local government unit in which the establishment is located. This notice is in addition to any notice required by WARN.

The law directs the Department of Trade and Economic Development to establish a program to help employers, employees and the community to respond quickly to the plant closing or layoff by providing information and technical assistance for dislocated workers. The law also provides information and technical assistance on accessing public and private services and programs for dislocated workers and establishes a grant program for examining the feasibility of alternatives to the plant closing. The dislocated worker programs are funded by a special payroll assessment that is paid with unemployment compensation taxes.

BANKRUPTCY NOTIFICATION

Under Minnesota law, an employer must notify employees and job applicants that it has filed a petition for bankruptcy or has had an involuntary bankruptcy petition filed against it. Failure to provide the required notice is a misdemeanor.

POSTER REQUIREMENTS

A number of federal and state statutes require that employers post certain notices in places on the company's premises where employees are likely to see them. Examples of these locations include bulletin boards, entrances and time clocks and other conspicuous places. Where a company has more than one work site, posters must be placed at each site. Poster requirements are listed below. Posters are available from the agencies listed, at the address and telephone number provided in the Resource Directory section of this Guide.

FEDERAL POSTER REQUIREMENTS

Fair Labor Standards

The U.S. Department of Labor requires employers to display posters on the federal minimum wage, overtime and child labor laws, and the Family and Medical Leave Act. Employees also must be notified of their rights under the Polygraph Protection Act of 1988. The Walsh-Healy Federal Contracts Act, the Davis Bacon and Related Acts, and the McNamara-O'Hara Service Contract Act require contractors to provide certain notices to employees working on government contracts. Posters and information are available from the U.S. Department of Labor, Wage and Hour Division.

Equal Employment Opportunity

Information on federal requirements including equal employment opportunity, age discrimination, federal contract compliance, and compliance with the Rehabilitation Act of 1973 may be obtained from the federal Equal Employment Opportunity Commission.

STATE POSTER REQUIREMENTS

Fair Labor Standards, Occupational Safety and Health, and Workers' Compensation

The State of Minnesota requires employers to display posters on the state minimum wage law, including the provision for an employee's right to the reason for termination, and on the state mandatory retirement law. The state also requires employers to display posters on the Occupational Safety and Health law and on workers' compensation rights of employees. All required posters including the unemployment compensation poster described below are available from the Department of Labor and Industry. The worker's compensation poster is available in many languages, including Spanish, Lao, Vietnamese, Cambodian, Hmong and English and can be downloaded from that Department's website, www.doli.state.mn.us

Unemployment Compensation

Posters on the state unemployment law may be obtained from the Minnesota Department of Labor and Industry.

CHECKLIST FOR HIRING AN EMPLOYEE

The following information generally outlines federal and state tax and other requirements that apply to the employment relationship. Detailed descriptions of these requirements, and any exceptions and special requirements that may apply, can be found in information bulletins and instruction booklets published by the agency listed. Addresses and telephone numbers appear in the Resource Directory section of this Guide. For specific advice on individual situations consultation with a qualified professional advisor is strongly recommended.

Note that corporations that are wholly-owned by the person who also performs services for that business are generally considered to be employers, and that owner is likewise generally considered to be an employee. Note also, as explained elsewhere in this Guide, persons working in the construction industry may be treated as employees for purposes of workers' compensation unless certain conditions are met.

1. Determine whether the worker is an employee.

Detailed discussion of whether a worker is an employee appears in the section of this Guide titled "Who is an Employee". A worker generally is considered an "employee" if the person who obtains the worker's services has the legal right to control the manner and means of performing the work. A worker may be considered an employee for certain purposes (e.g., payment of FICA taxes) and not for other purposes (e.g., income tax withholding). If a worker is an employee, the requirements described in this checklist will apply whether the person is employed full-time or part-time. Before determining that a worker is not an employee it is advisable to consult with your attorney or with the appropriate agency, e.g., Internal Revenue Service, Minnesota Department of Revenue, Minnesota Department of Economic Security, or the Minnesota Department of Labor and Industry.

The following forms and materials are available to assist in determining whether a worker is an employee.

Income tax withholding, FICA and Federal unemployment taxes:

Form: SS-8, Information for Use in Determining Whether a Worker is an Employee for Federal Employment Taxes and Income Tax Withholding.

Available from: Internal Revenue Service.

Filed with: The IRS Service Center designated on the form.

Minnesota unemployment compensation

Form: MDES-785, Information for Determination of Whether a Worker is an Employee.

Available from: Minnesota Department of Economic Security.

Filed with: Minnesota Department of Economic Security.

Workers' compensation

The Department of Labor and Industry has adopted rules addressing the conditions under which workers will be considered employees or independent contractors for workers' compensation purposes. These rules can be found at Minnesota Rules Chapter 5224. Copies of Minnesota Rules are available at law libraries and many public libraries, and may be purchased from the Minnesota Bookstore.

2. Obtain federal employer identification number.

Form: SS-4, Application for Employer Identification Number. (To obtain a federal employer identification number by telephone, call (toll free) 1-866-816-2065. Have a completed Form SS-4 available **before** making this call).

Available from: Internal Revenue Service.

Filed with: The IRS Service Center designated on the form.

How often: Once, unless business ownership or form of organization changes.

3. **Obtain Minnesota taxpayer identification number.**

Form: ABR, Application for Business Registration. (A Minnesota taxpayer identification number can also be obtained by calling (651) 282-5225 or (800) 657-3605.)

Available from: Minnesota Department of Revenue.

Filed with: Minnesota Department of Revenue.

How often: Once, unless business ownership or form of organization changes.

4. **Obtain Minnesota workers' compensation insurance.**

Form: None required.

Available from: Coverage is obtained through the employer's insurance company.

Filed with: Not applicable.

How often: Workers' compensation coverage is required for the entire time the employer has employees. Certain exemptions may exist. For information on these exemptions, contact your insurance company or the Minnesota Department of Labor and Industry, Workers' Compensation Division.

5. **Obtain Minnesota unemployment compensation employer identification number.**

Form: MDES-13, Report to Determine Liability.

Available from: Minnesota Department of Economic Security.

Filed with: Minnesota Department of Economic Security.

How often: Within 30 days of establishing or acquiring a business in Minnesota.

6. **Verify compliance with immigration law.**

Form: I-9, Employment Eligibility Verification, and Form M-274, Handbook for Employers with Instructions for Completing Form I-9.

Available from: United States Immigration and Naturalization Service.

Filed with: Form I-9 must be retained by the employer for three years following the date of hire or one year after the individual's employment is terminated, whichever is later.

How often: Generally, a new Form I-9 must be completed each time an individual is hired. An employer who rehires a person within three years of the date the I-9 was originally completed may be able to update and re-verify employment eligibility on the original Form I-9. Details are provided in the "M-274 Handbook for Employers" available from the Immigration and Naturalization Service.

7. Obtain employee withholding information (Form W-4; child support and spousal maintenance obligations).

Form W-4.

Form:	W-4, Employee's Withholding Allowance Certificate (used for both federal and Minnesota withholding).
Available from:	Internal Revenue Service.
Filed with:	In most cases, the W-4 is retained in the employer's file. A copy of the Form W-4 must be sent to the Internal Revenue Service and the Minnesota Department of Revenue if the employee claims exemption from withholding and has wages that would normally exceed $200 per week, or claims more than ten withholding allowances, or if the Internal Revenue Service or the Minnesota Department of Revenue notify the employer that the Form W-4 must be filed. In addition, the Minnesota Department of Revenue has indicated that it "requests" a copy of the Form W-4 given by an employee whom the employer "believes" is not entitled to the number of claimed exemptions. If the employee claims fewer allowances for Minnesota purposes than for federal purposes, two separate Form W-4s must be completed. Write "Minnesota Only" across the top of the form showing the Minnesota allowances and "Federal Only" across the top of the form showing federal allowances. An employee cannot claim more allowances for Minnesota purposes than are claimed for federal purposes.
How often:	The Form W-4 generally is valid until the employee provides a new one. However, employees who claim exemption from withholding must renew the exemption annually by filing a new Form W-4 by February 15 each year. Whenever an employee replaces an existing Form W-4 with a new one, the employer must put the new W-4 into effect no later than the start of the first payroll period ending on or after the 30th day after the day on which the replacement Form W-4 is received. If there is no payroll period, the replacement Form W-4 must be put into effect with the first payment of wages on or after the 30th day after the day on which the replacement Form W-4 is received. The replacement Form W-4 can be put into effect sooner, if the employer wishes.

Child Support, Medical Support, Spousal Maintenance.

With respect to the payment of child support, medical support, maintenance and related payments, Minnesota employers are required to report certain information to the Minnesota Department of Human Services on new employees and independent contractors, and on rehires, within fifteen days of hiring the employee or engaging the independent contractor. (This replaces the former requirement that Minnesota employers had to ask individuals who are hired for employment whether they have court-ordered support obligations that are required by law to be withheld from income, and to ask the terms of the court order.)

Employers must provide the Department of Human Services with employee or independent contractor's name, address, social security number, and if available, date of birth, along with the employer's own name, address and federal employer identification number.

In addition to the reporting to the Department of Human Services employers are required to ask all new employees whether they have court-ordered medical support or dependent insurance obligations that must be withheld from income, and the terms of any court order. If amounts for medical support must be withheld, the employer must do the appropriate withholding. If the employee is required to obtain dependent insurance the employer must tell the employee about the application process and enroll the employee and the dependents in the plan.

Note that employers are required to make such withholdings within a specified time period, and there are limits on the percentage of wages that can be withheld.

8. Advance payment of Earned Income Credit tax refund.

The Earned Income Credit (EIC) is a refundable tax credit for certain low-income workers. Workers who maintain a household, have dependent children and who are eligible for the EIC may elect to receive advance payments of the credit by filing Form W-5 with the employer. The amount of the advance EIC paid to the employee is applied against the employer's payroll tax payment. The amount of the advance EIC payment is recorded on the employee's Form W-2 at the end of the year. Note that the "Economic Growth and Tax Relief Reconcilation Act of 2001" made a number of changes to the calculation and availability of this credit.

Moreover, employers must notify employees who do not have income tax withheld that they may be eligible for a tax refund because of the EIC. Copy C (the employee's copy) of the official Form W-2 contains information about the EIC. Employers who use the official Form W-2, or a substitute Form W-2 that contains the exact wording under the heading "Earned Income Credit" on the back of Copy C, will not be required to issue Notice 797, Notice of a Possible Federal Tax Refund Due to the Earned Income Credit. Employers who do not use either the official Form W-2 or a substitute Form W-2 meeting the requirements set forth in the previous sentence are required to issue Notice 797 to their employees. If the employer is required to issue Notice 797 to its employees, the employer must do so within one week before or after the employer provides the employee with his or her Form W-2. Notice 797 is available from the Internal Revenue Service.

Form:	Form W-5, Earned Income Credit Advance Payment Certificate.
Available from:	Internal Revenue Service.
Filed with:	An eligible employee files Form W-5 with the employer.
How often:	Eligible employees must file a new Form W-5 with the employer each calendar year.

9. Welfare-to-Work tax credit.

The Welfare-to-Work (W2W) federal tax credit is available to employers as an incentive to hire long-term recipients of family assistance programs who meet certain eligibility requirements. Note that the W2W credit has recently been extended to December 31, 2001. As of the time this Guide went to press, it was unclear if it would be extended again.

Form:	IRS Form 8850, "Pre-Screening Notice and Certification Request for the Work Opportunity and Welfare-to-Work Tax Credits" **and either** U.S. Department of Labor ETA Form 9062, "Conditional Certification Form", if provided to the job seeker by a participating government agency, **or** U.S. Department of Labor ETA Form 9061 "Individual Characteristics Form", if the job seeker has not been given a conditional certification.
Available from:	IRS Form 8850, from the IRS, or may be downloaded (including the instructions) from www.doleta.gov/employer/wtwweb.htm; ETA Forms 9062 and 9061 are available from the U.S. Department of Labor, or may be downloaded from www.doleta.gov.
Filed with:	The state employment agency Welfare to Work (W2W) coordinator (which also handles the WOTC program, described below), which in Minnesota is Larry Cheetham, Minnesota Department of Economic Security/WorkForce Services Branch, 390 North Robert St., St. Paul, MN 55101.
How often:	One time: complete the IRS Form 8850 by the date the job offer is made, and mail it to the state employment agency W2W coordinator within twenty-one days of the date that the new employee begins work. Mail the ETA 9061 or 9062 to the state employment agency W2W coordinator.

10. Work Opportunity Tax Credit (WOTC)

The WOTC program provides employers with federal tax credits as an incentive to hire members of targeted groups who traditionally have difficulty in finding jobs. The Minnesota Department of Economic Security determines the eligibility of Minnesota residents, and gives certifications to employers, who may then claim the tax credits. Note that the WOTC has recently been extended to December 31, 2001. As of the time this Guide went to press, it was unclear if it would be extended again.

Form:	IRS Form 8850, "Pre-Screening Notice and Certification Request for the Work Opportunity and Welfare-to-Work Tax Credits" **and either** U.S. Department of Labor ETA Form 9062, "Conditional Certification Form", if provided to the job seeker by a participating government agency, **or** U.S. Department of Labor ETA Form 9061 "Individual Characteristics Form", if the job seeker has not been given a conditional certification.
Available from:	IRS Form 8850, from the IRS, or may be downloaded (including the instructions) from www.doleta.gov/employer/wtwweb.htm; ETA Forms 9062 and 9061 are available from the U.S. Department of Labor, or may be downloaded from www.doleta.gov.

Filed with: The state employment agency Work Opportunity Tax Credit (WOTC) coordinator, which in Minnesota is Larry Cheetham, Minnesota Department of Economic Security/WorkForce Services Branch, 390 North Robert St., St. Paul, MN 55101.

How often: One time: complete the IRS Form 8850 by the date the job offer is made, and mail it to the state employment agency WOTC coordinator within twenty-one days of the date that the new employee begins work. Mail the ETA 9061 or 9062 to the state employment agency WOTC coordinator.

11. Withhold federal income tax and FICA tax (employee share).
and
12. Withhold Minnesota income taxes.

Form: No specific form is required. These are accounting entries on the employer's books. The amounts also must be listed on the employee's pay statement. Tables showing amounts to be withheld are provided by the Internal Revenue Service and the Minnesota Department of Revenue. (Note that those withholding tables were revised on July 1, 2001). The taxes are paid through periodic deposits and quarterly tax returns. (See Steps 14 and 16.)

Available from: Not applicable.

Filed with: Accounting records are retained by the employer and are subject to inspection by the Internal Revenue Service and Minnesota Department of Revenue.

How often: Withholding must be done each time wages are paid.

13. Account for employer's share of payroll taxes.

Payroll taxes include the employer's share of the FICA (Social Security and Medicare) tax, federal unemployment tax (FUTA) and Minnesota unemployment tax.

Form: No specific form is required. These are accounting entries made on the employer's books each time wages are paid. The taxes are paid through deposits or with quarterly or annual tax returns. (See Steps 14, 15 and 19.)

Available from: Not applicable.

Filed with: These taxes must be deposited in a bank as specified by, or paid directly to, the Internal Revenue Service and the Minnesota Department of Economic Security. Note that electronic filing of these taxes may be required.

How often: The accounting entries are made each time wages are paid.

14. Deposit withheld federal income tax and employer's and employees' share of FICA tax.
and

15. Deposit federal unemployment (FUTA) tax.

Form: 8109, Federal Tax Deposit Coupon.

Available from: Preprinted deposit coupon payment books (Form 8109) are automatically sent to the employer after the Internal Revenue Service receives the application for an employer identification number. The Internal Revenue Service requires use of the Form 8109 when depositing at a financial institution. Note that EFTPS (Electronic Federal Tax Payment System) may be required (see below).

Filed with: Deposits are made to a financial institution authorized as a federal depository (usually the employer's bank or credit union).

How often: For federal income tax and FICA tax, the accumulated liability usually must be deposited monthly or semiweekly (or by the next day if the liability is $100,000 or more). For this purpose, the "liability" is the sum of the withheld federal income tax, the employees' and the employer's share of Social Security and Medicare, minus any advanced earned income credit paid by the employer. Generally, employers with a liability of $50,000 or less accrued during a designated four-quarter period will deposit monthly and employers whose liability is more than $50,000 are required to deposit semi-weekly. The employer will follow the appropriate deposit schedule for the entire calendar year. The specific rules may be found in IRS Publication 15, ***Circular E, Employer's Tax Guide*** which may be obtained from the Internal Revenue Service.

Note that there are new rules requiring the payment of federal taxes by electronic funds transfer (EFTPS). Under the new EFTPS requirements, if the total deposits of all federal taxes exceed $200,000 during a given calendar year, that taxpayer is required to use EFTPS for tax deposits for the next calendar year.

FUTA tax deposits are made quarterly (by the end of the month following the end of the quarter), unless the amount of FUTA tax owed but not deposited is $100 or less. If the tax is $100 or less at the end of the quarter, no deposit is required. The tax is added to the tax for the next quarter.

16. Deposit withheld Minnesota income tax.

Form: The employer can make Minnesota Tax Deposits in one of three ways: via the Department's eFILE system available at www.taxes.state.mn.us, by touchtone telephone (800) 570-3329, or by mailing in form MW-5, Withholding Tax Deposit Form.

Available from: Either www.taxes.state.mn.us (to use eFILE), or by telephoning (800) 570-3329, (to use touchtone telephone), or from the Department. (The Minnesota Department of Revenue sends a customized from book to employers registered for withholding tax. The Minnesota Department of Revenue requests that employers use the preprinted forms. It is not necessary to reorder MW-5 deposit forms. The Department of Revenue will mail you new forms when you need them.

Filed with: Minnesota Department of Revenue.

How often: The total amount of accumulated undeposited withholding tax will determine how often deposits must be made. Note that electronic payment may be required. For further information see the Minnesota Income Tax Withholding instruction booklet, available from the Minnesota Department of Revenue.

17. File federal quarterly withholding return.

Form: 941, Employer's Quarterly Federal Tax Return. (Different forms are required for employers of agricultural employees).

Available from: Internal Revenue Service.

Filed with: The IRS Service Center designated on the form.

How often: The employer must file a return quarterly (annually for employers of agricultural employees using Form 943).

18. File Minnesota quarterly withholding return.

Form: MW-1, Quarterly Withholding Tax Return (for the first three quarters of the year); MW-6, Year-End Withholding Return/Reconciliation (for the fourth quarter).

Available from: Minnesota Department of Revenue.

Filed with: Minnesota Department of Revenue either via the Internet, using the Department's eFILE (at www.taxes.state.mn.us) or by touchtone telephone, at (800) 570-3329.

How often: Quarterly. A return must be filed even if the employer paid no wages subject to withholding or had no employees during the quarter.

19. File Minnesota unemployment compensation tax report.

Form: MDES-1, Quarterly Tax Report and MDES-1D, Quarterly Wage Detail Report.

Available from: Minnesota Department of Economic Security.

Filed with: Minnesota Department of Economic Security.

How often: Quarterly.

20. File federal unemployment tax (FUTA) return.

Form: 940, Employer's Annual Federal Unemployment (FUTA) Tax Return or 940-EZ (Simplified Form).

Available from: Internal Revenue Service.

Filed with: The IRS Service Center designated on the form.

How often: Annually, by January 31 of each year.

See the section of this Guide on Unemployment Taxes for situations in which Form 940-EZ may be filed.

21. Provide Form W-2 to employee and others.

Form: W-2, Wage and Tax Statement.

Available from: Internal Revenue Service.

Filed with: Employee (three copies); Social Security Administration (one copy); Minnesota Department of Revenue (one copy). One copy is retained by the employer.

How often: The Form W-2 must be provided to the employee by January 31 each year. If the employee stops working for the employer and requests the W-2 before the January 31 deadline, it must be provided within 30 days following the request. The federal copy of the Form W-2, along with Form W-3, is filed with the Social Security Administration by February 28 each year.

22. File Minnesota Annual Withholding Return/Reconciliation.

Note: File this <u>**ONLY**</u> if you are not a quarterly filer (see checklist item 18) and you have been notified by the Minnesota Department of Revenue that you are an annual filer of income taxes withheld.

Form: File the Minnesota Annual Return/Reconciliation using the Internet (www.taxes.state.mn.us) or via touchtone telephone (800) 570-3329.

Available from: Minnesota Department of Revenue, in the customized forms book.

Filed with: Minnesota Department of Revenue by mail.

How often: Annually, by February 28 each year.

23. Information returns, pensions and other payments.

Employers who make payments to consultants, independent contractors, and others who are exempt from withholding may be required to provide a federal Form 1099-MISC to those individuals, and file the form with the Internal Revenue Service. Employers who pay pensions are required to issue Form 1099R to the recipients. The Internal Revenue Service and the Minnesota Department of Revenue have established special rules applicable to these situations.

BUSINESS TAXES

Common areas of small business tax liability include federal and state income taxes, state sales and use tax, FICA (Social Security and Medicare) tax, FUTA (federal unemployment) tax, state unemployment tax, and tax withholding. In addition, businesses may be liable for less commonly applicable taxes such as taxes on the sale of fuel, alcohol products and cigarettes, and the hazardous waste generator tax. These taxes are discussed in more detail in this section.

Note that businesses that operate in multiple jurisdictions, whether cities, states, or counties, need to be concerned about the taxes imposed by each of those jurisdictions, as well as the impact on the tax imposed by their home jurisdiction. This applies equally to businesses using the Internet to sell goods or services.*

SOURCES OF INFORMATION

Business owners who wish to learn more about federal and state taxation can attend workshops and seminars offered throughout the state. Telephone numbers for these workshops are listed in the Resource Directory section of this Guide.

Internal Revenue Service and Minnesota Departments of Revenue and Economic Security Business Education Workshops

The Internal Revenue Service and the Minnesota Departments of Revenue and Economic Security provide free tax workshops. Day and evening workshops are held in several cities across the state; also, daytime workshops are conducted at the Fort Snelling Federal Office Building. The evening workshops are three and one-half hours in length. Daytime workshops range from a half to a full day in length.

Basic Workshops. Both the evening and daytime workshop series offer sessions suitable for new businesses, new employers, and others interested in an introduction to business tax responsibilities.

- **Business Income Tax** discusses various types of business organizations, such as sole proprietorships, partnerships, and corporations, and the tax requirements of each type of business. Basic record keeping, estimated tax payments, business use of one's home and certain business expenses are discussed.

* For more information on using the Internet in business operations, see *A Legal Guide to the Internet*, published by and available without charge from the Minnesota Small Business Assistance Office, 500 Metro Square, 121 7th Place East, St. Paul, MN 55101-2146, telephone (651) 296-3871 or 1-800-657-3858 (ask for Small Business Assistance or available from www.dted.state.mn.us).

- **Sales Tax** provides a basic understanding of the types of goods and services subject to sales tax. Use tax requirements, record keeping, filing requirements, forms preparation and the use of purchases with exemption certificates will be discussed.
- **Employment Taxes and Employer Issues and Responsibilities** provides participants with a basic overview of federal and state employment tax requirements including those that relate to: corporation and S-corporation officers and employees; withholding and deposits; unemployment tax; quarterly and annual filings; and independent contractor/employee issues. The workshop also includes labor standards issues and the rules for employers with respect to employee child support and other obligations (further discussed in the "Issues for Employers" section of this Guide.)

Specialized Workshops. Generally, these workshops are held at Fort Snelling in South Minneapolis. Topics include: Business Assets/Depreciation; Partnerships; C corporations; S corporations; and Business Retirement Plans. These workshops offer advanced technical information.

Written Information

Both the Internal Revenue Service and the Minnesota Department of Revenue have written information on certain business topics.

Internal Revenue Service. The Internal Revenue Service provides small business tax kits for business owners. These kits contain the federal tax forms and instructions needed by most businesses. Kits may be obtained by contacting the Internal Revenue Service at the address and telephone number listed in the Resource Directory section of this Guide. A limited supply of forms and publications and walk-in assistance also may be obtained from the Internal Revenue Service field offices listed in the Resource Directory section of this Guide.

Minnesota Department of Revenue. Information on Minnesota taxes administered by the Minnesota Department of Revenue is published in instruction booklets for each type of tax.

In addition, the Sales Tax Division of the Minnesota Department of Revenue publishes Fact Sheets which provide technical application of the sales tax law to certain industries and taxable items. Likewise, the Individual Income Tax Division publishes Fact Sheets on individual income tax topics. The instruction booklets and Fact Sheets may be obtained by calling the Department of Revenue at the telephone numbers listed in the Resource Directory section of this Guide or by accessing the Department's web site (www.taxes.state.mn.us).

TAX IDENTIFICATION NUMBER

Many Minnesota businesses will need one or more tax identification numbers. These include the Federal Employer Identification Number, the Minnesota Taxpayer Identification Number, and the Minnesota Unemployment Compensation Employer Identification Number. New tax identification numbers must be obtained each time the ownership or form of business organization changes.

Federal Employer Identification Number

Sole proprietors who do not have employees, who are not required to file information returns, who do not have a retirement plan for themselves, and who are not required to pay federal excise taxes in connection with their business generally may use their social security number as their federal employer identification number. Likewise, single-member limited liability companies that have elected to be taxed as a sole proprietorship may follow the rule set out in the previous sentence. All other business entities are required to obtain a federal employer identification number by filing Form SS-4 with the Internal Revenue Service. Note also that an independent contractor doing commercial or residential building construction or improvements in the public or private sector is considered to be for workers' compensation purposes an employee of any person or entity for whom or which that independent contractor performs services unless, among other things, that independent contractor has a federal employer identification number.

Form SS-4 may be obtained from the Internal Revenue Service by calling the IRS at the telephone number listed in the Resource Directory section of this Guide. The completed form may be mailed to the appropriate IRS Service Center, as noted on the form. Processing time is approximately four weeks. Businesses that need their federal tax identification number sooner may obtain it by telephone. The business owner must first obtain and complete Form SS-4, and then call the appropriate IRS Service Center, as noted on the form where a service representative will ask for the information from Form SS-4 and issue the identification number over the phone. The business owner records this number on Form SS-4, then signs, dates and mails or faxes the form to the Internal Revenue Service to complete the process. The form must be sent to the Internal Revenue Service within five days of the phone call.

Minnesota Taxpayer Identification Number

A business needs to obtain a Minnesota tax identification number if it is required to file information returns for income tax purposes, has employees, makes taxable sales, or owes use tax on its purchases. Most businesses need a Minnesota tax identification number. However, a sole proprietorship or single member limited liability company which does not have any of these tax obligations does not need a Minnesota tax identification number.

A business can obtain a Minnesota tax identification number by calling the Minnesota Department of Revenue at (651) 282-5225, or at (800) 657-3605. Minnesota tax identification numbers can also be obtained by completing and mailing or faxing Minnesota Department of Revenue Form ABR.

Minnesota Unemployment Compensation Employer Identification Number

All business entities, other than sole proprietorships or single member limited liability companies without employees, must register with the Department of Economic Security. This Department issues identification numbers that are different from those issued by the Department of Revenue and the Internal Revenue Service. Registration is accomplished by filing Form MDES-13 (former DJT-13), Report to Determine Liability, with the Minnesota

Department of Economic Security at the address listed in the Resource Directory section of this Guide or by calling the Department of Economic Security at (651) 296-6141.

TAXPAYER BILL OF RIGHTS

Both the United States Congress and the Minnesota Legislature have enacted a Taxpayer Bill of Rights that governs many taxpayer relationships with the Internal Revenue Service and the Minnesota Department of Revenue. These laws formalize and standardize many audit, appeal, and collection procedures and clarify rights and protections available to taxpayers.

Information on the federal Taxpayer Bill of Rights and the legislation amending it known as the Taxpayer Bill of Rights II is provided in Publication 1, ***Your Rights as a Taxpayer***, which may be obtained by calling the Internal Revenue Service. Information on the Minnesota taxpayer rights law also may be obtained by calling the Minnesota Department of Revenue. Both are listed in the Resource Directory section of this Guide.

ELECTRONIC FILING OF TAXES

A business is required to file all its Minnesota electronically if it annually collects or owes more than the following amounts of any one type of Minnesota tax:

Sales and use tax	$120,000
Corporate estimated tax	20,000
MinnesotaCare tax	120,000
Cigarette or tobacco tax	120,000
Alcohol tax	120,000
Employee withholding	50,000
Distributor taxes	120,000
Insurance premium taxes	120,000
Fire insurance taxes	120,000

In other words, if a business collects more than $120,000 in sales taxes annually, but its only other tax is $10,000 in employee withholding taxes, both the sales tax and the withholding taxes must be paid electronically. For this purpose, the Department of Revenue measures the tax collected or owned for the period from July 1 to June 30 of the following year (i.e., not the calendar year). Any business exceeding one of the above thresholds is notified by the Department of Revenue, by letter, in the October following the end of the measuring period that as of the next January 1, all that business's taxes must be filed electronically.

Note that for federal tax purposes, many businesses will be required to file tax payments electronically, by means of the Electronic Federal Tax Payment System (EFTPS). See the section of this Guide titled "Business Taxes – Income Tax Withholding – Withholding Tax Deposit and Filing Requirements".

BUSINESS INCOME TAX RETURNS

This section describes the federal and state income tax returns that must be filed by various business entities. The business also may be liable for estimated tax payments, sales and use tax, and other taxes which are discussed later in this chapter.

SOLE PROPRIETORSHIP

For federal tax purposes, the sole proprietor reports income and expenses from the business on Schedule C or Schedule C-EZ (Form 1040) and any related forms and schedules. The net income or loss from the business is then transferred to the proprietor's individual Form 1040. The sole proprietor uses Schedule SE (Form 1040) to report net self employment income for purposes of computing the Social Security and Medicare self employment tax.

There is no separate form for reporting sole proprietorship income on the Minnesota tax return. To compute Minnesota income tax, the proprietor uses Form M-1, the individual income tax return form. A copy of the federal Form 1040, including a copy of Schedule C or Schedule C-EZ and other supporting schedules, must be attached to the Minnesota return.

PARTNERSHIP

For federal tax purposes, the partnership files Form 1065, which is an information return. No tax is paid by the partnership with this return. Other forms and schedules may be required, including Schedules K and K-1. Individual partners use Schedule E (Form 1040), which is prepared using information from their Schedule K-1 of Form 1065, to report their distributive share of partnership income, deductions, credits and losses on the individual Form 1040. Schedule SE (Form 1040) is used to compute Social Security and Medicare self employment tax.

For state tax purposes, the partnership completes Form M-3, Partnership Return and files it with the Department of Revenue along with a copy of federal Form 1065 and Schedules K and K-1. The partnership may also have to pay a minimum fee based on property, payroll, and sales attributable to Minnesota. If the partnership has items of income, credits or modifications that are different from its federal return, the partnership should also issue and file Schedule M-KPI and/or Schedule M-KPC. If the partnership has nonresident individual partners it may file a composite income tax on their behalf using Schedule M-KC. If it has nonresident individual partners who will not be included in such composite income tax, generally the partnership is required to withhold income tax on behalf of such partners and remit it with its Minnesota partnership return, by using Schedule MW-3NR. Individual partners who are not included on the composite income tax also complete Form M-1, the individual income tax return.

C CORPORATION

A C corporation is taxed under the provisions of Subchapter C of the Internal Revenue Code. For federal tax purposes, the C corporation reports its income, deductions and credits, and computes its tax on Form 1120 or Form 1120-A. Supporting forms and schedules may be required. If the corporation issues dividends, it must annually send its shareholders Form 1099-DIV, stating the amount of dividends paid. A copy of Form 1099-DIV also is filed with the Internal Revenue Service. Shareholders report dividends received from the corporation on their individual Form 1040.

The C corporation determines its state tax on Form M4, Corporation Income Tax return. The corporation also may have to pay a minimum fee based on property, payroll, and sales attributable to Minnesota.

S CORPORATION

An S corporation is a corporation that elects to be treated for federal tax purposes under Subchapter S of the Internal Revenue Code. As stated elsewhere in this Guide, a form making this election must be timely filed with the Internal Revenue Service. The S corporation generally is not separately taxed. The S corporation files Form 1120S and supporting forms and schedules, including Schedules K and K-1 (Form 1120S). Individual shareholders report their share of the S corporation's income, deductions, and credits on their individual Form 1040, using information contained on the Schedule K-1.

S corporations file Minnesota Form M-3S-4, S Corporation Return, with the state, along with copies of federal Form 1120S and supporting forms and schedules. In addition, the S corporation may have to pay a minimum fee based on property, payroll, and sales attributable to Minnesota. If the S corporation has items of income, credits or modifications that are different from the federal return it should also issue and file Schedule M-KS. If the S corporation has nonresident individual shareholders it may file a composite income tax on their behalf using Schedule M-KC. If it has nonresident individual shareholders who will not be included on such a Schedule, generally the S corporation is required to withhold income tax on behalf of such shareholders and remit it with the Minnesota S corporation return by using Schedule MW-3NR. Individual shareholders who are not included on the Schedule M-KC must also complete Form M-1, the individual income tax return.

LIMITED LIABILITY COMPANY

Under certain Treasury Regulations (26 C.F.R. § 301.7701-1 et seq. which became effective January 1, 1997), the organizers of a limited liability company can choose how the limited liability company will be taxed. Generally speaking an LLC with one member may be taxed either as a corporation or as a sole proprietorship. LLCs with two or more members may be taxed either as a partnership or as a corporation. Note that for one member LLCs, this decision will also impact whether the LLC needs a tax identification number. The Minnesota Department of Revenue has indicated that a Minnesota limited liability company will receive the tax treatment for state purposes that it receives for federal purposes. Persons considering forming a limited liability company are advised to consult with a tax professional regarding the state and federal tax treatment of such an entity. See also the sections of this Guide entitled "Choosing the Form of Business Organization – Tax and Non-Tax Considerations – Introduction" and "Choosing the Form of Business Organization – Tax and Non-Tax Considerations – Tax Considerations in Choosing the Form of Organization."

MINNESOTA INCOME TAX MODIFICATIONS AND DEDUCTIONS

Due to differences between state and federal law, it may be necessary to modify federal taxable income in order to arrive at Minnesota net income. Individuals use Schedule M-1M to list their income additions and subtractions. C corporations use Form M4-I to list their modifications. Partnerships and S corporations use Schedules M-KPI, M-KPC or M-KS to pass modifications through to their partners or shareholders.

For C corporations, an 80 percent deduction is allowed for dividends received during the year if the recipient owns 20 percent or more of the payor's stock. If the recipient owns less than 20 percent, the deduction is limited to 70 percent of the dividends received.

C corporations are allowed a deduction for:

- Contributions to the state of Minnesota or its political subdivisions for exclusively public purposes;
- Contributions to Minnesota charities;
- Gifts of Minnesota real property to the United States government.

Minnesota charities include war veterans organizations, fraternal associations, foundations, trusts, and corporations that are organized for charitable purposes. They must have their principal place of business in Minnesota and must perform substantially all of their activities in Minnesota.

C corporations also are allowed to deduct contributions to a non-Minnesota charitable foundation in proportion to that foundation's Minnesota activity. Contributions to charitable organizations that do not conduct substantially all of their activities in Minnesota are not deductible.

Contribution carryovers are not allowed.

NET OPERATING LOSSES

A corporation may carry forward a net operating loss (NOL) 15 years and may use the NOL to offset future years' income. A corporation's NOL cannot be used to offset tax paid on personal income in previous years.

An individual may carry back an NOL to offset previous years' income, and may carry it forward to offset future income. Federal guidelines are followed in making the NOL computation.

TAX CREDITS

Minnesota allows several credits which can reduce the tax otherwise payable by businesses. Some of these credits are available only to C corporations, while others may be taken by partnerships, partners, S corporations, S corporation shareholders, and owners of sole proprietorships. Certain credits may only be taken as a carryback or carryover of unused credits permitted in a prior year.

Credits presently available are:

- For C corporations, the alternative minimum tax (AMT) carryover credit (Minnesota Statutes § 290.0921, subd. 8);
- Alternative minimum credit for individuals (Minnesota Statutes § 290.091, subd. 6);
- Enterprise zone credit (Minnesota Statutes § 273.1314, subd. 9);
- Credit for research and experimental expenditures (Minnesota Statutes § 290.068);
- Credit for income tax withheld for nonresident partners or S corporation shareholders (Minnesota Statutes § 290.92, subd. 12(b)).
- Border city zone credit, to encourage businesses to locate in certain Minnesota cities (Breckenridge, Dilworth, East Grand Forks, Moorhead and Ortonville), rather than in other states. (Minnesota Statutes section 469.1732). Note that according to representatives of the Minnesota Department of Revenue, businesses claim this credit by filing a claim for refund (i.e., it's not claimed on the tax return).
- The RISE credit, to encourage businesses to hire graduates of job training programs meeting the requirements of Minnesota Statutes section 290.0673. Note that according to representatives of the Minnesota Department of Revenue, businesses claim this credit by filing a claim for refund (i.e., it's not claimed on the tax return); and
- Credit in an amount equal to thirty percent of the cost of transit passes provided by an employer, to its employees, for use in Minnesota (Minnesota Statutes § 290.06, subd. 28, added by 2000 Statutes Chapter 490, Article 4, Section 16).

Other, federal tax credits that may be of interest to businesses are:

- The Work Opportunity Tax Credit (WOTC) program provides employers with federal tax credits for hiring members of targeted groups the members of which traditionally have difficulty in securing employment. The Minnesota Department of Economic Security determines whether a particular job seeker qualifies under the program, and if so, then provides a certification to an employer, which is then eligible for the tax credit. At the time this Guide went to press, the WOTC had been extended to December 31, 2001. Note that this program has been extended in the past and could well be again.

The full credit is an amount equal to forty percent of the first $6,000 in wages paid to a newly-hired person within the first twelve months of employment, so long as that person has worked at least 400 hours in that twelve month period. Thus, the maximum tax credit is $2,400. A partial credit is available for a newly-hired person who does not work at least 400 hours; if that person has worked at least 120 hours, a credit is available in an amount equal to twenty-five percent of the first $6,000 in wages. Also, the tax credit for the summer youth target group is available only for the first $3,000 in wages.

Unused portions of the credit may be carried back three years, and forward fifteen years.

Targeted groups are: recipients of Aid to Families with Dependent Children (AFDC); veterans who received food stamps for at least three of the last fifteen months; economically disadvantaged ex-felons hired no later than one year after conviction or release from prison; vocational rehabilitation referrals; young people aged sixteen through seventeen, hired for the summer, who reside in an Empowerment Zone or Enterprise Community; individuals aged eighteen through twenty-five who reside in an Empowerment Zone or Enterprise Community; individuals aged eighteen through twenty-five who have received food stamps for at least three of the last five months, or; persons who have received Supplemental Security (SSI) benefits for at least one month within sixty days of their date of hire.

For more information on the WOTC program, contact the Minnesota Department of Economic Security/WorkForce Exchange Branch, 390 North Robert Street, St. Paul, MN 55101, (651) 296-8746, e-mail mdes.wotc@state.mn.us.

- The Welfare to Work Tax Credit (W2W) program is a federal tax credit offered to employers as an incentive to hire long-term family assistance recipients. W2W credits are available until December 31, 2001. Note that this program has been extended in the past and could well be again.

The Minnesota Department of Economic Security is responsible for determining whether an individual is a member of a group eligible for this credit, and for providing certifications to employers.

A credit is available in an amount equal to up to thirty-five percent of the first $10,000 in wages earned by the individual in the first year of employment, and up to fifty percent of the first $10,000 in wages earned by the individual in the second year of employment. Thus, the maximum credit is $8,500 per individual hired.

An individual is considered a qualifying long-term family assistance recipient if he or she is a member of a family:

- that has received family assistance (i.e., AFDC/TANF or a successor program) for at least eighteen consecutive months, ending on the date of hire;
- whose AFDC or TANF eligibility expired under federal or state law after August 5, 1997, but only so long as he or she was hired within two years after that eligibility expired, or;
- that received family assistance for a total of at least eighteen months, whether or not consecutive, after August 5, 1997 (i.e., such a person cannot qualify until at least February, 1999).

For more information on the W2W program, contact Larry Cheetham, Minnesota Department of Economic Security/WorkForce Services Branch, 390 North Robert Street, St. Paul, MN 55101, (651) 296-8746, e-mail mdes.wotc@state.mn.us.

Note that in some instances, the person hired will meet the requirements of both the W2W and the WOTC. In those situations, the employer may claim only one of the two credits in any given year, but may claim the credit that provides the largest tax advantage.

Note that the "Economic Growth and Tax Relief Reconciliation Act of 2001" made a number of changes to the federal tax credits available to employers. For instance, that legislation allows, in some instances, a credit to employers for providing certain types of child care assistance.

The **AMT carryover credit** and **alternative minimum credit for individuals** allow a reduction of regular tax for alternative minimum tax previously paid.

The **enterprise zone** legislation provides for creation of a number of zones in the state, with special consideration given to areas bordering on other states, in which special tax credits may be allowed: (1) sales tax exemption for construction equipment and material; (2) income tax credit based on the number of employees; (3) income tax credit for debt financing costs incurred to construct new facilities; (4) property tax credit for new business facilities or for expansion of facilities. It is available to partnerships and corporations and may be passed through to partners and S corporation shareholders.

The credit for **research and experimental expenditures** is available for "qualified research expenses" as defined in Section 41(b) and (e) of the federal Internal Revenue Code, except for those expenses incurred for basic research conducted outside the state of Minnesota. For more details on qualified research expenses, see Minnesota Statutes § 290.068. The credit is available only to C corporations. It is not available to S corporations or individuals.

The credit for **income tax withheld for nonresident individual partners** or **S corporation shareholders** is a credit on the individual's individual income tax return and is claimed on the "Minnesota income tax withheld" line of Form M-1.

More detailed information on these credits, carryovers, and carrybacks may be obtained from the Minnesota Department of Revenue.

NON-MINNESOTA BUSINESSES DOING BUSINESS IN MINNESOTA

Non-Minnesota businesses which do business in Minnesota or own property in Minnesota may be subject to taxation by Minnesota if they have sufficient "nexus" or connection with Minnesota to justify imposition of Minnesota tax laws. Activities that create nexus include but are not limited to:

- Having a place of business in Minnesota;
- Having employees or independent contractors conducting business in Minnesota;
- Owning or leasing real property, or tangible personal property, in Minnesota, and
- Obtaining or regularly soliciting business from within Minnesota. Obtaining or soliciting business within Minnesota includes activities like selling products or services to customers in Minnesota who receive the product or service in Minnesota; 76engaging in transactions with customers in Minnesota that involve intangible property and result in income; leasing tangible personal property in Minnesota, and; selling or leasing real property located in Minnesota. Methods of regularly soliciting business in Minnesota include direct mail and phone solicitation, and various forms of advertising, including via print publications and radio and television.

This issue can be complicated to resolve. Further information on the nexus standards and exceptions, and other requirements for non-Minnesota businesses may be obtained from the Department of Revenue.

TAXATION OF FIRMS DOING BUSINESS WITHIN AND OUTSIDE MINNESOTA

Weighted Apportionment Formula

Businesses which operate both inside and outside Minnesota apportion their net income to Minnesota using a weighted formula. Under this method, income is apportioned by determining the percent of property, payroll and sales attributable to doing business in Minnesota. The three factors are then weighted: property and payroll are each weighted 12.5 percent, and sales are weighted 75 percent. The sum of these weighted factors is the percentage of net income apportioned to Minnesota. Partnerships and S corporations also use the apportionment method to compute Minnesota source income. Individuals who are Minnesota residents and partners or S corporation shareholders pay Minnesota income tax on all of their income, regardless of source. Nonresident individuals who are partners or S corporation shareholders pay Minnesota income tax on only the portion of the partnership's or S corporation's income that is apportioned to Minnesota. For partnerships with corporate partners, the partnership must pass through to its corporate partners each such partner's pro rata share of the partnership's apportionment factors, so that the corporate partners can complete their Minnesota corporate tax returns.

Note that the 1999 legislature modified the statutes on apportionment. For instance, Minnesota Statutes section 290.17, subd. 3, now provides as a general rule that all income of a trade or business (other than non-business income, the definition of which has been modified to conform to the U.S. Supreme Court's most recent decision on this issue, *Allied Signal, Inc., v Director, Division of Taxation* (504 U.S. 768)) is subject to apportionment. Also, a corporation is now allowed a credit for taxes paid to another state: the amount of that credit equals the amount of "qualifying tax" paid to that other state, multiplied by the corporation's apportionment percentage under Minnesota Statutes section 290.191. For this purpose, the term "qualifying tax" means the amount of tax paid to the other state based on income also taxed by Minnesota.

Example

A corporation that has $1 million in net income from all sources, with 100 percent of its property and payroll in Minnesota and 10 percent of its sales attributable to Minnesota would apply the weighted apportionment formula as follows:

XYZ Corporation

Factor	Percent In Minnesota	Weighted Apportionment
Property	100%	x .125 = 12.5%
Payroll	100%	x .125 = 12.5%
Sales	10%	x .75 = 7.5%
Minnesota apportionment percentage		32.5%
Net income		$1,000,000
Minnesota net income ($1,000,000 x .325)		$325,000
Minnesota corporate income tax rate		9.8%
Tax liability ($325,000 x 9.8%)		$31,850

"Throwback Rule"

In determining what to include in "sales" for purposes of the weighted apportionment formula, above, most states (including Minnesota) look to destination in determining where sales should be assigned. In other words, if the sale was made within Minnesota, so that the "destination" of whatever was sold is Minnesota, that sale is included in the "sales" factor used in that apportionment formula. Sometimes, however, a "throwback" rule is used, which when used includes sales made in other states in that "sales" factor. This occurs because the taxing state "recaptures" sales made in other states that are not taxed, for whatever reason, in those other states. Minnesota does not use the "throwback" rule.

UNITARY CORPORATIONS

In past years, a C corporation which is part of a unitary business was required to file Minnesota schedules CI and ACI in addition to Form M4. Now, both unitary and nonunitary corporations file the same forms, although a unitary corporation will complete different parts of these forms. A single combined unitary return must be filed for the entire unitary group. For more information contact the Department of Revenue at the address and telephone number provided in the Resource Directory section of this Guide.

BUSINESS ACTIVITIES REPORT

Every corporation that has property or personnel in Minnesota or receives income from Minnesota sources is required to file with the Department of Revenue, Form M-4R, Business Activities Report, unless the corporation files a timely corporate income tax return (either Form M-4 or Form M-3S-4), has a certificate of authority to do business in Minnesota, or is otherwise exempt from this requirement. A corporation that is required to file a Business Activities Report and fails to do so does not have any cause of action upon which it may bring suit under Minnesota law and is prevented from using Minnesota courts for all contracts executed and all causes of action that arose before the accounting period for which the corporation failed to file the report. The Commissioner of Revenue may disclose to litigants whether a Business Activities Report has been filed by a party to a lawsuit.

Copies of Form M-4R may be obtained from the Minnesota Department of Revenue. Questions may be directed to the Department.

ESTIMATED TAX

Individuals who are sole proprietors, partners, S corporation shareholders, and members of limited liability companies generally will be required to make federal and Minnesota estimated tax payments if their income tax and, for federal purposes, self employment tax will exceed taxes paid through withholding and credits by $500 or more ($1,000 for federal individual income tax purposes). The tax is determined on income from all sources, not just on income from the business. Federal Form 1040-ES, Estimated Taxes for Individuals and Minnesota Form M-14, Individual Estimated Tax Payment Vouchers must accompany tax payments. Note that Federal Form 1040-ES contains a worksheet to use to compute estimated tax payments.

A C corporation whose estimated tax is expected to be $500 or more must make estimated tax payments. Federal estimated tax payments are deposited with an authorized financial institution or Federal Reserve Bank. Minnesota payments are filed with the Department of Revenue. Corporations use federal Form 1120-W and Minnesota Form M-18 to calculate and make estimated tax payments. Any C corporation must make electronic deposits of all depository taxes, including estimated tax payments, in 2002 by using the Electronic Federal Tax Payment System (EFTPS) either if: the corporation was required to use EFTPS in 2001 or; the corporation's total deposits of such taxes in 2000 exceeded $200,000. Partnerships and S corporations must make Minnesota estimated tax payments if their minimum fee and S corporation taxes are expected to be $500 or more, or if they have any nonresident individuals whose tax is expected to be $500 or more and who are included on the entity's composite income tax. Withholding of tax for nonresident partners or shareholders is not subject to estimated tax requirements. Payments are filed with the Minnesota Department of Revenue on Form M-71 for partnerships and Form M-72 for S corporations.

Forms, worksheets and instructions for completing the forms are available from the Internal Revenue Service and the Minnesota Department of Revenue at the addresses and telephone numbers provided in the Resource Directory section of this Guide.

INCOME TAX PENALTIES AND INTEREST

Both the Internal Revenue Service and the Department of Revenue may assess monetary penalties and interest for failure to pay a required tax, for a substantial underpayment of tax, for failure to file a return, for both failure to file and failure to pay, and for filing a fraudulent, false or frivolous return. The Internal Revenue Service also may impose a monetary penalty for underpayment of tax due to negligence or disregard of the tax rules, or for a substantial understatement of income. In addition, both the federal government and the state may impose criminal penalties for deliberately failing to file a return or deliberately filing a false return.

The interest rate on unpaid taxes is adjusted periodically by both the Internal Revenue Service and the state to reflect current market rates.

SALES AND USE TAX REGISTRATION

Every person who makes taxable retail sales or provides taxable services in Minnesota must obtain a Minnesota tax identification number and register for authorization to collect and remit Minnesota sales and use tax. This must be done before making any taxable sales in Minnesota. This includes not only all sellers located in Minnesota, but also any seller located outside Minnesota who:

- Has an office, place of distribution, sales or sample room, warehouse, or other place of business in Minnesota, either directly or by a subsidiary, or;
- Has an agent, representative, member, sales person, canvasser, solicitor or employee (either temporary or permanent) in Minnesota for any purpose, including the repair, sale, delivery, installation, or solicitation of orders for taxable items, or the leasing of tangible personal property located in Minnesota.

As described in further detail below, a business that does not pay sales tax at the time it purchases taxable goods and services is required to pay use tax. A business that is required to pay use tax must also obtain a Minnesota tax identification number and register for the sales and use tax authorization.

The required Minnesota tax identification number and registration for authorization to collect and remit Minnesota sales and use tax can be obtained by telephoning the Minnesota Department of Revenue at (651) 282-5225 or (800) 657-3605 or by calling or visiting any of the Department's regional offices. Alternatively, a business can complete Minnesota Department of Revenue Form ABR (Application for Business Registration) and mail or fax it to the Department of Revenue. The ABR form contains mailing and faxing instructions. The ABR form is also available (in a PDF version that can be printed; the required Adobe Acrobat software is included, free of charge) from the Department's web site, at www.taxes.state.mn.us. Note that the site also contains links to some federal tax forms.

THE MINNESOTA SALES TAX

The sales tax is a tax on the gross receipts from selling, leasing or renting tangible personal property at retail, or providing taxable services, in Minnesota. The end user of the personal property or services is responsible for paying the tax. Generally, a sale is at retail unless the customer purchases the property for purposes of reselling it, or plans to incorporate the property purchased into a new product for sale at retail. Sales by a manufacturer or wholesaler that are sold to customers who are not in the business of reselling the items purchased are sales at retail. However, some sales are specifically exempted by law from the sales and use tax. These exemptions are discussed later in this section.

The Department of Revenue has issued fact sheets on certain sales tax issues. Several fact sheets are industry specific. Copies of fact sheets can be obtained by telephoning (651) 296-6181 or (800) 657-3777, or from the Department's website, www.taxes.state.mn.us.

The general sales tax rate of 6.5 percent is imposed on the retail price of taxable goods and services. Some items, however, are taxed at special rates, as follows:

- Car rentals – in addition to the 6.5 percent tax, a 6.2 percent tax and a 3 percent fee are charged.
- Liquor sales – 9 percent.
- Mobile homes – 4.225 percent, based on the dealer's cost.
- Park trailers – 4.225 percent.

Note that many services are taxable. For information on what services are taxable or to request fact sheets written for businesses that provide taxable services, contact the Department of Revenue at (651) 296-6181 or (800) 657-3777, or access its website at www.taxes.state.mn.us.

MOTOR VEHICLE SALES TAX

Motor vehicles are subject to a motor vehicle sales tax. The tax on sales of most motor vehicles is 6.5 percent. Passenger vehicles ten years old and older, collector vehicles, and certain other types of vehicles are taxed at lower or special rates. For further information on the motor vehicle sales tax, contact the Minnesota Department of Public Safety, Driver and Vehicle Services Division at the address provided in the Resource Directory section of this Guide, or the nearest motor vehicle licensing office.

THE MINNESOTA USE TAX

The use tax complements and is similar to the sales tax. It applies when a buyer does not pay Minnesota sales tax to a vendor on tangible personal property purchased for storage, use or consumption in Minnesota. The use tax rate, 6.5 percent, is the same as the sales tax rate. The rate is applied to the cost of the taxable purchases on which the sales tax is not paid. The buyer pays use tax directly to the state. **Both businesses and individuals are subject to use tax.** For more information, request the Department's Use Tax Fact Sheets (Fact Sheet 146, Use Tax for Businesses, or Fact Sheet 156, Use Tax for Individuals).

Use tax must be paid on:

- Items purchased outside Minnesota from retailers who do not collect Minnesota sales tax, if the items are for use, storage or consumption in Minnesota.
- Items originally purchased for resale, if the items are taken out of inventory for business or personal use. When items are taken out of inventory, use tax is calculated on the purchase prices of the items.
- Items originally purchased for use in agricultural or industrial production, if the items are put to a taxable use. The use tax must be paid when the item is put to taxable use.
- Items and taxable services purchased from a Minnesota seller who does not collect the sales tax, if the items are put to a taxable use.

Businesses that have registered for sales and use tax should report the cost of the use tax items on their sales and use tax return. Individuals must file a Form UT-1, Consumer's Use Tax Return, which is due April 15 following the end of the calendar year. Local use tax is also due if the items are used in an area that imposes a local sales and use tax. Note that with the exception of Duluth local use taxes, all local use taxes are required to be reported on the taxpayer's state return.

EXEMPTION CERTIFICATES

Generally, all sales of taxable merchandise are presumed to be subject to the sales tax. However, certain customers are not required to pay the tax at the time of purchase. To show they are authorized to buy goods without paying the tax, these customers must give the seller a properly completed exemption certificate. There are several different exemptions. The most common are for: purchases of items that become part of a new product that will be sold at retail (a "Certificate of Exemption" Form ST-3 is used), or purchases of goods that will be resold at retail (a "Resale Exemption Certificate" Form ST-5 is used).

Unless the customer gives the seller a properly completed exemption certificate, the seller is required to collect the sales tax. It is not sufficient for the customer to provide only its sales and use tax number. Copies of blank exemption certificates are available from the Department of Revenue at the address and telephone number listed in the Resource Directory section of this Guide or from its web site, www.taxes.state.mn.us.

An exemption certificate may be for either a single purchase or a blanket exemption. Customers who frequently make exempt purchases from one seller should give that seller a blanket exemption certificate to cover future purchases. That way, the seller will not need to collect a new certificate each time the customer makes a purchase.

A properly completed exemption certificate should be retained in the seller's files to substantiate the exemption. Certificates are subject to inspection by the Department of Revenue, but they should not be mailed to the Department.

EXEMPTIONS AND EXEMPT ORGANIZATIONS

Certain sales are exempt from sales and use tax. Exemptions commonly encountered by Minnesota businesses are listed below. Detailed information on the exemptions may be obtained from the Minnesota Department of Revenue at the address and telephone number provided in the Resource Directory section of this Guide or from the Department's web site, www.taxes.state.mn.us.

Food, Clothing and Prescription Drugs

Generally, the sale of clothing, prescription drugs and most food is exempt from the sales and use tax. However, the exemption for sales of food does not apply to food purchased from restaurants, bars, delicatessens or caterers, or from vending machines, and it does not include candy or soft drinks.

Refund for Tax Paid On Capital Equipment Purchases

Purchasers of "capital equipment" as defined in Minnesota Statutes section 297A.01, subd 16, may be eligible for a refund of the sales tax paid at the time of purchase. The sales or use tax must first be paid at the full rate. The purchaser may then file a claim for refund (Form ST-11) with the Department of Revenue for the sales or use tax paid.

In order to qualify for the refund, the capital (or replacement capital) equipment must be used by the purchaser or lessee primarily for manufacturing, fabricating, mining, or refining tangible personal property to be sold ultimately at retail, or for electronically transmitting results retrieved by a customer of an on-line computerized data retrieval system. Capital equipment includes all machinery and equipment that is essential to the integrated production process; also included are repair and replacement parts, materials used for foundations that support machinery or equipment, and materials used to construct and install special purpose buildings used in the production process.

Resource Recovery

An exemption from sales and use tax is allowed for purchases of equipment used for processing solid or hazardous waste at a resource recovery facility. Such an exemption requires prior approval by the Minnesota Department of Revenue. For more information, contact the Minnesota Department of Revenue, Sales and Use Tax Division.

Sales to Non-Profit Organizations

Nonprofit organizations may, in certain instances, be exempt from paying sales tax. Nonprofit organizations that purchase otherwise taxable goods or services will not have to pay sales tax on such purchases if: the organization is organized exclusively for a charitable, religious, or educational purpose; and the organization receives prior authorization from the Department for the exemption. The exemption does not apply to the purchases of meals, lodging, waste collection or disposal services, or motor vehicles, and also does not apply to the additional 6.2% tax or 3% fee on short term rental of vehicles. Qualifying exempt organizations must provide an exemption certificate.

Sales to Government Agencies; "Direct Pay" Permits

All sales made directly to the federal government are exempt from sales tax. To claim that exemption, an agency of the federal government merely needs to provide a purchase order or payment voucher indicating that the purchase is made directly by the federal government; alternatively, the purchasing federal agency may provide a Certificate of Exemption form (Form ST-3). Sales to employees of the federal government are not exempt from sales tax.

Although sales made directly to the State of Minnesota are not exempt from sales tax, Minnesota State agencies use a direct pay permit, which means that those agencies do not pay the tax to the seller, but instead pay the tax directly to the Department of Revenue. Purchase orders used by Minnesota State agencies contain information about the direct pay permit, so it is not necessary for vendors to obtain a copy of it. There are exceptions to the use of direct pay permits. Sellers of prepared food or beverages, lodging and related services, admissions to amusement or athletic events, motor vehicles or certain services to the State of Minnesota must collect sales tax on those sales from the purchasing Minnesota State agency.

Most sales to local governments (such as cities, counties, townships) are not exempt from sales tax.

Most purchases by public schools, local government hospitals and nursing homes are exempt from sales tax. To claim the exemption, these purchasers must provide a Certificate of Exemption (Form ST-3) to their sellers. However, sales of meals, lodging, or waste collection services to those entities are not exempt.

Fund Raising Sales by Non-Profit Organizations

Under certain conditions, non-profit organizations are not required to collect sales tax on sales of tangible personal property, admission charges, and sales of food, meals, or drinks at fund raising events sponsored by the organization. Fund raising sales by certain youth and senior citizen organizations also are exempt. The exemption is subject to strict requirements, and failure to meet the requirements can make taxable the entire gross receipts from fund raising for the year. For more information, contact the Department of Revenue at (651) 296-6181 or (800) 657-3777.

FILING THE SALES AND USE TAX RETURN

Any individual or business having a sales tax permit must file a sales and use tax return, even if no sales or use tax is due. How often a return must be filed during the year depends on the amount of tax due. For businesses averaging less than $100 per month in sales and use tax, the return is due annually. Returns are due quarterly if the sales and use tax averages between $100 and $500 per month; and due monthly if sales and use tax averages more than $500 per month. Special rules apply to businesses that operate seasonally. In addition, if sales and use tax liability is at least $120,000 per year, the tax must be paid by means of electronic funds transfers. Also, taxpayers who are required to pay other Minnesota taxes electronically are required to pay their sales and use taxes electronically as well. These taxpayers will be notified by the Department of Revenue. See the section of this Guide titled "Business Taxes – Electronic Filing of Taxes."

All sales and use tax returns must be filed electronically, by using either the Internet (www.taxes.state.mn.us), and scroll down to "e-FILE Minnesota" or the telephone (800) 570-3329. For annual filers, the return is due on February 5 of the following year. For monthly or quarterly filers, the return must be filed by the 20th day of the following month (for monthly filers) or of the month following the end of the quarter (for quarterly filers). If the due date falls on a legal holiday or weekend, the return is due the next business day.

LOCAL SALES AND USE TAXES

Any local government that imposes a local sales tax must also impose a local use tax. The Minnesota Department of Revenue administers and collects the local taxes on behalf of all the local governments listed below, with the exception of the city of Duluth. Note that all local taxes listed below are in addition to the 6.5% state general sales tax and the 9% state tax on intoxicating liquor. Local taxes are subject to the same penalty, interest and enforcement provisions as the state sales tax. These cities and the special sales or sales and use taxes they are authorized to impose are listed below. If you make taxable sales or perform taxable services in any of the cities or the county listed below (other than Duluth), include that information in your registration for a Minnesota tax identification number.

Cook County – One percent general sales and use tax.

Duluth – One percent general sales and use tax, with guidelines similar to the state sales tax guidelines; one percent sales tax on food and beverages (for sales of up to $100,000, and 2-1/2% tax thereafter); five percent sales tax on lodging for facilities with up to thirty units; six and one-half percent sales tax for facilities with thirty or more units. Note: Beginning July 1, 2003, Duluth taxes will be administered by the Department of Revenue. Until them: Do not include any Duluth sales or use tax on your Minnesota sales and use tax return. Instead, contact the city of Duluth: Duluth Sales Tax, 105 City Hall, Duluth, MN 55802 or (218) 723-3271.

Hermantown – One-half percent general sales and use tax.

Mankato – One-half percent general sales and use tax.

Minneapolis – One-half percent general sales and use tax with guidelines similar to the state sales tax guidelines; two percent tax on transient lodging with more than 50 rooms; three percent entertainment tax; three percent downtown restaurant tax; and three percent downtown liquor tax. The restaurant and liquor taxes are imposed only in a special downtown taxing area.

New Ulm – One-half percent general sales and use tax.

Proctor – One-half percent general sales and use tax.

Rochester – One-half percent general sales and use tax; three percent sales tax on transient lodging.

St. Cloud – One percent sales tax on liquor and food sold at restaurants and places of refreshment within the city limits.

St. Paul – One-half percent general sales and use tax.

Two Harbors – One-half percent general sales and use tax.

Willmar – One-half percent general sales and use tax.

Winona – One-half percent general sales and use tax.

All Cities and Towns – Any city or town may impose a lodging tax. Some cities are authorized by the legislature to impose other special taxes, which are administered by those cities, not the Department of Revenue.

FICA TAX

The Social Security and Medicare benefit programs are financed by taxes paid by employers and employees under the Federal Insurance Contributions Act (FICA), and by self employed individuals through the self employment tax.

FICA taxes are levied on both the employer and the employee. The employer is responsible for the employer's share of FICA taxes, and also is required to collect and pay the employee's part of the tax, which is withheld from the employee's pay in much the same way as income tax is withheld. Self employed individuals compute their self employment tax on Internal Revenue Service Schedule SE of Form 1040.

FICA tax for both employers and employees for 2002 is 7.65 percent of the first $84,900 of wages paid each employee, plus an additional 1.45 percent of wages paid over $84,900.

For 2002, the self employment tax rate is 15.3 percent. A self employed individual may take a deduction in computing his or her net earnings from self employment. This deduction is an amount equal to one-half of the self employment tax multiplied by the earnings from self employment. In addition, a self-employed individual may deduct one-half of his or her self employment tax liability for the year as an adjustment to income in arriving at adjusted gross income.

The self employment tax is imposed on net earnings of $400 or more. The maximum amount of earnings subject to self employment tax in 2002 is $84,900 at 15.3 percent and an additional rate of 2.9 percent for earnings over $84,900.

Special rules apply to tipped employees, and to persons who receive both wages and self employment income. Special rules also apply to payments in kind made by employers, such as the furnishing of meals, lodging, clothing or services to employees.

It should be noted that the FICA rates and wage base limitations stated above are current as of December, 2001. However, these amounts are subject to change by congressional action. Typically wage base limitations change each year. It is therefore wise to consult the IRS for the correct rate at the time of withholding or payment.

The following IRS publications can provide additional information on FICA contributions, withholding and self employment taxes: Publication 15, ***Employer's Tax Guide (Circular E);*** Publication 15-A, ***Employer's Supplemental Tax Guide;*** and Publication 533, ***Self Employment Tax.*** To obtain these publications contact the Internal Revenue Service at the address and telephone number provided in the Resource Directory section of this Guide.

INCOME TAX WITHHOLDING

INTRODUCTION

Employers must withhold federal and Minnesota income tax and the employee's share of the FICA tax from their employees and pay those taxes to the federal and state government. The amount of withholding is based on the wages or salary paid the employee, and the number of withholding allowances claimed by the employee on Form W-4, Withholding Allowance Certificate, which the employee completes at the time of hiring. (Withholding Allowance Certificates are discussed later in this section.) Employers are required to withhold both federal and state income taxes and FICA tax from their employees' wages as soon as they are paid. Note that special rules may apply to the withholding of taxes on "supplemental" wages (e.g., on a bonus paid to an employee).

The Internal Revenue Service and the Minnesota Department of Revenue provide withholding tables to enable the employer to determine the appropriate withholding amount. These tables are available from those agencies. Those agencies also send periodic newsletters or notices to employers about changes in the law or procedures. Employers must comply with those changes.

TAX IDENTIFICATION NUMBER

All business entities that have employees must obtain a federal employer identification number. Firms that employ anyone who works in Minnesota, or any Minnesota resident, must also obtain a Minnesota tax identification number. Employers should apply for their tax identification numbers well before they expect to hire their first employee, to allow for adequate processing time. A penalty may be assessed for failure to apply on time.

A federal identification number is obtained by filing Form SS-4 with the Internal Revenue Service. A state tax identification number is obtained by filing Form ABR with the Minnesota Department of Revenue or by calling that Department, at (651) 282-5225, or at (800) 657-3605. Further information on the procedure for obtaining these numbers is provided in the section of this Guide on Business Taxes or may be obtained from the Internal Revenue Service or Minnesota Department of Revenue at the address and telephone numbers provided in the Resource Directory section of this Guide.

Following receipt and processing of the applications for tax identification numbers, the Internal Revenue Service and the Minnesota Department of Revenue provide the employer with respective identification numbers, income tax withholding instructions, withholding tax tables, and enough forms for immediate use. Employers must file and pay Minnesota taxes electronically or via a touchtone telephone and thus will not receive any booklet of customized forms; instead, that electronic filing system makes such forms unnecessary. For all employers, the Internal Revenue Service will provide a coupon book containing deposit forms and quarterly returns. The federal forms will be preprinted with the company's name, address, and tax identification number, and should be used for making required deposits. Employers should withhold and remit federal and state taxes as soon as they begin paying wages, even if they have not yet received their identification number or forms.

WITHHOLDING ALLOWANCE CERTIFICATES

Federal Form W-4, Employee's Withholding Allowance Certificate, is completed by the employee at the time of hiring, and is used by the employer to determine how much tax to withhold from the employee's paycheck. Form W-4 may be obtained by contacting the Internal Revenue Service at the address and telephone number provided in the Resource Directory section of this Guide.

Employees can claim fewer exemptions for their Minnesota withholding than for their federal withholding. If an employee wishes to do so, the employee should complete two W-4 forms and mark one "state copy" and one "federal copy." An employee cannot claim more exemptions for Minnesota withholding than for federal withholding.

In most cases Form W-4 need not be sent to either the Internal Revenue Service or the Minnesota Department of Revenue. Two exceptions to this rule are: (1) when the employee claims more than ten withholding allowances, and (2) when the employee claims exemption from withholding and his or her wages normally would exceed $200 per week. In these situations the employer must send a copy of the Form W-4 to the Internal Revenue Service and the Department of Revenue.

If the employer is required to send a copy of Form W-4 to the Internal Revenue Service, it should be sent with the quarterly Form 941, along with any written statements from the employee in support of the claims made on Form W-4. The copy should also be sent to the Department of Revenue at the same time. Employers must complete boxes 8 and 10 on any copies of Form W-4 sent to the IRS and the Minnesota Department of Revenue.

The employer should honor the employee's Form W-4 until either the Internal Revenue Service and/or the Department of Revenue notifies the employer that the certificate is not valid. The Internal Revenue Service and the Department of Revenue will notify the employee in writing of their determination. If the employer is notified that the certificate is not valid, it cannot honor that certificate or any future certificates filed by the employee claiming more allowances than determined by the Internal Revenue Service and/or the Department of Revenue unless the employer is authorized by either agency to do so. The employer may allow the employee only the number of allowances which the Internal Revenue Service and/or the Department of Revenue determines the employee is entitled to claim.

An employer who fails to send the required copy of a withholding allowance certificate to the Internal Revenue Service or the Department of Revenue is subject to a monetary penalty for each certificate that is not sent. Any employee who files a withholding allowance certificate which he or she knows is incorrect is subject to a $500 penalty for each incorrect certificate filed.

FURNISHING WAGE AND TAX STATEMENT TO EMPLOYEES

The employer must issue a wage and tax statement (federal Form W-2) to each employee on or before January 31 of the following year, or within 30 days of a written request from the employee if his or her employment was terminated. The federal copy of Form W-2, together with Form W-3, Transmittal of Income and Tax Statements, must be filed annually with the Social Security Administration by February 28. The state copy of Form W-2 must be filed with the Minnesota Department of Revenue by February 28. No other forms should be sent with the W-2s.

Forms W-2 and W-3 may be obtained from the Internal Revenue Service at the address and telephone number provided in the Resource Directory section of this Guide.

DEFINITION OF EMPLOYER AND EMPLOYEE

Generally, an employer is a person or organization for whom a worker performs a service as an employee. The employer usually provides the tools and place to work and has the right to hire and discharge an employee. A person may be an employer for purposes of one kind of tax but not for another.

Generally, employees can be defined either under common law or under special statutes for special purposes. Generally speaking, a common law employee is anyone who performs services that can be controlled by an employer (what will be done and how it will be done). This is true even when the employer gives the employee freedom of action. What matters is that the employer has the legal right to control the method and result of the services.

Further information on determining whether an individual is an employee is provided in the sections of this Guide titled "Issues for Employers" and "Checklist for Hiring an Employee" or refer to Federal Publication 15A, *Employer's Supplemental Tax Guide.*

ISSUES FOR NONRESIDENT EMPLOYERS AND EMPLOYEES

Wisconsin, North Dakota and Michigan Residents Working in Minnesota

Minnesota has tax reciprocity agreements with these states. Under these agreements, residents of Wisconsin, North Dakota or Michigan who work in Minnesota are not required to have Minnesota income tax or nonresident entertainer tax withheld from their Minnesota compensation. Instead, they pay state tax to the state in which they live. The reverse is true also for Minnesota residents who work in Wisconsin, North Dakota or Michigan. They pay tax to Minnesota only.

A Wisconsin, North Dakota or Michigan resident who does not want Minnesota income tax withheld from his or her wages must complete and give to the employer Form MW-R, Reciprocity Exemption/Affidavit of Residency. The employer must retain one copy for his or her records and forward one copy to the Minnesota Department of Revenue. Form MW-R should be filled out by the employee each year by February 28 or within 30 days of beginning work. The employer must send a copy of Form MW-R to the Minnesota Department of Revenue no later than March 31, or within thirty days after a new employee, or an employee who changes his or her address, files the form with the employer.

Employees of Interstate Carrier Companies

Interstate carrier companies that have employees such as truck drivers, bus drivers or railroad workers who travel across state borders in their work must withhold state income tax for the employee's state of residence.

Interstate air carrier companies must withhold tax in any state in which an employee has his or her residence and in any state in which the employee earns more than fifty percent of his or her compensation.

Tax on Nonresident Entertainment Entities

Nonresident entertainers such as musicians, actors, dancers, athletes and public speakers may be subject to a two percent tax on compensation they receive for entertainment performed in Minnesota. The tax is imposed on the entertainment entity. The person who has legal control of the payment of the compensation is responsible for withholding and depositing the tax.

Further information on the nonresident entertainer tax may be obtained from the Department of Revenue.

Minnesota Residents Employed Outside Minnesota

In Other States. An employer of a Minnesota resident who does not work in Minnesota but works in another state and who withholds federal income tax from the wages of that employee may also be required to withhold Minnesota income tax. The employer may also be required to withhold taxes in the other state in which the work is being performed.

An employer who is required to withhold both Minnesota income tax and income tax for another state should first determine the amount of income tax to be withheld for each state. If the amount of Minnesota income tax to be withheld is greater than the amount to be withheld from the state in which the employee is working, the employer should send the difference to Minnesota to the Department of Revenue and the amount due to the state in which the employee is working to that state. If the amount due to Minnesota is less than the amount due to the other state, the employer should send to that state the amount due to the other state and should not withhold any Minnesota income to that state tax.

Outside the United States. A Minnesota resident who is transferred to a location outside the United States remains a Minnesota resident unless: (1) the employee is a "qualified individual" for the foreign earned income exclusion of Section 911(d)(1) of the Internal Revenue Code, and (2) the employee does not have an interest in any homesteaded property in Minnesota. If the employee does not meet these criteria, the employer must continue to withhold Minnesota income tax from the employee's wages.

Any Minnesota income tax withheld from these employees must be sent to the Department of Revenue according to the same rules as tax withheld from employees working in Minnesota. (See the section titled "Withholding Tax Deposit and Filing Requirements" below.)

If the employee changes his or her domicile and requests that you stop withholding Minnesota income tax, a copy of the employee's W-4 and a letter explaining in detail why the employee thinks his or her domicile has changed must be sent to the Department of Revenue.

WITHHOLDING TAX DEPOSIT AND FILING REQUIREMENTS

Overview

Both the Internal Revenue Service and the Minnesota Department of Revenue require employers to deposit withheld tax on a periodic basis, and to file periodic returns. Deposit and filing requirements are discussed below. Employers should note that for purposes of determining the frequency of payment, federal and state withholdings are totaled separately.

Deposit Requirements

Annual Requirement (Federal only). Agricultural employers who accumulate less than $1,000 federal tax liability during the year may pay the tax and file the return annually.

Annual Requirement (Minnesota only). Minnesota employers with less than $500 in Minnesota tax in a year may be notified by the Department of Revenue that they qualify for annual filing. If an employer is so notified, at any time during the year in which its Minnesota withholding tax exceeds $500, the employer is required to make a deposit at the end of the month following the month in which withholding tax exceeded $500. To make that deposit, the employer should use the Minnesota Department of Revenue's Internet e-FILE mechanism (www.taxes.state.mn.us) or telephone (800) 570-3329.

Quarterly Requirement. Employers with federal deposit liability of less than $2,500 in the current quarter or state withholdings of $1500 or less in the prior quarter pay the entire amount to the Internal Revenue Service or Minnesota Department of Revenue quarterly. The payment is due the last day of the month following the end of the quarter.

General Rule for Making Deposits (Minnesota). If an employer withholds more than $1500 in Minnesota tax during the previous quarter, the employer is required to make Minnesota deposits in the next quarter as often as it is required to make federal deposits.

Monthly Requirement (Federal). New employers and employers whose total federal tax liability for the four quarters in the lookback period is $50,000 or less are required to deposit employment taxes for each month by the fifteenth day of the following month. The look back period is the four quarters beginning July 1 of the second preceding year and ending June 30 of the prior year. Employers should consult IRS Publication 15, *Circular E,* and the Minnesota Department of Revenue for specific rules and exceptions.

Semi-weekly Requirement (Federal only). Employers whose total tax liability for the lookback period is more than $50,000 are required to deposit employment taxes on Wednesday and/or Friday, according to their payroll day. Employers should consult IRS Publication 15, *Circular E, **Employer's Tax Guide**,* for specific rules.

One-Day Requirement (Federal only). Employers who accumulate taxes of $100,000 or more on any day during a deposit period are required to make the deposit by the close of the next banking day, whether they are a monthly or semi-weekly depositor.

Electronic Federal Tax Payment System (EFTPS). EFTPS is the system sponsored by the U.S. Department of Treasury under which taxpayers may initiate federal tax payments electronically (i.e., instead of by using paper coupons). Since January 1, 2000, taxpayers are required to use EFTPS if the aggregate of their 1998 federal tax payments was at least $200,000; thereafter, a taxpayer is required to use EFTPS on January 1 if the aggregate of their federal tax payments for the year before the prior year was $200,000.

Note also that EFTPS is voluntary for other taxpayers. Since January 1, 2000, the IRS has expanded the types of nondepository tax payments for which voluntary payment may be made via EFTPS to include nondepository payments of federal income, estate and gift, employment, and certain excise taxes.

IRS Publication 15, Circular E, *Employer's Tax Guide* contains information about EFTPS.

Filing Requirements

Quarterly Withholding Tax Return. Each quarter, all employers (except annual agricultural filers) must file federal Form 941, Employer's Quarterly Federal Tax Return with the Internal Revenue Service. In addition, all employers (except Minnesota annual filers) must file Minnesota Quarterly Tax Withholding Return for the first three quarters, and a Year-End Withholding Return Reconciliation for the fourth quarter. These returns may be filed via the Internet, using eFILE (at www.taxes.state.mn.us) or the telephone (800) 570-3329.

End of Year Filing. Federal Form W-3, Transmittal of Income and Tax Statements, must be filed annually with the federal copies of each employee's Form W-2. The state copies of each employee's Form W-2 should be mailed separately using the W-2 label from the coupon book. The federal Form W-3 must be filed no later than February 28 in the year following the taxable year, or within 30 days of going out of business.

Annual Filing. If you have been notified by the Minnesota Department of Revenue that you are an annual filer, you should not file quarterly returns. You will file only an Annual Withholding Return/Reconciliation, with Federal Form W-2, by February 28 of the year following the end of the taxable year. That Annual Withholding Return/Reconciliation must be filed via the Internet or via the telephone, using the same eFILE or toll-free telephone number.

Forms

Deposits are made with federal Form 8109, Federal Tax Deposit Coupon. Deposits of Minnesota taxes are made via the Internet or by touchtone phone. Quarterly returns are made with federal Form 941, Employer's Quarterly Federal Tax Return. All state returns must be filed via the Internet or touchtone telephone. Note that both federal and state returns must be filed, even if all amounts due have already been paid via deposits.

Due Dates

All federal 941 forms are due April 30, July 31, October 31 and January 31. The first three Minnesota quarterly returns are due April 30, July 31, and October 31. The Year-End and fourth-quarter return, along with the return for annual filers are due February 28. Federal returns and deposits and state deposits will be considered on time if received or postmarked on or before the due date. The postmark must be a United States postmark and must not be from a postage meter. If deposits are made electronically, refer to the specific instructions for the type of deposit.

WITHHOLDING TAX PENALTIES AND INTEREST

Both the Internal Revenue Service and the Minnesota Department of Revenue assess penalties and interest for the failure to make deposits on time, the failure to file required returns on time, and the failure to file W-2 and 1099 forms. The amount of penalty for late deposits or late filing is based on the length of time the payment or return is late. The Internal Revenue Service imposes a penalty on failure to provide correct information on W-2 forms, and failure to provide a correct Taxpayer Identification Number.

Any person responsible for paying over the withholding may be held personally liable for failure to do so. A penalty equal to 100 percent of the amount withheld from employee's paycheck, also may be imposed.

Interest is assessed on unpaid withholding tax (plus penalties). Interest accrues from the date the payment should have been made to the date the payment actually is made. The interest rate is adjusted to reflect market rates.

CONTRACTOR AND SUBCONTRACTOR CLEARANCE

A prime contractor, contractor or subcontractor who performs work on a project for the State of Minnesota or any of Minnesota's political or governmental subdivisions (e.g., counties, cities, school districts) must file a Withholding Affidavit for Contractors, Form IC-134, with the Department of Revenue certifying that the contractor has complied with Minnesota's withholding tax laws in order to receive final payment for the work.

A **contractor** is a person who is awarded a contract to perform work and who performed the work personally or through his or her employees. A **prime contractor** is a contractor who is awarded a contract to perform work but who subcontracts all or part of the work to other contractors. A **subcontractor** is hired by a prime contractor to perform all or part of the work on a contract. A **subcontractor** files Form IC-134 when the subcontractor completes its part of the project. A **prime contractor** or **contractor** files Form IC-134 when the entire project is completed.

Information on filing procedures and certification forms may be obtained from the Department of Revenue at the telephone number provided in the Resource Directory section of this Guide.

SUCCESSOR LIABILITY FOR CERTAIN TAXES WHEN A BUSINESS OR ITS ASSETS ARE TRANSFERRED

Whenever a business or its assets are transferred outside the ordinary course of business, and a lien for unpaid sales or withholding taxes has been filed, in certain situations the new owner can be liable for the amount of the lien and any related interest and penalties, and any other unpaid sales or withholding taxes. In order to avoid liability for these taxes, the potential new owner must send a notice to the Commissioner of the Department of Revenue at least twenty days before taking possession of the assets or paying the purchase price. That notice must contain information regarding the transfer of the business or its assets, the terms and conditions of that transfer, and the tax identification number of the business being transferred.

The Commissioner then has twenty days to notify the potential new owner of any additional sales or withholding taxes (including interest and penalties); the Commissioner may also notify the potential new owner of the amount needed to satisfy the lien, or that there are no taxes due in addition to the amount shown on the lien, or that additional tax returns are due. If the Commissioner fails to give the required notice within the twenty-day period, the potential new owner is not liable for any taxes other than those shown on the lien.

These rules apply to transfers of businesses or business assets, whether by sales or gift. In the case of sales transfers, the amount of the tax liability cannot exceed the purchase price. In the case of gift transfers, the tax liability is presumed to be the value of the transferred assets or business. Also, for transfers by gift, the tax liability can be avoided by returning the gifted property. These rules also apply to changes in the type of business entity or changes to the name of the business, so long as one business is being discontinued and another one started.

REVOCATION OR PREVENTION OF LICENSE ISSUANCE OR RENEWAL

Existing licenses can be revoked if the Department of Revenue notifies the licensing authority that the license holder owes the state for back taxes, penalties or interest.

In addition, the Commissioner of Revenue is authorized to stop, by issuing a Notice of Requirement for Tax Clearance, the issuance or renewal of any business, trade, occupational or professional license issued by the state, a county or a municipality to businesses that have a state tax liability of more than $500 (Minnesota Statutes § 270.72).

If a licensing agency receives a Notice of Requirement for Tax Clearance for a business, a license may not be issued, renewed or transferred until the agency receives a tax clearance certificate from the Commissioner of Revenue. A tax clearance certificate is issued only upon resolution of the tax delinquency.

The Commissioner of Revenue is responsible for all negotiations, disputes and appeals resulting from a license denial under this statute. Further information regarding the requirements or application of this law may be obtained from the Minnesota Department of Revenue's Collection Enforcement group, at the address and telephone number provided in the Resource Directory section of this Guide.

UNEMPLOYMENT TAXES

Unemployment benefits are paid to eligible workers who lose their jobs. Funds to pay unemployment benefits are provided by unemployment taxes paid by employers (i.e., no deductions can be made from a employee's wages to cover these taxes). Federal unemployment compensation taxes (often referred to as FUTA) are collected by the Internal Revenue Service on behalf of the U.S. Department of Labor. State unemployment compensation taxes and the state economic security law are administered by the Department of Economic Security. Information on the federal and state programs may be obtained from the Internal Revenue Service (FUTA) and the Minnesota Department of Economic Security (state program) at the address and telephone number provided in the Resource Directory section of this Guide.

FEDERAL UNEMPLOYMENT TAXES

Filing Requirements

The employer is responsible for paying the federal unemployment tax (FUTA). It is not withheld from the employees' pay. The FUTA tax return is filed once a year on federal Form 940 or Form 940-EZ. The return generally is due one month after the year ends.

Form 940-EZ is a simplified version of Form 940. Form 940-EZ can be used by employers that pay by the due date of Form 940 all unemployment contributions to only one state and that do not have taxable FUTA wages that are exempt from state unemployment tax.

A FUTA tax return must be filed by any employer that meets any one of the following tests:

- The employer pays $1,500 or more in wages in any one calendar quarter for the reporting year or the preceding year, or
- The employer had one or more employees for some part of a day in any of 20 different weeks during the reporting year or during the preceding calendar year. For this test, all regular, temporary, and part-time employees are counted. Partners of a partnership are not counted. (This test is known as the "general" test).
- The employer paid cash wages of $20,000 or more to farm workers during any calendar quarter for the reporting year or the prior year, or
- The employer had 10 or more farm workers for some part of a day in each of 20 different weeks in the reporting year. Aliens admitted to the United States on a temporary basis to perform farm labor are counted. (This test is known as the "farm workers" test).

- The employer paid cash wages of $1,000 in any calendar quarter in the reporting year or the preceding year for household work done in a private home, local college club, or local chapter of a fraternity or sorority. (This test is known as the "household employees" test).

Figuring the Tax

The federal unemployment tax is figured on the first $7,000 in wages paid to each employee during the year. (The wage base is subject to change.) The tax is imposed on the employer – it must not be collected or deducted from the wages of the employee.

The federal unemployment tax rate for 2002 is 6.2 percent of the wage base. However, the employer is given a credit of up to 5.4 percent for the state unemployment tax it pays. The tax rate, therefore, can be as low as 0.8 percent (6.2 percent minus 5.4 percent) if the state is not subject to a credit reduction. If the state tax rate is less than 5.4 percent, the employer is still allowed the full 5.4 percent credit. An employer may not, however, take the credit for any tax the employer did not actually pay.

An employer who takes over the business of an employer who was subject to the federal unemployment tax may, in figuring the wage base for FUTA, count wages paid by the first employer to employees who continue to work for the second employer.

Paying the Tax

FUTA tax is reported on Form 940 or Form 940-EZ. The form covers one year and generally is due one month after the year ends. An employer may, however, have to make deposits of the tax before filing the return. If at the end of any calendar quarter the employer owes but has not yet deposited more than $100 in FUTA tax for the year, the employer must make a deposit by the end of the following month. If the tax is $100 or less at the end of a quarter, it does not need to be deposited. Instead, it is added to the tax for the next quarter. If the total undeposited tax is more than $100 in the next quarter, a deposit is required. Form 8109 is used to make federal tax deposits.

Penalties

An employer can avoid penalties and interest by making tax deposits when they are due, filing a correct return, and paying the proper amount of tax when due. Penalties may be imposed for late deposits and late filing unless the employer can show reasonable cause for the delay. Information on penalties may be obtained from the Internal Revenue Service at the address and telephone number provided in the Resource Directory section of this Guide.

STATE UNEMPLOYMENT TAXES

Coverage

All firms or organizations having services performed for them in Minnesota are subject to the provisions of the Minnesota economic security law, and most firms or organizations are required to pay taxes or reimburse benefits in lieu of taxes. Tax liability depends on the amount and type of employment, the amount of wages paid and other factors present in special situations.

Report to Determine Liability

An entity that conducts business in Minnesota is required to complete Form MDES-13, Report to Determine Liability, within 30 days, even though it may not be liable to this state for unemployment taxes. The Department of Economic Security will subsequently advise the entity of its liability.

Report to Determine Succession

A firm that buys a business or otherwise acquires the assets or any part of an existing business that is subject to the economic security law must at the time of the acquisition complete and file Form MDES-13S, Report to Determine Succession. By statute, an individual or organization that acquires all or part of the organization, trade or business or any part of the assets from a Minnesota employer is jointly and severally liable for any unpaid tax, interest and penalties due and not paid by the predecessor employer, in an amount not to exceed the reasonable value of that part of the organization, trade, business or assets acquired.

An organization that plans to acquire any part of an existing business can obtain information on the predecessor's account by filing a written release from the predecessor with the Department of Economic Security. An organization that acquires assets in the normal course of the seller's business is not, by reason of the acquisition, subject to this provision of the law.

How Much Tax

By statute, each new employer must pay tax equal to the state's average cost rate unless the business was acquired from a liable predecessor and the new employer is eligible to have an experience rate computed based on all or part of the predecessor's experience record. Employers in high experience rating industries are assigned a separate benefit cost rate. The state's average cost rate is based on benefits paid to all Minnesota unemployment benefit applicants and on all wages reported that were subject to taxation, within the computation period. The average cost rate cannot be less than 1.00 percent.

New employers in high experience rating industries are assigned a separate tax rate. High experience rating industries include residential, commercial or industrial construction; sand, gravel, or limestone mining; manufacturing of concrete, concrete products or asphalt; and road building, repair or resurfacing, including residential and commercial driveways and parking lots. The tax rate for new employers in these industries is 8.00 percent, plus the minimum tax rate equal to the current minimum "experience rate" assessed against existing employers under the experience rating plan (i.e., a minium rate of one-tenth of one percent to six-tenths of one percent; see the discussion below in the paragraph beginning "An experience rating plan. . .")

The computation period is 60 months, ending on June 30 of the year prior to the year for which the rate is applicable.

An experience rating plan is in effect for those employers who have been liable under the law for a sufficient period of time to establish some measure of their experience with employment. Experience rates increase or decrease according to the employer's experience with unemployment applications. Experience rates range from a minimum rate of one-tenth of one percent to six-tenths of one percent (depending on the balance in the Unemployment Compensation Fund on June 30 of the preceding calendar year) to a maximum rate of 9.50 percent. The publication MDES-130 ***Minnesota Employers' Unemployment Handbook*** provides more information. The handbook is available from the Minnesota Department of Economic Security at the address and telephone number provided in the Resource Directory section of this Guide.

New employers who acquire a business by purchase, change of legal entity or by any other means, should also pay particular attention to the section entitled "Experience Rating Successorships" in the MDES-130 publication.

If the entire business was acquired and the predecessor and successor share 25% or more common ownership, the successor will be required to inherit the employment experience record of the predecessor. Common ownership includes ownership by a spouse, parent, child, brother, sister, aunt, uncle, niece, nephew or first cousin by birth, marriage or adoption. If this is the case and the predecessor's rate was high, so too will be the successor's rate, until the successor establishes a better experience record during the following years. If a distinct severable portion of the business of a commonly owned predecessor is acquired, the successor may apply for the portion of the predecessor's experience record that is applicable to the portion of the business acquired.

Solvency Assessment

If the Minnesota Unemployment Compensation Fund balance is less than $150 million on June 30 of any year, a solvency assessment will be in effect for the following calendar year. The rate of assessment, payable by all taxpaying employers, will be ten percent of the tax due. The assessment is to be combined and paid with the quarterly tax.

Special Assessment for Dislocated Worker Fund

A special assessment of seven one-hundredths of one percent of taxable payroll (before 2001, one-tenth of one percent of taxable payroll) is imposed on all taxpaying employers. This assessment is paid with the quarterly tax. Proceeds are used to fund programs designed to assist dislocated workers.

Records

True and accurate employment records must be kept by all Minnesota employing units, whether they are covered under the law or not. Since an employer's liability cannot be properly determined without such records, the records must be open at any time to inspection by the Department of Economic Security. The law provides penalties to ensure compliance.

Records must show, for each individual, the following: name; social security number; days and number of hours in which the individual performed personal services; location where the services were performed; gross wages paid and wages due but not paid for personal services; rate and base unit of pay; amounts paid as allowances or reimbursement for expenses; the date of separation and the reason for the termination; and the complete resident address. Wages paid and wages due but not paid must be broken down to show the character of each payment. For example, meals, lodging, bonuses and gifts must be shown separately.

Records must also show for each pay period: the beginning and ending dates of the period; the total amount of wages paid and wages due but not paid for personal services performed; and the date of payment. Employment records must be preserved for at least eight years after the calendar year in which the wages were paid or became payable.

Quarterly Tax Reports

Unlike the federal government, which uses annual unemployment tax returns, Minnesota requires most employers to file employment tax returns on a quarterly basis. When an employer becomes liable, it must file quarterly tax reports and pay tax on the wages reported. The Unemployment Quarterly Tax Report consists of two parts: the Quarterly Tax Report for reporting summary information, and the Wage Detail Report for reporting specific information for each employee. The amount of tax due is based upon wages for all employees, whether permanent or temporary, except those excluded by law. Examples of excluded employment are listed in publication MDES-130, ***Minnesota Employer's Unemployment Handbook.***

The employer's name is placed on a regular mailing list, and at the end of each quarter the necessary report forms are mailed. Failure to receive blank forms does not relieve the employer of the responsibility for filing tax reports. In such cases, a facsimile form may be used.

The report is due and the tax is payable within one month after the end of each calendar quarter. The report is due and the tax is payable, therefore, on or before April 30, July 31, October 31 and January 31.

The employer is also required to report the total number of covered workers who worked or received pay during the quarter. Only the persons who worked or received pay during the payroll period which included the 12th of the month should be included in these totals.

All wages paid to employees during the calendar quarter must be reported. This includes commissions, bonuses, tips and the cash value of remuneration other than cash. Wages must be reported for both full and part-time workers.

The taxable wage base is shown on the report. An employer is required to pay tax on each employee's annual wages up to the wage base limit and must keep track of each employee's earnings on both a quarterly and an annual basis.

Employers are required to file quarterly wage reports detailing the wages paid to each employee. The information required each calendar quarter includes each employee's name, social security number, total wages paid to the employee, and the number of hours worked in the quarter by the employee.

Instructions for completing the Quarterly Tax Report are on the form itself. Information and assistance on specific problems not covered by the instructions may be obtained from the Tax Processing Unit of the Department of Economic Security at the address and telephone number provided in the Resource Directory section of this Guide.

Interest Charged on Late Tax Payments

If the taxes due are not paid by the due date, the employer is charged interest at the rate of one and one-half percent per month, or any part thereof, from the due date until payment is made to the Department of Economic Security. The department is required to assess such interest charge and collect it, in addition to taxes, by court action if necessary. Interest charges may be waived if a late payment is attributable to certain extenuating circumstances as provided in department rules. Requests for waiver must be in writing, and the reasons for late payment must be substantiated.

Penalties for Failure to File Timely Reports

An employer who knowingly fails to file a Quarterly Tax Report or a Wage Detail Report by the due date is required to pay a penalty in addition to the interest charged for not paying the tax. An employer who files the Wage Detail Report but knowingly fails to include any of the required information or knowingly enters erroneous information, is also subject to a penalty. Reports are required from liable employers, even though they had no employees during the quarter, and therefore owe no tax. Even though no tax is due, the penalty will still apply if the report is filed late.

Information on penalties is provided in the publication ***MDES-130, Minnesota Employer's Unemployment Handbook*** from the Department of Economic Security at the address and telephone number provided in the Resource Directory section of this Guide.

Adjustments and Refunds

An employer that overpays the tax due may apply for an adjustment within four years from the date the tax was paid. To obtain an adjustment the employer should obtain and complete Form MDES-506, Employer's Application for Wage Adjustment. These forms may be obtained from any Minnesota WorkForce Center listed in publication MDES-130, or from the state office of the Department of Economic Security. The form should be prepared in duplicate. One copy is retained for the employer's records and the original, properly signed, copy is mailed to the Department of Economic Security. Upon approval of the application by the department, the employer will be mailed a credit notice that can be applied against future taxes. The department will issue a refund check for the full amount of the credit, if so requested by the employer.

An employer that fails to include all wages in a previous report should prepare Form MDES-506 in duplicate, and mail the original to the Department of Economic Security. Upon receipt of the completed form, the necessary adjustments will be made.

As a result of a Department's audit of an employer's quarterly reports, overpayments or underpayments may also be disclosed. In such cases the adjustment permitted by law will automatically be made, and the employer will be notified of any overpayment or underpayment.

Adjustments for a prior quarter should not be made on a Quarterly Tax Report. All adjustments should be made on form MDES-506.

Audits

The Department of Economic Security field auditors perform regular examinations of employer records. An audit to verify wage items and employment is generally confined to a single year but may be expanded if errors are found. All the employer's records, including subsidiary records, must be made available to the auditor.

Field auditors may also inspect records for the purpose of establishing an employer's liability under the law, to obtain information regarding a claim for benefits and in connection with fraud investigations.

The Minnesota economic security law provides that the records of any employing unit must be open to inspection, audit and verification at any reasonable time, and as often as may be necessary.

Personal Liability for Payment of Unemployment Tax

In the event that a corporation or limited liability company fails to pay its unemployment compensation tax, individual officers, directors, employers, governors, members or owners who are responsible for filing tax returns and paying unemployment taxes may be held personally liable for the unpaid taxes.

Contractor Penalty for Failure to Pay Unemployment Compensation Tax

An employer on any nonresidential construction, repair, or remodeling project that fails to provide unemployment compensation coverage for employees may be sued for damages by any losing bidder on the project. The losing bidder may be entitled to recover the amount of profit the winning contractor expected to make on the project, as well as costs and attorneys fees.

HAZARDOUS WASTE GENERATOR TAX

Anyone who generates more than 100 pounds (10 gallons) per year of hazardous waste in the state of Minnesota is subject to a hazardous waste tax. Persons who generate hazardous waste outside the state of Minnesota, but who ship it to Minnesota for storage or treatment must also pay a hazardous waste tax. See the section titled "Pollution Control Programs" earlier in this Guide. The tax is paid at a flat base rate for very small quantity generators. Small quantity and large quantity generators must compute the calculated quantity rate and pay the larger of the base rate or calculated quantity rate. The tax is based on the volume of hazardous waste generated and on its method of disposal. Very small quantity generators presently pay a base rate of $50; small quantity generators' base rate is $200; large quantity generators' base rate is $500.

Hazardous waste is any refuse or discarded material which cannot be handled by routine waste management techniques because it poses a present or potential hazard to human health or other living organisms. Specific definitions and criteria exist for these wastes. For more information see the section titled "Hazardous Waste" earlier in this Guide.

Revenues from the tax are deposited in a special fund to be used for clean up of hazardous waste and hazardous waste spillage in the state of Minnesota.

The hazardous waste quantity tax does not apply to hazardous wastes which are destined for recycling fuel blending or incineration at a permitted hazardous waste incineration facility in Minnesota. The hazardous waste quantity tax does not apply to hazardous wastes that are pretreated to a nonhazardous state prior to discharge to a publicly – owned treatment facility. The tax does not apply to waste that is not hazardous after it is neutralized. Also, the tax does not apply to hazardous wastes generated as a result of a response action or generated as a result of lead acid battery smelting.

The tax must be paid on or before April 15th of the year following the year in which the waste was generated. For the metropolitan area, the tax is computed on a Minnesota Hazardous Waste Tax Generator Annual Tax Return and is filed with the Minnesota Department of Revenue. For generators outside the metropolitan area, the generator tax and the generator fee are paid to the Department of Revenue on a Combined Billing Statement.

If the tax for a calendar year is expected to exceed $1,000, it must be paid in four equal installments which total at least 80 percent of the actual amount due. The Declaration of Estimated Tax, Form HZ-18 and first installment payment are due on or before March 15 of that year. The remaining three equal installments are due on or before the 15th day of June, September and December.

For further information, call or write the Minnesota Department of Revenue Special Taxes Office, at the address and telephone number provided in the Resource Directory section of this Guide.

OTHER MINNESOTA TAXES

There are several other taxes that may apply to small businesses. Businesses that sell gasoline, propane or diesel fuel collect the tax from the customer and remit it to the state. Wholesalers and distributors of alcohol products and cigarettes also collect and pay taxes to the state. There are other less commonly used taxes.

FEDERAL HIGHWAY USE TAX

A federal tax is imposed on the use of highways by certain trucks, truck tractors, and buses. The tax applies to trucks having taxable gross vehicle weights of 55,000 pounds or more. Therefore, pickup trucks, panel trucks and trucks of that nature are not subject to the highway use tax. In addition, the tax applies to vehicles used on public roads more than 5,000 miles per year (7,500 miles per year for agricultural vehicles). The tax is reported on federal IRS Form 2290, Heavy Vehicle Use Tax Return.

Owners of heavy trucks are required to prove that they have paid their federal highway use tax before state motor vehicle departments will register a taxable vehicle. Generally, a copy of Schedule 1 of Form 2290, stamped after payment and returned to the taxpayer by the Internal Revenue Service, is acceptable proof of payment.

FEDERAL TAX REQUIREMENTS

YOU MAY BE LIABLE FOR	IF YOU ARE OR ARE TAXED AS*	USE FORM	DUE ON OR BEFORE
Tax Identification Number	Sole proprietor with employees; Partnership; Corporation If you are a sole proprietor with no employees use your Social Security Number as your tax identification number	SS-4, Application for Identification Number	See Instructions on Form SS-4
Individual – Income Tax Return	Sole proprietor	Schedule C (Form 1040), Profit or loss from business	April 15th or the 15th day of the 4th month after the end of the tax year
	Partner or S corporation shareholder	Schedule E (Form 1040), Supplemental Income or Loss	Same as above
Business – Income Tax Return	Partnership	Form 1065, U.S. Partnership Return of Income	15th day of the 4th month following the close of the tax year
	S corporation	Form 1120-S, U.S. Income Tax Return for S corporation	15th day of the 3rd month after the end of the tax year
	Corporation	Form 1120, U.S. Corporation Income Tax Return	15th day of the 3rd month after the end of the tax year
Estimated Taxes – Individual	Sole Proprietor or individual who is a partner or S corporation shareholder	Form 1040ES, Estimated Tax For Individuals	15th day of the 4th, 6th, and 9th months of tax year, 15th day of 1st month after end of tax year
Estimated Taxes – Corporation	Corporation	Form 1120-W, Corporation Estimated Tax	15th day of the 4th, 6th, 9th and 12th months of tax year
Withholding of Income Tax and FICA Deposits	Business with Employees	Form 8109, Federal Tax Deposit Coupon	See withholding and deposit instructions issued by IRS
Return for Reporting Withholding of Employee's Income Tax and FICA	Business with Employees	Form 941, Employer's Quarterly Tax Return	End of month following end of quarter
Reporting Information on Wage and Tax Statements (Form W-2)	Business with Employees	W-3, Transmittal of Income and Tax Statements	February 28
Unemployment Tax (FUTA)	Business with Employees	Form 940, Employer's Annual Federal Unemployment (FUTA) Tax Return	January 31
Unemployment Tax Deposits	Business with Employees	Form 8109 Federal Tax Deposit Coupon	See FUTA Deposit Instructions issued by IRS
Information Returns	Business Required to File Form 1099, U.S. Information Returns	Form 1096, Annual Summary and Transmittal of U.S. Information Returns	February 28
Other Federal Taxes call the IRS			

* Note that generally speaking, single-member LLCs may choose to be taxed as a sole proprietorship or a corporation. LLCs with at least two members may choose to be taxed either as a corporation or as a partnership.

STATE OF MINNESOTA TAX REQUIREMENTS

YOU MAY BE LIABLE FOR	IF YOU ARE OR ARE TAXED AS*	USE FORM	DUE ON OR BEFORE
Tax Identification Number	Making taxable sales or withholding taxes; Partnership, Corporation	ABR, Application for Business Registration	See instructions for completing Form ABR.
Income Tax	Sole Proprietor	M-1, Individual Income Tax Return	April 15, or the 15th day of 4th month after the end of the tax year
	Individual who is a partner or S corporation shareholder	M-1	Same as above
	C Corporation	M-4, Corporation Franchise Tax Return	15th day of 3rd month after end of the tax year; for cooperative associations, the 15th day of the 9th month after end of the tax year
		M-7 (insurance companies)	15th day of 3rd month after end of tax year
	S corporation	M-3S-4, S Corporation Return	15th day of 3rd month after end of tax year
	Partnership	M-3 Partnership Return	15th day of 4th month after the end of tax year.
Sales and Use Tax	Organization that makes retail sales or provides taxable services	ST-1, Sales and Use Tax Return	Due date is based on filing cycle assigned by Department of Revenue – see instructions.
	Business that purchases taxable property for use in Minnesota with - out paying sales tax	ST-1, Sales and Use Tax Return	Included on Sales and Use Tax Return
	Consumer who purchases taxable property without paying sales tax	UT-1, Consumer's Use Tax Return	April 15th of following year
Estimated Tax	Sole proprietor or individual who is a partner or S corporation shareholder	M-14, Tax Payment Voucher-Individual	15th day of 4th, 6th, and 9th months of tax year; and 15th day of 1st month after end of tax year
	Corporation	M-18, Corporation/ Banks Declaration of Estimated Tax Payment Vouchers	15th day of 3rd, 6th, 9th, and 12th months of tax year
Withholding of Income Tax	Sole proprietor, corporation, S corporation or partnership	MW-5, Income Tax Withholding Deposit Form	See withholding instructions issued by the Department of Revenue
		MW-1, Employer's Quarterly Income Tax Withholding Return	End of month following end of quarter
Nonresident Partner or Shareholder Withholding	Partnership S corporation	M-3 (Schedule MW-3NR) M-S3-4 (Schedule MW-3NR)	Due date of tax return
Providing Information on Withholding of Tax	Sole proprietor, corporation, S corporation, or partnership	MW-6, Year End Withholding Reconciliation; MW1-A, Minnesota Employer's Income Tax Withholding Annual Return/Reconciliation	February 28 for both

* Note that generally speaking, single-member LLCs may choose to be taxed as a sole proprietorship or a corporation. LLCs with at least two members may choose to be taxed either as a corporation or as a partnership.

STATE OF MINNESOTA TAX REQUIREMENTS

YOU MAY BE LIABLE FOR	IF YOU ARE OR ARE TAXED AS*	USE FORM	DUE ON OR BEFORE
Unemployment Tax	Sole proprietor, corporation, S corporation, partnership, limited liability partnership	MDES-13, Report to Determine Liability	Prior to hiring employees
		MDES-1, Unemployment Quarterly Tax Report	One month after end of each calendar quarter
Minimum Fee	Corporation	M-4	Due date of tax return
	S Corporation	M-3S-4	
	Partnership	M-3	
Other Taxes	Call Department of Revenue		

* Note that generally speaking, single-member LLCs may choose to be taxed as a sole proprietorship or a corporation. LLCs with at least two members may choose to be taxed either as a corporation or as a partnership.

SOURCES OF INFORMATION AND ASSISTANCE

STATE PROGRAMS

MINNESOTA SMALL BUSINESS ASSISTANCE OFFICE

The Minnesota Small Business Assistance Office, specifically created by Minnesota Statutes § 116J.66, provides accurate, timely and comprehensive information and assistance to businesses in all areas of start-up, operation and expansion. Functionally, the office has two bureaus for service delivery: the Bureau of Business Licenses and the Bureau of Small Business. The specific services of the Bureau of Business Licenses and the Bureau of Small Business are described below. For further information on these programs or to order any of the publications, call or write the Minnesota Small Business Assistance Office at the address and telephone number listed in the Resource Directory section of this Guide.

The Minnesota Small Business Assistance Office also administers the Small Business Development Center program. For further information on this program, call or write Minnesota Small Business Development Centers at the address and telephone number listed in the Resource Directory section of this Guide.

Bureau of Business Licenses

The Bureau of Business Licenses provides a number of services at no charge. It publishes the ***State of Minnesota Directory of Licenses and Permits*** reproduced in this Guide. That Directory is also available electronically at www.dted.state.mn.us. The Bureau provides comprehensive information on the number and kind of licenses required for a business venture, the agencies which issue them and the affirmative burdens imposed on applicants. The Bureau will also provide opinions from licensing agencies on their use of discretion in issuing licenses, and the potential issues and difficulties in obtaining licenses based on a review of a potential applicant's business concept. Master application procedures for obtaining related and similar licenses from different licensing agencies of the state are available, as well as consolidation of hearings involved in obtaining multiple licenses and information on related licensing requirements of federal and local governments.

Bureau of Small Business

The Bureau of Small Business serves as a focal point within state government for information. It publishes ***Checklist for Hiring an Employee*** (reprinted in this Guide), an outline of the federal and state requirements governing the hiring of an employee; ***A Guide to Intellectual Property Protection***, a primer for the inventor and the entrepreneur on the protection of new ideas and the products which result from them; ***A Legal Guide for the Software Developer,*** intended to familiarize small businesses and independent inventors who develop new computer software with the basic legal issues involved in developing, protecting and distributing their inventions and products; ***A Legal Guide to the Internet,*** designed to alert Minnesota companies, employers and residents to issues which commonly are in conjunction with operating on the Internet; ***An Employer's Guide to Employment Law Issues in Minnesota,*** designed to alert Minnesota employers to issues which commonly arise in the employment relationship; ***An Employer's Guide to Employee Handbooks in Minnesota,*** a discussion of some of the major issues associated with the development of employee handbooks, including the handbook functions, the concept of "at will" employment, and determining appropriate handbook provisions; ***Leave Comparison for Minnesota Employers,*** designed to provide guidance on employee leaves, including those mandated by state and federal laws, and published in four different formats because federal and state employee leave laws vary depending on the number of employees an employer has; ***An Employers' Guide to Employee Benefits*** discusses employee benefits, including pension and welfare plans; ***A Manufacturer's Guide to Products Liability Law in Minnesota,*** addressing theories of liability, types of claims that may be brought against manufacturers, possible defenses, damages that can be recoverable at trial, and preventive strategies that manufacturers can use to reduce the risk that a product liability lawsuit will be brought against them; ***An Introduction to Franchising,*** a discussion of the practical business, legal and procedural considerations involved in the establishment, marketing and operation of a franchise; ***Securities Law Considerations when Raising Capital – An Entrepreneur's Guide,*** providing a general overview of the various federal and state securities law considerations involved in raising capital and including such areas as "taking a company public," "due diligence," the investment agreement and tax consequences of capital financing; ***Incorporating and Operating a Minnesota Business Corporation,*** intended to help shareholders, directors and officers of new Minnesota corporations identify and address various post-incorporation issues; ***Doing Business in the European Union,*** designed to assist Minnesota businesses as they formulate plans for their companies' international operations in Europe; ***Doing Business in the United Kingdom,*** which provides U.S. business persons with an overview of the major legal, business and other considerations involved in conducting business activities in the United Kingdom; ***Small Business Notes,*** an electronic format serial publication presenting a brief overview of recent trends, developments and issues affecting small businesses. ***Small Business Notes*** is available on the web at www.dted.state.mn.us (click on "Business", click on "Publications", click on "Business and Economic Development"). Note that a number of these publications, along with Occasional Papers and E-Alerts detailing various issues of interest to businesses, are also available on the Minnesota Department of Trade and Economic Development's website at www.dted.state.mn.us. (Click on "Business," click on "Publications," and click on "Business and Economic Development.") The Bureau continually produces new publications throughout the year. Contact the Bureau for a current publications list. All publications are available free of charge. The Bureau also sponsors seminars and workshops on small business issues.

Small Business Development Centers

The Minnesota Small Business Development Centers provide one-on-one business counseling and group training seminars on management topics to small businesses throughout Minnesota. Most Small Business Development Centers are located within an hour's drive of a county seat. Counseling services are free. Training seminars are provided at nominal cost. Fees may be charged for out-of-pocket costs and specialized services.

Counseling services primarily focus on assisting new and growing businesses in the areas of business planning, financial analysis and loan packaging, and marketing. Directly and through collaboration with other organizations, the Small Business Development Centers also offer assistance and referrals in areas like regulatory compliance assistance, federal research and development opportunities, information technology, exporting, and government procurement. Counseling is customized to meet the needs of the client, and may be provided by staff or private sector counselors.

Training seminars offered by the Small Business Development Centers are designed to help small business owners and managers strengthen their management skills. Topics change to meet the needs of participants. Recent topics have included access to capital, understanding and using financial statements, market analysis and planning, workplace communication, employment issues, international trade, selling to the government, taxation, and federal research and development opportunities. Small Business Development Centers also offer access to pre-business workshops to help those who are considering starting a business to explore the possibilities and determine whether to pursue the venture. Training seminars offered by the Small Business Development Centers are listed on the Department of Trade and Economic Development Internet site, http://www.dted.state.mn.us.

Resource libraries at Small Business Development Centers offer access to business books and periodicals and to computerized data bases. Many Small Business Development Centers have computers and business software that may be used by clients to develop business plans. The Small Business Development Centers are accessible by Internet, and most offer on-line counseling.

The Small Business Development Centers are a partnership of the U.S. Small Business Administration, the Minnesota Department of Trade and Economic Development, and the colleges, universities, and other organizations where Small Business Development Centers are located. Businesses served by the Small Business Development Centers must meet size standards and other requirements for assistance established by the U.S. Small Business Administration.

Addresses and telephone numbers for members of the Small Business Development Center network are listed in the Resource Directory section of this Guide.

MINNESOTA TRADE OFFICE

The Minnesota Trade Office (MTO), a division of the Department of Trade and Economic Development, promotes international trade and provides information, training and counseling to Minnesota businesses that desire to sell their products and services in the international marketplace.

The MTO provides assistance for businesses new to exporting entirely or new to specific markets. It also offers ongoing support for businesses that have built an export base in other countries but require further assistance to strengthen their position or expand their global reach. Programs and services focus on the countries and industries that have the greatest potential for developing and improving Minnesota's export opportunities.

The MTO's Export Promotion unit, which is staffed with a team of export professionals with broad international business experience, provides a variety of valuable services, all of which are designed to help Minnesota businesses establish themselves more quickly and easily in foreign markets.

The Export Promotion Unit identifies markets for Minnesota products and services; provides one-on-one counseling to companies either at the Trade Office or at the company's location; assists businesses with trade leads; provides referrals regarding export services; arranges and leads trade missions to promote Minnesota's products and services; promotes Minnesota products and services at national and international trade shows; hosts foreign delegations; plans itineraries and arranges meetings to help foreign buyers find compatible Minnesota companies; provides market intelligence and personalized export consultation; assists Minnesota agricultural providers in developing agricultural markets; helps foreign companies locate facilities in Minnesota buy finding appropriate government, legal, real estate and business services, and maintains an international information network.

The MTO's Education and Information unit conducts intensive export-training seminars and workshops statewide to familiarize potential exporters with the fundamentals of international trade. The unit also maintains the International Research Center, an exhaustive repository of detailed and up-to-date information on foreign markets, current trends and general export information and statistics.

An invaluable tool for exporters at all levels, the center is open to the public and provides professional researchers to assist patrons as they gather background information on foreign markets and economies, marketing, regulations, standards and culture. Materials are available to help exporters learn the basic mechanics of exporting and the art of conducting business in countries around the globe. The center has economic data, export statistics, international trade periodicals, information on trade shows, "How-to-Export" guides and company directories.

Contact the Minnesota Trade Office at the address and telephone number provided in the Resource Directory section of this guide.

EMPLOYMENT AND TRAINING PROGRAMS

Minnesota WorkForce Centers

Minnesota WorkForce Centers help bring together employers and qualified workers. The Job Service offices are part of the WorkForce Center System, a one-stop, integrated site where employers and job seekers can have their employment and training needs met. WorkForce Centers are found all over Minnesota and provide customer-driven services in cooperation with community and business partners. A list of WorkForce Centers is provided in the Resource Directory section of this Guide.

Services of Job Service offices are funded by the FUTA tax. Most services are provided free of charge. Employer services available through Job Service include job posting, recruitment assistance, pre-screening and testing of job applicants, labor market information, informational seminars, reemployment insurance information, and youth employment programs. Job openings are listed in a computerized job bank.

Employers can access Minnesota's Job Bank and America's Job Bank through the Internet. To market their qualifications, job seekers enter resumes into this national network, which is then searched by employers looking for workers to meet their needs. The internet address can be found in the Resource Directory section of this Guide.

Services provided by Minnesota WorkForce Centers include:

- Regional Analysts are used by business and economic development communities to deliver customized presentations relating to relocation or expansion in certain regions. They answer questions related to labor availability, demographics, employment projections, and other issues related to regional economics. Regional Analysts also participate in special projects statewide, such as the Northeast Minnesota Skills Assessment, worker shortage issues, and regional labor market surveys. For more information contact the Regional Analysts at the phone number listed in the Resource Directory section of this Guide.
- The Regional Analysis unit can assist in answering many questions for businesses, such as: what is the availability of workers with specific skills, education, etc? What are the prevailing wage rates in a specific skill area or region? What training programs are available in a specific area? What is the unemployment rate in a given area? How many persons are employed in a specific occupational area, or within a specific region? How many persons are being trained in a specific region, or within certain occupational areas?
- Minnesota's Job Bank allows job seekers to enter their resumes, and validated employers and private employment agencies to search for workers who meet their needs. The job openings portion allows employers to electronically post job openings. These services are provided to the public through Minnesota WorkForce Centers. The Internet address for these services is http://www.mnworks.org.
- The WorkForce Center Resource Areas contain a wide range of information and tools such as books, videos, directories, tapes, periodicals, and self-help tutorials for widely-used computer applications. Personal computers with Internet access to job listings, applicant listings, local employer home pages, and education and career education are also available at no cost for job seekers, employers and students.

- Tax and employment seminars are regularly scheduled. For more information, contact your nearest WorkForce Center.
- Job Skills Analysis, Applicant and Employee Assessment, and Customized Training Services. A service from the Minnesota Department of Economic Security and Minnesota State Colleges and Universities can help employers hire the best employees by undergoing job analysis exercises, creating position descriptions, and the like. For more information and a free consultation, call the appropriate number listed in the Resource Directory section of this Guide.

Apprenticeship and Training Programs

Voluntary apprenticeship programs are operated by employers, employer associations and/or unions to provide occupational training in industry and trade areas. Apprentices learn a skilled trade through on the job work experience and related classroom or correspondence instruction, working with and learning from skilled individuals.

Employers enter into an apprenticeship agreement with a person who is at least 16 years of age. The apprenticeship agreement provides for not less than 2000 hours of reasonably continuous on the job employment and 144 hours of related instruction per year in an approved training program. Apprentices who complete a state-certified program receive certificates of completion.

The Division of Voluntary Apprenticeship of the Minnesota Department of Labor and Industry works with the prospective sponsor in establishing an apprenticeship program, and provides supportive services throughout the apprenticeship.

The Division of Voluntary Apprenticeship develops and promotes equal opportunity in apprenticeship in accordance with the Minnesota Plan for Equal Opportunity in Apprenticeship. The division is also the approving agency in the State of Minnesota for the Veterans Administration for Apprenticeship and other on-the-job training programs.

For further information contact the Department of Labor and Industry Division of Voluntary Apprenticeship at the address and telephone number provided in the Resource Directory section of this Guide.

WorkForce Investment Act (WIA Title I) Programs

Programs offered under Title I of the WorkForce Investment Act offer financial incentives to employers for hiring and training low-income and unemployed people. The programs are federally funded and locally planned and operated. On-the-job training or customized classroom training is available.

To utilize the program, employers describe their business employment needs to WIA representatives. These representatives are aware of the local labor market, and are able to match qualified applicants with available openings. Once the employer makes the final selection, an agreement is prepared between the parties.

The subsidy and training time is determined according to a certified training schedule, and payment is received within a few weeks. For customized training, other arrangements are made to cover costs. Funds are available to pay for specialized classroom training of the employer's choice or to reimburse an employer up to 50 percent of wages paid for some of the costs associated with training WIA Title I-eligible clientele.

WIA Title I services also include vocational evaluation and assessment. This service permits individualized assessment of a client's skills, as well as assessing the client's potential interests and ability to perform certain occupations.

Job training services are available free of charge to all employers. For further information on WIA Title I programs, contact the local office listed under "WorkForce Investment" in the Resource Directory section of this Guide.

MINNESOTA EXTENSION SERVICE

The Extension Service provides education through technical assistance, counseling or referral assistance in agricultural, community and economic development, forestry, family living, home-based businesses, small business and tourism. Services are provided through offices in each county, area technical specialists, state specialists, and referrals to other agencies, institutions and the private sector. Limited individual counseling is provided in agri-business, forestry related businesses, various other small businesses and tourism-recreation. Seminars on economic development and business management are conducted in cooperation with other agencies, local interest groups and various firms on topics most desired by local business groups needing assistance.

Contact the Minnesota Extension Service at the address and telephone number listed in the Resource Directory section of this Guide for the nearest Extension office.

MINNESOTA JOB SKILLS PARTNERSHIP

The Minnesota Job Skills Partnership serves as a catalyst between businesses and educational institutions in developing cooperative training projects that provide training for new jobs or to retrain existing employees. The Partnership makes grants to educational institutions, which are the eligible applicants and recipients, which have partnered with a business to identify specific training needs of the business. A cash or in-kind contribution from the business must match the Partnership's funds on a one-to-one basis. For additional descriptive information and application procedures contact the Job Skills Partnership at the address and telephone number given in the Resource Directory section of the Guide.

DISLOCATED WORKER PROGRAM

The Dislocated Worker Program is designed to provide workforce investment activities that will increase the employment, retention, and earning of employees dislocated from work. The program seeks to improve the quality and skill of Minnesota's workforce in an effort to improve productivity while at the same time reducing the burden on other social service networks. This program also offers employers the skilled and retrained workers they need to remain competitive. The program provides funds to be used for services for employees affected by both small (fewer than 50) and large (50 or more workers) layoffs. The state's Rapid Response team immediately investigates these layoffs and creates a plan for providing these services to those workers. The plans are designed to allow flexibility in tailoring specific services to the workers affected. For additional information and procedural guidelines contact the Dislocated Worker Program at (651) 296-2953 or write to Dislocated Worker Program, 500 Metro Square Building, 121 7th Place East, St. Paul, MN 55101.

GOVERNMENT PROCUREMENT ASSISTANCE

Governmental agencies at the federal, state and local level are major consumers of a variety of goods and services. Many such agencies have special set-aside or preference programs for small businesses in general and/or businesses which are owned, controlled and operated by minorities or otherwise disadvantaged individuals. The requirements for participation in these programs vary greatly as do the definitions and standards of eligibility.

In addition, many units of government are increasingly using electronic data interchange in their procurement processes. Businesses will need to prepare to participate in electronic data interchange and electronic payment systems if they intend to be able to compete for government business.

FEDERAL PROCUREMENT

The Small Business Act authorizes federal agencies to conduct procurement that are exclusively reserved for small businesses called "small business set asides." There are different programs under which these set asides are authorized.

The Small Business Reserve is a statutory provision that requires all agency purchases valued between $2,500 and $100,000 be reserved for small businesses. It applies when there are two or more responsible small businesses that can satisfy the agency's requirement at a fair market price. Contracts in this dollar range are made using simple procedures that make it easier for small businesses to participate. Procurement opportunities valued above $100,000 are subject to more complicated procedures.

The Small Business Competitive Demonstration Program (implemented in 1999) consists of two major components: (a) unrestricted competition in four designated industry groups and (b) enhanced small business participation in 10 agency targeted industry groups through the use of set-asides. If purchases are made in one of the designated industry groups, agencies are required to use open competition as long as the annual small business participation in that industry group equals a designated percentage of that agency's contracted dollars. If the participation falls below that percentage, the agency is authorized to conduct small business set-asides until that percentage is achieved.

The Very Small Business (VSB) Program is an extension of the small business set-aside program administered by the SBA as a pilot to increase opportunities for VSB concerns. Procurement requirements, including construction requirements, estimated to be between $2,500 and $50,000 must be reserved for eligible VSB concerns if certain criteria are met.

Several other federal procurement programs exist for small businesses. These programs address the areas of contractor responsibility, subcontracting opportunities, innovation research, technology, business development and disadvantaged businesses.

The Certification of Competency Program requires the government to purchase goods and services from responsible contractors, meaning that the contractor has the capacity, financial resources, business acumen and required eligibility to perform a federal prime contract.

A significant amount of dollars awarded to prime contractors are expended to promote and support the process of subcontracting to small businesses for goods and services.

Under the Small Business Innovation Research (SBIR) Program, federal agencies having research and development budgets in access of $100 million set aside a percent for awards to small high-technology firms. The SBIR program is discussed in the Sources of Information and Assistance section of this Guide.

Under the Small Business Technology Transfer Program (STTP) federal agencies having annual research and development budgets of more than $1 billion will set aside a percentage for awards to small high-technology firms that collaborate with non-profit research institutions.

The 8(a) Business Development Program is designed to provide business assistance and training to help socially and economically disadvantaged citizens gain access to the economic mainstream. This nine year program, consisting of a four year developmental stage and a five year transition stage, provides specialized businesses training, counseling and the ability to obtain contracts through sole-source and restricted competition procedures.

The Small Disadvantaged Business Program is designed to help Small Disadvantaged Businesses (SBDs) obtain government contracts. The SBA must certify a small business that seeks to obtain SBD status. Certified firms are eligible to receive a price evaluation credit when competing for contracts in certain designated industries.

Recent Reforms

Older preference programs for small businesses, specially disadvantaged businesses, were once effective in promoting small business market-share. The Supreme Court's *Adarand* decision restricted federal affirmative action practices that use ethnic or racial criteria as a basis for decision- making. In procurement, using race as a determining factor in awarding contracts is now subject to strict scrutiny and must serve a compelling government interest.

The Federal Acquisition Streamlining Act established the requirement for the creation of the FACNET, a government-wide electronic contracting system. The objective is to provide a paperless system for the electronic exchange of data to support procurement transactions.

Eventually, all firms must be able to receive electronic payments in order to be eligible to contract with the government. Programs are in place to help small businesses make the conversion to electronic commerce and interface with government EDI (Electronic Data Interchange) systems.

Micro-purchases (government purchases at or below $2,500, $2,000 for construction) are made using the simplest and most direct buying techniques. Micro-purchases may be made by telephone, over the counter, by Internet transactions, or other means of electronic communication. A government wide commercial purchase card is expedient to have for these purchases.

Simplified acquisitions procedures apply to procurement with an estimated value of $100,000 and below. As mentioned above, procurement valued between $2,500 and $100,000 are reserved exclusively for small businesses. Simplified acquisitions are made using oral or written solicitations along with commercial purchase cards or electronic purchasing techniques.

The largest volume of dollars expended by the federal government is made through the use of formal procedures for acquisitions above the $100,000 simplified acquisition threshold. Formal procedures include sealed bidding where an Invitation for Bids is used and negotiations where a Request for Proposals is used. Under sealed bidding procedures, contractors submit bids that are opened publicly at a time and place designated by the purchasing agency. Award is made to the lowest priced responsible bidder. In a negotiation, a statement of work outlining the goals to be achieved by the contractor describes the requirements. Negotiations has been proven to be an effective technique for obtaining a range of solutions.

There is also a growing trend among federal agencies to negotiate long-term Multiple-Award Task Order contracts. These contracts frequently combine a wide range and large volume of work that had previously been the subject of individual contracts.

Resources

Procurement actions expected to exceed the sole-source 8(a) award requirements threshold or designated SDB-eligible are published in the U.S. Department of Commerce's "Commerce Business Daily" (CBD). This publication can be obtained from the U.S. Government Printing Office or on the (free) CBD website at: http://cbdnet.gpo.gov.

Many federal agencies publish their requirements on their own home pages.

The Small Business Act requires that agencies annually publish a list of their requirements for upcoming fiscal years. These requirements can be accessed through individual agency websites or the SBA website.

The U.S. Department of Defense also has a Central Contractor Registration through the Internet.

STATE PROCUREMENT

The state of Minnesota has a program for enabling small businesses and small businesses owned by targeted groups to participate in the state procurement process. Under this program, the state may set aside certain contracts for award to small businesses, may grant preferences for bids by small targeted group businesses, and may require state contractors to subcontract with small firms.

The small business procurement program and the targeted group procurement program are administered by the Department of Administration. Information and an application package may be obtained by contacting the Materials Management Division of that Department at the address and telephone number provided in the Resource Directory section of this Guide. Also, note that that Division's web site is a good source of information (www.mmd.admin.state.mn.us).

Purchases from Small Business in General

Each fiscal year the Department of Administration must ensure that small businesses receive at least 25 percent of the total value of anticipated total state procurement of goods and services, including printing and construction. In addition, every state agency must for each fiscal year designate for awarding to small businesses at least 25 percent of the anticipated procurements of that agency for professional and technical services.

Note that at the time this Guide went to press, the Department of Administration was in the process of formulating modifications of existing Rules to reflect changes to the state procurement process (which Rules would define a "small" business) made under Chapter 386 from the 1998 legislative session.

To be eligible for the small business procurement program, a business must have its principal place of business in Minnesota; be a manufacturer, manufacturer's representative, dealer, jobber, distributor, contractor, or business engaged in a joint venture; not be a broker, third party lessor, or franchise; and comply with revenue or sales limitations for the industry established by the Department of Administration.

Purchases from Small Targeted Group Businesses

The purpose of the targeted group procurement program is to remedy the effects of past discrimination against members of targeted groups. Periodically, the Department of Administration studies whether effects of past discrimination continue to dampen the participation of members of targeted groups. The last such study was submitted to the legislature in February, 1999, and the resulting report is titled "State of Minnesota Disparity Study." To be considered under the program, a business must be so designated by the Commissioner of the Department of Administration; businesses can be designated under one of two possible avenues. First, for businesses majority owned and operated by women, persons with a substantial physical disability, or specific minorities, the designation is made on the basis of "purchasing categories". A business is eligible under the program if the Commissioner "determines there is a statistical disparity between the percentage of purchasing from businesses owned by group members and the representation of businesses owned by group members among all businesses in the state in the purchasing category." Second, the Commissioner may designate a business if the Commissioner "determines that inclusion is necessary to remedy discrimination against the owner based on race, gender, or disability in attempting to operate a business that would provide goods or services to public agencies." (Note that the statute specifically provides that such designations of purchasing categories and businesses are not rules for purposes of Chapter 14 of Minnesota Statutes, and are not subject to the rulemaking provisions of that Chapter.)

To be eligible for the small targeted group procurement program, a business must be majority owned and operated by women, or by persons with a disability, or by specific minorities; and have its principal place of business in Minnesota. Also, to qualify a business must: not be a manufacturer, manufacturer's representative, dealer, jobber, distributor, contractor, or business engaged in a joint venture; not be a broker, third party lessor, or franchise; comply with revenue or sales limitations for the industry established by the Department of Administration; and be certified as eligible according to procedures and criteria established by the Department of Administration.

To qualify for the targeted group and economically disadvantaged procurement programs, the business must file an application for certification and supporting documentation with the Materials Management Division of the Department of Administration. The application and supporting documentation are reviewed by the staff of the Materials Management Division for conformity with applicable laws. A business that is certified by the Department of Administration is eligible to participate in small business procurement programs of the Department of Administration, and could be eligible to participate in similar programs of the state Department of Transportation and some metropolitan agencies, without further certification. Certified businesses must submit an annual report to the Materials Management Division verifying information on file with the Division.

The incentive for targeted group vendors is the pricing preference received on state contracts. Specifically, the Commissioner of Administration may award up to a six percent preference in the amount bid for specified goods or services (i.e., a bid for $106 is treated the same as a bid for $100 by a non-targeted business), when the bidder is a small targeted group business. Likewise, a pricing preference of up to six percent (four percent for construction projects) may be awarded for bids submitted by a small business located in an "economically disadvantaged area". For this purpose, a business can qualify by meeting one of three tests: the owner resides in or the business is located in a county in which the median income for married couples is less than 70% of the state median income for married couples; the owner resides in or the business is located in an area designated a "labor surplus" area by the U.S. Department of Labor; or, the business is a rehabilitation facility or work activity program. Also, the Department of Administration may designate a "targeted neighborhood" (so designated pursuant to Minnesota Statutes section 469.202) or an "enterprise zone" (so designated pursuant to Minnesota Statutes section 469.167) as "economically disadvantaged" for purposes of that 6% preference.

All laws and rules pertaining to solicitations, bid evaluations, contract awards, and other procurement matters apply equally to procurements from small businesses. Before making an award under the small targeted group business program, the Department of Administration is directed by statute to evaluate whether the small business scheduled to receive the award is able to perform the contract. The determination includes consideration of production and financial capacity and technical competence.

LOCAL PROCUREMENT

Businesses interested in selling their goods or services to local units of government should contact each locality. Outside the immediate Twin Cities area the local city clerk or county auditor is the best first step in determining the potential for sales to local governments. For the cities of Minneapolis and St. Paul, procurement contacts are listed in the Resource Directory section of this Guide.

RESEARCH AND DEVELOPMENT PROGRAMS

MINNESOTA PROJECT INNOVATION, INC.

Minnesota Project Innovation, Inc. (MPI) is a private non-profit organization that assists Minnesota businesses in:

- Maximizing the receipt of federal funds through the Small Business Innovation Research (SBIR) program, the Small Business Technology Transfer (STTR) programs, and other research and development funding programs; and
- Increasing the receipt of contracts available through federal, state and local governments.

Federal Research and Development Funding

MPI assists high technology companies to increase receipt of federal research and development grants through the SBIR and STTR programs. Each year approximately $1.2 billion will be available to small businesses through the SBIR and STTR programs. The SBIR and STTR programs offer emerging, high technology companies up to $850,000 each to conduct research and development activities to lead to a commercial product. Each year, the SBIR and STTR programs offer more than 500 research topics. MPI offers several services to maximize the receipt of federal funds by Minnesota companies through these programs including workshops, information databases, one-on-one consulting, business development assistance, and corporate partnering.

Government Procurement Assistance

MPI's Government Procurement program assists businesses to successfully bid on federal and state contracts as prime and/or subcontractors. This program can help businesses identify relevant government procurement activities and agencies that match a company's products and services, provide awareness of active solicitations, and furnish procurement price histories for reference. MPI also provides electronic commerce and electronic data interchange training and implementation for government procurement. In addition to the Minneapolis office, this program has satellite offices in Mankato, Moorhead, Burnsville, St. Cloud, St. Paul and Virginia.

MINNESOTA SEED CAPITAL NETWORK

For a fee, the Minnesota Seed Capital Network, administered by MPI, introduces private investors to high technology companies seeking to raise seed capital ranging from $250,000 to $2.5 milion.

MINNESOTA TECHNOLOGY, INC.

Minnesota Technology, Inc. (MTI) is a state technology-based economic development organization. MTI's mission is to strengthen and diversify the state's economy by helping industry apply, develop and commercialize technology. MTI's staff of industry and business specialists works with companies throughout Greater Minnesota to provide them with productivity/automation solutions and help them keep pace with domestic and global competition through advanced manufacturing and technology. In the Twin Cities area, MTI promotes the growth of the technology community by identifying and supporting technology networks, hosting Technology Awareness forums and providing information, references and referrals for emerging Twin Cities technology companies. The addresses and telephone numbers for MTI offices are listed in the Resource Directory section of this Guide.

Manufacturing and Technology Assistance

Minnesota Technology, Inc. is an affiliate of the U.S. Department of Commerce's National Institute of Standards and Technology (NIST) and is the state's Manufacturing Extension Partnership (MEP) center. MTI offers:

- Customized, on-site technology assistance – Working one-on-one with companies to help manage projects through expertise and technology to streamline processes, improve product quality, reduce manufacturing costs, rework inventory and waste, identify new markets and help companies grow.
- Accessing federal lab technologies – MTI's staff works closely with Federal Research Laboratories located within NASA, the U.S. Department of Energy and the U.S. Department of Defense. This partnership enables small- to- medium-sized Minnesota companies secure federal lab technology and expertise and adapt it to their needs, leading to solutions for product development, engineering issues, testing and research and development.
- Leveraging technology expertise at colleges and universities – MTI bridges the gap between business needs and academia by connecting small companies to the technology expertise and R&D resources at our colleges and universities. Through MTI staff located at the University of Minnesota's Institute of Technology and Academic Health Center, as well as other institutions, MTI brings companies together with faculty, students and research laboratories.
- eBusiness strategies and tools – the eBusiness Institute, a partnership with the University of Minnesota-Crookston, provides senior managers of small- to-medium size firms with information on how the Internet can help them grow their businesses. In addition, MTI's eBusiness specialists provide customized services to companies.

- Minnesota Technology Directory – MTI publishes a directory of Minnesota technology-intensive companies. The Directory contains valuable on-line profiles of 2,000 firms and can be used to identify technology leaders, uncover new customers, profile competitors, track emerging technologies and create valuable partnerships. The web site is: www.minnesotatechnology.org/directories/directory.
- Sharing knowledge, insight, perspective on-line – MTI's web site includes information on the state's technology community and assets through the "MN Tech Scene" and "Trends and Analysis."
- FastTrac Manufacturing – Through a joint effort between MTI and the University of St. Thomas, the FastTrac-Manufacturing™ program is available to owners and managers of Minnesota manufacturing firms. FastTrac-Manufacturing is a national education program created by experienced business owners to help manufacturers look at their entire manufacturing operation and develop a plan for growth. FastTrac-Manufacturing™ is a hands-on learning experience that gives manufacturers the opportunity to put proven business practices to work immediately because they use their own company as the case study in the program. Topics covered in this 11-session program include management, marketing research and tactics, financial tools and management, managing growth, and money sources.
- The Small Manufacturers Success – MTI and the Minnesota Department of Trade and Economic Development have formed a partnership to help small manufacturing and technology business owners and managers successfully grow their businesses by identifying the company's areas of excellence and recommending opportunities for improvements. The service will be delivered by several of the Small Business Development Centers (SBDCs) in Greater Minnesota. In addition to the direct assistance to these companies, training programs or workshops will be based on the most important collective needs of small manufacturers aimed to help them be successful.

ACCOUNTING AND TAX ASSISTANCE

PUBLIC ACCOUNTANTS

A Certified Public Accountant (CPA) is a person licensed and certified by the state for professional competence and experience in the field of accounting whose education and experience background includes: completion of a college accounting program; passing a rigorous exam in accounting, auditing, income taxes and business law; qualifying for certification by the State Board of Accountancy; practicing according to a strict code of ethics; meeting continuing education requirements; and passing a peer review of their policies and procedures every three years. A Licensed Public Accountant (LPA) is also licensed by the state without having passed an examination. An LPA provides many of the same functions as a CPA and is also required to meet ongoing continuing professional education and peer review.

CPAs are qualified to provide a variety of services, but their services are particularly beneficial to start-up situations in three general areas: financial statement services; tax-related services; and financial planning and consulting services.

Financial Statement Services

Accounting is the language of business. It ties together the marketing and management operations of a business. CPAs and LPAs use this language to communicate needed information to their clients. The financial statements are the medium through which pertinent information is transmitted to businesses. They usually include the accountant's report; balance sheet; income statement; cash flow statement; and notes to the financial statements.

Each statement gives a different aspect of the condition or result of operations for a period of time. The more one understands and respects the language, the more benefit one derives from the financial statements. The present and prospective activities of the business will often dictate that a CPA give independent, objective opinions on financial statements prepared by management. The reports rendered by the CPA on the financial statements are generally at one of three levels:

- **An Audit.** A positive assertion on financial statements that the financial statements do or do not present fairly the financial position, results of operations, and cash flows in accordance with generally accepted accounting principles or another comprehensive basis of accounting consistently applied.
- **A Review.** Limited assurance that nothing came to the accountant's attention to indicate the statements were not in accordance with generally accepted accounting principles or another comprehensive basis of accounting.
- **A Compilation.** An indication that the financial statements were compiled from information represented by management and that no assurance is given on them.

The level of reporting plays a significant role because it indicates the degree of assurance that the CPA or LPA is rendering on the financial statements. Where a business has borrowed from a financial institution, the size of the debt will usually dictate what level of assurance the bank would like to see.

Tax-Related Services

The entrepreneur often doesn't realize that tax planning is a source of business capital. Careful planning and the use of a CPA or LPA can enhance this source of funds. Income taxes must be paid on business profits; hence, they are expenses of a business. These income taxes, if properly planned, can be kept to a minimum, thus leaving cash available for financing your business. In addition, if a business should fail, you will want the most advantageous treatment of these losses. The CPA and LPA must always be aware of current changes in the tax law and can provide the proper vehicle for making the most of this source of funds. For example, the CPA and LPA can: assist in structuring the initial organization of proprietorships, partnerships (whether general, limited or limited liability) or corporations; assist in structuring a possible tax-free incorporation; assist in structuring business purchase, sale or liquidation transactions; prepare various compliance tax reports, such as individual, partnership and corporate income tax, payroll, sales tax, property taxes; handle tax examinations and tax planning strategies; assist in estate planning and personal tax planning; and assist in the implementation of executive compensation, retirement plans and employee benefit programs.

Financial Planning and Consulting Services

A CPA or LPA can assist a business in choosing the form of business organization; setting up an accounting system and procedures; defining and obtaining reporting, operational and cost control needs; developing and evaluating the business plan, forecasts and budgets; strategic planning; preparing special purpose reports including statements prepared on comprehensive bases of accounting other than generally accepted accounting principles; preparing reports with opinion on specific financial statement elements such as accounts receivable and inventory reports; discussing results of applying agreed-upon procedures to specific financial statement elements; implementing cash flow and management reports; structuring and implementing financing plans for the start-up, operation, and expansion stages; preparing reports to management on the strengths and weaknesses of internal accounting controls along with recommendations to correct the weaknesses; preparing bank loan applications for initial or expansion capital needs; computer selection, implementation and training; and providing advice on business valuations and mergers and acquisitions.

The Minnesota Society of Certified Public Accountants maintains a free referral service to put businesses in contact with qualified CPAs. In addition, that organization has developed a free informational kit for small businesses, titled ***"Starting a Small Business in Minnesota***. Contact the MNCPA at the telephone number listed in the Resource Directory section of this Guide.

ENROLLED AGENTS

Enrolled Agents are trained and experienced tax professionals who have either passed a comprehensive examination given by the Department of the Treasury or have had five continuous years of experience with the Internal Revenue Service at the audit level. Enrolled Agents must maintain their credentials through continuing tax education which is reported directly to the Internal Revenue Service. Enrolled Agents are trained to handle complex tax returns for individuals, partnerships, corporations and other tax entities, and are authorized to represent taxpayers at all administrative levels before the Internal Revenue Service. Information and referrals may be obtained from the National Association of Enrolled Agents referral hotline telephone number provided in the Resource Directory Section of this Guide or from the Minnesota Society of Enrolled Agents at the website provided in the Resource Directory section of this Guide.

TAXPAYER EDUCATION WORKSHOPS

The Internal Revenue Service and the Minnesota Departments of Revenue and Economic Security sponsor free workshops on tax issues for small businesses. For more information on these workshops contact either the Minnesota Department of Revenue at (800) 888-6231, or (651) 297-4213 in the metro area.

ACCOUNTABILITY MINNESOTA

AccountAbility Minnesota is a nonprofit organization that assists low-income individuals and small business owners with their accounting issues and tax filing requirements. Low-cost accounting set-up and support is provided by accounting consultants or by volunteers who donate their time and expertise to work with clients on broader business and management issues.

AccountAbility Minnesota also offers small business workshops on tax and accounting-related topics. These classes are provided periodically and are open to the public.

Eligibility. Depending on the type of business, direct services are limited to business owners whose household income, including gross business revenue, is less than $30,000. If the business involves selling a product or requires the hiring of an employee(s) or renting office space, this income ceiling may be as much as $40,000. However, each business will be evaluated on a case-by-case basis to determine eligibility.

The assistance is not meant to be ongoing as one would expect from an accounting or bookkeeping service. Up to 25 hours of consulting services will be provided. The goal of AccountAbility Minnesota is to equip entrepreneurs with the tools to manage their financial record keeping and reporting systems at a level with which they are comfortable.

Typical Services. Typical service areas include record keeping systems; financial statements and helping clients to understand them; reporting and filing requirements; financial management; business planning; accounting software; payroll tax returns and income tax preparation.

To apply for help, business owners must complete an application form and submit a $25 application fee. To obtain this form or for more information, contact AccountAbility Minnesota at the address and telephone number provided in the Resource Directory section of this Guide. Class schedules and other information is also available on their website.

LIBRARIES

LIBRARY SERVICES

Although libraries are often overlooked by many business owners and operators, in fact libraries and librarians in many cases can be an invaluable source of assistance. Virtually every library is a point of access and assistance to print materials, electronic data bases, CD Roms, national and international distribution channels. While many of these items can be used by patrons themselves, it is important not to discount the fact that librarians are the most familiar with these resources and are in many cases the only experts skilled in the use of these resources. Skilled professionals know the complexities, the strengths and pitfalls of the resources. These tricks of the trade can save the entrepreneur or small business person time, hassle and money.

Traditional library materials, books or journals explore a range of topics of interest to any business person – starting a business, product protection, employee rights and responsibilities, accounting, taxation, marketing, quality management, writing a business plan, economic trends or emerging technologies. Libraries also offer reference tools including indexes to business, finance, scientific and technical journals, lists of trade and professional associations, guides to government publications, annual reports, files on Minnesota companies, information on local and regional resources. Those reference tools are valuable in preparing a business plan, researching competitors and trends performing analysis of customers and many other situations.

Today's libraries also offer access to online data bases of business, technical, geographic and demographic information; the data may be full text, references to other sources, or numeric information. In most cases, a skilled searcher is a great asset to the novice user exploring online information sources and, again, librarians are experts in the use of online resources.

Many Minnesota libraries also serve as depositories for specified government data and information from state and federal agencies. Depository libraries include print publications and, increasingly, access and software to manipulate electronic data bases.

A rapidly increasing number of library collections can be searched from remote locations. At present the University of Minnesota, the State Colleges and Universities libraries, state agencies and the Minneapolis Public Library can be searched from any dial-up terminal. Plans call for increased extension of remote access in the near future.

While most users appropriately think first of the local public library that library can itself point to other library collections, some of which feature special business collections and business reference tools. College and university libraries frequently serve the broader communities in which they reside. Libraries in government agencies offer unique publications and professional assistance. Special libraries also serve larger corporations, law firms, medical institutions and a vast array of specific target user populations. Many of these libraries participate in multitype library systems that link them with the broader library and information community. As a result, library patrons can access materials from many different sources, and in many cases that access will be the result of a search by a librarian.

A list of libraries and library networks can be found in the Resource Directory section of this Guide.

ADDITIONAL SOURCES OF ASSISTANCE

MANAGEMENT ASSISTANCE FOR MINORITY BUSINESSES

There are a number of organizations which offer business planning and business management assistance specifically targeted to businesses owned and operated by racial minorities, women, disabled individuals, and other socially or economically disadvantaged persons. A listing of these organizations can be found in the Resource Directory section of this Guide.

INCUBATORS

Sometimes called enterprise centers, innovation centers or business and technology centers, incubators offer new, small firms a way to minimize both fixed and variable costs by providing low cost office and production space, shared office services, management assistance and – in some cases – financial assistance.

INVENTORS RESOURCES

The Minnesota Inventors Congress (MIC) provides information and assistance for inventors. It serves as a focal point for an invention support system in the state by providing literature and guidance about the invention process. An annual Inventors Conference provides an opportunity for inventors to meet with manufacturers and financiers and to test market their inventions. The MIC also conducts educational seminars and workshops and publishes a quarterly newsletter ***MIC MEMO***.

For assistance or further information contact the Minnesota Inventors Congress at the address and telephone number listed in the Resource Directory section of this Guide.

MINNESOTA TECHNICAL ASSISTANCE PROGRAM

The Minnesota Technical Assistance Program (MnTAP), was created in 1984 at the University of Minnesota with support from the Minnesota Office of Environmental Assistance as a resource for pollution prevention assistance. MnTAP helps Minnesota businesses protect the environment and stay competitive by providing practical alternatives for minimizing industrial waste and preventing pollution of our land, air, and water. MnTAP is not a regulatory agency, and its services are provided at no cost to any Minnesota business. Staff at MnTAP includes scientists and engineers with industry experience.

MnTAP offers the following types of assistance to Minnesota companies that need help with their solid, hazardous, and nonhazardous industrial waste problems:

- **Telephone assistance:** MnTAP staff can provide information on:
  - Alternative raw materials to use in manufacturing processes
  - Process redesign to improve process efficiency and prevent pollution, including reducing hazardous waste, air emission and wastewater loading
  - Decreasing waste management costs
  - Efficient technologies being used in your industry
- **On-site assistance:** MnTAP staff will visit your facility to evaluate your operation and help identify pollution prevention opportunities and proper waste management practices.
- **Student intern program:** MnTAP will hire and pay a college student to work at your company to solve waste problems by developing effective waste reduction solutions.
- **Information resources:** MnTAP can offer technical resources on process equipment, options for process change, chemical substitution or waste management. Case studies, fact sheets reference lists, and the MnTAP newsletter, *SOURCE*, provide useful information on pollution prevention, waste management, and regulatory compliance. Access MnTAP publications and useful links at MnTAP's web site: www.mntap.umn.edu. MnTAP also conducts workshops and seminars with trade associations. These provide information on pollution prevention opportunities for specific industries or industrial processes.

- **Materials exchange program:** The materials exchange program is a free service that links companies with unneeded, reusable goods to other organizations who can use them. Through the exchange companies save on disposal or raw material purchasing costs. This information is listed on the web site www.mnexchange.org.

For more information, contact MnTAP at the address and telephone number listed in the Resource Directory section of this Guide.

MINNESOTA STATE COLLEGES AND UNIVERSITIES

All colleges and universities within the MnSCU system provide programs for small business owners. These programs range from the certificate level to the master's degree. Some programs are focused on comprehensive business management such as the business marketing and management (A.A.S. degree) and the business administration master's degree. Other programs contain a number of courses which small business owners or those intending to become small business owners would find useful.

In addition to the above programs which result in an academic credential, MnSCU's community and technical colleges also offer a large variety of non-credit workshops and seminars worthwhile to small business owners. These educational opportunities are available either through open enrollment to the public or through customized contracts with individual business.

REGIONAL DEVELOPMENT COMMISSIONS

Regional development commissions are established by statute to coordinate and conduct regional planning activities for the counties, cities and towns which comprise the region.

The commissions are responsible for preparing and adopting a regional development plan which prescribes the policies, goals, standards, and programs for the orderly development of the region. By statute, the plan must address the physical, economic and social needs of the region, including land use, parks and open space, access to sunlight for solar energy systems, airports, highways, transit facilities, hospitals, libraries, schools, housing and public buildings.

The commissions review applications for federal and state loans and grants, conduct urban and rural research, coordinate civil defense, community shelter planning and flood plain management within the region and may contract to provide services and technical assistance to local units of government in the conduct of local planning and development activities.

A list of the regional development commissions, the counties they include, and the office addresses can be found in the Resource Directory section of this Guide.

TRADE INFORMATION CENTER

The Trade Information Center is a resource for information on federal export assistance programs. The Center is operated by the U.S. Department of Commerce for the 19 agencies comprising the Trade Promotion Coordinating Committee (those agencies responsible for managing federal promotion programs and activities).

The Trade Information Center is an access point for information including export counseling, sources of international market research and trade leads, overseas and domestic trade events, sources of export financing and advice on export licenses and controls. Through the Center's trade specialists, businesses can learn how to access reports from the computerized National Trade Data Bank, which includes over 200,000 government documents related to export promotion and international markets. The staff can also direct businesses to state and local trade organizations that provide additional export assistance.

Information on reaching the Center is located in the Resource Directory section of this Guide. The Center is open from 8:30 a.m. to 5:30 p.m., Monday through Friday, Eastern Time. A fax retrieval system, available 24 hours a day, provides general and country-specific export information as well as documents on international trade agreements.

SCORE ASSOCIATION OFFICES (SERVICE CORPS OF RETIRED EXECUTIVES)

SCORE is a nationwide organization of retired and active business men and business women who volunteer their services to help either new or existing businesses. In Minnesota there are 500 members in seven SCORE chapters located in principal metropolitan areas of the state. These chapters operate branches in smaller communities. Approximately 8,500 people per year are helped in Minnesota through one of the following SCORE programs:

- Going into business workshops.
- Business seminars on specific subjects.
- Free, confidential one on one counseling in all areas of business management.

SCORE is a resource partner with the U.S. Small Business Administration (SBA) and receives direct support from Economic Development Specialists from the U.S. Small Business Administration office in Minneapolis.

A list of SCORE offices and branches can be found in the Resource Directory section of this Guide.

SCORE sponsors seminars for small businesses. The "Going Into Business" seminar is designed to help people minimize risks in the start-up and operation of a business. The "Business Loan" seminar offers an overview of SBA loan guarantee programs and details of the preparation necessary to obtain SBA and other loans. SCORE's "International Trade" seminar outlines the details of exporting. The "Marketing" workshop provides details on how to run an effective, low cost marketing program for a small business. SCORE seminars and workshops are listed on the Minnesota SCORE website: www.SCOREMINN.org.

The Minneapolis, St. Paul, and South Metro chapters of SCORE hold workshops and seminars periodically throughout the year at a number of locations in the Twin Cities metro area. There is a nominal charge for these seminars. For details on dates and locations, call the Minneapolis office at (952) 938-4570, the St. Paul office at (651) 632-8937, or the South Metro office at (952) 808-5595.

Additionally, SCORE presents a free "Business Loan" seminar every Thursday (except Thanksgiving Day). These seminars begin at 10:00 a.m. and are held at the U.S. Small Business Administration Office, 210-C Butler Square, 100 North Sixth Street, in downtown Minneapolis. For details call the SBA at (612) 370-2324.

BUSINESS INFORMATION CENTER

The Business Information Center (BIC) is administered by Minnesota Project Innovation and the U.S. Small Business Administration, and can provide access to the internet, training, and a network of business consultants (including SCORE volunteers). The BIC is located at 105 Mill Place, 111 Third Avenue South, Minneapolis 55401-2551, telephone (612) 347-6775.

RESOURCE DIRECTORY

RESOURCE DIRECTORY

CONTENTS

COOPERATIVES

Minnesota Association of Cooperatives
30 East 7th Street, Suite 1720
St. Paul, MN 55101-4933
(651) 228-0213
(877) MNCOOPS
Internet site: www.wfcmac.org

ENVIRONMENTAL

See Government, State
Minnesota Environmental Quality Board
Minnesota Office of Environmental Assistance
Minnesota Pollution Control Agency
Minnesota Technical Assistance Program (MnTAP)

EXPORT ASSISTANCE

Trade Information Center
U.S. Department of Commerce
14th Street and Constitution Avenue Northwest
Ronald Regan Bldg.
Washington, DC 20230
(800) 872-8723
(800) 833-8723 (TDD)
Internet site: http://tradeinfo.doc.gov

Minneapolis U.S. Export Assistance Center
U.S. Department of Commerce
Plaza VII, Suite 2240
45 South 7th Street
Minneapolis, MN 55402
(612) 348-1638
Internet site: www.exportassistance.gov

See Government, State (Minnesota Trade Office)

FINANCING, FEDERAL SOURCES

Certified Development Companies

Central Minnesota Development Company
277 Coon Rapids Boulevard, Suite 212
Coon Rapids, MN 55433
(763) 784-3337

Minneapolis Economic Development Company
Minneapolis Community Development Agency
Crown Roller Mill
105 5th Avenue South, Suite 600
Minneapolis, MN 55401-2534
(612) 673-5181

Minnesota Business Finance Corporation
616 Roosevelt Rd., Suite 200
St. Cloud, MN 56301
(320) 255-1685

Prairieland Economic Development Corp.
One Prairie Drive
Slayton, MN 56172
(507) 836-6656
(800) 507-9003

South Central Minnesota Business Finance EDC
209 Second St. S., Suite 311
Mankato, MN 56002-0666
(507) 625-6056
(800) 749-9015

St. Paul Metro East Development Corp. (SPEDCO)
2233 North Hamline Avenue, Suite 420
Roseville, MN 55113
(651) 631-4900

Southeastern Minnesota 504 Development, Inc.
220 South Broadway, Suite 100
Rochester, MN 55904
(507) 288-6442

Twin Cities Metro Certified Development Company
Arden Woods Professional Building
4105 Lexington Avenue North, Suite 170
Arden Hills, MN 55126
(651) 481-8081
(800) 641-6258

Rural Development

U.S.D.A. Rural Development
410 AgriBank Building
375 Jackson Street
St. Paul, MN 55101-1853
(651) 602-7800
Internet site: www.rurdev.usda.gov

Area & Regional Offices

900 Robert Street N.E., Suite 103 (Regional Office)
Alexandria, MN 56308
(320) 763-3191

101 - 21st St. SE
Austin, MN 55912
(507) 437-8247

3217 Bemidji Avenue North
Bemidji, MN 56601
(218) 751-2689

512 Northeast "C" Street
Brainerd, MN 56401
(218) 829-9273

306B Brighton Avenue South
Buffalo, MN 55313
(763) 682-1151

380 South Garfield Street
Cambridge, MN 55008
(763) 689-4937

809 8th Street Southeast
Detroit Lakes, MN 56501
(218) 847-9392

4850 Miller Trunk Highway, Suite 1B
Duluth, MN 55811
(218) 720-5278

1810 30th St. NW, #3
Faribault, MN 55021
(507) 332-7418

1424 East College Drive
Marshall, MN 56258
(507) 532-3234

38694 12 Tanger Drive
North Branch, MN 55056
(651) 674-7051

201 Sherwood Avenue South
P.O. Box 486
Thief River Falls, MN 56701
(218) 681-2843

First Bank Building, Suite 104
203 1st Street South
Virginia, MN 55792
(218) 741-3929

Marketplace of Waite Park (Regional Office)
110 South 2nd Street, Suite 102
Waite Park, MN 56387
(320) 255-9111

1001 High Ave. (Regional Office)
P.O. Box 1013
Willmar, MN 56201
(320) 235-5612

1508 North Douglas
P.O. Box 158
Worthington, MN 56187
(507) 372-7783

Small Business Administration
210C Butler Square Building
100 North 6th Street
Minneapolis, MN 55403
(612) 370-2324
Internet site: www.sba.gov

Small Business Investment Companies

Affinity Ventures III, L.P.
901 Marquette Avenue, Suite 1810
Minneapolis, MN 55402
(612) 252-9897

Agio Capital Partners, I, L.P.
Interlachen Corporate Center
5050 Lincoln Drive, Suite 420
Edina, MN 55436
(952) 938-1628

Bayview Capital Partners, L.P.
641 Lake Street, Suite 230
Wayzata, MN 55391
(952) 345-2000

Capstone Ventures SBIC, L.P.
60 South Sixth Street
Minneapolis, MN 55401
(612) 371-77832

Convergent Capital Partners I, L.P.
5353 Wayzata Blvd., Suite 205
Minneapolis, MN 55416
(612) 595-8022

Doughtery Opportunity Fund II, L.P.
7200 Metro Blvd.
Edina, MN 55439
(952) 831-6499

Medallion Capital, Inc.
7831 Glenroy Road, Suite 480
Minneapolis, MN 55439-3132
(952) 831-2025

Milestone Growth Fund, Inc.
401 Second Avenue South, Suite 1032
Minneapolis, MN 55401
(612) 338-0090

Norwest Equity Partners VII, L.P.
3600 IDS Center
80 South 8th Street
Minneapolis, MN 55402
(612) 215-1600

Norwest Venture Partners VI, L.P.
3600 IDS Center
80 South 8th Street
Minneapolis, MN 55402
(612) 215-1600

Norwest Venture Partners VII, L.P.
3600 IDS Center
80 South 8th Street
Minneapolis, MN 55402
(612) 215-1600

Norwest Venture Partners VIII, L.P.
3600 IDS Center
80 South 8th Street
Minneapolis, MN 55402
(612) 215-1600

Piper Jaffray Healthcare Capital, L.P.
Mailstation: J10122-32
800 Nicollet Mall, Suite 800
Minneapolis, MN 55402-7020
(612) 303-5686

Jaffray Healthcare Fund III, L.P.
Mailstation: J10122-32
800 Nicollet Mall, Suite 800
Minneapolis, MN 55402-7020
(612) 303-5686

Piper Jaffray Technology Capital SBIC, L.P.
Mailstation: J10122-32
800 Nicollet Mall, Suite 800
Minneapolis, MN 55402-7020
(612) 303-5686

U.S. Bancorp Capital Corporation
U.S. Bankplace
601 Second Avenue South
Minneapolis, MN 55402
(612) 973-4568

Wells Fargo SBIC, Inc.
3600 IDS Center
80 South 8th Street
Minneapolis, MN 55402
(612) 215-1600

Small Business Innovation Research (SBIR) Program
c/o Minnesota Project Innovation, Inc.
111 Third Ave. S. #100
Mpls, MN 55401
(612) 349-2603

FINANCING, STATE SOURCES

Environmental Assistance, Office of
520 Lafayette Road North, 2nd Floor
St. Paul, MN 55155-4100
(651) 296-3417
(800) 657-3843
website: www.moea.state.mn.us

Trade and Economic Development, Department of
500 Metro Square
121 7th Place East
St. Paul, MN 55101-2146
Internet site: www.dted.state.mn.us

Capital Access Program
(651) 296-6858

Minnesota Investment Fund
(651) 297-1391

Rural Initiatives Program
Regional Revolving Loan Program
(651) 297-1170

Tourism Loan Program
(651) 296-6858

Urban Initiative Program
(651) 297-1170

Urban Initiative Program Certified Partners
Anoka County Econ. Dev. Partnership
277 Coon Rapids Blvd. #104
Coon Rapids MN 55433
(763) 786-0869

Metropolitan Econ. Dev. Assoc.
Suite 106
250 South Second Ave.
Minneapolis, MN 55401
(612) 332-6332

Milestone Growth Fund
Suite 1032
401 Second Ave. S.
Minneapolis, MN 55401
(612) 338-0090

Minneapolis Consortium of Community Developers
2308 Central Avenue, N.E.
Minneapolis, MN 55418-3710
(612) 789-7337

Minneapolis Entrepreneurs Fund
30 East 7th Street, Suite 950
St. Paul, MN 55101
(651) 647-0013

Minneapolis Urban League
2000 Plymouth Avenue North
Minneapolis, MN 55411
(612) 302-3107

Neighborhood Development Center
651 1/2 University Avenue
St. Paul, MN 55104
(651) 291-2480

North End Area Revitalization
1061 Rice Street
St. Paul, MN 55107
(651) 488-1039

Phillips Community Development Corp.
1014 E. Franklin Avenue
Minneapolis, MN 55404
(612) 871-2435

Riverview Economic Development Assn.
176 Concord Street
St. Paul, MN 55107
(651) 222-3727

Women Venture
2324 University Avenue
St. Paul, MN 55104
(651) 646-3808

FINANCING, LOCAL SOURCES

Anoka County
Anoka County Economic Development Partnership
277 Coon Rapids Boulevard, Suite 104
Coon Rapids, MN 55433
(763) 786-0869

Anoka/Sherburne County Capital Fund
277 Coon Rapids Boulevard, Suite 104
Coon Rapids, MN 55433
(763) 786-0869

Duluth
TEAM Duluth
118 East Superior Street
Duluth, MN 55802
(218) 722-5501

Request– *Small Business Resource Directory 1995* from:
University of Minnesota – Duluth
Center for Economic Development
11 E Superior Street, Suite 210
Duluth, MN 55802
(218) 726-7298
Internet site: www.umdced.com

Minneapolis – Request *Helping Small Businesses Grow* from:
Minneapolis Community Development Agency
Business Finance Department
Crown Roller Mill, Suite 200
105 5th Avenue South
Minneapolis, MN 55401-2534
(612) 673-5095
Internet site: www.mcda.org

The Minneapolis Foundation's Enterpreneurs Fund
Loantech
(612) 278-7180
Offers matching services, a loan fund and technical assistance to small for-profit businesses located in seven Minneapolis neighborhoods.

St. Paul

Department of Planning and Economic Development
Business Resource Center
25 W. Fourth St.
Fourteenth Floor
St. Paul, MN 55102
(651) 266-6600
Internet site: ww.stpaulbusiness.org

Two Harbors

Two Harbors Development Commission
522 1st Avenue
Two Harbors, MN 55616
(218) 834-3489
Offers financial and technical assistance to for-profit businesses located, or to be located, in the Two Harbors area.

FINANCING, PRIVATE SOURCES

Rural Initiative Organizations

Central Minnesota Foundation
405 First Street, S.E.
Little Falls, MN 56345-3043
(320) 632-9255
Serves Benton, Cass, Chisago, Crow Wing, Isanti, Kanabec, Mille Lacs, Morrison, Pine, Sherburne, Stearns, Todd, Wadena, and Wright counties.

Northland Foundation
610 Sellwood Building
202 West Superior Street
Duluth, MN 55802
(218) 723-4040
Serves Aitkin, Carlton, Cook, Lake, Koochiching, Itasca and St. Louis counties.

Northwest Minnesota Foundation
4225 Technology Drive
Bemidji, MN 56601
(218) 759-2057
(800) 659-7859
Internet site: www.nwmf.org
Serves Beltrami, Clearwater, Hubbard, Kittson, Lake of the Woods, Mahnomen, Marshall, Norman, Pennington, Polk, Red Lake, and Roseau counties.

Southern Minnesota Initiative Fund
525 Florence Avenue
P.O. Box 695
Owatonna, MN 55060-0695
(507) 455-3215
Internet site: www.semif.org
Serves Blue Earth, Brown, Dodge, Faribault, Fillmore, Freeborn, Goodhue, Houston, LeSueur, Martin, Mower, Nicollet, Olmsted, Rice, Sibley, Steele, Wabasha, Waseca, Watonwan, and Winona counties.

Southwest Minnesota Foundation
1390 Hwy 15 South
P.O. Box 428
Hutchinson, MN 55350
(320) 587-4848
(800) 594-9480
Serves Big Stone, Chippewa, Cottonwood, Jackson, Kandiyohi, Lac Qui Parle, Lincoln, Lyon, McLeod, Meeker, Murray, Nobles, Pipestone, Redwood, Renville, Rock, Swift, and Yellow Medicine counties.

West Central Initiative Fund
Norwest Bank Building, Suite 205
220 West Washington Avenue
Fergus Falls, MN 56537
(218) 739-2239
(800) 735-2239
Internet site: www.wcif.org
Serves Becker, Clay, Douglas, Grant, Otter Tail, Pope, Stevens, Traverse, and Wilkin counties.

Small Business Administration Microloan Intermediaries

Minneapolis Consortium of
Community Developers, Inc.
2308 Central Avenue N.E.
Minneapolis, MN 55418-3710
(612) 789-7337
Internet site: www.cando.org
Service Area: City of Minneapolis.
Call for location eligibility

Northeast Entrepreneur Fund, Incorporated
Olcott Plaza
820 9th Street North
Virginia, MN 55792
(218) 749-4191
(800) 422-0374
Internet site: www.neefund.org
Service Area: Koochiching, Itasca, St. Louis, Aitkin, Carlton, Cook and Lake counties.

Northwest Minnesota Foundation
4225 Technology Drive, NW
Bemidji, MN 56601
(218) 759-2057
(800) 659-7859
Internet site: www.nwmf.org
Service Area: Beltrami, Clearwater, Hubbard, Kittson, Lake of the Woods, Mahnomen, Marshall, Norman, Pennington, Polk, Red Lake, and Rousseau counties.

WomenVenture
2324 University Avenue
St. Paul, MN 55114
(651) 646-3808
Internet site: www.womenventure.org
Service Area: Cities of Minneapolis and St. Paul, the counties of Anoka, Carver, Chisago, Dakota, Goodhue, Hennepin, Isanti, Ramsey, Scott, Sterns, Steele, Washington and Wright.

(Non Lending Technical Assistance Provider)
Neighborhood Development Center, Inc.
651 1/2 University Ave.
St. Paul, MN 55104
(651) 291-2480
Internet site: www.WINDNDC.org
Service Area: City of St. Paul and Minneapolis.

Northeast Entrepreneur Fund, Inc.
Olcott Plaza
820 Ninth Street North
Virginia, MN 55792
(218) 749-4191
(800) 422-0374

William C. Norris Institute
2001 Killebrew Drive
Suite 302
Bloomington, MN 55425
(952) 876-0621

GOVERNMENT, FEDERAL

Copyright Office, U.S.
Library of Congress
101 Independence Avenue S.E.
Washington, D.C. 20559-6000
(202) 707-3000
Internet site: www.lcweb.loc.gov/copyright

Equal Employment Opportunity Commission
330 2nd Avenue South, Suite 430
Minneapolis, MN 55401
(612) 335-4040
Internet site: www.eeoc.gov

1801 L Street N.W.
Washington, DC 20507
(202) 663-4900

Immigration and Naturalization Service
Attn. Employer Relations Officer
2901 Metro Drive, Suite 100
Bloomington, MN 55425
(612) 313-9052

Internal Revenue Service
General Information
(800) 829-1040
Internet site: www.irs.gov

Forms or Publications
(800) 829-3676
(800) 829-4059 (TTY)
(703) 368-9694 (fax)

Taxpayer Education Workshops
(651) 312-7637

Walk-in assistance and forms may be obtained from Taxpayer Assistance Offices at the field offices listed below. Call (800) 829-1040 for information on the days and hours the field offices are open. Forms may also be obtained by fax at (703) 368-9694.

2001 Killebrew Drive, Suite 239
Bloomington, MN 55425

Room 105 Federal Building
515 1st Street West
Duluth, MN 55802

Suite 408, Northwestern Office Building
209 2nd Street South
Mankato, MN 56001

Towle Building, Suite 275
330 2nd Avenue South
Minneapolis, MN 55401

Breckenridge Skyway Plaza, Room 304
21 2nd Street Southwest
Rochester, MN 55902

720 West St. Germain, Room 212
St. Cloud, MN 56301

Room 385 Federal Building
316 North Robert Street
St. Paul, MN 55101

Regional Service Center for businesses with their principal place of business in Minnesota:

Internal Revenue Service
Ogden, Utah 84201

To obtain a federal taxpayer identification number by telephone, call toll free 1-866-816-2065. Have a completed Form SS-4 available before making this call.

Labor, Department of
Employment Standards Administration
Wage and Hour Division
TriTech Office Center, Suite 920
331 Second Avenue So.
Minneapolis, MN 55401-2233
(612) 370-3371
Internet site: www.dol.gov

Pension and Welfare Benefits Administration
200 Constitution Avenue Northwest
Washington, DC, 20210-1111
(202) 219-8776
Internet site: www.dol.gov/dol/pwba

Patent and Trademark Office, U.S.
General Information Services Division
USPTO Crystal Plaza 3, Room 2C02
Washington, D.C. 20231
(800) 786-9199
(703) 305-7785 (TTY)
Internet site: www.uspto.gov

Securities and Exchange Commission
Office of Small Business
450 5th Street Northwest, Mail Stop 3-4
Washington, D.C. 20549
(800) SEC-0330
(202) 942-2950
Internet site: www.sec.gov

Midwest Regional Office
1400 Citicorp Center
500 West Madison Street
Chicago, Il 60661-2511
(312) 353-7390

Small Business Administration
210C Butler Square Building
100 6th Street North
Minneapolis, MN 55403-1525
(612) 370-2324
Internet site: www.sba.gov

GOVERNMENT, STATE
www.state.mn.us

Administration, Department of
Materials Management Division
Customer and Vendor Services Helpline
112 Administration Building
50 Sherburne Avenue
St. Paul, MN 55155
(651) 296-2600
(651) 282-5799 (TTY)
Internet site: www.mmd.admin.state.mn.us

Agriculture, Department of
Dairy and Food Inspection Division
90 West Plato Boulevard
St. Paul, MN 55107
(651) 296-2627
Internet site: www.mda.state.mn.us

Bookstore, Minnesota's
Room 110 A
117 University Avenue
St. Paul, MN 55155
(651) 297-3000
(800) 657-3757
(651) 282-5077 (TTY)
(800) 657-3706 (TTY)
Internet site: www.comm.media.state.mn.us

Bureau of Business Licenses
See Small Business Assistance Office, Minnesota

Commerce, Department of
85 7th Place East, Suite 500
St. Paul, MN 55101
Internet site: www.commerce.state.mn.us

General Information
(651) 296-4026

Enforcement Division
(651) 296-2488
(800) 657-3602

Franchise Registration
(651) 296-6328

Insurance Information
(651) 297-7161

Securities Registration
(651) 296-4973

Economic Security, Department of
390 North Robert Street
St. Paul, MN 55101
Internet site: www.mnwfc.org

General Information
(651) 296-2919

Information on Taxes (Tax Liability)
(651) 296-6141

Environmental Assistance, Office of
520 Lafayette Road North, 2nd Floor
St. Paul, MN 55155-4100
(651) 296-3417
(800) 657-3843

Environmental Quality Board
300 Centennial Office Building
658 East Cedar Street
St. Paul, MN 55155
Internet site: www.mnplan.state.mn.us/eqb

General Information
(651) 296-3985

Sustainable Development Initiative
(651) 297-5228

Environmental Review
(651) 296-8253

Human Rights, Department of
Army Corps of Engineers Centre
190 East 5th Street, Suite 700
St. Paul, MN 55101
(651) 296-5663
(651) 296-1283 (TTY)
(800) 657-3704
Internet site: www.humanrights.state.mn.us

Labor and Industry, Department of
443 Lafayette Road North
St. Paul, MN 55155-4307
Internet site: www.doli.state.mn.us

General Information
(651) 284-5000
(651) 297-4198 (TTY)
(800) 342-5354

Apprenticeship
(651) 284-5090
(800) 657-3607

Labor Standards
(651) 284-5070

Prevailing Wage Standards
(651) 284-5091

Workplace Safety Consultation
(651) 284-5060
(800) 657-3776

OSHA Compliance
(651) 284-5050
(877) 470-6742 (toll free)

OSHA Duluth Area Office
5 North Third Avenue West, Suite 402
Duluth, MN 55802
(218) 723-4678

OSHA Mankato Area Office
Nichols Office Center
410 Jackson Street, Suite 520
Mankato, MN 56001
(507) 389-6501

Posters
(651) 284-5042

Workers' Compensation Information
(651) 284-5005 (Twin Cities)
(800) 342-5354 (Outside Twin Cities Area)
(218) 723-4670 (Duluth)
(800) 365-4584 (Duluth Office)

Investigative Services
(651) 297-5797 (Twin Cities)
(888) 372-8366 (Toll Free)

Minnesota State Colleges and Universities (MnSCU)
500 World Trade Center
30 E. Seventh Street
St. Paul, MN 55101
(651) 296-8012
(888) 667-2848
Internet site: www.mnscu.edu

Pollution Control Agency
520 Lafayette Road
St. Paul, MN 55155-4194
Internet site: www.pca.state.mn.us

Information (Front Desk)
(651) 296-6300
(800) 657-3864
(651) 282-5332 (TDD)

Customer Assistance Center
(Air, Water, Tanks, and Hazardous Waste)
(651) 297-2274
(800) 646-6247

Solid Waste Permits
(651) 296-8584

Small Business Ombudsman
(651) 297-8615
(800) 985-4247

Small Business Assistance Program
(651) 282-6143
(800) 657-3938

Revenue, Department of
600 N. Robert St.
St. Paul, MN 55146
Internet site: www.taxes.state.mn.us

Central Registration
(Business Tax ID numbers)
Mail Station 4410
St. Paul, MN 55146-4410
(651) 282-5225
(800) 657-3605
(651) 297-2265 Fax

Collection Enforcement Group
P.O. Box 64447
St. Paul, MN 55146
(651) 296-1980

Corporations Unit
(651) 297-7000

Forms Distribution Office
Mail Station 1421
St. Paul, MN 55146-1421
(651) 296-9118
(800) 657-3676

Individual Income Tax Division
(651) 296-3781
(800) 652-9094

Minnesota Business Tax Education Program
Mail Station 6340
St. Paul, MN 55146-6340
(651) 297-4213
(800) 888-6231
(651) 296-1938 (Fax)

Partnership Unit
(651) 296-3475

Petroleum Tax Office
Mail Station 3333
St. Paul, MN 55146-3333
(651) 296-0889
(800) 657-3596

Sales Tax Division
Mail Station 6330
St. Paul, MN 55146-6330
(651) 296-6181
(800) 657-3777
(651) 296-1938 (Fax)

Special Taxes Division
Mail Station 3331
St. Paul, MN 55146-3331
(651) 297-1882

Withholding Division
Mail Station 6501
St. Paul, MN 55146-6501
(651) 282-9999
(800) 657-3594

Secretary of State, Office of
180 State Office Building
100 Constitution Avenue
St. Paul, MN 55155-1299
Internet site: www.sos.state.mn.us
(651) 296-2803
(877) 551-6767

Fax Forms Library
(651) 296-2803

Public Information (Lists)
(651) 284-4087 or
(651) 215-1442

Small Business Assistance Office, Minnesota
500 Metro Square
121 7th Place East
St. Paul, MN 55101-2146
Internet site:
www.dted.state.mn.us (Click on Business, click on Technical Assistance, Click on Assistance for Small Business)
(651) 296-3871 (Voicemail Publication Order Line)
(651) 282-2103 (Information and Assistance)
(800) 657-3858 (Ask for Small Business Assistance)

Technical Assistance

Minnesota Technical Assistance Program (MnTAP)
University of Minnesota
McNamara Alumni Center
200 Oak St. S.E., Suite 350
Minneapolis, MN 55455
(612) 624-1300
(800) 247-0015
Internet site: www.mntap.umn.edu or www.mnexchange.org

Trade and Economic Development, Department of
500 Metro Square
121 7th Place East
St. Paul, MN 55101-2146
Internet site: www.dted.state.mn.us

General Information
(651) 297-1291
(800) 657-3858

Job Skills Partnership
(651) 296-0388

WorkForce Development Division
(651) 296-2953
Fax: (651) 215-3842

Rapid Response Team
(651) 297-3416
(800) 657-3858

Small Business Assistance Office
(651) 296-3871 (Voicemail Publication Order Line)
(651) 282-2103 (Information and Assistance)
(800) 657-3858 (Ask for Small Business Assistance)

Small Business Development Centers
(651) 297-5770
(800) 657-3858 (Ask for Small Business Development Center Office)

Tourism Office
(651) 296-5029
(800) 657-3700

Trade Office
1000 World Trade Center Building
30 East 7th Street
St. Paul, MN 55101-4902
(651) 297-4222
(800) 657-3858

GOVERNMENT, REGIONAL

Regional Development Commissions

Northwest Regional Development Commission
115 South Main Avenue, Suite 1
Warren, MN 56762
(218) 745-6733
Region 1. Serves Kittson, Marshall, Norman, Pennington, Polk, Red Lake, and Roseau counties.

Headwaters Regional Development Commission
403 4th Street Northwest
P.O. Box 906
Bemidji, MN 56619
(218) 444-4732
Region 2. Serves Beltrami, Clearwater, Hubbard, Lake of the Woods, and Mahnomen counties.

Arrowhead Regional Development Commission
221 West 1st Street
Duluth, MN 55802
(218) 722-5545
(800) 232-0707
Region 3. Serves Aitkin, Carlton, Cook, Itasca, Koochiching, Lake, and St. Louis counties.

Region 5 Development Commission
611 Iowa Avenue, N.E.
Staples, MN 56479
(218) 894-3233
Region 5. Serves Cass, Crow Wing, Morrison, Todd, and Wadena counties.

Mid-Minnesota Development Commission
333 Southwest 6th Street
Willmar, MN 56201
(320) 235-8504
(800) 450-8608
Region 6E. Serves Kandiyohi, McLeod, Meeker, and Renville counties.

Upper Minnesota Valley Regional Development Commission
323 West Schlieman Avenue
Appleton, MN 56208
(320) 289-1981
Region 6W. Serves Big Stone, Chippewa, Lac Qui Parle, Swift, and Yellow Medicine counties.

East Central Regional Development Commission
100 South Park Street
Mora, MN 55051
(320) 679-4065
Internet site: www.region7erdc.org
Region 7E. Serves Chisago, Isanti, Kanabec, Mille Lacs, and Pine counties

Southwest Regional Development Commission
2401 Broadway Avenue, Suite 1
Slayton, MN 56172
(320) 289-1981
Internet site: www.umdrdc.org
Region 8. Serves Cottonwood, Jackson, Lincoln, Lyon, Murray, Nobles, Pipestone, Redwood, and Rock counties.

Region 9 Development Commission
Nichols Office Center
410 Jackson Street, Box 3367
Mankato, MN 56002-3367
(507) 387-5643
(800) 450-5643
Internet site: www.rndc.org
Region 9. Serves Blue Earth, Brown, Faribault, LeSueur, Martin, Nicollet, Sibley, Waseca, and Watonwan counties.

Metropolitan Council
Mears Park Center
230 East 5th Street
St. Paul, MN 55101
(651) 602-1000
Internet site: www.metrocouncil.org
Region 11. Serves Anoka, Carver, Dakota, Hennepin, Ramsey, Scott, and Washington counties.
Note: Regions 4, 7W and 10 are dissolved.

INSURANCE

Minnesota Joint Underwriting Association
Pioneer P.O. Box 1760
North Central Life Tower
445 Minnesota Street, Suite 514
St. Paul, MN 55101
(651) 222-0484
(800) 552-0013

Minnesota Market Assistance Program
P.O. Box 117
Fifty Lakes, MN 56448
(218) 763-3749
(800) 257-1838

INVENTORS

Minnesota Inventors Congress
805 East Bridge Street
P.O. Box 71
Redwood Falls, MN 56283
(507) 637-2344
(800) INVENT-1 (468-3681)
Internet site: www.invent1.org
See also, Technology

U.S. Patent and Trademark Depository Library
Minneapolis Public Library
Technology/Science/Government Documents Division
300 Nicollet Mall
Minneapolis, MN 55401
(612) 630-6120
NOTE: Sometime in 2002, this library will be demolished and rebuilt on the same site. Contact the library for information on an interim location.

JOB SERVICES AND JOB TRAINING DEPARTMENT OF ECONOMIC SECURITY

WorkForce Centers

Internet site: www.mnworkforcecenter.org
Job Skills Analysis, Assessment and Customized Training
Call (651) 221-1304. For the WorkForce Center nearest you, call 1-800-GET-JOBS (1-888-438-5627)
(TTY) 1-800-657-3973

1649 West Main Street, Skyline Mall
Albert Lea, MN 56007-1868
(507) 379-3409
(507) 379-3409 (TTY)

701 Broadway Street, Suite 101
Alexandria, MN 56308-1811
(320) 762-7800
(320) 762-7805 (TTY)

1900 8th Avenue Northwest, Riverland Community College
Austin, MN 55912-1473
(507) 433-0555
(507) 433-0556 (TTY)

Beltrami County Community Services Center
616 America Ave, Suite 210
Bemidji, MN 56601
(218) 759-8200
(218) 759-8200 (TTY)

1201 89th Ave. N.E., Suite 235, Anoka County Human Services Bldg.
Blaine, MN 55434
(763) 783-4800
(763) 785-5987 (TTY)

4220 W. Old Shakopee Rd.
Bloomington, MN 55437
(952) 346-4000
(952) 346-4043 (TTY)

1919 South 6th Street
P.O. Box 767
Brainerd, MN 56401-4526
(218) 828-2450
(218) 855-5030 (TTY)

7115 Northland Terrace, Suite 100
Brooklyn Park, MN 55428
(763) 536-6000
(763) 536-6005 (TTY)

14551 County Rd. 11
Burnsville, MN 55337
(952) 997-4850
(952) 997-4873 (TTY)

1575 East Highway 95, Suite C
Cambridge, MN 55008-1756
(763) 689-7136
(763) 689-7141 (TTY)

715 Cloquet Avenue
Cloquet, MN 55720-1629
(218) 879-5201
(218) 879-0870 (TTY)

1730 University Ave.
Crookston, MN 55716-0604
(218) 281-6020
(218) 281-6020 (TTY)

801 Roosevelt Avenue
Detroit Lakes, MN 56501-3703
(218) 846-7379
(218) 846-0772 (TTY)

320 West 2nd Street, Suite 205
Duluth, MN 55802-1494
(218) 723-4730
(218) 723-4725 (TTY)

406 Third St. N.W.
East Grand Forks, MN 56721-0666
(218) 773-9841
(218) 773-9841 (TTY)

923 North State Street, Suite 110
P.O. Box 767
Fairmont, MN 56031-0767
(507) 235-5518
(507) 235-5518 (TTY)

Faribo Town Square
201 Lyndale Avenue, Suite 1
Faribault, MN 55021-5758
(507) 333-2047
(507) 333-2047 (TTY)

125 West Lincoln Avenue, Suite 1
P.O. Box 418
Fergus Falls, MN 56538-0418
(218) 739-7560
(218) 739-7287 (TTY)

1215 Southeast 2nd Avenue
P.O. Box 678
Grand Rapids, MN 55744-0678
(218) 327-4480
(218) 327-4480 (TTY)

3920 13th Avenue East
P.O. Box 68
Hibbing, MN 55746-0068
(218) 262-6777
(218) 262-6777 (TTY)

2 Century Avenue
P.O. Box 550
Hutchinson, MN 55350-0550
(320) 587-4740
(320) 587-4740 (TTY)

407 4th Street
International Falls, MN 56649-2413
(218) 283-9427
(218) 283-3436 (TTY)

114 Holcombe Avenue North, Room 170
Litchfield, MN 55355-2273
(320) 693-2859
(320) 693-2859 (TTY)

Coburns Complex
315 12th St. NE
Little Falls, MN 56345-2910
(320) 616-2400
800-627-3529 (TTY)

Mankato Place
12 Civic Center Plaza, Suite 1600
Mankato, MN 56001
(507) 389-6723
(507) 389-6512 (TTY)

607 W. Main Street, Lyon County Courthouse
Marshall, MN 56258-2087
(507) 537-6236
(507) 537-6237 (TTY)

Minneapolis
Call for nearest location:
(612) 520-3500
(612) 821-4000

129 West Nichols
Montevideo, MN 56265-0636
(320) 269-8819
(320) 269-8819 (TTY)

Marquette Bank Building
106 Pine Street
Monticello MN 55362-8302
(763) 271-3700
(763) 271-3745 (TTY)

715 11th Street North, Suite 201, Clayton County Family Service Center
Moorhead, MN 56560-2086
(218) 236-2191
(218) 236-2001 (TTY)

903 E. Forest Avenue
Mora, MN 55051
(320) 679-6484
(320) 679-6494 (TTY)

1618 South Broadway
New Ulm, MN 56073-3756
(507) 354-3138
(507) 354-3138 (TTY)

2098 E. 11th Ave.
N. St. Paul, MN 55109-5100
(651) 779-5666
(651) 779-5223 (TTY)

110 West Fremont
Owatonna, MN 55060-2328
(507) 455-5850
(507) 455-5850 (TTY)

1011 East 1st Street
Park Rapids, MN 56470-1712
(218) 732-3396
(218) 732-9761 (TTY)

1606 West 3rd Street
Red Wing, MN 55066-0033
(651) 385-6480
(651) 385-6404 (TTY)

300 11th Avenue Northwest, Suite 112
Civic Drive Plaza
Rochester, MN 55901
(507) 285-7315
(507) 280-3584 (TTY)

205 2nd Avenue Northwest
P.O. Box 68
Roseau, MN 56751-0068
(218) 463-2233
(218) 463-2266 (TTY)

3333 West Division Street, Suite 212
P.O. Box 67
St. Cloud, MN 56302-0067
(320) 654-5320
(320) 654-5147 (TTY)

St. Paul
Call for nearest location:
(651) 642-0363

752 Canterbury Rd. S.
Shakopee, MN 55379
(952) 445-7087
(952) 402-9801

Washington County Government Center
14949 62nd Street, N., Room 20
Stillwater, MN 55082-0006
(651) 430-6850
(651) 430-6872 (TTY)

1301 Highway 1 East
Northland Community College
Thief River Falls, MN 56701-0679
(218) 681-0909
(218) 681-0919 (TTY)

820 North 9th Street, Suite 250
Virginia, MN 55792-2345
(218) 748-2200
(218) 748-2222 (TTY)

Wadena County Social Services Building
124 SE 1st St., Suite 2
Wadena, MN 56482
(218) 631-7660
(218) 631-7677 (TTY)

60 E. Marie, Suite 209
W. St. Paul, MN 55118-5900
(651) 552-5000
(651) 552-5005 (TTY)

33 E. Wentworth
W. St. Paul, MN 55118
(651) 450-2667
(651) 450-2914

Kandiyohi County
Human Services Bldg.
2200 23rd St., N.E., Suite 2040
Willmar, MN 56201-9423
(320) 231-5174
(320) 231-5174 (TTY)

1250 Homer Road, Suite 200, Winona Technical College
Winona, MN 55987-4897
(507) 453-2920
(507) 453-2930 (TTY)

511 10th Street
Worthington, MN 56187-2342
(507) 376-3116
(507) 376-3116 (TTY)

Twin Cities Metro Area
Centralized Job Bank Office
(651) 296-8400

WorkForce Investment Act Title I

Northwest Private Industry Council, Inc./ WorkForce Council
721 S. Minnesota St.
P.O. Box 604
Crookston, MN 56716
(218) 281-6020 (218) 281-6020 (TTY)

Rural Minnesota Concentrated Employment Program (CEP), Inc.
803 Roosevelt Avenue
P.O. Box 1108
Detroit Lakes, MN 56501
(218) 846-7400 (218) 846-0772 (TTY)

Northeast Minnesota Office of Job Training
820 N. 9th Street, Suite 240
Olcott Plaza
P.O. Box 1028
Virginia, MN 55792
(218) 748-2200 (218) 748-2222 (TTY)

City of Duluth
Duluth Job Training
332 City Hall
411 West First Street
Duluth, MN 55802-1102
(218) 723-3419 (218) 723-4725 (TTY)

Central Minnesota Jobs & Training Services
106 Pine Street
P.O. Box 116
Monticello, MN 55362
(763) 271-3711 (763) 271-3745 (TTY)

Southwest Minnesota Private Industry Council
607 West Main
Marshall, MN 56258
(507) 537-6987 (507) 537-6237 (TTY)

South Central WorkForce Council
Nichols Office Center
101 First Street, E.
Route Box 1
Vernon Center, MN 56090
(507) 549-3452

Southeastern Minnesota WorkForce Development Council, Inc.
300 11th Avenue NW., Suite 110
Rochester, MN 55901
(507) 292-5153 (507) 280-3584 (TTY)

Hennepin/Scott/Carver Employment and Training Consortium
Hennepin County Training and Employment Assistance Department
300 S. Sixth Street
Minneapolis, MN 55487-0012
(612) 348-5203
TTY: (612) 348-5435

Minneapolis Employment and Training Program
250 South 4th Street – Room 510
Minneapolis, MN 55415-1372
(612) 673-5700

Anoka County
Minnesota WorkForce Center/Anoka County
1201 - 89th Avenue NE., Suite 235
Blaine, MN 55434
(763) 783-4800 FAX: (763) 783-4844
TTY: (763) 783-4724

Dakota County
Dakota County WorkForce Services
60 East Marie Avenue, Suite 220
West St. Paul, MN 55118
(651) 450-2633 FAX: (651) 450-2656
TTY: (651) 450-2616

Ramsey County
Ramsey County Consolidated
2098 - 11th Avenue South
North St. Paul, MN 55109
(651) 779-5651 (651) 779-5223 (TTY)

Washington County
Washington County WorkForce Center
Washington County Government Center
14949 - 62nd Street North
P.O. Box 6
Stillwater, MN 55082-0006
(651) 430-6850 FAX: (651) 430-6864
TTY: (651) 439-3220

Stearns-Benton
Stearns-Benton Employment and Training Council
3333 W. Division, Suite 212
St. Cloud, MN 56301
(320) 654-5320 (320) 654-5147 (TTY)

Winona County Training and Employment WorkForce Council
1250 Homer Road
Winona, MN 55987
(507) 453-2920 FAX (507) 453-2960
TTY (507) 453-2936

Statewide Contact
WorkForce Services Branch
390 N. Robert Street, Room 125
St. Paul, MN 55101
(651) 297-7851 or (800) 456-8519
FAX: (651) 296-5745
TTY: (651) 296-2796

LEGAL ASSISTANCE

Minnesota State Bar Association
Attorney Referral Service
514 Nicollet Avenue, Suite 300
Minneapolis, MN 55402
(800) 292-4152
(612) 333-1216 (TDD)
Serves all Minnesota counties other than Hennepin, Ramsey and Dakota.

For referrals in Hennepin County: (612) 752-6666
For referrals in Ramsey County: (651) 224-1775
For referrals in Dakota County: (952) 431-3200

LIBRARIES

Primary Metropolitan Libraries

Anoka County Library
711 Highway 10 Northeast
Blaine, MN 55434-2398
(763) 717-3267

Bayport Public Library
582 North 4th Street
Bayport, MN 55003
(651) 439-7454

Carver County Library
Chaska Library
4 City Hall Plaza
Chaska, MN 55318
(952) 448-9395

Columbia Heights Public Library
820 40th Avenue Northeast
Columbia Heights, MN 55421
(763) 706-3690
(763) 706-3692 (TDD)

Dakota County Library
1340 Wescott Road
Eagan, MN 55123
(651) 688-1500
Internet site: www.co.dakota.mn.us/library/index.htm

Forest Lake Public Library
220 North Lake Street
Forest Lake, MN 55025
(651) 464-4088
Internet site: www.washington.lib.mn.us

Hennepin County Library
Southdale Area Library
7001 York Avenue South
Edina, MN 55435-4287
(952) 847-5933
Internet site: www.hennepin.lib.mn.us

Minneapolis Public Library
300 Nicollet Mall
Minneapolis, MN 55401
(612) 630-6200
Internet site: www.mpls.lib.mn.us
NOTE: This library will be closing in 2002, and moving to an interim location.

James J. Hill Reference Library
80 West 4th Street
St. Paul, MN 55102
(651) 265-5500
www.jjhill.org

Ramsey County Public Library
2180 Hamline Avenue North
Roseville, MN 55113
(651) 628-6803

Scott County Library
13090 Alabama Avenue South
Savage, MN 55378
(952) 707-1770
Internet site: www.scott.lib.mn.us

St. Paul Public Library
90 West 4th Street – CLOSED UNTIL MID 2002
St. Paul, MN 55102
(952) 266-7000
Internet site: www.stpaul.lib.mn.us

St. Paul Public Library
Lexington Branch
1080 W. University
St. Paul, MN 55104
(651) 642-0359
Internet site: www.stpaul.libraries.mn.us

Shakopee Public Library
235 South Lewis Street
Shakopee, MN 55379
(952) 233-3850
Internet site: www.scott.lib.mn.us

South St. Paul Public Library
106 3rd Avenue North
South St. Paul, MN 55075
(651) 554 3240

Stillwater Public Library
223 North 4th Street
Stillwater, MN 55082-4806
(651) 439-1675
Internet site: www.washington.lib.mn.us

Washington County Library
2150 Radio Drive
Woodbury, MN 55125
(651) 731-8487
Internet site: www.washington.lib.mn.us

Minnesota Library Systems

Arrowhead Library System
701 11th Street North
Virginia, MN 55792
(218) 741-3840
Internet site: www.arrowhead.lib.mn.us

Central Minnesota Libraries Exchange
St. Cloud State University
MC 1300 720 Fourth Avenue S.
St. Cloud, MN 56301-4498
(320) 255-2950
Internet site: http://lrs.stcloudstate.edu/cmle/

East Central Regional Library
244 South Birch Street
Cambridge, MN 55008
(763) 689-7390
Internet site: http://ecrl.lib.mn.us

Great River Regional Library
405 W. St. Germain
St. Cloud, MN 56301
(320) 650-2500
Internet site: www.griver.org

Kitchigami Regional Library
P.O. Box 84
Pine River, MN 56474
(218) 587-2171
Internet site: http://nlln.org/aurora/krl/krl.html

Lake Agassiz Regional Library
118 South 5th Street, P.O. Box 900
Moorhead, MN 56561-0900
(218) 233-3757
Internet site: www.nlln.org/aurora/larl/index.html

MELSA
1619 Dayton Avenue, Suite 314
St. Paul, MN 55104-1849
(651) 645-5731
Internet site: www.melsa.lib.mn.us

Metronet
1619 Dayton Ave., Suite 314
St. Paul, MN 55104
(651) 646-0475
Internet site: www.metronet.lib.mn.us

North Country Library Cooperative
Olcott Plaza
820 North 9th Street, Suite 110
Virginia, MN 55792
(218) 741-1907

Northern Lights Library Network
801 Jenny Avenue SW
Perham, MN 56573
(218) 347-6315
Internet site: http://nlln.org

Northwest Regional Library
210 LaBree Avenue N.
Thief River Falls, MN 56701
(218) 681-1066
Internet site: http://nlln.org/aurora/nwrl

Pioneerland Library System
410 5th Street Southwest
P.O. Box 327
Willmar, MN 56201-0327
(320) 235-6106

Plum Creek Library System
P.O. Box 697
Worthington, MN 56187
(507) 376-5803
Internet site: www.plumcreeklibrary.org

SELCO/SELS
2600 19th Street N.W.
Rochester, MN 55901
(507) 288-5513
Internet site: www.selco.lib.mn.us

Southcentral Minnesota Interlibrary Exchange (SMILE)
110 South Broad Street
P.O. Box 3031
Mankato, MN 56002-3031
(507) 389-5108

Southwest Area Multi-County Multi-Type Interlibrary Exchange (SAMMIE)
BAC 282
Southwest State University
Marshall, MN 56258-1515
(507) 532-9013
Internet site: www.sammie.org

Traverse des Sioux Library System
P.O. Box 4396
Mankato, MN 56002-4396
(507) 625-6169
(800) 450-6169
Internet site: www.tds.lib.mn.us

Viking Library System
204 North Cascade
Fergus Falls, MN 56537
(218) 739-5286
Internet site: www.viking.lib.mn.us

Law Libraries

Anoka County Law Library
325 E. Main St.
Anoka, MN 55303
(763) 422-7549

The Minnesota State Law Library
25 Constitution Avenue
Room G25 Minnesota Judicial Center
St. Paul, MN 55155
(651) 296-2775
Internet site:
www.lawlibrary.state.mn.us/index.html

Dakota County Law Library
Judicial Center
1560 W. Highway 55
Hastings, MN 55033
(651) 438-8080

Hamline University School of Law Library
1536 Hewitt Avenue
St. Paul, MN 55104-1284
(651) 523-2125
Internet site:
www.hamline.edu/law/library/index.html

Hennepin County Law Library
C-2451 Government Center
300 South 6th Street
Minneapolis, MN 55487
(612) 348-2903
Internet site:
www.co.hennepin.mn.us/lawlibrary/lawlib.htm

Ramsey County Law Library
1815 Courthouse
St. Paul, MN 55102
(651) 266-8391

St. Louis County Law Library
100 North 5th Avenue West, Room 515
Duluth, MN 55802-1202
(218) 726-2611

Scott County Law Library
Scott County Government Center
200 4th Street
Shakopee, MN 55379
(952) 496-8713

Stearns County Law Library
P.O. Box 262
725 Courthouse Square, Room 105
St. Cloud, MN 56303
(320) 656-3678

University of Minnesota Law Library
229 19th Avenue South
Minneapolis, MN 55455
(612) 625-4300
Internet site: www.law.umn.edu/library/home.html

U.S. Courts Library
Federal Courts Building, Room 541
St. Paul, MN 55101
(651) 848-1320

Washington County Law Library
Government Center
14949 62nd St., N., P.O. Box 6
Stillwater, MN 55082-0006
(651) 430-6330

William Mitchell College of Law Library
871 Summit Avenue
St. Paul, MN 55105
(651) 227-9171
(888) WMCL-LAW
Internet site: www.wmitchell.edu/library

Note: There are county law libraries in each county, the management of which is usually assigned to courthouse employees. The above list has full-time law library staffing. A complete list can be found at internet site: www.lawlibrary.state.mn.us/clldir.html.

Government Document Depository Libraries

Bemidji State University
A.C. Clark Library
1500 Birchmont Drive
Bemidji, MN 56601-2699
(218) 755-3342
Internet site: www.bemidji.msus.edu

Anoka County Library
711 Highway 10 N.E.
Blaine, MN 55434-2398
(763) 717-3267

St. John's University
Alcuin Library
Collegeville, MN 56321-2500
(320) 363-2122

Duluth Public Library
520 West Superior Street
Duluth, MN 55802-1578
(218) 723-3802
Internet site: www.duluth.lib.mn.us

University of Minnesota Duluth Library
10 University Drive
Duluth, MN 55812-2495
(218) 726-8100
Internet site: www.d.umn.edu/lib/collections.html

Dakota County Library
1340 Wescott Road
Eagan, MN 55123-1099
(651) 688-1500

Hennepin County Library System
Southdale Library
7001 York Avenue South
Edina, MN 55435-4287
(952) 847-5933

Minnesota State University, Mankato
Memorial Library
Ellis and Maywood Avenue
P.O. Box 8400, ML 3097
Mankato, MN 56002-8419
(507) 389-5952
Internet site: www.lib.mnsu.edu/lib/govdoc/govhome.html

Southwest State University
Library, Government Documents
1501 State Street
Marshall, MN 56258
(507) 537-7278
Internet site: www.2.southwest.msus.edu

Minneapolis Public Library
Technology/Science/Government Documents Division
300 Nicollet Mall
Minneapolis, MN 55401-1992
(612) 630-6120
NOTE: This library will close in 2002 and move to an interim location.

University of Minnesota
Government Publications Library
10 Wilson Library
Minneapolis, MN 55455-0414
(612) 624-5073
Internet site: http://govpubs.lib.umn.edu/index.phtml

Moorhead State University
Livingston Lord Library - Documents Dept.
1104 7th Avenue S.
Moorhead, MN 56563
(218) 236-2461
Internet site: www.mnstate.edu/library

University of Minnesota-Morris
Rodney A. Briggs Library
Morris, MN 56267-2134
(320) 589-6180
Internet site: www.mrs.umn.edu/library/gordocs.shtml

Carleton College
Lawrence McKinley Gould Library
One North College Street
Northfield, MN 55057-4097
(507) 646-4266
Internet site: www.library.carleton.edu/collections/govdocs.html

St. Olaf College
Rolvaag Memorial Library
1510 St. Olaf Avenue
Northfield, MN 55057-1093
(507) 646-3795

Ramsey County Library
Roseville Library
2180 North Hamline Avenue
Roseville, MN 55113-4241
(651) 628-6803

St. Cloud State University
Learning Resources and Technical Services
James W. Miller Learning Resources Center, MC130-B
720 4th Avenue South
St. Cloud, MN 56301-4998
(320) 255-2063
Internet site: http://lrs.stcloudstate.edu/guides/govt.html

Hamline University
School of Law Library
1536 Hewitt Avenue
St. Paul, MN 55104
(651) 523-2125

Minnesota State Law Library
Minnesota Judicial Center
G25 Constitution Avenue
St. Paul, MN 55155
(651) 296-2775
Internet site: www.lawlibrary.state.mn.us/gpl.html

St. Paul Public Library
Government Publications – CLOSED UNTIL MID 2002
90 West 4th Street
St. Paul, MN 55102
(651) 632-5179

University of Minnesota
St. Paul Campus Central Library
Government Documents
1984 Buford Avenue
St. Paul, MN 55108
(612) 624-1212
Internet site: http://magrath.lib.umn.edu

William Mitchell College of Law
871 Summit Avenue
St. Paul, MN 55105
(651) 227-9191
Internet site: www.wmitchell.edu/library/tour/gordocs.html

Gustavus Adolphus College Library
800 College Avenue
St. Peter, MN 56082
(507) 933-7569
Internet site: www.gac.edu/oncampus/academics/Resources/library/govdocs/gdfm.html

Winona State University
Maxwell Library - Government Documents
Johnson and Sanborn Streets
Winona, MN 55987
(507) 457-5146
Internet site: www.winona.msus.edu/library/index.html

MANAGEMENT ASSISTANCE, GENERAL

SCORE Offices

Minnesota SCORE District Office
Small Business Administration
210-C Butler Square Building
100 North 6th Street
Minneapolis, MN 55403
(612) 370-2324
Website: www.scoreminn.org

Albert Lea SCORE Office
Albert Lea Chamber of Commerce
202 North Broadway
Albert Lea, MN 56007
(507) 373-3939

Alexandria SCORE
Alexandria Technical College
1601 Jefferson Street
Alexandria, MN 56308
(320) 762-4510

Austin SCORE Office
Austin Chamber of Commerce
329 Main Street North, Suite 102
Austin, MN 55912
(507) 437-4561

Detroit Lakes SCORE Office
Northwest Technical College
900 Hwy 34E
P.O. Box 832
Detroit Lakes, MN 56501
(218) 846-7415

Fairmont SCORE Office
Fairmont Area Chamber of Commerce
206 North State Street
P.O. Box 826
Fairmont, MN 56031
(507) 235-5547

Mankato SCORE Chapter #328
Mankato Chamber of Commerce
112 Riverfront Drive
P.O. Box 999
Mankato, MN 56001
(507) 345-4519

Minneapolis SCORE Chapter #2
Bremmer Bank Building, Suite 103
8800 Hwy 7
Minneapolis, MN 55426
(952) 938-4570

New Ulm SCORE Office
New Ulm Chamber of Commerce
1 North Minnesota Street
New Ulm, MN 56073
(507) 233-4300

Owatonna SCORE
Owatonna Chamber of Commerce
320 Hoffman Drive, P.O. Box 331
Owatonna, MN 55060
(507) 451-7970

Red Wing SCORE
Pottery Office & Center
2000 West Main, Suite 326
Red Wing, MN 55066
(651) 385-2236

Rochester SCORE Chapter #406
Rochester Area Chamber of Commerce
220 South Broadway, Suite 100
Rochester, MN 55904
(507) 288-1122

St. Cloud SCORE Chapter #468
Whitney Senior Center
1527 Northway Drive
St. Cloud, MN 56303
(320) 240-1332

St. Paul SCORE Chapter #391
Liberty State Bank, Suite 300
176 N. Snelling Avenue
St. Paul, MN 55104
(651) 632-8937

South Metro SCORE Chapter #628
Burnsville Executive Suites
350 Burnsville Parkway, Suite 400
Burnsville, MN 55337
(952) 808-5595

Willmar SCORE Chapter #2
Kandiyohi County Economic Development Partnership
2104 Highway 12E
Willmar, MN 56201

Winona SCORE Office
Winona Chamber of Commerce
67 Main Street
P.O. Box 870
Winona, MN 55987
(507) 452-2272

Worthington SCORE
Worthington Chamber of Commerce
1121 3rd Avenue
Worthington, MN 56187
(507) 372-2919

Small Business Development Centers

Small Business Development Centers
State Administrative Office
500 Metro Square
121 7th Place East
St. Paul, MN 55101-2146
(651) 297-5770
(800) 657-3858 (ask for Small Business Development Centers)

Bemidji State University
Small Business Development Center
3801 Bemidji Avenue North
Bemidji, MN 56601
(218) 755-4900

Central Lakes College
Small Business Development Center
501 West College Drive
Brainerd, MN 56401
(218) 855-8142

University of Minnesota Duluth
Small Business Development Center
Duluth Technology Village
11 E. Superior St., Suite 210
Duluth, MN 55802
(218) 726-7298

University of Minnesota Duluth –CED
Natural Resources Research Institute
Small Business Develoment Center
5013 Miller Trunk Highway
Duluth, MN 55611
(218) 726-7298

Vermilion Community College
Small Business Development Center
1900 East Camp Street, Room CS105A
Ely, MN 55731
(218) 365-7295

Itasca Development Corporation
Small Business Development Center
12 Northwest Third Street
Grand Rapids, MN 55744
(218) 327-2241

Hibbing Community College
Small Business Development Center
1515 East 25th Street
Hibbing, MN 55746
(218) 262-6703

Rainy River Community College
Small Business Development Center
1501 Highway 71
International Falls, MN 56649
(218) 285-2255

Region Nine Development Commission
Small Business Development Center
410 Jackson Street, P.O. Box 3367
Mankato, MN 56002-3367
(507) 389-8875

Southwest State University
Small Business Development Center
1501 State Street – ST105
Marshall, MN 56258
(507) 537-7386

University of St. Thomas
Small Business Development Center
1000 LaSalle Avenue, MS 25 H 225
Minneapolis, MN 55403
(651) 962-4500

Minnesota State University, Moorhead
Small Business Development Center
1104 7th Avenue South, MSU Box 303
Moorhead, MN 56563
(218) 236-2289

Owatonna Incubator Incorporated
Small Business Development Center
1065 24th Avenue Southwest
Owatonna, MN 55060
(507) 451-0517

Pine Technical College
Small Business Development Center
1100 4th Street
Pine City, MN 55063
(320) 629-4510

Rochester Community and Technical College
Small Business Development Center
Riverland Hall
851 30th Avenue Southeast
Rochester, MN 55904
(507) 285-7536

Southeast Minnesota Development Corporation
Small Business Development Center
111 West Jessie Street, P.O. Box 684
Rushford, MN 55971
(507) 864-7557

St. Cloud State University
Small Business Development Center
616 Roosevelt Road, Suite 100
St. Cloud, MN 56301
(320) 255-4842

North Shore Business Enterprise Center
Small Business Development Center
1313 Fairgrounds Road
Two Harbors, MN 55616
(218) 834-3494

Mesabi Range Community and Technical College
Quad Cities Small Business Develoment Center
1001 Chestnut Street West, L 119
Virginia, MN 55792
(218) 749-7152

Minnesota State Colleges and University (MNSCU)

500 World Trade Center
305 East Seventh Street
St. Paul, MN 55101
(651) 296-8012
888-667-2848 (Toll free)
Internet site: www.mnscu.edu

University of Minnesota

Extension Service
Education Development System
405 Coffey Hall
St. Paul, MN 55108-1030
Internet site: www.extension.umn.edu
(612) 625-2787

MANAGEMENT ASSISTANCE FOR MINORITY BUSINESSES

Asian Development Corporation
1437 Marshall Avenue, #103
St. Paul, MN 55104
(651) 647-1140

Council on Asian Pacific Minnesotans
525 Park St., Suite 105
St. Paul, MN 55103
(651) 296-0538

Minneapolis/St. Paul Minority Business
Development Center MBDC-MEDA
250 2nd Ave. So., Suite 106
Minneapolis, MN 55401
(612) 332-6332
Internet site: www.meda.net

Native American Business Development Center
P.O. Box 217
Cass Lake, MN 56633
(218) 335-8583
Internet site: www.nabdcmn.org

Minnesota Minority Supplier Development Council
(MMSDC)
250 2nd Ave. S., Suite 106
Minneapolis, MN 55401
(612) 332-6332
Internet site: www.mmsdc.org

WomenVenture
2324 University Avenue, Suite 200
St. Paul, MN 55114
(651) 646-3808

PROCUREMENT ASSISTANCE

Department of Administration, Materials Management Division

See entry under Government, State

Federal and State Procurement Contacts www.access.gpo.gov or www.mpi.org

Minnesota Project Innovation Incorporated
2720 Riverwoods Lane
Burnsville, MN 55337
(651) 384-8555

Minnesota Project Innovation Incorporated
23990 Geldner Lane
RR 1 Box 187C
Cleveland, MN 56017
(507) 931-5106

Minnesota Project Innovation, Incorporated
111 3rd Avenue South, Suite 100
Minneapolis, MN 55401-2551
(612) 347-6745
website: www.mpi.org

Minnesota Project Innovation Incorporated
MSU Box 303
615 11th Street South
Moorhead, MN 56563-0001
(218) 299-5801

Minnesota Project Innovation Incorporated
921 1st Street North, Suite 104
St. Cloud, MN 56303
(320) 202-6496

Minnesota Project Innovation Incorporated
1821 University Avenue West, Suite S-340
St. Paul, MN 55104
(651) 603-6763 (Toll free)

Minnesota Project Innovation Incorporated
14823 Credit View Drive
Savage, MN 55378
(952) 226-3337
(877) 312-0337

Minnesota Project Innovation, Inc.
200 Olcott Plaza
820 North Ninth Street
Virginia, MN 55792
(218) 742-3427

Local Procurement Offices

Minneapolis

City of Minneapolis
Purchasing Department
Towle Building, Suite 552
330 Second Avenue So.
Minneapolis, MN 55401
(612) 673-2500

St. Paul/Ramsey County

City of Saint Paul
Vendor Outreach Program
15 West Kellogg Boulevard, Suite 900
St. Paul, MN 55102
(651) 266-8967

Metropolitan Agencies

Metropolitan Airports Commission
Attn: Office of Diversity
6040 28th Avenue South
Minneapolis, MN 55450
(612) 726-8175

Metropolitan Council
Office of Diversity and EEO
F.T. Heywood Office
560 Sixth Avenue N.
Minneapolis, MN 55411
(612) 349-7463

Counties

Anoka County Purchasing
2100 3rd Avenue
Anoka, MN 55303
(763) 323-5318

Hennepin County Purchasing
A-2205 Government Center
300 6th Street South
Minneapolis, MN 55487
(612) 348-3181

SMALL BUSINESS INNOVATION RESEARCH PROGRAM

See Technology

TAX AND ACCOUNTING ASSISTANCE

Minnesota Association of Public Accountants
1711 West County Road B, Suite 300N
Roseville, MN 55113
(651) 635-0706

Minnesota Society of Certified Public Accountants
7900 Xerxes Avenue South, Suite 1230
Bloomington, MN 55431
(952) 831-2707
(800) 331-4288

National Association of Enrolled Agents
EA Referral Hotline (800) 424-4339
Minnesota Society of Enrolled Agents
P.O. Box 104
Clearwater, MN 55320
Website: www.mnsea.org

AccountAbility Minnesota
2314 University Avenue, Suite 12
St. Paul, MN 55114
(651) 287-0187
Website: www.accountability.org

TECHNOLOGY

Minnesota Project Innovation, Incorporated
111 3rd Avenue South, Suite 100
Minneapolis, MN 55401-2551
(612) 347-6751

Minnesota Technology, Inc.
111 3rd Avenue South
Minneapolis, MN 55401-2551
(612) 373-2900
(800) 325-3073
www.minnesotatechnology.org.

Minnesota Technology Regional Offices

725 Center Avenue
Moorhead, MN 56560
(218) 236-8584

1030 East Bridge Street
Redwood Falls, MN 56283
(507) 637-2010

851 30th Avenue Southeast
Rochester, MN 55904
(507) 285-7184

300 East St. Germain, Suite 200
St. Cloud, MN 56304
(320) 654-5201

140 Olcott Plaza
820 North 9th Street
Virginia, MN 55792
(218) 741-4241

DIRECTORY OF LICENSES AND PERMITS

DIRECTORY OF LICENSES AND PERMITS

REGULATED ACTIVITY	DEPARTMENT	CONTACT
Aboveground Storage Tank Installations /		
Aboveground Storage Tanks (see TANKS)		
Abstracter		
Abstracter	Commerce, Minnesota Dept. of	(651) 296-6319 or (800) 657-3978
Accountants		
Certified / Licensed Public Accountant	Accountancy, Minnesota State Board of	(651) 296-7938
Acupuncture		
Acupuncture Practitioner	Medical Practice, Minnesota State Board of	(612) 617-2130
Adjuster (see INSURANCE)		
Adoption		
Private Child-Caring or Child Placing License (Rule 4)	Human Services, Minnesota Dept. of	(651) 296-3971
Advertising Devices, Signs		
Advertising Device Permit	Transportation, Minnesota Dept. of	(651) 582-1443
Air Quality		
Hot Mix Asphalt Permit	Pollution Control Agency, Minnesota	(651) 297-2274 or
Individual Part 70 Operating Permit or State Operating Permit		(800) 646-6247
Registration Permits (Options A, B, C, or D)		
Aircraft		
Aircraft Dealer's License	Transportation, Minnesota Dept. of	(651) 296-8061
Airports		
Airport License: Personal-Use Airport	Transportation, Minnesota Dept. of	(651) 296-8061
Airport License: Private Airport		
Airport License: Public Airport		
Commercial Aviation Operators License		
Alarm and Communication Contractors		
Alarm and Communication Contractor	Electricity Board, Minnesota	(651) 642-0800
Alcohol (see LIQUOR)		
Permit to Purchase or Possess Ethyl Alcohol	Public Safety, Minnesota Dept. of	(651)296-6159
Alcohol and Drug Treatment Providers		
Chemical Dependency Rehab Treatment (Rule 35)	Human Services, Minnesota Dept. of	(651) 296-3971
Outpatient Alcohol and Drug Treatment (Rule 43)		
Alcoholism		
Alcohol and Drug Counselor License	Health, Minnesota Dept. of	(651) 282-5619
All Terrain Vehicles (see UTILITY VEHICLES)		
Alternative Health Care		
Unlicensed Complementary and Alternative Health Care Practitioners	Health, Minnesota Dept. of	(651) 282-5623
Ambulance Service (see EMERGENCY MEDICAL SERVICES)		
Ammonia		
Anhydrous Ammonia Storage System Permit	Agriculture, Minnesota Dept. of	(651) 297-7275

REGULATED ACTIVITY	DEPARTMENT	CONTACT
Animals		
Abandoned Animals License	Animal Health, Minnesota Board of	(651) 296-2942
Animal Exhibition Permit		
Animal Sales for Research: Class B (Dogs and Cats)		
Feed Foodwaste to Animals License		
Hatchery Permit		
Import Poultry Permit		
Kennel License (Dogs and Cats)		
Livestock Markets and Consignment Sales Permit		
Pet Food Processing Permit		
Poultry Dealer Permit		
Pullorum-Typhoid Testing Authorization		
Rendering Plant Permit		
Apiaries		
Apiary Certificate of Inspection	Agriculture, Minnesota Dept. of	(651) 296-0591
Apiary Permit for Importation		
Appraiser		
Real Estate Appraiser	Commerce, Minnesota Dept. of	(651) 296-6319 or (800) 657-3978
Aquaculture		
Aquaculture License	Natural Resources, Minnesota Dept. of	(651) 297-4935
Aquatic Farms		
Aquaculture License	Natural Resources, Minnesota Dept. of	(651) 297-4935
Archaeology		
Archaeological Site Permit	Office of the State Archaeologist, Minnesota	(612) 725-2411
Architecture		
Architect	Architecture, Engineering, Land Surveying, Landscape Architecture, Geoscience and Interior Design, Board of	(651) 296-2388
Asbestos		
Asbestos Contractor License	Health, Minnesota Dept. of	(651) 215-0900
Asbestos Inspector Certificate		
Asbestos Management Planner Certificate		
Asbestos Project Designer Certificate		
Asbestos Site Supervisor Certificate		
Asbestos Training Course Permit		
Asbestos Worker Certificate		
Notification of Asbestos-Related Work and Amendments		
ASPHALT (see WATER QUALITY)		
Assessors		
Assessor Certification: Various Classes	Assessors, Minnesota State Board	(651) 296-3010
Athletic Training		
Athletic Trainer (registration)	Medical Practice, Minnesota State Board of	(612) 617-2130
Attorney		
Attorney Registration	Lawyers Professional Responsibility, Office of (Minnesota Supreme Court)	(651) 296-3952 or (800) 657-3601
Auctioneer		
Auctioneer	Contact local County Auditor office.	
Audiology		
Audiologist Registration	Health, Minnesota Dept. of	(651) 282-5629

REGULATED ACTIVITY	DEPARTMENT	CONTACT
Aviation		
Aircraft Dealer's License	Transportation, Minnesota Dept. of	(651) 296-8061
Airport License: Personal-Use Airport		
Airport License: Private Airport		
Airport License: Public Airport		
Commercial Aviation Operators License		
Bailbondsmen		
Insurance Agent (Line item for Bailbondsmen)	Commerce, Minnesota Dept. of	(651) 296-6319 or (800) 657-3978
Bait		
Exporting Minnow Dealer	Natural Resources, Minnesota Dept. of	(651) 297-4935
Minnow Dealer's License		
Minnow Retailer		
Nonresident License to Purchase, Possess and Transport Frogs		
Nonresident Minnow Hauler License		
Resident Frog Dealer (Take, Possess, Transport, Sell)		
Resident License to Purchase, Possess and Transport Frogs		
Banks (see also COMMERCIAL MORTGAGE BROKERING, CREDIT UNIONS, CURRENCY EXCHANGE, DEBT PRORATING AGENCY, INSURANCE, LOANS (NON-BANK LENDERS), MORTGAGE ORIGINATOR OR SERVICER, SAFE DEPOSIT COMPANY)		
Electronic Financial Terminal Authorization (Nonfinancial Institutions)	Commerce, Minnesota Dept. of	(651) 296-2715
Electronic Financial Terminal Notification (State-Chartered Financial Institutions)		
Detached Banking Facility Authority	Commerce, Minnesota Dept. of	(651) 297-3779
Electronic Funds Transmission Facility Authorization		
Interstate Banking and Branching Authority		
Interstate Trust-Trust Office or Representative Trust Office		
Minnesota Bank or Trust Company Mergers		
State Bank Charter or Trust Company Charter or Industrial Loan & Thrift Company With Deposit-Taking Powers		
State Bank Trust Authority Approval Trust Service Office Authority		
Barbering (not cosmetology)		
Barbers and Barbershops: Various Classes	Barber Examiners, Minnesota Board of	(651) 642-0489
Bed and Breakfast		
Bed and Breakfast Registration (to serve liquor)	Public Safety, Minnesota Dept. of	(651) 296-6159 or (651) 296-9519
Food, Beverage and Lodging License	Health, Minnesota Dept. of	(651) 215-0865
Bees (see APIARIES)		
Bingo (see GAMBLING)		
Bingo Halls		
Bingo Hall License	Gambling Control Board, Minnesota	(651) 639-4000
Boat Dealer		
Boat Dealer License	Natural Resources, Minnesota Dept. of	(651) 297-3227
Boats for Hire		
Tour Boat Liquor License	Public Safety, Minnesota Dept. of	(651) 296-6159 or (651) 296-6939
Boiler Operating Engineer		
Boiler Engineer: Six Classes	Labor and Industry, Minnesota Dept. of	(651) 284-5137

REGULATED ACTIVITY	DEPARTMENT	CONTACT
Brokers (see also MOTOR VEHICLE DEALER)		
Food Broker License	Agriculture, Minnesota Dept. of	(651) 296-1592
Agent, Broker-Dealer, Investment Advisor	Commerce, Minnesota Dept. of	(651) 296-2283
Residential Mortgage Originator or Servicer License	Commerce, Minnesota Dept. of	(651) 296-2297
Commercial Mortgage Limited Broker	Commerce, Minnesota Dept. of	(651) 296-6319 or
Real Estate Salesperson; Real Estate Broker		(800) 657-3978
Viatical Settlement Broker	Commerce, Minnesota Dept. of	(651) 297-7058 or (651) 297-3976
Motor Vehicle Dealers License	Public Safety, Minnesota Dept. of	(651) 296-2977
NOTE: For the purposes of the motor vehicle dealers license, a "Dealer" includes licensed new motor vehicle dealers, used motor vehicle dealers, motor vehicle brokers, wholesalers, auctioneers, lessors of new or used motor vehicles, scrap metal processors, used vehicle parts dealers, and salvage pools.		
Brokers License	Public Safety, Minnesota Dept. of	(651) 296-6159
Building Mover		
Building Mover License	Transportation, Minnesota Dept. of	(651) 405-6060 or (888) 472-3389
Building Official		
Accessibility Specialist	Administration, Minnesota Dept. of	(651) 296-7099
Certified Building Official		
Certified Building Official Limited		
Burning		
Open Burning Permit	Contact the local city government, fire department, local forestry office or fire warden.	
Bus Shelters		
Bus Shelter Permit	Transportation, Minnesota Dept. of	(651) 582-1443
Camps		
Children's Camp Permit	Health, Minnesota Dept. of	(651) 215-0870
Recreational Camping Area License	Health, Minnesota Dept. of	(651) 215-0859
Camps and Campgrounds		
Membership Campground Registration	Commerce, Minnesota Dept. of	(651) 296-6332
Membership Campground Agent Licensing	Commerce, Minnesota Dept. of	(651) 296-6319 or (800) 657-3978
Carriers		
Common Carrier License	Public Safety, Minnesota Dept. of	(651) 296-6159 or
Common Carrier License - Intoxicating or 3.2%		(651) 296-6939
Common Carrier License (and Sunday)		
Commercial Driver's License (CDL)	Public Safety, Minnesota Dept. of	(651) 297-5029
Moving Buildings Over Highways Permit When Over Legal Size(s) or Legal Weight	Transportation, Minnesota Dept. of	(651) 405-6000 or (800) 657-3959
Oversized Vehicles: Single Trip Permit, Job Permit, and Annual Permit		
Special Transportation Certificate (STS)	Transportation, Minnesota Dept. of	(651) 405-6060 or (888) 472-3389
Catering		
Caterer's Permit (to serve liquor)	Public Safety, Minnesota Dept. of	(651) 296-6159 or (651) 296-6939
Food, Beverage and Lodging License	Health, Minnesota Dept. of	(651) 215-0865
Charitable Organizations		
Charitable Organizations Registration	Attorney General, Minnesota Office of	(651) 296-6172
Charitable Trusts	Attorney General, Minnesota Office of	(651) 296-8019
Professional Fundraiser Registration		
Check-Cashing Company		
Currency Exchange License	Commerce, Minnesota Dept. of	(651) 296-2297

REGULATED ACTIVITY	DEPARTMENT	CONTACT
Cheese		
Cultured Dairy Food / Farmstead Cheese Permit	Agriculture, Minnesota Dept. of	(651) 296-2627
Chemical Dependency		
Alcohol and Drug Counselor License	Health, Minnesota Dept. of	(651) 282-5619
Chemical Dependency Rehab Treatment (Rule 35)	Human Services, Minnesota Dept. of	(651) 296-3971
Outpatient Alcohol and Drug Treatment (Rule 43)		
Chemigation		
Chemigation Permit & Chemigation Substantial Alteration Permit	Agriculture, Minnesota Dept. of	(651) 297-2614
In-home Child Care		
Child Care		
Child Care Center License (Rule 3)	Human Services, Minnesota Dept. of	(651) 296-3971
Family Child Care and Group Family Child Care (Rule 2)		
In Home Child Care	Contact County Social Services or Human Services Department	
Child Placement		
Private Child-Caring or Child Placing License (Rule 4)	Human Services, Minnesota Dept. of	(651) 296-3971
Chiropractic		
Doctor of Chiropractic	Chiropractic Examiners, Minnesota Board of	(612) 617-2222
Chloroflurocarbons (CFCs)		
CFC and Freon Regulation Information	Pollution Control Agency, Minnesota	(651) 297-8661 or (800) 657-3864
CFC Recyclers and CFC Recovery Equipment Certification	U.S. Environmental Protection Agency	(312) 886-6818 or (800) 296-1996
Cigarette		
Unfair Cigarette Sales Act Fee	Commerce, Minnesota Dept. of	(651) 297-3866
Cigarette & Tobacco Distributor & Subjobber Licenses	Revenue, Minnesota Dept. of	(651) 297-1882
Clubs (Buying Clubs, Health Clubs, Social Referral Clubs)		
Buying Clubs, Health Clubs, Social Referral Clubs Registration	Attorney General, Minnesota Office of	(651) 296-7575
Collection Agency		
Collection Agency and Debt Collector	Commerce, Minnesota Dept. of	(651) 296-6319 or (800) 657-3978
Collection Agency Certificate of Exemption		
Commercial Drivers		
Commercial Driver's License (CDL)	Public Safety, Minnesota Dept. of	(651) 297-5029
Commercial Driver Training		
Commercial Driver Training School License	Public Safety, Minnesota Dept. of	(651) 296-3966
Commercial Mortgage Brokering		
Commercial Mortgage Limited Broker	Commerce, Minnesota Dept. of	(651) 296-6319 or (800) 657-3978
Communication Contractors		
Alarm and Communication Contractor	Electricity Board, Minnesota	(651) 642-0800
Complementary Health Care		
Unlicensed Complementary and Alternative Health Care Practitioners	Health, Minnesota Dept. of	(651) 282-5623

REGULATED ACTIVITY	DEPARTMENT	CONTACT
Composting		
Compost Facility Permit	Pollution Control Agency, Minnesota	(651) 296-6300 or (800) 657-3864
Contractors		
Residential Building Contractor / Remodeler	Commerce, Minnesota Dept. of	(651) 296-6319 or (800) 657-3978
Corn		
Hybrid Field Corn Seed Variety Registration	Agriculture, Minnesota Dept. of	(651) 296-6123
Corporate Take-Overs		
Corporate Take-Over Offers Registration	Commerce, Minnesota Dept. of	(651) 296-4051
Cosmetologist		
Cosmetologist, Salons and Schools	Commerce, Minnesota Dept. of	(651) 296-6319 or (800) 657-3978
Counselors		
Alcohol and Drug Counselor License	Health, Minnesota Dept. of	(651) 282-5619
Unlicensed Mental Health Practitioners	Health, Minnesota Dept. of	(651) 282-5621
Courier (see also CARRIERS and MOTOR CARRIERS)		
Household Goods Mover Permit Limousine Service Permit Motor Carriers of Property or Passengers: Single State Registration System (SSRS) Passenger Carrier Registration (Intrastate) Property Carrier Registration (Intrastate)	Transportation, Minnesota Dept. of	(651) 405-6060 or (888) 472-3389
Credit Services Organization		
Credit Services Organization Registration	Commerce, Minnesota Dept. of	(651) 296-6319 or (800) 657-3978
Credit Unions		
Credit Union Certificate of Organization	Commerce, Minnesota Dept. of	(651) 296-2297
Currency Exchange		
Currency Exchange License	Commerce, Minnesota Dept. of	(651) 296-2297
Dairy		
Cultured Dairy Food/Farmstead Cheese Permit Dairy Plant License Grade A Milk Production Permit Milk and Cream Buyer and Tester License	Agriculture, Minnesota Dept. of	(651) 296-2627
Day Care		
Adult Day Care Center License (Rule 223) Child Care Center License (Rule 3)	Human Services, Minnesota Dept. of	(651) 296-3971
Adult Foster Care License (Rule 203) Family Child Care and Group Family Child Care (Rule 2) In-home Child Care	Contact County Social Services or Human Services Department	
Debt Collection		
Collection Agency and Debt Collector Collection Agency Certificate of Exemption	Commerce, Minnesota Dept. of	(651) 296-6319 or (800) 657-3978
Debt Prorating Agency		
Debt Prorating Agency License	Commerce, Minnesota Dept. of	(651) 296-2297
Dentistry		
Dentist; Dental Hygienist; Dental Assistant	Dentistry, Minnesota Board of	(612) 617-2250

REGULATED ACTIVITY	DEPARTMENT	CONTACT
Deputy Registrar		
Deputy Registrar Appointment	Public Safety, Minnesota Dept. of	(651) 296-6911
Detectives (see PRIVATE DETECTIVES)		
Dietitians		
Dietitian License	Dietetics & Nutrition Practice, State Board of	(612) 617-2175
Doctors		
Physician (Medical Doctor and Doctor of Osteopathy)	Medical Practice, Minnesota State Board of	(612) 617-2130
Dogs and Cats (see ANIMALS)		
Drainage		
Drainage Permit	Transportation, Minnesota Dept. of	(651) 582-1443
Drive-Away In Transit		
Minnesota Drive-Away In Transit (Motor Carriers)	Public Safety, Minnesota Dept. of	(651) 296-2977
Driveways		
Access Permit	Transportation, Minnesota Dept. of	(651) 582-1443
Drugs (Human and Veterinary)		
Controlled Substance Researcher	Pharmacy, Minnesota Board of	(612) 617-2201
Drug Manufacturing License		
Drug Wholesaler License		
Medical Gas Distributor		
Pharmacist License		
Pharmacy License		
Pharmacy Technician License		
Electric High Voltage Transmission Lines		
Route Permit	Environmental Quality Board (MN Planning)	(651) 296-3714
Electricians		
Electrical Contractor Class A	Electricity Board, Minnesota	(651) 642-0800
Electrical Contractor Class B		
Electrical Installer Class A		
Electrical Installer Class B		
Journeyman Electrician Class A		
Lineman		
Maintenance Electrician		
Master Electrician Class A		
Elevators		
Elevator Constructor	Electricity Board, Minnesota	(651) 642-0800
Elevator Contractor		
Master Elevator Constructor		
Emergency Medical Services		
Emergency Medical Technician Registration Minnesota Ambulance Service License	Emergency Medical Services Regulatory Board	(612) 627-6000 or (800) 747-2011
Employment Agency		
Employee Leasing Company Registration	Commerce, Minnesota Dept. of	(651) 296-4523
Employment Agency (Temporary) Exemption Certificate		
Employment Agency License for Operation	Labor and Industry, Minnesota Dept. of	(651) 284-5005
Employment Search Firm		
Search Firm License	Labor and Industry, Minnesota Dept. of	(651) 284-5005

REGULATED ACTIVITY	DEPARTMENT	CONTACT
EMTs (see EMERGENCY MEDICAL SERVICES)		
Energy		
Energy Audit Certification	Commerce, Minnesota Dept. of	(651) 297-1771
Energy Facilities		
Certificate of Need	Public Utilities Commission, Minnesota	(651) 297-4562
Site Permit for Large Electric Generating Power Plant	Environmental Quality Board (MN Planning)	(651) 296-3714
Site Permit for Large Wind Energy Conversion Systems	Environmental Quality Board (MN Planning)	(651) 296-5089
Engineering		
Engineer-In-Training Professional Engineer	Architecture, Engineering, Land Surveying, Landscape Architecture, Geoscience and Interior Design, Board of	(651) 296-2388
Entertainment Agency		
Entertainment Agency License	Labor and Industry, Minnesota Dept. of	(651) 284-5144
Environmental Health Specialist/Sanitarian Registration		
Environmental Health Specialist/Sanitarian Registration License	Health, Minnesota Dept. of	(651) 215-0843
Explosives		
Explosives License Ownership or Possession of an Explosive Device or Incendiary Device Application	Public Safety, Minnesota Dept. of	(651) 642-0610
Explosives Permit	Contact the local Sheriff's Office or local Police Department	
Family Therapy (see MARRIAGE AND FAMILY THERAPY)		
Feed, Commercial		
Commercial Feed License (Includes Pet and Specialty Pet Foods)	Agriculture, Minnesota Dept. of	(651) 296-6124
Feedlots		
Feedlot Interim Permit Feedlot NPDES Permit (General and Individual) Registration (Feedlot Program) State Disposal System Permit	Pollution Control Agency, Minnesota	(651) 296-7203 or (800) 657-3876
Fertilizer		
Fertilizer License	Agriculture, Minnesota Dept. of	(651) 296-8379
Soil and Plant Amendment Registration Specialty Fertilizer Registration	Agriculture, Minnesota Dept. of	(651) 297-4871
Bulk Pesticide/Fertilizer Storage Facility or Substantial Alteration Permit	Agriculture, Minnesota Dept. of	(651) 297-7274
Agricultural Liming Material License Anhydrous Ammonia Storage System Permit	Agriculture, Minnesota Dept. of	(651) 297-7275
Financial Counselors/Planners		
Financial Counselor or Planner Disclosure Document	Commerce, Minnesota Dept. of	(651) 296-2283
Fire Protection (see FIREWORKS DISPLAY, SPRINKLER SYSTEMS, TANKS)		
Firearms (see also EXPLOSIVES)		
Federally Licensed Gun Dealers	Bureau of Alcohol, Tobacco and Firearms National Licensing Center	(404) 417-2751

REGULATED ACTIVITY	DEPARTMENT	CONTACT
Fireworks Display		
FireworksDisplay Operator	Fire Marshall division (MN Dept. of Public Safety)	(651) 215-0500
Fish		
Fish Smoking Operation Permit	Agriculture, Minnesota Dept. of	(651) 296-1592
Aquaculture License	Natural Resources, Minnesota Dept. of	(651) 297-4935
Commercial Netting of Fish		
Fish Packer License		
Fish Vendor		
International Fish Buyer - Retail		
International Fish Buyer - Wholesale		
Lake Superior Fish Buyer - Retail		
Lake Superior Fish Buyer - Wholesale		
Lake Superior Fishing Guide License		
Food		
Fish Smoking Operation Permit	Agriculture, Minnesota Dept. of	(651) 296-1592
Food Broker License		
Meat Custom Processor Permit		
Retail Food Handler License		
Wholesale Food Handler License		
Wholesale Food Processor or Manufacturer License		
Livestock Meat Packing Company Agent License	Agriculture, Minnesota Dept. of	(651) 296-2292
Livestock Meat Packing Company License		
Cultured Dairy Food / Farmstead Cheese Permit	Agriculture, Minnesota Dept. of	(651) 296-2627
Grade A Milk Production Permit		
Milk and Cream Buyer and Tester License		
Non-Resident Frozen Food		
Minnesota Wholesale Produce Dealer's License	Agriculture, Minnesota Dept. of	(651) 296-8620
Minnesota Grown Logo Labeling License	Agriculture, Minnesota Dept. of	(651) 297-5510
Food, Beverage and Lodging License	Health, Minnesota Dept. of	(651) 215-0865
Environmental Health Food Manager Certification	Health, Minnesota Dept. of	(651) 215-0870
Wild Rice Dealer License	Natural Resources, Minnesota Dept. of	(651) 297-4935
Forest Products		
Permit to Cut Timber	Natural Resources, Minnesota Dept. of	(651) 296-4498
Special Product and Use Permits (Fuelwood)		
Foster Care		
Adult Foster Care License (Rule 203)	Contact County Social Services or Human Services Department	
Family Foster Care and Group Family Foster Care License (Rule 1)		
Franchises		
Franchise Offer or Sale Registration	Commerce, Minnesota Dept. of	(651) 296-6328
Frogs		
Nonresident License to Purchase, Possess and Transport Frogs	Natural Resources, Minnesota Dept. of	(651) 297-4935
Resident Frog Dealer (Take, Possess, Transport, Sell)		
Resident License to Purchase, Possess and Transport Frogs		
Fuels		
Refuse Derived Fuel Processing Permit	Pollution Control Agency, Minnesota	(800) 657-3864
Fuels Distributors License	Revenue, Minnesota Dept. of	(651) 296-0889
Special Fuel License		
Fundraising		
Charitable Organizations Registration	Attorney General, Minnesota Office of	(651) 296-6172
Professional Fundraiser Registration	Attorney General, Minnesota Office of	(651) 296-8019

REGULATED ACTIVITY	DEPARTMENT	CONTACT
Funeral Directors		
Mortuary Science (Mortician) License	Health, Minnesota Dept. of	(651) 282-3829
Funeral Establishments		
Crematory License	Health, Minnesota Dept. of	(651) 282-3829
Funeral Establishment License		
Fur		
Fur Farm Registration	Agriculture, Minnesota Dept. of	(651) 296-1592
Fur Tanning and Dressing License	Natural Resources, Minnesota Dept. of	(651) 297-4935
Game and Fur Farm License		
Nonresident Individual Fur Buyer		
Raw Fur Buyer		
Supplemental Raw Fur Dealer		
Gambling / Gambling Equipment		
Bingo Hall License	Gambling Control Board, Minnesota	(651) 639-4000
Distributor's License		
Excluded Bingo		
Excluded Raffle		
Exempt Permit		
Gambling Manager's License		
Manufacturer's License		
Organization License		
Manufacture and/or Distributor of Gambling Devices	Public Safety, Minnesota Dept. of	(651) 296-6159
Temporary Possession of a Gambling Device		
Gambling Tax Permit	Revenue, Minnesota Dept. of	(651) 282-5225 or (800) 657-3605
Gas Storage Underground		
Permit to Store Gas or Liquid Underground Using Natural Geologic Formations as a Storage Reservoir	Natural Resources, Minnesota Dept. of	(651) 296-0434
Gasoline		
Fuels Distributors License	Revenue, Minnesota Dept. of	(651) 296-0889
Genetically Engineered Organisms		
Agricultural Based Genetically Engineered Organism Release Permit	Agriculture, Minnesota Dept. of	(651) 296-1277
Non-Agricultural Based Genetically Engineered Organism Release Permit	Environmental Quality Board (Minnesota Planning)	(651)296-2871
Geology		
Geologist	Architecture, Engineering, Land Surveying, Landscape Architecture, Geoscience and Interior Design, Board of	(651) 296-2388
Geologist-In-Training		
Ginseng, Buying and Selling		
License to Buy or Sell Wild Ginseng	Natural Resources, Minnesota Dept. of	(651) 297-4935
Grain		
Grain Bank License	Agriculture, Minnesota Dept. of	(651) 297-2314
Grain Buying and Storing License		
Independent Grain Buyer's License		
Greenhouses		
Greenhouse Certificate	Agriculture, Minnesota Dept. of	(651) 296-8619
Grocery Stores (see FOODS)		
Group Homes		
Board and Lodging License	Health, Minnesota Dept. of	(651) 215-0865
Boarding Care Home	Health, Minnesota Dept. of	(651) 215-8701

REGULATED ACTIVITY	DEPARTMENT	CONTACT
Group Homes (continued)		
Supervised Living Facility		
Chemical Dependency Rehab Treatment (Rule 35)	Human Services, Minnesota Dept. of	(651) 296-3971
Group Home License (Rule 8)		
Habilitation (Waivered Services) for the Developmentally Disabled License		
Guides		
Guide Bear Hunters, License to	Natural Resources, Minnesota Dept. of	(651) 297-4935
Guide Turkey Hunters, License to		
Lake Superior Fishing Guide License		
Hazardous Materials		
Hazardous Material Shipper's: Uniform Program Credentials (UPR)	Transportation, Minnesota Dept. of	(651) 405-6060 or (888) 472-3389
Transporters of Hazardous Materials: Uniform Program Credential (UPM, UPMM)		
Hazardous Waste		
Hazardous Waste Treatment, Storage or Disposal Permit	Pollution Control Agency, Minnesota	(651) 296-6300 or (800) 657-3864
Hazardous Waste Generator License	Pollution Control Agency, Minnesota	(651) 297-8330
Underground Storage Tank Contractor / Supervisor Certificate	Pollution Control Agency, Minnesota	(651) 296-7902
Hazardous Waste Transporter: Uniform Program Credential (UPW)	Transportation, Minnesota Dept. of	(651) 405-6060 or (888) 472-3389
Health Care Facilities		
Board and Lodging License	Health, Minnesota Dept. of	(651) 215-0865
Boarding Care Home	Health, Minnesota Dept. of	(651) 215-8701
Freestanding Outpatient Surgical Centers		
Group Home License (Rule 8)		
Hospitals		
Housing with Services Establishment Registration		
Nursing Homes		
Supervised Living Facility		
Maternity Shelter License (Rule 6)		
Mental Health Center and Clinic Certification (Rule 29)		
Health Care Providers		
Home Care and Hospice	Health, Minnesota Dept. of	(651) 215-8701
Health Clubs (see CLUBS)		
Health Maintenance Organizations (HMO)		
Accountable Provider Network License	Health, Minnesota Dept. of	(651) 282-6327
Community Integrated Service Network License		
Health Maintenance Organization Certificate of Authority		
Hearing Aids		
Hearing Instrument Dispenser Certification	Health, Minnesota Dept. of	(651) 282-5620
Hearing Instrument Dispenser Trainee		
Herbs		
License to Buy or Sell Wild Ginseng	Natural Resources, Minnesota Dept. of	(651) 297-4935
Home Health Care		
Home Care and Hospice	Health, Minnesota Dept. of	(651) 215-8701
Hospice (see HOME HEALTH CARE)		
Hospitals		
Hospitals	Health, Minnesota Dept. of	(651) 215-8701

REGULATED ACTIVITY	DEPARTMENT	CONTACT
Hotels (see HOTELS, MOTELS AND RESTAURANTS)		
Hotels, Motels and Restaurants		
Food, Beverage and Lodging License	Health, Minnesota Dept. of	(651) 215-0865
Bed and Breakfast Registration (to serve liquor)	Public Safety, Minnesota Dept. of	(651) 296-6159 or (651) 296-9519
Environmental Health Food Manager Certification	Health, Minnesota Dept. of	(651) 215-0870
Hybrid Seed		
Hybrid Field Corn Seed Variety Registration	Agriculture, Minnesota Dept. of	(651) 296-6123
Insurance		
Insurance Premium Financing License	Commerce, Minnesota Dept. of	(651) 296-2297
Catastrophe Adjuster	Commerce, Minnesota Dept. of	(651) 296-6319 or
Crop Hail Adjuster		(800) 657-3978
Insurance Adjuster		
Insurance Agency		
Insurance Agent		
Insurance Agent (Line item for Bailbondsmen)		
Third Party Administrator License	Commerce, Minnesota Dept. of	(651) 296-8592
Insurance Certificate of Authority	Commerce, Minnesota Dept. of	(651) 296-9429
Utilization Review Organization License	Commerce, Minnesota Dept. of	(651) 297-3976
Viatical Settlement Broker		
Viatical Settlement Provider License		
Interior Designer		
Certified Interior Designer	Architecture, Engineering, Land Surveying, Landscape Architecture, Geoscience and Interior Design, Board of	(651) 296-2388
Invention Development Services		
Invention Development Service Disclosure	Attorney General, Minnesota Office of	(651) 296-3353
Investment Advisor		
Agent, Broker-Dealer, Investment Advisor	Commerce, Minnesota Dept. of	(651) 296-2283
Jewelry (see PRECIOUS METALS)		
Junk Dealers, Pawnbrokers, and Second Hand Dealers		
May be regulated by both city and county where business is located.	Contact local city or county government offices	
Kennels (see ANIMALS)		
Laboratories		
Environmental Laboratory Certification	Health, Minnesota Dept. of	(612) 676-5200
Land Surveyor		
Land Surveyor	Architecture, Engineering, Land Surveying, Landscape Architecture, Geoscience and Interior Design, Board of	(651) 296-2388
Land Surveyor-In-Training		
Lands (Public)		
License to Cross Public Lands and Waters	Natural Resources, Minnesota Dept. of	(651) 296-0237
Permit to Cut Timber	Natural Resources, Minnesota Dept. of	(651) 296-4498
Special Product and Use Permits (Fuelwood)		
Easement Across State-Owned Land Managed by the Minnesota Department of Natural Resources	Natural Resources, Minnesota Dept. of	(651) 296-4807
Lease of State-Owned Land Managed by the	Minnesota Department of Natural Resources	
State Industrial Minerals Lease		
State Iron Ore/Taconite Lease		
State Metalic Minerals Lease		

REGULATED ACTIVITY	DEPARTMENT	CONTACT
Lands (Public) (continued)		
State Peat Lease Resource Management Access Permit Special Events Permit	Natural Resources, Minnesota Dept. of	(651) 296-6157
Landscape Architect		
Landscape Architect	Architecture, Engineering, Land Surveying, Landscape Architecture, Geoscience and Interior Design, Board of	(651) 296-2388
Lawn Service Companies (see FERTILIZER and PESTICIDES)		
Lawyer		
Attorney Registration	Lawyers Professional Responsibility, Office of (Minnesota Supreme Court)	(651) 296-3952 or (800) 657-3601
Lead		
Independent Examination Permit Lead Firm Certificate Lead Inspector License Lead Project Designer License Lead Risk Assessor License Lead Supervisor License Lead Training Course Permit Lead Worker License	Health, Minnesota Dept. of	(651) 215-0909
Liming Material		
Agricultural Liming Material License	Agriculture, Minnesota Dept. of	(651) 297-7275
Limousine Service (see MOTOR CARRIER)		
Liquor		
Bed and Breakfast Registration Brand Label Registration Brew Pub License Brokers License Caterer's Permit Certification On Sale and/or Sunday Liquor License Club On Sale Liquor License Common Carrier/Planes/Boats/Trains License Common Carrier/Planes/Boats/Trains License - Intoxicating or 3.2% Common Carrier/Planes/Boats/Trains License (and Sunday) Consumption and Display Permit County On Sale Liquor License Farm Winery License Malt Beverage Importer's License Manufacturer of Wine License Manufacturer / Wholesaler Intoxicating Liquor Branch License Manufacturer / Wholesaler Intoxicating Liquor License Manufacturer's Warehouse Permit Micro Brewery License Minnesota Brewer's License Off Sale Liquor License On Sale Wine License Renewal of Liquor, Wine or Club License Representative or Salesman Identification Card Retailers Identification Card Temporary On Sale Liquor License Permit Temporary One Day Consumption and Display Permit Tour Boat Liquor License Wholesaler of 3.2% Malt Liquor Wine and Distilled Spirits Importers License	Public Safety, Minnesota Dept. of	(651) 296-6159

REGULATED ACTIVITY	DEPARTMENT	CONTACT
Livestock		
Livestock Dealer License	Agriculture, Minnesota Dept. of	(651) 296-2292
Livestock Dealer's Agent License		
Livestock Market Agency License		
Livestock Meat Packing Company Agent License		
Livestock Meat Packing Company License		
Livestock Markets and Consignment Sales Permit	Animal Health, Minnesota Board of	(651) 296-2942, Ext. 31
Loans (Non-Bank Lenders)		
Accelerated Mortgage Payment Provider Authorization	Commerce, Minnesota Dept. of	(651) 296-2297
Consumer Small Loan Lender		
Industrial Loan and Thrift Company Authorization		
Motor Vehicle Sales Finance Company License		
Regulated Lender License		
Lobbyists		
Lobbyist Registration	Campaign Finance and Public Disclosure Board, Minnesota	(651) 296-5615 or (800) 657-3889
Mail Order		
Mail or Telephone Order Merchandise Rule	U.S. Federal Trade Commission	(877) 382-4357
Managed Care		
Workers' Compensation Managed Care Organizations Certification	Labor and Industry, Minnesota Dept. of	(651) 284-5159
Manufactured Homes		
Manufactured Home Dealer -Limited License	Administration, Minnesota Dept. of	(651) 297-7081
Manufactured Home Dealer -Subagency License		
Manufactured Home Dealer License		
Manufactured Home Manufacturer License		
Manufactured Home Installer	Commerce, Minnesota Dept. of	(651) 296-6319 or (800) 657-3978
Manufactured Home Park License	Health, Minnesota Dept. of	(651) 215-0859
Manufacturing Facility		
Manufacturing General Permit	Pollution Control Agency, Minnesota	(651) 297-2274 or (800) 646-6247
Manure		
Commercial Animal Waste Technician	Agriculture, Minnesota Dept. of	(651) 297-7175
Massage		
Massage Therapists	Contact local city government offices.	
Marriage and Family Therapy		
Marriage and Family Therapist	Marriage and Family Therapy, Minnesota Board	(612) 617-2220
Marriages (see also MINISTERS)		
Marriage License	Clerk of District Court	
Maternity Shelters (see also HEALTH CARE FACILITIES and RESIDENTIAL SERVICES PROGRAMS)		
Maternity Shelter License (Rule 6)	Human Services, Minnesota Dept. of	(645) 296-3971
Meat Packing		
Meat Custom Processor Permit	Agriculture, Minnesota Dept. of	(651) 296-1592
Livestock Meat Packing Company Agent License	Agriculture, Minnesota Dept. of	(651) 296-2292
Livestock Meat Packing Company License		
Medical Gas Distribution		
Medical Gas Distributor	Pharmacy, Minnesota Board of	(612) 617-2201

REGULATED ACTIVITY	DEPARTMENT	CONTACT
Medicine, Practice of		
Physician (Medical Doctor and Doctor of Osteopathy)	Medical Practice, Minnesota State Board of	(612) 617-2130
Physician Assistant (registration)		
Respiratory Care Practitioner (registration)		
Mental Health Services		
Unlicensed Mental Health Practitioners	Health, Minnesota Dept. of	(651) 282-5621
Mental Health Center and Clinic Certification (Rule 29)	Human Services, Minnesota Dept. of	(651) 296-3971
Residential Treatment for Emotionally Disturbed Children (Rule 5)		
Residential Treatment for Mentally Ill Adults (Rule 36)		
Midwifery		
Traditional Midwife License	Medical Practice, Minnesota State Board of	(612) 617-2130
Mining and Minerals		
Permit for Removal of Stockpiled Iron-Bearing Materials	Natural Resources, Minnesota Dept. of	(218) 262-6767
Permit to Mine - Iron Ore and Taconite	Natural Resources, Minnesota Dept. of	(651) 296-4807
Permit to Mine - Nonferrous Metallic Minerals		
Permit to Mine - Peat		
Registration of Exploratory Borer		
State Industrial Minerals Lease		
State Iron Ore/Taconite Lease		
State Metallic Minerals Lease		

Ministers

Ministers, of any religious denomination, must file with the court administrator of the Minnesota District court of the county in which the ceremony is to be performed a copy of their credentials of license or ordination in order to solemnize a marriage. See *Minnesota Statutes* 517.

Minnows (see BAIT)

Mobile Homes (see MANUFACTURED HOMES)

REGULATED ACTIVITY	DEPARTMENT	CONTACT
Money Transmitting		
Money Transmitter	Commerce, Minnesota Dept. of	(651) 296-2297
Mortgage Originator or Servicer		
Residential Mortgage Originator or Servicer License	Commerce, Minnesota Dept. of	(651) 296-2297
Morticians		
Mortuary Science (Mortician) License	Health, Minnesota Dept. of	(651) 282-3829

Motels (see HOTELS, MOTELS AND RESTAURANTS)

REGULATED ACTIVITY	DEPARTMENT	CONTACT
Motor Carrier		
Motor Carrier Direct Pay Certificate	Revenue, Minnesota Dept. of	(651) 296-5343
Moving Buildings Over Highways Permit When Over Legal Size(s) or Over Legal Weight	Transportation, Minnesota Dept. of	(651) 405-6000 or (800) 657-3959
Building Mover License	Transportation, Minnesota Dept. of	(651) 405-6060 or (888) 472-3389
Hazardous Material Shipper's: Uniform Program Credentials (UPR)		
Hazardous Waste Transporter: Uniform Program Credential (UPW)		
Household Goods Mover Permit		
Interstate Motor Carriers of Exempt Commodities: Bingo Stamp Credential (D-1)		
Limousine Service Permit		
Motor Carriers of Property or Passengers: Single State Registration System (SSRS)		
Passenger Carrier Registration (Intrastate)		

REGULATED ACTIVITY	DEPARTMENT	CONTACT
Motor Carrier (continued)		
Property Carrier Registration (Intrastate)		
Transporters of Hazardous Materials: Uniform Program Credential (UPM, UPMM)	Transportation, Minnesota Dept. of	(651) 405-6060 or (888) 472-3389
Oversized Vehicles: Single Trip Permit, Job Permit, and Annual Permit		
Motor Vehicle Dealers		
Motor Vehicle Dealers License	Public Safety, Minnesota Dept. of	(651) 296-2977
NOTE: A "Dealer" includes licensed new motor vehicle dealers, used motor vehicle dealers, motor vehicle brokers, wholesalers, auctioneers, lessors of new or used motor vehicles, scrap metal processors, used vehicle parts dealers, and salvage pools.		
Motorized Vehicles		
ATV Dealer License	Natural Resources, Minnesota Dept. of	(651) 297-3227
ATV Manufacturer License		
OHM Dealer License		
OHM Manufacturer License		
ORV Dealer License		
ORV Manufacturer License		
Snowmobile Dealer License		
Snowmobile Manufacturer License		
Nonresidential Services Programs		
Habilitation (Waivered Services) for the Developmentally Disabled License	Human Services, Minnesota Dept. of	(651) 296-3971
Independent Living Assistance for Youth (245A.22)		
Semi-Independent Living Services for the Developmentally Disabled License		
Training and Habilitation Services for the Developmentally Disabled License		
Notary Public		
Notary Public Commission	Commerce, Minnesota Dept. of	(651) 296-6319 or (800) 657-3978
Nurseries		
Greenhouse Certificate	Agriculture, Minnesota Dept. of	(651) 296-8619
Nursery Stock Dealer Certificate		
Nursery Stock Grower Certificate		
Minnesota Grown Logo Labeling License	Agriculture, Minnesota Dept. of	(651) 297-5510
Nursing		
Licensed Practical Nurse (LPN)	Nursing, Minnesota Board of	(612) 617-2180
Public Health Nurse Registration Certificate		
Registered Nurse (RN)		
Approval of Practical Nursing Programs	Nursing, Minnesota Board of	(612) 617-2294
Approval of Professional (Registered) Nursing Programs		
Nursing Home Administrators		
Nursing Home Administrator	Nursing Home Administrators, Minnesota Board of	(612) 617-2117
Nursing Homes		
Nursing Homes	Health, Minnesota Dept. of	(651) 215-8701
Nutritionist		
Nutritionist License	Dietetics & Nutrition Practice, State Board of	(612) 617-2175
Occupational Therapy		
Occupational Therapy Practitioner License	Health, Minnesota Dept. of	(651) 282-5624

REGULATED ACTIVITY	DEPARTMENT	CONTACT
Optometry		
Optometrist	Optometry, Minnesota State Board of	(612) 617-2173
Osteopaths (see DOCTORS)		
Pawnbrokers		
Pawnbrokers Code of Conduct	Contact local city or county government offices	
Payroll Services		
Payroll Services Registration (Third Party Bulk Filer)	Revenue, Minnesota Dept. of	(651) 282-5225 or (800) 657-3605
Peat		
Permit to Mine - Peat	Natural Resources, Minnesota Dept. of	(651) 296-4807
State Peat Lease		
Pesticide		
Pesticides Registration	Agriculture, Minnesota Dept. of	(651) 296-4292
Aquatic Pest Control Applicator/Company License	Agriculture, Minnesota Dept. of	(651) 297-7175
Commercial Pesticide Applicator License		
Noncommercial Pesticide Applicator License		
Pesticide Dealer License		
Private Pesticide Applicator Certificate		
Structural Pest Control Applicator/Company License		
Bulk Pesticide/Fertilizer Storage Facility or Substantial Alteration Permit	Agriculture, Minnesota Dept. of	(651) 297-7274
Pet Food		
Commercial Feed License (Includes Pet and Specialty Pet Foods)	Agriculture, Minnesota Dept. of	(651) 296-6124
Pet Food Processing Permit	Animal Health, Minnesota Board of	(651) 296-2942, Ext. 31
Petroleum (see FUELS AND STORAGE)		
Pharmacy		
Pharmacist License	Pharmacy, Minnesota Board of	(612) 617-2201
Pharmacy License		
Pharmacy Technician License		
Physical Therapy		
Physical Therapist License	Physical Therapy, Minnesota State Board of	(612) 627-5406
Physician Assistants		
Physician Assistant (registration)	Medical Practice, Minnesota State Board of	(612) 617-2130
Pipefitter		
High Pressure Pipefitter Journeyman Contractor	Labor and Industry, Minnesota Dept. of	(651) 284-5124
Pipelines		
Pipeline Routing Permit	Environmental Quality Board (Minnesota Planning)	(651) 296-5089
Placement Services		
Employee Leasing Company Registration	Commerce, Minnesota Dept. of	(651) 296-4523
Employment Agency (Temporary) Exemption Certificate		
Employment Agency License for Operation	Labor and Industry, Minnesota Dept. of	(651) 284-5005
Search Firm License		
Plants		
Brand Name for Seed Variety Registration	Agriculture, Minnesota Dept. of	(651) 296-6123
Hybrid Field Corn Seed Variety Registration		
Minnesota Seed Permit		

REGULATED ACTIVITY	DEPARTMENT	CONTACT
Plants (continued)		
Noxious Weed Transportation Permit Screenings Purchase Permit Greenhouse Certificate Nursery Stock Dealer Certificate Nursery Stock Grower Certificate	Agriculture, Minnesota Dept. of	(651) 296-8619
Plumbers		
Plumber, Journeyman License Plumber, Master License Plumber's Apprentice Registration	Health, Minnesota Dept. of	(651) 215-0841
Podiatric Medicine, Practice of		
Podiatrist	Podiatric Medicine, Practice of	(612) 617-2200
Police		
Part-time Peace Officer License Peace Officer License	Peace Officer Standards and Training, Minnesota Board of	(651) 643-3060
Poultry		
Hatchery Permit Import Poultry Permit Poultry Dealer Permit Pullorum-Typhoid Testing Authorization	Animal Health, Minnesota Board of	(651) 296-2942, Ext. 20
Power Plant Siting		
Site Designation and Certificate of Site Compatibility	Environmental Quality Board (Minnesota Planning)	(651) 296-2096
Precious Metal		
Precious Metal Dealer License	Regulated by County Auditor	

NOTE: A Precious Metal Dealer is any person(s) engaged in the business of buying secondhand items containing precious (silver, gold and platinum) metal. *Minnesota Statutes* 325F.73

REGULATED ACTIVITY	DEPARTMENT	CONTACT
Private Detectives		
Private Detective License	Private Detective and Protective Agent Services, Minnesota Board of	(651) 215-1753
Protective Agents		
Protective Agent Services License	Private Detective and Protective Agent Services, Minnesota Board of	(651) 215-1753
Psychology, Practice of		
Licensed Psychologist; Licensed Psychological Practitioner	Psychology, Minnesota Board of	(612) 617-2230
Racing (Horse)		
Racing Class A License (Ownership and Operation) Racing Class B License (Racing & Card Club Operation) Racing Class C License (Occupational) Racing Class D License (County Agricultural Associations)	Racing Commission, Minnesota	(952) 496-7950
Veterinarian	Veterinary Medicine, Minnesota Board of	(612) 617-2170
Radiation		
Radiation Equipment/Sources Registration	Health, Minnesota Dept. of	(651) 643-2127 or (651) 643-2151
Out-of-State Radioactive Material Source Temporary Registration	Health, Minnesota Dept. of	(651) 643-2151

Radiologic Technicians (note: contact American Registry at (651) 687-0048, Minnesota is not a licensing state).

Raffles (see CHARITABLE ORGANIZATIONS AND GAMBLING)

REGULATED ACTIVITY	DEPARTMENT	CONTACT
Radio Monitoring		
Mobile Monitor Permit - Individual	Public Safety, Minnesota Dept. of	(651) 603-0178
Mobile Monitor Permit - Media		
Mobile Monitor Permit - Non-Law Monitoring		
Railroad Crossing		
Railroad Grade Crossing Operating License	Transportation, Minnesota Dept. of	(651) 296-2472
Real Estate		
Real Estate Appraiser	Commerce, Minnesota Dept. of	(651) 296-6319 or (800) 657-3978
Real Estate Closer		
Real Estate Salesperson; Real Estate Broker		
Subdivided Land Agent Designation		
Subdivided Land Registration	Commerce, Minnesota Dept. of	(651) 296-6332
Recreational Camping Area (see CAMPS)		
Recyclers (see CHLOROFLUROCARBONS (CFCs) AND MOTOR VEHICLE DEALER)		
Refuse-Derived Fuel Processing		
Refuse Derived Fuel Processing Permit	Pollution Control Agency, Minnesota	(800) 657-3864
Registrars, Deputy (see DEPUTY REGISTRARS)		
Rehabilitation Consultants, Firms and Vendors		
Qualified Rehabilitation Consultants, QRC Firms, and Registered Rehabilitation Vendors	Labor and Industry, Minnesota Dept. of	(651) 284-5036
Rendering Plant (see ANIMALS)		
Research, Drug		
Controlled Substance Researcher	Pharmacy, Minnesota Board of	(612) 617-2201
Residential Services Programs		
Housing with Services Establishment Registration	Health, Minnesota Dept. of	(651) 215-8701
Maternity Shelter License (Rule 6)	Human Services, Minnesota Dept. of	(651) 296-3971
Residential Services for the Developmentally Disabled License		
Residential Treatment for Emotionally Disturbed Children (Rule 5)		
Residential Treatment for Mentally Ill Adults (Rule 36)		
Respiratory Therapist		
Respiratory Care Practitioner (registration)	Medical Practice, Minnesota State Board of	(612) 617-2130
Restaurants		
Food, Beverage and Lodging License	Health, Minnesota Dept. of	(651) 215-0865
Bed and Breakfast Registration (to serve liquor)	Public Safety, Minnesota Dept. of	(651) 296-6159 or (651) 296-9519
Environmental Health Food Manager Certification	Health, Minnesota Dept. of	(651) 215-0870
Roads and Highways		
Railroad Grade Crossing Operating License	Transportation, Minnesota Dept. of	(651) 296-2472
Construction of Tunnels Under Highways Permit	Transportation, Minnesota Dept. of	(651) 296-8655
Utility Permit on Trunk Highway Right of Way		
Moving Buildings Over Highways Permit When Over Legal Size(s) or Over Legal Weight	Transportation, Minnesota Dept. of	(651) 405-6000 or (800) 657-3959
Oversized Vehicles: Single Trip Permit, Job Permit, and Annual Permit		
Access Permit	Transportation, Minnesota Dept. of	(651) 582-1443
Advertising Device Permit		
Drainage Permit		

REGULATED ACTIVITY	DEPARTMENT	CONTACT
Roofers		
Residential Roofer	Commerce, Minnesota Dept. of	(651) 296-6319 or (800) 657-3978
Safe Deposit Company		
Safe Deposit Company License	Commerce, Minnesota Dept. of	(651) 296-2297
Sales and Use Tax		
Sales and Use Tax Permit (Business Tax ID Number)	Revenue, Minnesota Dept. of	(651) 282-5225 or (800) 657-3605
Resale Exemption Certificate	Revenue, Minnesota Dept. of	(651) 296-6181 or (800) 657-3777
Sales and Use Tax Exempt Status Certificate	Revenue, Minnesota Dept. of	(651) 296-6184
Salons		
Cosmetologist, Salons and Schools	Commerce, Minnesota Dept. of	(651) 296-6319 or (800) 657-3978
Salvage, Motor Vehicle (see MOTOR VEHICLE DEALER)		
Sand and Gravel		
Non-Metallic Mineral Processing General Permit	Pollution Control Agency, Minnesota	(651)297-2274 or (800)646-6247
Sanitarians		
Environmental Health Specialist / Sanitarian Registration License	Health, Minnesota Dept. of	(651) 215-0843
Satellite Television Systems (see ALARM AND COMMUNICATION CONTRACTORS)		
Scanners		
Mobile Monitor Permit - Individual Mobile Monitor Permit - Media Mobile Monitor Permit - Non-Law Monitoring	Public Safety, Minnesota Dept. of	(651) 603-0178
School Administrator		
School Administrator (Directors, Superintendents of Schools, Principals, or Related Services Personnel)	Children, Families and Learning, Minnesota Dept. of	(651) 582-8691
Schools		
Private For Profit Post-Secondary Career Education Institutions Private and Non-Minnesota Public Post-Secondary Institutions	Higher Education Services, Minnesota Office of	(651) 642-0584 or (800) 657-3866 Ext. 3172
Approval of Practical Nursing Programs Approval of Professional (Registered) Nursing Programs	Nursing, Minnesota Board of	(612) 617-2294
Commercial Driver Training School License	Public Safety, Minnesota Dept. of	(651) 296-3966 (651) 642-0584
Screenings		
Screenings Purchase Permit	Agriculture, Minnesota Dept. of	(651) 296-6123
Second Hand Dealers		
May be regulated by both city and county where business is located.		
Securities Sales		
Securities for Sale Registration	Commerce, Minnesota Dept. of	(651) 296-4520
Security Guards		
Protective Agent Services License	Private Detective and Protective Agent Services, Minnesota Board of	(651) 215-1753
Security Systems (see ALARM AND COMMUNICATIONS CONTRACTORS)		

REGULATED ACTIVITY	DEPARTMENT	CONTACT
Seeds		
Brand Name for Seed Variety Registration Hybrid Field Corn Seed Variety Registration Minnesota Seed Permit Screenings Purchase Permit	Agriculture, Minnesota Dept. of	(651) 296-6123
Shelters (see BUS SHELTERS AND HEALTH CARE FACILITIES)		
Shooting Preserves		
Commercial Shooting Preserve License Private Shooting Preserve License	Natural Resources, Minnesota Dept. of	(651) 297-4935
Signs (see ADVERTISING DEVICES)		
Social Work		
Social Worker License (Various Classes)	Social Work, Minnesota Board of	(612) 617-2100
Soil Science		
Professional Soil Scientist Soil Scientist-In-Training	Architecture, Engineering, Land Surveying, Landscape Architecture, Geoscience and Interior Design, Board of	(651) 296-2388
Solid Waste		
Type IV Waste Disposal Operator or Inspector Certificate Type V Waste Disposal Operator or Inspector Certificate	Pollution Control Agency, Minnesota	(651) 296-9269
Type II Landfill Operator or Inspector Certificate Type III Landfill Operator or Inspector Certificate	Pollution Control Agency, Minnesota	(651) 297-5754
Industrial Solid Waste Land Disposal Permit Mixed Municipal Solid Waste Land Disposal Permit Municipal Solid Waste Combustor Ash Land Disposal Permit Solid Waste Storage Permit Solid Waste Transfer Facility Permit	Pollution Control Agency, Minnesota	(800) 657-3864
Special Events on DNR lands		
Special Events Permit	Natural Resources, Minnesota Dept. of	(651) 296-6157
Special Transportation Services		
Special Transportation Certificate (STS)	Transportation, Minnesota Dept. of	(651) 405-6060 or (888) 472-3389
Speech Pathology		
Speech-Language Pathologist Registration	Health, Minnesota Dept. of	(651) 282-5629
Sprinkler Systems		
Fire Protection Sprinkler System Contractor License Fire Protection Sprinkler System Design Contractor License Fire Sprinkler Systems Plan Review Managing Employee Certificate Sprinkler Fitter (Conditional Journeyman) Certificate Sprinkler Fitter (Journeyman) Certificate Sprinkler Fitter (Limited Journeyman) Certificate	Fire Marshall Division (MN Dept. of Public Safety)	(651) 215-0500
Storage (see also WAREHOUSES)		
Permit to Store Gas or Liquid Underground Using Natural Geologic Formations as a Storage Reservoir	Natural Resources, Minnesota Dept. of	(651) 296-0434

REGULATED ACTIVITY	DEPARTMENT	CONTACT
Subdivided Lands		
Subdivided Land Agent Designation	Commerce, Minnesota Dept. of	(651) 296-6319 or (800) 657-3978
Subdivided Land Registration	Commerce, Minnesota Dept. of	(651) 296-6332
Tanks		
Flammable Liquid Tanks Plan Review	Fire Marshall Division (MN Dept. of Public Safety)	(651) 215-0500
Underground Storage Tank Contractor/Supervisor Certificate	Pollution Control Agency, Minnesota	(651) 296-7902
Aboveground Storage Tank (AST) Registration Underground Storage Tank (UST) Registration	Pollution Control Agency, Minnesota	(651) 297-8664
Tanning Facilities		
Safety and equipment standards established by Minn. Stat. 325H.01 et. seq. For licensing information contact the municipality where the facility is located.		
Taxes		
Unfair Cigarette Sales Act Fee	Commerce, Minnesota Dept. of	(651) 297-3866
Gambling Tax Permit Tax Identification Number (Sales Tax and Use Permit)	Revenue, Minnesota Dept. of	(651) 282-5225 or (800) 657-3605
Fuels Distributors License Special Fuel License	Revenue, Minnesota Dept. of	(651) 296-0889
Motor Carrier Direct Pay Certificate	Revenue, Minnesota Dept. of	(651) 296-5343
Sales and Use Tax Exempt Status Certificate	Revenue, Minnesota Dept. of	(651) 296-6184
Cigarette & Tobacco Distributor & Subjobber Licenses	Revenue, Minnesota Dept. of	(651) 297-1882
Taxidermy		
Taxidermist License	Natural Resources, Minnesota Dept. of	(651) 297-4935
Teachers		
School Administrator (Directors, Superintendents of Schools, Principals, or Related Services Personnel) Teacher	Children, Families and Learning, Minnesota Dept. of	(651) 582-8691
Telemarketing		
Telemarketing Sales Rule	U.S. Federal Trade Commission	(877) 382-4357
Telephone Installers (see ALARM AND COMMUNICATION CONTRACTORS)		
Telecommunications / Telephone Services		
Certificate of Authority	Commerce, Minnesota Dept. of	(651) 296-6173
Alternate Operator Service Certificate of Authority Interexchange and Long Distance Service Certificate of Authority Local Telephone Service Certificate of Authority	Public Utilities Commission, Minnesota	(651) 296-6913
Timber (see also FOREST PRODUCTS)		
Tobacco		
Unfair Cigarette Sales Act Fee	Commerce, Minnesota Dept. of	(651) 297-3866
Cigarette & Tobacco Distributor & Subjobber Licenses	Revenue, Minnesota Dept. of	(651) 297-1882
Tow Truck Operators		
Vehicle Tower	Contact local city or county government offices.	
Trailer Parks		
Manufactured Home Park License	Health, Minnesota Dept. of	(651) 215-0859
Tunnels		
Construction of Tunnels Under Highways Permit	Transportation, Minnesota Dept. of	(651) 296-8655

REGULATED ACTIVITY	DEPARTMENT	CONTACT
Turtle and Tortoise		
Turtle and Tortoise License	Natural Resources, Minnesota Dept. of	(651) 297-4935
Underground Storage Tanks (see TANKS)		
Utilities		
Utility Permit on Trunk Highway Right of Way	Transportation, Minnesota Dept. of	(651) 296-8655
Utility Crossings of Public Lands and Waters		
License to Cross Public Lands and Waters	Natural Resources, Minnesota Dept. of	(651) 296-0237
Utility Vehicles		
ATV Dealer License	Natural Resources, Minnesota Dept. of	(651) 297-3227
ATV Manufacturer License		
Boat Dealer License		
OHM Dealer License		
OHM Manufacturer License		
ORV Dealer License		
ORV Manufacturer License		
Snowmobile Dealer License		
Snowmobile Manufacturer License		
Vending Machines		
Retail Food Handler License	Agriculture, Minnesota Dept. of	(651) 296-1592
Unfair Cigarette Sales Act Fee	Commerce, Minnesota Dept. of	(651) 297-3866
Cigarette & Tobacco Distributor & Subjobber Licenses	Revenue, Minnesota Dept. of	(651) 297-1882
Veterinary Medicine		
Veterinarian	Veterinary Medicine, Minnesota Board of	(612) 617-2170
Viatical Settlements		
Viatical Settlement Broker	Commerce, Minnesota Dept. of	(651) 297-7058 or (651) 297-3976
Viatical Settlement Provider License		
Warehouses		
Grain Bank License	Agriculture, Minnesota Dept. of	(651) 297 2311
Grain Buying and Storing License		
Independent Grain Buyer's License		
Storage of General Merchandise License		
Manufacturer's Warehouse Permit	Public Safety, Minnesota Department of	(651) 296-6159 or (651) 296-6939
Waste		
Hazardous Waste Treatment, Storage or Disposal Permit	Pollution Control Agency, Minnesota	(651) 296-6300 or (800) 657-3864
Feedlot Interim Permit	Pollution Control Agency, Minnesota	(651) 296-7203 or (800) 657-3876
Feedlot NPDES Permit (General and Individual)		
State Disposal System Permit		
Individual Sewage Treatment Systems License (Designers, Installers, Inspectors, and Pumpers)	Pollution Control Agency, Minnesota	(651) 296-7309
Type IV Waste Disposal Operator or Inspector Certificate	Pollution Control Agency, Minnesota	(651) 296-9269
Type V Waste Disposal Operator or Inspector Certificate		
Wastewater Operator Certification		
Type II Landfill Operator or Inspector Certificate	Pollution Control Agency, Minnesota	(651) 297-5754
Type III Landfill Operator or Inspector Certificate		
Hazardous Waste Generator License	Pollution Control Agency, Minnesota	(651) 297-8330
Compost Facility Permit	Pollution Control Agency, Minnesota	(800) 657-3864
Demolition Debris Land Disposal Facility Permit		
Industrial Solid Waste Land Disposal Permit		
Mixed Municipal Solid Waste Land Disposal Permit		
Municipal Solid Waste Combustor Ash Land Disposal		

REGULATED ACTIVITY	DEPARTMENT	CONTACT
Waste (continued)		
Permit		
Solid Waste Storage Permit		
Solid Waste Transfer Facility Permit		
Water Appropriation		
Water Appropriation Permit - Long Term (Exceeding two years)	Natural Resources, Minnesota Dept. of	(651) 297-2835
Water Appropriation Permit - Temporary (1-2 year maximum)		
Water Conditioning		
Water Conditioning Contractor	Health, Minnesota Dept. of	(651) 215-0841
Water Conditioning Installer		
Water Quality		
NPDES General Industrial Storm Water Permit	Pollution Control Agency, Minnesota	(651) 296-3960 or (800) 657-3864
NPDES General Construction Storm Water Permit	Pollution Control Agency, Minnesota	(651) 296-6798 or (800) 657-3864
NPDES/SDS Asphalt General Permit (MNG49)	Pollution Control Agency, Minnesota	(651) 296-7162 or (800) 657-3864
NPDES/SDS Permit		
NPDES/SDS Pretreatment General Permit (MNP)		
Sanitary Sewer Extension Permit		
Feedlot Interim Permit	Pollution Control Agency, Minnesota	(651) 296-7203 or (800) 657-3876
Feedlot NPDES Permit (General and Individual)		
Registration (Feedlot Program)		
State Disposal System Permit		
Wastewater Operator Certification	Pollution Control Agency, Minnesota	(651) 296-9269
Underground Storage Tank (UST) Registration	Pollution Control Agency, Minnesota	(651) 297-8664
Water Supply		
Water Supply System Operator Certificate	Health, Minnesota Dept. of	(651) 215-0751
Water Wells and Borings		
Vertical Heat Exchanger Contractor	Health, Minnesota Dept. of	(651) 215-0818
Wells and Borings: Dewatering Well Contractor License		
Wells and Borings: Drive Point / Dug Well Contractor License		
Wells and Borings: Elevator Shaft Contractor License		
Wells and Borings: Explorer License (Exploratory Borings)		
Wells and Borings: Monitoring Well Contractor Registration		
Wells and Borings: Pump Installer License		
Wells and Borings: Screen & Pitless Contractor License		
Wells and Borings: Well Contractor License		
Wells and Borings: Well Sealing Contractor License		
Waters		
Dam Safety Permit	Natural Resources, Minnesota Dept. of	(651) 296-4800
Public Waters Work Permit (Protected Waters Permit)		
Weeds		
Noxious Weed Transportation Permit	Agriculture, Minnesota Dept. of	(651) 296-6123
Weighing and Measuring Equipment		
Placing in Service Permit	Commerce, Minnesota Dept. of	(651) 639-4010
Wild Rice Dealer		
Wild Rice Dealer License	Natural Resources, Minnesota Dept. of	(651) 297-4935

REGULATED ACTIVITY	DEPARTMENT	CONTACT
Wildlife Exhibit		
Permit to Exhibit Captive Wildlife	Natural Resources, Minnesota Dept. of	(651) 772-7906
X-Ray Machines (see RADIATION)		
Radiation Equipment/Sources Registration X-Ray Machine Operator Certification (Basic Skills Exam Information)	Health, Minnesota Dept. of	(651) 643-2127 or (651) 643-2151

INDEX